ISLAM
AND
HUMAN RIGHTS

FOURTH EDITION

ISLAM
AND
HUMAN RIGHTS

Tradition and Politics

Ann Elizabeth Mayer
University of Pennsylvania

Westview
PRESS

A Member of the Perseus Books Group

Copyright © 2007 by Westview Press, a Member of the Perseus Books Group.

Published in the United States of America by Westview Press, a Member of the Perseus Books Group, 5500 Central Avenue, Boulder, Colorado 80301-2877, and in the United Kingdom by Westview Press, 12 Hid's Copse Road, Cumnor Hill, Oxford OX2 9JJ.

Find us on the world wide web at www.westviewpress.com

Westview Press books are available at special discounts for bulk purchases in the United States by corporations, institutions, and other organizations. For more information, please contact the Special Markets Department at the Perseus Books Group, 11 Cambridge Center, Cambridge, MA 02142, or call (617) 252-5298, (800) 255-1514 or email special.markets@perseusbooks.com.

Library of Congress Cataloging-in-Publication Data
Mayer, Ann Elizabeth.
    Islam and human rights : tradition and politics / Ann Elizabeth Mayer.—
4th ed.
        p. cm.
    Includes bibliographical references and index.
    ISBN-13: 978-0-8133-4335-8 (pbk. : alk. paper)
    ISBN-10: 0-8133-4335-6 (pbk. : alk. paper) 1. Human rights—Islamic countries. 2. Human rights—Religious aspects—Islam. I. Title.
KBP2460.M39 2007
341.4'80917671—dc22   2006016091

The paper used in this publication meets the requirements of the American National Standard for Permanence of Paper for Printed Library Materials Z39.48-1984.

10   9   8   7   6   5   4   3   2

*To my mother
and her mother*

Contents

Human Rights Concerns in the Middle East, 199
Summary, 202

Preface

Perspicacious readers will note that the title of this book is a misnomer. A more accurate title might be "A Comparison of Selected Civil and Political Rights Formulations in International Law and in Actual and Proposed Rights Schemes Purporting to Embody Islamic Principles, with a Critical Appraisal of the Latter with Reference to International Law, Evolving Islamic Thought, and Relevant State Practice." The actual title stands as it is simply because it is the kind of rubric that people tend to consult when looking for material on human rights in Muslim milieus. That is, it has been selected for purely practical reasons despite its not being very informative.

The reference to "Islam" in the book title is potentially misleading, since I repudiate the commonly held view that Islam by itself determines the attitudes one finds in the Muslim world on human rights issues. In fact, I see Islam as only one factor in the reception of human rights in Muslim societies. The reason this book focuses on Islamic human rights schemes is that my own research interests happen to center on the role of Islamic law in contemporary Middle Eastern societies, the subset of Muslim societies that is of concern here.

A central thesis of this book is that one should not speak of "Islam" and human rights as if Islam were a monolith or as if there existed one established Islamic human rights philosophy that caused all Muslims to look at rights in a particular way. The precepts of Islam, like those of Christianity, Hinduism, Judaism, and other major religions possessed of long and complex traditions, are susceptible to interpretations that can and do create conflicts between religious doctrine and human rights or that reconcile the two. In reality, one cannot predict the position that a person will take on a human rights problem simply on the basis of the person's religious affiliation—and this is as true of Muslims as of members of other faiths. Even where the discussion is limited, as it is here, to Muslims living in the area stretching from North Africa to Pakistan, Muslims' attitudes toward human rights run the gamut from total rejection to wholehearted embrace.

Indeed, by now there should be far greater awareness of the fact that the relationship between Islamic tenets and human rights is intensely contested than there was at the time of earlier editions of this book. Political developments have illustrated how diverse Muslims' views are regarding the applicability of international human rights law to Muslim societies.

The public debates and the literature wrestling with the relationship of Islam and human rights have vastly proliferated over recent years, making it necessary to incorporate new material in this edition. In updating the previous edition while staying within the page limits that I have been given, I have been obliged to make extensive cuts, but I have still been unable to cover all the new developments and publications that deserve attention. For example, although the US invasion and occupation of Afghanistan and Iraq are relevant aspects of this topic, as are US policies in combating terrorism, I lack sufficient space to do these justice. I hope that the annotated bibliography that is included in this edition will somewhat compensate for the undertreatment of some related topics.

The focus here is the political use of Islam in the era since the founding of the United Nations in formulations of distinctive Islamic human rights schemes—meaning combinations of elements connected by design. As I point out, these schemes embody highly selective and often less-than-coherent appropriations of Islamic principles, many in combination with unacknowledged borrowings from international human rights documents. I critically appraise these schemes. The problems that I discuss include inserting human rights nomenclature into the context of philosophies inimical to rights and freedom, misrepresentations of comparative legal history, oversimplifying and stereotyping Islamic doctrines, failures to address actual patterns of rights abuses, insufficient grasp of international rights principles, imprecise legal methodologies, evasive and ambiguous rights formulations, and misleading rhetoric. All these flaws should be ascribed to the failings of the human authors, not to Islam per se.

Reacting to the unfair and often grotesque demonization of Islam in the West, some are disposed to attribute any critical perspectives on the ascendancy of political Islam in the Middle East to ugly Western prejudices. Due to the inhibiting effect of such attitudes, much of the secondary literature on the relationship between Islam and human rights was for a considerable period informed by an uncritical approach that contributed little to an understanding of the subject. In many ways, the approach taken in this book has been inspired by common defects in the secondary literature. Since I am consciously endeavoring to compensate for what I see as defects in the secondary literature, these defects should be summarized.

Many authors who write on Islam and human rights offer slipshod or apologetic accounts, refusing to acknowledge the problematic records of Muslim countries or of Islamist ideologues. Many fail to analyze and explain the criteria that are being employed to decide what qualifies as "Islamic law," a term with a variety of potential connotations. One encounters failures to perceive the need to distinguish between principles set forth in the Islamic sources, the historical patterns of interpreting these sources, and the results of contemporary governments converting Islamic law into statutes and policies. One sees authors who neglect to distinguish ideals from the actual laws, legal institutions, and policies in place in Muslim countries. Treating Islamic law as static, authors may dismiss the relevance of new understandings of the sources as if these necessarily fell outside the bounds of the Islamic tradition. The enormous disparities in views among contemporary Muslims on rights questions are rarely given their due, and the existence of Muslim thinking that is supportive of a secular public domain and of international human rights law is largely overlooked.

Writing in this area often reveals an unfamiliarity with international human rights law and how it developed and a lack of awareness of how Muslims helped formulate the international human rights system, mistakenly identifying this system with the United States. The result is the simplistic characterization of international human rights law as a "Western" creation or even as an artifact of US culture. Comparisons of Islamic rights standards with their international counterparts, if undertaken at all, tend to be careless and underdeveloped, with common tendencies to misrepresent international law and to minimize the extent to which Islamic versions of human rights deviate from it. Specific analyses of how Islamic versions of human rights relate to actual rights abuses in the Middle East are usually wanting, so that discussions remain at the level of vague, decontextualized generalizations. Moreover, there is a disinclination to take into account the skewed balance of power between the government and the governed in the political systems of the contemporary Middle East and the implications of that situation for rights issues. Failing to acknowledge the central role of the nation-state, an institution that all Muslim countries have borrowed from the West, authors tend to speak of the Islamic community as it existed in the early centuries of Islamic history.

The weaknesses in the secondary literature correlate with the inclination on the part of Western students of the Middle East and Islam to imagine that a distinctive Islamic cultural particularism shapes all Muslims' thinking, leading to taking at face value supposedly Islamic rationales for denying human rights. A corollary seems to be that the proper level of empathy for Muslims and their beliefs requires uncritically accepting any "Islamic" rubrics for legal rules and policies that deny human rights to Muslims. In contrast, in Muslim countries, skeptical scrutiny of Islamic rationales for policies that disregard international human rights is routine. Thus, although governments may claim that their opposition to international human rights is justified by Islamic culture, the Muslims whom they govern may dismiss such claims as cynical appeals to religion, attempts to legitimize the vices of undemocratic political systems.

In the following study, I am critical of governmental and ideological claims that unimpeachable Islamic authority warrants violations of human rights, even though I understand that individual Muslims may freely decide to accept the authority of interpretations of Islamic sources that place Islamic law at odds with international human rights law. Muslims' right to have such private beliefs must be respected. However, the situation becomes different when claims that Islamic rules should supersede human rights are made in a context where they are used to strip people of human rights that they aspire to enjoy and to which they are entitled under international law. Here one is not talking about personal religious beliefs but programs affecting the domains of politics and law. Projected or actual programs based on distinctive Islamic versions of human rights can engender conflicts with international law, and it is these conflicts that are examined in this book.

What currently distinguishes Muslims' approaches to rights is their frequent recourse to interpretations of religious sources to develop positions supporting or condemning rights. Although human rights are debated in purely secular terms in many Muslim milieus, in the wake of the Islamic resurgence, questions of human rights, like other great political issues facing Muslim societies, cannot easily be severed from disputes that are raging about the implications of Islamic theology and law for contemporary problems. "Islam" has become the vehicle both for political protest against undemocratic regimes and for the repression meted out by such regimes, simultaneously expressing aspirations for democracy and equality and providing rationales for campaigns to crush democratic freedoms and perpetuate old patterns of discrimination.

At a time when Islamic themes and terminology dominate political discourse in Muslim societies, it can be difficult for insiders and outsiders alike to distinguish between what are properly classified as political issues and ones that should be deemed religious issues. Nonetheless, when one carefully assesses disputes in Muslim societies about the implications of Islam for political controversies, one discerns that under the surface of the debates about "Islam," political struggles are going on that have much in common with the history of campaigns for democracy and equality in non-Muslim countries. It is also noteworthy that the results flowing from policies of upholding the supremacy of Islamic law at the expense of human rights and freedoms have largely replicated patterns already familiar under repressive and undemocratic regimes outside the Muslim world. Dissent is silenced, opponents are imprisoned or killed, free elections are barred, and a rigid ideological orthodoxy is imposed. The patterns of discrimination against women and religious minorities and persecutions of religious dissidents that proponents of Islamization currently insist are mandated by rules of Islamic law likewise mimic patterns of discrimination that have existed elsewhere, including in Western societies. The fact that Islamic rationales are offered for these garden-variety human rights violations should not immunize them from critical scrutiny.

In assessing Islamic human rights schemes, I have endeavored to treat all sources and arguments objectively, but that does not mean that I feel obligated to withhold judgment or to suppress my own opinions. My own views—with supporting reasoning—are expressed at various points in this book. On human rights questions, I do not consider that it is possible or even advisable to withhold all judgment on the moral rightness of positions. In clarification, I would say that one can write on questions of slavery and torture in a serious and fair manner without withholding all judgment about whether slavery and torture are benign or evil institutions and without suppressing all one's moral judgments and philosophical convictions.

I believe in the normative character of the human rights principles set forth in international law and in their universality. Many such principles—though hardly all—do have roots in rights formulations initially codified in the West, but this does not mean that the values that have since won international consensus after inputs from countries around the globe are irremediably Western and at odds with the needs and values of people living outside the West. On the contrary, Muslims made important contributions to the genesis of international human rights law and have been increasingly outspoken in their demands to enjoy the protections that it affords. Thus, the assertion that international human rights are "too Western" for use in Muslim societies seems particularly ill informed. Believing that international human rights law is universally applicable, I naturally also believe that Muslims are entitled to the full measure of human rights protections offered under international law. This inclines me to be critical of any actual or proposed rights policies that violate international human rights law, including US actions and policies affecting Muslims that are at odds with this law. I welcome the emergence of principled human rights advocacy in Middle Eastern countries and the growing tendency to interpret Islamic sources in ways that harmonize Islamic law and international human rights. However, I recognize at all times that I am an outside observer commenting on developments in another tradition, one in which my views can have no normative or prescriptive value. Therefore, I do not endorse any particular reading of Islamic doctrine, nor do I presume to signal which interpretations Muslims should deem authoritative.

Since the ideas of liberal reformist Muslims are under constant attack by powerful and extremely well-financed conservative forces determined to delegitimize their programs, their beleaguered positions cannot escape being subjected to the harshest possible critical scrutiny. One encounters lobbyists and hirelings assiduously working to discredit Muslim critics of the human rights abuses of Middle

Eastern governments and to boost the prestige of Islamist ideologues who aim to dismantle human rights. In reaction to this imbalance, I think it appropriate critically to examine the use of Islam by governments and ideologues to legitimize policies antithetical to rights, a political use of Islam that people in Middle Eastern countries can assail only at great risk to their personal safety and freedom.

Over the past several decades, international human rights law has won a wide following among Muslims. I learned about Muslims' growing involvement in international human rights through Muslim friends, who drew me into human rights networks. I have participated in a variety of efforts to try to secure greater respect for human rights in Middle Eastern countries—and not just in those countries pursuing Islamization. Aside from my formal study of how Islam relates to human rights issues, my work in support of human rights and the research I have done in Libya and Tunisia have convinced me that Islam itself is not the cause of the human rights deficiencies in the Middle East. Human rights abuses may be every bit as pervasive and just as severe in countries where Islamic law is in abeyance and religious impulses are suppressed as in countries where it figures, at least officially, as the legal norm. One must recognize that, depending on the political context, supporters of Islamization may easily turn out to be the victims of rights violations committed by secular regimes, and the violations of their human rights must be taken as seriously as any other rights violations. However, rights violations that do not take place under the rubric of applying Islamic law lie outside the scope of this volume.

This book focuses on the legal dimensions of human rights problems, examining the questions within the framework of comparative law and comparative legal history. Given the centrality of law in the Islamic tradition, the legal emphasis is warranted. However, there is no intention to imply that Islam is exclusively a legal tradition or that comparative legal history is the only legitimate way to approach this topic. In a more comprehensive study on the relationship of Islam to human rights, one would ideally want to include analyses of how principles of Islamic theology, philosophy, and ethics tie in with the treatment of human rights. This would carry one into areas beyond the comparative legal analysis of civil and political rights that is the sole concern of this work. The reader who conscientiously attempts to follow all the arguments and the specific comparisons in the following chapters will probably concur that the arduous task of sorting out the existing material is sufficient.

Ann Elizabeth Mayer

Acknowledgments

The genesis of this book lies in my four decades of study of Middle Eastern history and law. My interest in the subject of human rights in the Middle East emerged only belatedly, stimulated by talks with Middle Easterners. The attitudes toward human rights expressed by Middle Easterners of various backgrounds struck me as being different from what my academic training in the West had led me to expect, and their perspectives were often hard to reconcile with Western descriptions of Middle Eastern culture and Islamic political thought. I became intrigued by the comments that my interlocutors made about their aspirations for democratic freedoms. I noticed a common—though not unanimous—tendency to demand the same kinds of rights protections that exist in liberal democracies in the West and a general impatience with all official rationales that governments exploited to justify repression and discrimination. Ultimately, I concluded that Muslims' ideas of human rights deserved more systematic investigation, and I reoriented my research accordingly.

There are so many Middle Eastern friends and colleagues to whom I owe debts of gratitude for their generous efforts to enlighten me about their aspirations to enjoy human rights and their understandings of the Islamic tradition that it would be impossible to list them all here. It is also prudent not to mention names in a book on this sensitive topic, when human rights issues are now so bitterly contested and when speaking out on these issues can be dangerous. I hope that the many friends and colleagues who have assisted me in my study of Islam and human rights appreciate that I acknowledge owing them a great debt.

I also wish to thank Oceana Press for kindly granting me permission to reprint excerpts from the translation of the Iranian Constitution published in their collection.

A.E.M.

ISLAM
AND
HUMAN RIGHTS

CHAPTER 1

Comparisons of Rights Across Cultures

Background Issues

In the Muslim Middle East there have been strong but mixed responses to the ideals of human rights. These responses have included reformulations of human rights in Islamic terms. A selection of Islamic human rights schemes is analyzed in this book. Despite the fact that they share certain features in common, Islamic human rights schemes turn out to reflect the influences of the contexts in which they have arisen. Therefore, what I analyze here is not how Islam per se pertains to civil and political rights, but rather how various documents shaped by particular circumstances delineate where Islam stands on human rights.

The Islamic religion was a deeply ingrained feature of the culture of the traditional Middle East. In the course of the difficult modernization process to which all Muslim countries have been subjected, societies in the Middle East have been transformed. Extensive adjustments have been made to Islamic institutions during that process, and Islamic thought has been reformulated in response to changed realities and to globalization.[1] Some of the problematic features of Islamic human rights schemes are a direct result of the authors' failure to take into account these societal transformations.

Those formulating Islamic doctrine in the Middle East today confront a situation where Muslims are calling for greater freedom and protections for their rights. The latter are seeking relief from oppression and discrimination at the hands of contemporary governments that hold unprecedented power. Muslims' resentment of unaccountable, despotic governments has prompted a surge in activism supporting democratization and human rights.[2] This agitation has threatened established elites, who often seek to legitimize their policies by appeals to Islamic authority. Governments seeking to deploy Islam as a weapon against

1

mounting demands for reforms are motivated to support the production of Islamic human rights schemes that endorse their positions.

Debates about the relationship between the Islamic legal tradition and human rights have gained in practical significance in the wake of the Islamic resurgence that began after the Arab-Israeli war of 1967. Prior to that time, studying the nexus between Islam and human rights seemed to be an academic concern, because the movement toward secularization of legal systems had been very consistent, leaving only small islands of Islamic substantive rules in what were basically modern, secularized legal systems. In a dramatic turnabout, the Islamic resurgence led to calls for the rejection of Western legal models and for the Islamization of laws. Proliferating Islamization measures have made the topic of Islamic law and human rights a matter of intense controversy. To date, the major debates have centered around civil and political rights, where, depending on interpretations, the rules of Islamic law and international human rights law may sharply diverge. How Islam factors into the important areas of economic and social rights or solidarity rights has so far provoked less interest and controversy.

Distinctive Islamic human rights schemes need to be evaluated in the context of Muslims' diverging opinions on the relationship between Islamic and international law, there being no settled Islamic consensus in the area. Muslims have espoused a wide range of opinions on rights—from the assertion that international human rights replicate values already inherent in Islamic teachings and are fully compatible with Islam to the claim that international human rights law is the product of alien, Western culture and represents values that are repugnant to Islam. In between these extremes, one finds a range of compromise positions that in effect maintain that Islam accepts many but not all aspects of international human rights law or that it endorses human rights with certain reservations and qualifications.

Views that are representative of this middle ground constitute the primary focus of this book. In the following chapters, I analyze specific aspects of selected Islamic human rights schemes that purport to represent definitive Islamic countermodels of human rights, replacing the international formulations. None of these have been ratified by a universal consensus or by a democratic referendum; instead, they have been promoted by members of educated elites and by undemocratic governments. The fact that I focus on the middle-ground positions does not mean that they are more authentically Islamic than other views on the relationship of Islam and human rights. They are simply more attractive subjects for investigation, because they reveal the conflicting trends presently at work in shaping Islamic approaches to rights. Middle-ground positions illustrate the problems of taking elements from international human rights law and transplanting these into a matrix of values and principles that are being retained from the premodern Islamic legal heritage, trying to customize the secular transplants to make them fit in a framework that is derived from aspects of the Islamic heritage that are based on very dissimilar premises. Such middle-ground positions are also of great practical importance, because they closely correlate with stances on human rights that have been adopted by many governments. Middle Eastern governments are motivated to compromise in order to maintain their position in the United Nations system of international law, which requires respect for international human rights law. However, the same governments may simultaneously intend to accord overriding priority to Islamic law.

It is possible to have a regional system of human rights that affords more extensive rights protections than international law, as is the case in the European Union, but countries belonging to the Organization of the Islamic Conference that endorse Islamic human rights have not to date shown interest in devising schemes affording more extensive protections for human rights. On the contrary, Islamic human rights schemes, such as the one promoted by the Organization of the Islamic Conference, have consistently used distinctive Islamic criteria to cut back on the rights and freedoms guaranteed by international law, as if the latter were excessive.

Cross-comparisons between actual and proposed Islamization measures and more theoretical statements of Islamic human rights are undertaken in later chapters. Various Islamic human rights schemes are compared with international human rights standards to elucidate where they coincide with or diverge from each other and to highlight where they obfuscate rather than clarify their intent to undermine the protections afforded by international law. Some theoretical discussions of how the Islamic tradition relates to human rights are also examined. The literature arguing that Muslims may have human rights, but only according to Islamic principles, provides the rationales for many recent laws and government policies.

Comparative legal history, the mainstay of the following analyses, is an academic field where major political controversies are rarely encountered. As an eminent comparatist has stated, comparative law looks at the relationships among legal systems and their rules, and ultimately it is concerned with similarities and differences in legal systems and rules in the context of historical relationships.[3] In the main, scholars can expect such studies to be of interest to specialists and can assume that any controversies they may provoke will center on issues of scholarship. If scholars are comparing, say, German law and Japanese law, they do not expect the mere undertaking of such comparisons to be condemned by their academic peers. Nor do they expect that their work will be denounced as politically unsound if they objectively record the similarities and differences they have uncovered or state whether aspects of one system were historically derived from the other. Those writing on comparative legal history are used to working in a discipline free from ideologically inspired precensorship. Thus, they may express their conclusions without worrying about pressures to adjust them to fit the canons of a prevailing orthodoxy.

At a time when all Muslim countries belong to the United Nations system of international law, there should be no barrier to evaluating Islamic human rights schemes and Islamization measures using international human rights standards. Since this type of study is quite conventional in the field of comparative legal history, one might not expect that researching and commenting on Islamic human rights schemes would resemble stepping into an ideological minefield. In actuality, a Western scholar discovers that referring to international law to make critical assessments of Islamic approaches to rights provokes hostile reactions. Such assessments may be condemned as ethnocentric ventures designed to prove that Western laws are superior to Islamic law. Due to the mistaken assumption that accepting the authority of international human rights instruments necessarily requires Muslims to abandon their own cherished values and to submit to distinctively Western priorities, some read support for the universality of human rights as tantamount to an endorsement of Western imperialism. This can inspire attacks on Western scholars who undertake critical analyses of Islamic human rights as minions of Western hegemonic projects or purveyors of Orientalist ideas. Persons who are determined to defend Islamic schemes circumscribing human rights against critical appraisals do not hesitate to resort to grotesque distortions or to disseminate arrant falsehoods in efforts to deter the publication of negative assessments.[4] This hostile environment may account for why such appraisals have been slow to emerge.[5]

In these circumstances, it is not surprising that much of what has been written on Islam and human rights has been characterized by an uncritical mind-set and an unwillingness to tackle real problems. Fortunately, the climate that has inhibited scholarship from treating international human rights norms as applicable to Muslim societies has recently started to improve.[6] As Muslims have spoken out in ever greater numbers to denounce their governments for violating international human rights law, it has become harder to argue that criticizing governments for using Islamic doctrine to undermine and evade international human rights law is equivalent to promoting the ideologies of Orientalism and Western imperialism.

In light of the rank disinformation being disseminated, it is essential both to offer a preliminary response to the kinds of objections that are typically raised by those seeking to discredit critical assessments of Islamic human rights schemes and to establish the nature and goals of this comparative legal study.

Why Comparative Analyses Engender Controversies

What are the reasons why critical scholarly comparisons of international human rights law and Islamic human rights schemes have been effectively ruled off-limits? These informal but effective pressures for precensorship are less likely to come from scholars in the fields of international and comparative law than from specialists in area studies such as the study of the Middle East or Islam, especially from anthropologists. Islamologists and other students of the Middle East tend to become acculturated by their academic milieus in ways that lead them to conclude that such comparisons are objectionable. They may uncritically assimilate ideas voiced by many spokespersons for Middle Eastern groups and institutions that reject the universality of human rights and offer what are ostensibly culture-based objections to international human rights law. Scholars who are conscientiously seeking to understand Middle Eastern attitudes may discard a critical perspective, fearing that it will reflect Western bias and will impede the understanding of Middle Eastern societies on their own terms. In contrast, I maintain that a critical and even skeptical perspective should be maintained in the face of assertions that human rights do not apply outside Western countries or claims that Muslims perceive these as alien and incompatible with their traditions.

Reacting to the perceived arrogance and hypocrisy of Western judgments, those who are aiming for a balanced approach may agree with complaints that the West has its own history of egregious human rights violations—including an extensive record of patterns of torture, genocide, religious persecution, racism, sexism, and centuries of slavery—not to mention the abusive treatment of Muslims during the colonial era. Having reached this conclusion, scholars may reflexively classify criticisms of Islamic human rights schemes as products of Western prejudices or campaigns to tarnish the image of Islam and to portray Islamic culture as primitive and cruel. Many perceive the ultimate goal of these critiques to be to demonstrate that Western culture is advanced and inherently superior and that Western political, economic, and cultural hegemony was and is a natural and beneficial phenomenon for humankind. Pointing out where Islamic human rights schemes fall short of international standards may be understood as efforts to prove that Western domination of Muslim countries in the past was justified and to legitimize current neo-imperialist projects.

Assumptions will inevitably be made that there is a link between scholarship that critiques human rights deficiencies in the Middle East and the US deployment of human rights rhetoric to justify invading Afghanistan and Iraq. These invasions were preceded by US governmental statements professing outrage over the human rights violations perpetrated by the Taliban and Saddam Hussein and were officially justified by US claims to be engaged in spreading the blessings of democracy and human rights in the region. Many observers see hypocrisy in US claims that these takeovers were motivated by concern for the human rights of the oppressed populations of Afghanistan and Iraq. Such claims rang hollow at a time when US policy accommodated gross human rights abuses by governments in the region that cooperated with US foreign policy strategies, when US military actions and mismanagement were costing a staggering toll in terms of death and human suffering among the "liberated" populations, and when Muslim prisoners were being brutally mistreated in US prison camps in places like Abu Ghraib, Bagram, and Guantánamo, where detainees were incarcerated without even the most rudimentary rights protections.

The case of Iraq is particularly problematic, because for several decades the United States had been willing to cooperate with Saddam Hussein's thuggish dictatorship and tolerate its egregious rights violations as long as it served US strategic goals. Only when US interests in the region were redefined did American policy reverse course to encompass regime change. The 2003 invasion of Iraq was characterized as "Operation Iraqi Freedom," and the ostensible human rights rationale was promoted after other pretexts for invading, such as Saddam's supposed connections to al-Qaeda and his alleged project of manufacturing weapons of mass destruction, proved illusory. Given the gross inconsistencies in US policy on human rights, official US claims to be advancing human rights in the Middle East have little credibility.

Seeing yet another chapter in the history of the imperialist West cynically invoking human rights deficiencies in Middle Eastern countries to justify self-interested intervention in the region, observers may automatically associate all academic writing dealing with human rights deficiencies in the Middle East with White House strategies. However, having conceded that the US government employs cynical human rights rhetoric, I do not see why independent Western scholars should be barred from assessing human rights issues in Middle Eastern societies if they are applying standards consistently to all parties—including the United States. If a scholar's study of foreign culture were to be disqualified simply by the fact that the foreign policy of his or her country of origin was characterized by hypocrisy, then most such study would be barred.

The argument that private criticisms of the treatment of rights in Muslim milieus are of a piece with hypocritical governmental policy is especially weak in the case of this study, which includes criticisms of the use of Islam to deny rights by regimes that were US allies. With respect to these, the United States was hypocritical not in the sense of judging their records particularly harshly but, rather, the reverse—it glossed over human rights abuses committed by strategically important governments that were either friendly or at least cooperative.

The United States provided the strongest military and economic support for President Zia's regime in Pakistan from his 1977 coup until his death in 1988 and was relatively tolerant of the rights violations perpetrated under his Islamization program. Washington has generally been reluctant publicly to denounce rights abuses in Saudi Arabia, one of the most valued US allies. In the case of Sudan, the United States was a staunch mainstay of the Nimeiri government in 1983–1985, when Nimeiri was pursuing his Islamization campaign, showing a readiness to accommodate its abuses. The Reagan administration even gave President Nimeiri a cordial reception in the White House in spring 1985 after Nimeiri had ordered the execution of a peaceable seventy-six-year-old Sudanese religious leader as a "heretic." Islamization was resumed in 1989 when a cabal of Islamists and General Omar al-Bashir overthrew the elected government. Its notorious record of human rights violations earned Bashir's regime pariah status until its willingness to assist the United States in fighting terrorism led to a dramatic warming of ties between the Sudanese dictatorship and the second Bush administration, which was willing to overlook retrograde Islamization measures and atrocities such as genocide and mass rapes in order to secure Sudanese cooperation.

Moreover, when Afghan factions fighting the Soviets and aiming to establish Afghanistan as an Islamic state showed disregard for human rights, the United States was still willing to underwrite their campaign. Despite the atrocious abuses perpetrated by the Taliban, plans for a UNOCAL oil pipeline across Afghan territory and other strategic concerns muted US condemnations until after September 11, 2001, when the regime was accused of shielding al-Qaeda terrorists.[7] Such treatment indicated that the United States in practice tolerated Islamic rationales for gross human rights violations—as long as the regimes served US policies. It also illustrated how the lives of Muslims and non-Western peoples may be devalued in the calculations of Washington officials. Thus, consistent critical appraisals of the human rights records in these countries hardly correlate with US policies, which have responded to human rights abuses in a selective and politicized manner.

Sensibilities about the linkage between critical assessments of Islam and imperialist projects have been exacerbated by the pervasive influence of Edward Said's seminal work, *Orientalism*.[8] In this book, Said argued that much of Western scholarship on the Orient, meaning the Islamic Middle East, has not been conducted in a spirit of scientific research but has been based on a racist assumption of fundamental Western superiority and Oriental inferiority. By positing ineradicable distinctions between the West and the Orient, Orientalist scholarship obscures the common humanity of people in the West and the Orient and, in Said's view, thereby dehumanizes Orientals in a way that serves the goals of Western imperialism.

Although Said was not a lawyer and did not examine the extensive studies of Islamic law that Europeans carried out when European imperialism was at its height, people influenced by his arguments have often tended to expand them carelessly to encompass the domain of legal scholarship. Said's work does have implications for the study of law in Muslim countries—but not the implications that his less perceptive acolytes tend to assume it has.[9] Although Said did not maintain that all critical examinations of Islamic institutions are infected by Orientalist biases, his disciples seem inclined to draw this inference from his book. In consequence, they may rush to condemn comparative analyses of Islamic law and international law—the latter being identified with the West—concluding that Orientalist prejudices are guiding such projects and mistakenly assuming that all Muslims regard international law as alien.

Notwithstanding common impressions to the contrary, the use of international human rights as authoritative standards is seen as entirely legitimate by the numerous supporters of human rights working within Middle Eastern countries. A case in point is the Casablanca Declaration produced by the First International Conference of the Arab Human Rights Movement, "Prospects for the Future," which took place in Casablanca, Morocco, on April 23–25, 1999, under the auspices of the Cairo Institute for Human Rights Studies with the collaboration of the Moroccan Organization for Human Rights. It was attended by one hundred representatives of human rights nongovernmental organizations (NGOs) from across the Arab world. After noting the need to examine the human rights conditions in the Arab world and the responsibilities and prospects of the Arab human rights movement, the Casablanca Declaration offered the following statement, which is representative of the views of Middle Eastern human rights activists more generally: "After extensive discussions, the Conference declared that the only source of reference in this respect is international human rights law and the United Nations instruments and declarations. The Conference also emphasized the universality of human rights."[10]

What opponents of human rights universality often miss is that treating international human rights as universal implies that peoples in the West and the East share a common humanity and that they are equally deserving of rights and freedoms. As the sharp international criticism of the US practice of extraordinary rendition and the US mistreatment of Muslims detained for suspected involvement in terrorism or insurgency has shown, international human rights law can be turned against Western powers that deny Muslims their human rights. To maintain that international human rights are inherently inconsistent with the traditional values of Muslim societies is to accept the quintessentially Orientalist notion that the concepts and categories employed in the West to understand societies and cultures are irrelevant and inapplicable in the East. To believe that Islam precludes "Orientals" from claiming the same rights and freedoms as people in the West is to commit oneself to perpetuating what Edward Said saw as the Orientalist tenet that Islam is a static, uniform system that dominates Oriental society, the coherence and continuity of which should not be imperiled by foreign intrusions such as democratic ideas and human rights.[11] Those who charge that comparisons of international and Islamic law, as they relate to human rights, are Orientalist implicitly endorse the same elitist stance as the cultural relativists—discussed below—which is that international human rights are the sole prerogative of members of Western societies. Therefore, they are distorting Said's message that categories such as "Islam" and "Oriental" should not be allowed to obscure the common humanity of peoples in the East and in the West.[12]

Cultural Relativism

At the core of many efforts to delegitimize comparisons of Islamic and international law is the conviction that such comparisons violate the principles of cultural relativism. Not all cultural relativists approach questions in an identical fashion, but in general they are inclined to endorse the idea that all values and principles are culture-bound and that there are no universal standards by which cultures may be judged. Similarly, they deny the legitimacy of using alien values to judge a culture and specifically reject any application of standards taken from Western culture to judge the institutions of non-Western cultures. For strong cultural relativists, evaluative comparisons of Islamic rights concepts and international ones are impermissible because such comparisons are believed to involve evaluating expressions of one culture by alien criteria. As a corollary, based on an identification—actually a misidentification—of human rights with distinctive Western values, they also oppose the idea that human rights norms are universal.[13] To impose on Third World societies principles taken from the Universal Declaration of Human Rights involves, according to this perspective, "moral chauvinism and ethnocentric bias."[14] Cultural relativists seeking support for their position might take comfort from statements like that of Iran's UN representative, Said Raja'i-Khorasani, defending Iran from charges that it was violating human rights. His argument that international standards could not be used to judge Iran's human rights record was paraphrased as follows:

The new political order was . . . in full accordance and harmony with the deepest moral and religious convictions of the people and therefore most representative of the traditional, cultural, moral and religious beliefs of Iranian society. It recognized no authority . . . apart from Islamic law . . . conventions, declarations and resolutions or decisions of international organizations, which were contrary to Islam, had no validity in the Islamic Republic of Iran. . . . The Universal Declaration of Human Rights, which represented secular understanding of the Judaeo-Christian tradition, could not be implemented by Muslims and did not accord with the system of values recognized by the Islamic Republic of Iran; his country would therefore not hesitate to violate its provisions.[15]

Raja'i-Khorasani identified the official position of the Iranian government rejecting international human rights with upholding Islamic religion and traditional culture. Similar assertions that governmental resistance to international human rights represents a defense of traditional culture and morality have been made by other governmental spokespersons in international conferences in attempts to defend governmental records of human rights violations, thereby demonstrating the political usefulness of the cultural relativist stance for foes of human rights.[16]

Employing a cultural relativist stance to deny the universality of human rights and to challenge the validity of comparative examination of international and Islamic versions of rights is problematic. An initial point that needs to be made is that cultural relativism, like Said's idea of Orientalism, is not a concept developed by legal specialists for application in the field of law. Cultural relativism is a principle that developed within fields such as cultural anthropology and moral philosophy.[17] There are several reasons why cultural relativism should not be invoked to delegitimize critical assessments of whether Middle Eastern governments are adhering to international human rights law.

As Jack Donnelly has noted, the interesting issue for cultural relativists is when there are practices that are internally defensible within the cultural system but unacceptable by external standards.[18] The opposition of cultural relativists to critical comparisons of Islamic and international rights concepts rests on an assumption that the curbs placed on human rights by restrictive Islamic versions of rights are accepted by Muslims—perhaps in the same way that Muslims accept the difficulties of month-long fasting—as part of their religious obligations. They assume that the internal Islamic cultural position on rights entails practices that are violative of external norms, in this case international law. The underlying assumptions are that Muslims do not think as Westerners do about rights and do not aspire to have them on the same terms. That is, cultural relativists assume that there exists a single authoritative, identifiably "Islamic" cultural position on rights issues—and they may imagine that Islamic human rights schemes express this position. In so doing, they tend to devote insufficient critical attention to what "culture" means in the context of modern state societies, wrongly equating Islamic culture with governmental representations of culture, and to discount the complexity and diversity of non-Western cultures more generally.[19]

An instructive illustration of the kinds of debates that go on within the world of Middle East specialists can be found in an article that reproduces e-mail exchanges in an on-line discussion—sharply edited, unfortunately—about Iran's official Islamic dress rules. The debates among specialists in the Gulf region were provoked when one commentator asserted that the Iranian government promoted women's rights and argued that the government-mandated *hejab* was a popular preference of Iranian women.[20] As the exchanges demonstrated, many professed experts on the Middle East refuse to distinguish between governmental representations of Islamic culture that are deployed to legitimize oppression and the actual attitudes of the Muslims affected by that oppression. They also exposed the Western tendency to disregard the significance of demands by people in Middle Eastern societies to enjoy human rights, in this case demands by Iranian women to make their own determinations about what their faith calls for in the way of dress. A priori generalizations about an Islam necessarily opposed to human rights were relied on, when what was needed were investigations of whether Muslims truly wanted to be governed by versions of rights that were said to be Islamic but that left them vulnerable to discrimination, mistreatment, and oppression.

Muslim Responses to and Involvement in the UN Human Rights System

Muslims since the 1980s have produced a large literature trying to define where Islam stands on human rights and comparing Islamic and international human rights. The very existence of this literature demonstrates that Muslims believe that such comparisons are both timely and legitimate. The frequent references to international human rights, even by Muslims who quarrel with these, show that these concepts are already percolating through Islamic culture and becoming part of the apparatus that Muslims use internally in debating laws and policies.

It is natural that rights concepts should have become a preoccupation of contemporary Islamic thought because they are intimately related to the actual political and legal problems facing all Muslim societies, which are struggling through incomplete transitional stages. As part of these transitions, Western-style governmental institutions have been imported and Islamic law and institutions have been increasingly displaced and marginalized, provoking a strong backlash in some circles. Among the cluster of institutions transplanted since the nineteenth century from the West, the foremost was the model of the modern nation-state. Importing this institution, with its great centralized power over society, broke with Islamic tradition; how to constrain such a leviathan had not been contemplated in Islamic jurisprudence. The nation-state is now ubiquitous in the Muslim world, along with its many accoutrements, including the establishment of national governments through constitutions, nationality creating ties to a particular country, and modern legislative and judicial institutions. Given this history, contemporary international human rights formulations are not incongruous in the context of the substantially Westernized legal systems of Muslim countries.

When one compares Islamic human rights concepts with international law, one is not judging an institution of an intact traditional culture by alien Western standards but examining Muslims' reworkings of concepts taken from Western legal systems that have already reshaped local models of governance. In these circumstances, to maintain that human rights are somehow alien to Muslim societies implies that the only legitimate Islamic models are those resembling the traditional Islamic institutions of previous centuries—thereby ignoring the vast changes that have occurred as a result of modernization and the institutional borrowings that accompanied that process. To maintain that respect for Islamic culture requires turning back the clock to the early nineteenth century, before "pure" Islam was compromised by adjustments to the modern world, is a view acceptable to only a few extremist groups, such as the Afghan Taliban.

The numerous recent efforts by governments of Muslim countries to justify their rejection of international human rights law on the basis of their alleged obligation to uphold Islamic principles are paradoxical, because those same governments have already indicated in various ways their acceptance of international law. Since Muslim countries have, without exception, joined the international community of nations formed under the auspices of the United Nations, they have agreed to be bound by international law. Muslim nations, like other nations, contribute to the formulation of public international law through their active participation in the United Nations and its affiliated organizations, including the drafting of legal instruments relating to human rights. Furthermore, Muslim countries have ratified many international human rights conventions.

Indeed, in a welcome development, a number of recent studies on the genesis of the international human rights system have amplified our appreciation of how input from representatives of Muslim countries influenced foundational UN human rights instruments. The studies document the relatively minor role played by Western powers such as the United States and highlight the significant contributions made by representatives of countries outside the North Atlantic region—including several Muslim countries. Of course, the personal leadership of Eleanor Roosevelt was vital in moving the human rights project forward at the UN, but the French jurist René Cassin, the Lebanese statesman Charles Malik, and the Chinese diplomat Peng Chen Chang were more influential in the drafting of the Universal Declaration of Human Rights (UDHR).[21] Far from finding human rights culturally alien, Chang, an expert on Confucianism, believed that Confucianism had laid the groundwork for human rights.[22] As Mary Ann Glendon observes, this deeply cultured man rejected stereotyping the East and the West as separate monoliths, each with a uniform culture. He asserted, "Culturally, there are many 'Easts' and many 'Wests' and they are by no means all necessarily irreconcilable."[23]

Interestingly, Cassin's assistant was his Iranian student, Fereydoun Hoveyda, who would later become a diplomat and earn a reputation as a man of letters. Hoveyda published his recollections of working on the project, and from his insider's account, it seems that Muslim countries were less inclined to find the UDHR religiously objectionable than to deem it problematic due to its unrealistic and utopian character. They found it hard to imagine that it could be implemented in their own countries, but they likewise did not see how one could expect Western countries to adhere to it.[24]

Susan Waltz conducted research on the participation of Muslim countries in the creation of the Universal Declaration and found that their representatives made important substantive contributions.[25] Muslims who want to discredit international human rights law promote the notions that Muslims were excluded from the process of producing this law, that the International Bill of Human Rights—comprising the UDHR and the two major covenants that were subsequently derived from it—expresses distinctively Western values, and that calling for human rights universality means supporting Western civilizational hegemony. Waltz's research shows that these charges are distortions and gross oversimplifications.

The representatives of Muslim countries apparently did not claim that the Islamic tradition precluded their accepting proposed human rights principles. However, they occasionally did try to block or modify some provisions; clashes with Islamic law would have been one likely basis for their objections, as in the cases of freedom to change religion and women's equality. A proclivity for such quibbling and disagreement was not limited to one faction, however; other representatives also disagreed on various proposed rights provisions, both in the UDHR and in the later covenants.

In typical Western accounts of the genesis of the UDHR, the objections and complaints made by the Saudi delegate, Jamil Baroody, are often noted, leading to generalizations about "Islamic" challenges to human rights universality or "Islamic" hostility to the UDHR.[26] In fact, the record is more complicated. Considering the opposition voiced by Baroody to the freedom to change religion that was eventually to be guaranteed in Article 18 of the UDHR, some observers have attributed his views to Islam—or, at least, Saudi Islam. However, Baroody was neither a Saudi nor a Muslim but a Syrian Christian. In any case, he did not expressly invoke Islam as a reason for his opposition. Johannes Morsink has found that the objections to Article 18 made by Baroody included ones completely unrelated to Islam, such as his assessment that in a provision affording freedom of religion, the language concerning the freedom to *change* religion was superfluous and that it was inconsistent to provide for the right to *change* religion as part of the freedom of religion when there were no corresponding provisions guaranteeing the right to *change* positions in the provisions on freedom of thought and conscience.[27] Some other delegations supported Baroody's objections, and not all of these were from Muslim countries.[28] Thus, leaping from Baroody's stated positions to generalizations about an "Islamic" hostility to the UDHR is unwarranted.

Since Islamic law as traditionally understood bars Muslims from converting to other faiths, one might have expected some Muslim countries to state that Islam stood in the way of their accepting the proposed Article 18 guaranteeing the right to freedom of religion and to change religion, but none seem to have chosen to do so—although Afghanistan, Egypt, Iraq, Pakistan, and Syria joined Baroody in expressing some qualms. Delegates from Muslim countries were not unanimous. As Waltz observed, at one point Sir Muhammed Zafrullah Khan, speaking for the Pakistani delegation, insisted that the Qur'an itself supported freedom of religion.[29] Significantly, no Muslim countries actually voted against Article 18 when it was finally put to a vote, suggesting that whatever objections they did have were not deemed vital.

As Waltz has noted, some objections were registered regarding Article 16 of the UDHR on marriage and the family. Among other things, this article provides that spouses are to have equal rights in marriage, that it should be entered into only with the free and full consent of both spouses, and that men and women have the right to marry and found a family "without any limitation due to race, nationality or religion." Elements in the article conflicted with Islamic laws in force in many Muslim countries that discriminated against women in various ways—such as giving the husband superior rights and barring Muslim women from marrying non-Muslim men, whereas Muslim men were allowed to marry Christians and Jews. Egypt, Iraq, Saudi Arabia, and Syria were among those objecting. Although the Egyptian delegate did not specifically cite Islamic rules, he argued that religious restrictions on who could marry whom should be acceptable.[30] Among Baroody's proposals was the idea that in lieu of being accorded equal rights, women should be entitled to "the full rights as defined in the marriage laws of their country"—a proposal that prompted a strong objection by the Pakistani delegate to the Third Committee on the grounds that Baroody's wording "would enable countries with laws discriminating against women to continue to apply them."[31] Again, Muslim opinion was divided. It was not only Muslim countries that quibbled; the United States, where states at the time had laws criminalizing interracial marriage, objected to a proposal for prohibiting limitations on marriage based on race, nationality, or religion.[32] Significantly, such an objection, which showed that the United States was unwilling to accommodate one of the most basic human rights ideals, has rarely been highlighted in accounts of the work leading up to the UDHR.

Baroody did make what sounded like a resentful complaint that the authors of Article 16 were, for the most part, using standards recognized by Western civilization and ignoring "more ancient civilizations," and he challenged the right of the committee to "establish uniform standards for all the countries of the world" or to proclaim "the superiority of one civilization" over others.[33] However, this challenge, which anticipates the later Asian values debate, seems to have had little resonance. No Muslim countries voted against Article 16, nor did any assert that the idea of women's equality in marital matters would clash with Islam. That is, although there is evidence that some Muslim delegates may have had religious grounds for objecting to certain aspects of Article 16, delegates from Muslim countries seem to have steered away from complaining that it conflicted with Islamic law.

Although Baroody was prone to quarrel with several proposals, his was not an absolute rejectionist stance; in fact, his comments revealed a certain ambivalence. Far from insisting that the UDHR would engender an irremediable clash of cultures, Baroody proposed that, although the declaration was "frequently at variance with the patterns of culture of Eastern states, that did not mean, however, that the declaration went counter to the latter, even if it did not conform to them."[34] Moreover, the emphasis on Baroody's carping in the secondary literature does not paint a balanced picture. The representatives of Muslim states generally supported the consensus behind the UDHR, and they, along with an array of small to medium-sized states, stayed engaged in the drafting process in the Third Committee, which worked to finalize the text. In contrast, the major powers had largely ceased their involvement after the UDHR project moved from the initial phase in the Human Rights Commission to the Third Committee.[35]

When the UDHR as a whole was submitted to the General Assembly, no Muslim country cast a vote against it, and Saudi Arabia was alone among Muslim countries in abstaining, being joined only by South Africa and various Eastern Bloc countries. All in all, it is inaccurate to claim that when the foundations of the modern UN human rights system were being laid, Muslim countries were foes of human rights universality. Indeed, the event was lauded by the Syrian delegate at the time, who exclaimed as the UDHR was approved: "[C]ivilization [has] progressed slowly, through centuries of persecution and tyranny, until, finally, the present declaration [has] been drawn up . . . Now at last the peoples of the world [will] hear it proclaimed that their aim [has] been reached by the United Nations."[36] In a similar vein, the Pakistani delegate proclaimed that Pakistan fully supported the adoption of the declaration because it was imperative that the peoples of the world should recognize the existence of a code of civilized behavior that would apply not only in international relations but in domestic affairs.[37]

As Waltz has established, after the UDHR was approved, representatives of a number of Muslim countries played influential and largely constructive roles working on the Third Committee in the subsequent development of the two main covenants, the International Covenant on Civil and Political Rights (ICCPR) and the International Covenant on Economic, Social and Cultural Rights (ICESCR). Although there was continued quibbling on the part of some Muslim countries regarding aspects of freedom to change religion and women's rights in marriage and divorce, all Muslim countries voted in favor of the covenants—even Saudi Arabia. Meanwhile, the United States—immersed in a phase of isolationism and suspicion of international institutions—had bowed out of the covenant drafting process altogether and announced in 1953 its decision not to ratify either covenant.[38]

In a relatively progressive move, several Middle Eastern countries sent women as UN delegates to work on human rights, including Iraq, Libya, Morocco, and

Pakistan. One of the outstanding contributors to the formulation of the two covenants was the Iraqi delegate, Bedia Afnan, who insisted that the equality of women be unequivocally affirmed and to whom women are indebted for her advocacy of the strong provisions on women's equality in Article 3 of both covenants.[39] In debates over women's rights in the ICCPR, the Libyan delegate turned out to be a vigorous advocate of equality of rights for both spouses in marriage.[40] The fact that these delegates' strong support for women's equality has largely been ignored while Baroody's more problematic stances have been emphasized is another indication of how accounts of the development of the International Bill of Human Rights have tended to reinforce presuppositions about the hostility of a hypostatized Islam to the values of human rights.

Waltz observed that Muslim countries took varied stances on human rights issues in the work producing the International Bill of Human Rights rather than following any Islamic consensus on rights. However, they did share a tendency to identify with the victims of human rights violations. They were naturally enthusiastic backers of the principle of self-determination and were united in denouncing the human rights violations that European colonialism had perpetrated and the hypocrisy of European powers speaking on behalf of human rights that they were unwilling to grant to subjugated populations in their colonies.[41] Muslim countries' positions on self-determination and the wrongs of colonialism were emphatically endorsed by a majority of UN members and became enshrined in many international human rights documents. At the same time, Western countries did not always take the stances that are associated with a pro-human rights philosophy and sometimes joined those opposing minority rights, measures to ensure effective implementation of human rights, and bans on discrimination.[42]

It is often overlooked that the package of rights in the International Bill includes economic and social rights. Muslim countries generally endorsed the ideas of economic and social rights, which the United States has always opposed as being antithetical to its capitalist ethos. When demands were made that, instead of preparing a single covenant elaborating on the rights set forth in the UDHR, economic and social rights should be set forth in a separate covenant, Muslim countries opposed the splitting of the domain of human rights.[43] Their position ultimately proved to be a losing one, but in recent years, supporters of human rights have tended to see human rights as being mutually reinforcing, concluding that splitting the UDHR into two separate covenants was misguided and harmful for rights. Thus, the position of Muslim delegates, the more progressive position, has belatedly won some vindication.

Despite the recent plethora of efforts to convince the world that there is a distinctive Islamic ethos that determines positions on human rights, in the years since the International Bill of Human Rights was produced, there has been relatively little difference between the stances of Muslim countries on human rights and those of non-Muslim countries. In recent years many Muslim countries have ranked among the more conservative countries when it comes to dimensions of civil and political rights that seem to challenge traditional family structures and sexual mores. In this they are not alone. They often wind up in alliances with the Vatican and conservative Catholic countries and on occasion with the United States, which under Republican leadership has often joined coalitions of countries opposing rights for women, children, and homosexuals, seeing these as offensive to religion and morality.[44] Muslim countries have uneven records of ratifying the major human rights conventions, with some countries having ratified most conventions and others few, but the very unevenness and dissimilarities in the patterns of ratifications indicate that, from the perspective of governments, there is no uniform interpretation of Islamic rights principles that dictates which international human rights to accept or reject.[45]

It is worth noting that various non-Muslim countries, including Angola, Belize, China, Japan, Liechtenstein, Luxembourg, Singapore, and the United States, as well as the Vatican, have had relatively poor records of ratifying human rights conventions. Muslim countries can hardly be said to be less likely to ratify than non-Muslim countries when the ratification records of Algeria, Egypt, Iran, Iraq, Jordan, Mali, Morocco, Niger, Syria, and Tunisia compare favorably with that of the United States. Even Saudi Arabia, which found itself unable to endorse the UDHR, has subsequently ratified many of the specific conventions, including the Women's Convention and the Convention on the Rights of the Child, neither of which the United States has ratified. Saudi Arabia, like many other Muslim countries, qualifies its adherence to human rights treaties with major reservations, but the United States has long had a similar habit.

Significantly, well after they all had achieved independence, Muslim countries speaking as a bloc formally recommitted themselves to the UN legal system. The 1972 Charter of the Organization of the Islamic Conference (OIC), the international organization to which all Muslim countries belong, expressly endorses international law and fundamental human rights, treating them as compatible with Islamic values. In the preamble of the charter, two adjacent paragraphs assert that the members are

RESOLVED to preserve Islamic spiritual, ethical, social and economic values, which will remain one of the important factors of achieving progress for mankind;

REAFFIRMING their commitment to the UN Charter and fundamental Human Rights, the purposes and principles of which provide the basis for fruitful cooperation amongst all people.

Having formally accepted the UN Charter, the cornerstone of the system of international human rights, governments of Muslim countries agreed to abide by UN standards. Nevertheless, some years later, Muslim countries seemed disposed to proclaim that they were bound by Islamic law, ascribing to it a higher authority than their commitments to international law.

International human rights law does not cease to bind states when their representatives formally claim that they are bound by conflicting religious law. Countries are not permitted to opt out of their international legal obligations at will or on pretexts of their own devising. As I discuss in Chapter 4, international law sets the standards for derogation from international human rights, and derogation is permitted only under specific, narrow conditions, which do not allow the appeal to religious rules to circumscribe or cancel human rights.

Muslim countries' challenges to the universality of human rights are attributed by cultural relativists to the particular dictates of Islamic culture, but this ignores a wider pattern of belated resistance to international human rights law, exemplified by the 1990s Asian values debate. Several non-Muslim Asian countries that had previously endorsed universal human rights later rejected them on the grounds that they were incompatible with their distinctive cultural values. Muslim countries were allied in this enterprise with the atheistic, Marxist leaders of the People's Republic of China, whose appeals to Chinese culture were patently cynical.[46]

One possible explanation for the timing of governmental attempts to wriggle out of commitments to international human rights law on grounds of alleged cultural particularisms lies in the forces of globalization, which dramatically altered the international scene. As Karen Engle's analysis indicates, when invoked against human rights universality, "culture" could be a proxy for many different concerns, including preserving national sovereignty, prioritizing economic and social rights, protecting the right to development over civil and political rights, or opposing Western double standards in applying rights.[47] Thus, the invocation of traditional Islamic values as a pretext for deviating from international human rights law may be a product of broader concerns.

Cultural relativists, many of whom sympathize when governmental spokespersons invoke "Islam" or "Eastern culture" to justify deviating from the human rights that they voluntarily chose to endorse, tend to deprecate and dismiss the positions of Muslims who support human rights universality and who protest the exploitation of Islam to deprive them of rights. However, these positions are being ever more assertively put forward, making them more difficult to ignore.

Evidence of these demands for the human rights afforded in international law can be found in the outcome of a 2003 conference in Beirut organized by the Cairo Institute for Human Rights Studies (CIHRS) in collaboration with the Association for the Defense of Rights and Freedoms (ADL). It was attended by thirty-six Arab NGOs, eleven international NGOs and intergovernmental organizations, fifteen legal, academic, and media experts, as well as seven government officials and parliamentarians acting as observers. Representatives from the Arab League and the United Nations High Commissioner for Human Rights also attended. The conference was supported by the European Union and held in close coordination with the International Federation for Human Rights (IFDH) and the Euro-Mediterranean Human Rights Network (EMHRN). The result of the conference was the Beirut Declaration on the Regional Protection of Human Rights in the Arab World, which affirmed human rights universality and included as Principle 3 an unqualified rejection of the use of "culture" or "Islam" to restrict human rights, asserting the following:

> Civilization or religious particularities should not be used as a pretext to cast doubt and to question the universality of human rights. The "particularities" that deserve celebration are those which make a citizen have a sense of dignity, equality and enrich his/her culture and life, and promote his/her participation in their own country's public affairs. Assuring the tolerant principles of Islam and religions in general should not be put in a false contradiction to human rights principles. The conference [warns against adherence to] aged interpretations of Islam that distort Islam and insult Muslims and lead to violations of human rights, particularly when excluding women and not allowing freedom of thought, belief, creative art, literature and scientific research.[48]

Another example can be found in the views articulated by the eminent Iranian human rights lawyer Shirin Ebadi, whose courageous work in highly perilous circumstances to advance human rights was crowned by a Nobel Prize in 2003. In the course of an interview granted in 2004, she succinctly stated her position on the compatibility of Islam and human rights:

> I am Muslim, to begin with. It's perfectly OK that there are certain people who do not accept Islam at all. Therefore, to announce that I am a Muslim can rub some people the wrong way. But my aim is to show that those governments that violate the rights of people by invoking the name of Islam have been misusing Islam. They violate these rights and then seek refuge behind the argument that Islam is not compatible with freedom and democracy. But this is basically to save face. In fact, I'm promoting democracy. And I'm saying that Islam is not an excuse for thwarting democracy.[49]

Muslims who defend the proposition that Islamic restrictions must be used to circumscribe human rights often argue that international human rights models are "too Western" to win Muslims' acceptance.[50] When asked to comment on this argument, Ebadi answered:

The idea of cultural relativism is nothing but an excuse to violate human rights. Human rights is the fruit of various civilizations . . . Those who are invoking cultural relativism are really using that as an excuse for violating human rights and to put a cultural mask on the face of what they're doing. They argue that cultural relativism prevents us from implementing human rights. This is nothing but an excuse. Human rights is a universal standard. It is a component of every religion and every civilization.[51]

Muslims like Ebadi who support international human rights may be dismissed by cultural relativists who brand them as Westernized or, even worse, as cultural traitors. In this stance, the cultural relativists betray their Orientalist proclivities, which, as discussed above, dispose them to view the peoples of the Orient and Occident as having inherently different natures and to consider the adoption of modern ideas and institutions by persons classified as Orientals as somehow incongruous and unnatural.[52]

The cultural relativist mind-set conditions Westerners to assume that "the natives" are content with systems that Westerners would find oppressive. As an Argentinean observer of the attitudes of cultural relativists has noted, the cultural relativists' position implies that

countries that do not spring from a Western tradition may somehow be excused from complying with the international law of human rights. This elitist theory of human rights holds that human rights are good for the West but not for much of the non-Western world. Surprisingly, the elitist theory of human rights is very popular in the democratic West, not only in conservative circles but also, and even more often, among liberal and radical groups. The right-wing version of elitism embodies the position, closely associated with colonialism, that backward peoples cannot govern themselves and that democracy only works for superior cultures. The left-wing version, often articulated by liberals who stand for civil rights in Western countries but support leftist dictatorships abroad, reflects a belief that we should be tolerant of and respect the cultural identity and political self-determination of Third World countries (although, of course, it is seldom the people who choose to have dictators; more often the dictators decide for them).

The position of relativist scholars who are human rights advocates illustrates an eloquent example of concealed elitism.

Such persons find themselves in an impossible dilemma. On the one hand they are anxious to articulate an international human rights standard, while on the other they wish to respect the autonomy of individual cultures. The result is a vague warning against "ethnocentrism," and well-intentioned proposals that are deferential to tyrannical governments and insufficiently concerned with human suffering. Because the consequence of either version of elitism is that certain national or ethnic groups are somehow less entitled than others to the enjoyment of human rights, the theory is fundamentally immoral and replete with racist overtones.[53]

Why are Western cultural relativists so ready to mistake official, ideologized representations of Islamic culture for authentic manifestations of indigenous culture and tradition? The currently voguish romantic communitarianism may dispose some in Western academia to accept uncritically any arguments on behalf of preserving cultural identity at the expense of human rights.[54] However, there are reasons to distinguish Islamist ideologies and governmental policies aiming to restrict human rights in the name of upholding Islamic law from efforts to preserve the cultural traditions valued by local communities. In order to enforce their "Islamic" rules, states such as Iran have to resort to coercive measures like threats, beatings, jailings, torture, and executions. Where governmental recourse to harsh sanctions is used to enforce compliance, the standards involved cannot embody authentic tradition. Authentic tradition imposes itself on its own authority and is normative because it has authority.[55] Thus, authentic living tradition is automatically accepted as such and does not have to be imposed with police-state tactics on a resisting population. The imposition of an official Islam by coercive governmental measures is more akin to "traditionalism," or the *ideology* of tradition. Thus, for example, throughout the Middle East, traditional dress is voluntarily worn by men and women who adhere to tradition as an expression of their cultural identity, whereas the uniform modest dress style that Iran's ruling clerics impose is enforced by aggressive police measures, often very brutal ones, which would be totally unnecessary if the dress rules actually corresponded to a popular sense of cultural identity.

If traditional Islamic values are being selectively utilized and manipulated for political ends by governments, this should be seen as part of a broader phenomenon in the Third World. Jack Donnelly's remarks are worth citing in this regard. He warned that "while recognizing the legitimate claims of self-determination and cultural relativism, we must be alert to cynical manipulations of a dying, lost, or mythical cultural past" and suggested that "traditional" culture may be more complex than is commonly imagined:

In the Third World today, more often than not we see dual societies and patchwork practices that seek to accommodate seemingly irreconcilable old and new ways. Rather than the persistence of traditional culture in the face of modern intrusions, or even the development of syncretic cultures and values, we usually see instead a disruptive and incomplete westernization, cultural confusion, or the enthusiastic embrace of "modern" practices and values.[56]

Western cultural relativists may lapse into fantasies of a "mythical cultural past," treating an idealized vision of tradition as if it had normative effect, when in fact it no longer corresponds to the day-to-day realities in the Middle East. They may fail to perceive how rapid urbanization, industrialization, and factors such as access to international media are creating conditions that foster the de-sire for human rights among people in the Middle East. Many Muslims have risked imprisonment, torture, and even death to stand up for the same human rights principles that cultural relativists maintain are incompatible with cultural values in the Muslim world. Cultural relativists would do well to consider ques-tions posed by a scholar familiar with Arab human rights activism:

> There are thousands of militants of the cause of human rights across the Arab world, people who subscribe to the notion of universal human rights. Who has the authority to decree that their belief in the ideal of universal human rights is a betrayal of their culture? They have achieved a synthesis of the cul-ture they were raised in on the one hand, and of values that promote equality and non-discrimination among all citizens on the other hand. The fact that there are thousands of them, in many areas of the Arab world, shows that this synthesis is not alien to our most fundamental values, those that are embed-ded in the traditional culture. Who has the right to declare them to be cultural apostates?[57]

Leaders in the Muslim world have reacted in ways that indicate their aware-ness of the mounting popularity that human rights enjoy. Concerned about their legitimacy, several have found it prudent to make concessions—although often merely cosmetic ones—to their citizens' demands for the observance of in-ternational human rights. For example, in June 1988, after years of trampling on human rights, Libya's long-standing military dictator Mu'ammar al-Qadhafi tried to reinvent himself as a champion of human rights, issuing his own Libyan human rights charter, releasing hundreds of political prisoners, and seeking to distance himself from his own sorry record by publicly denouncing the human rights abuses that had previously been carried out under his regime.[58] He even established a lavishly funded human rights prize to be bestowed in his name. Of course, as Qadhafi's stranglehold on power continued and his determination to crush all dissent remained fervid, the human rights initiatives turned out to be devoid of practical effect. However, Qadhafi is sensitive to shifting political cur-rents, and the fact that a leader guilty of so many egregious human rights viola-tions should deem it worth his while to try to wrap himself in the mantle of human rights is an indication of mounting pressures for expanded human rights.

Increasingly, human rights groups and Islamist movements compete for the loyalties of disaffected Muslims, and sometimes their appeals to the disaffected share common themes.[59] In many Muslim countries, Islam has become the most potent language of political protest against oppressive dictatorships and military regimes. Popular support for groups calling for "Islamization" in situations where they oppose undemocratic secular governments may signal more a repudiation of governmental policies than the intent to support the specifics of the Islamization programs that are pursued by these groups once they come to power. As I have noted elsewhere, when proponents of Islamization are in the opposition and are seeking to win backing for their programs, they tend to treat Islamization "as a scheme for reorganizing society that, because of its divine origins, can serve as a panacea for political, economic, and social ills."[60] Islamist groups trade on the positive connotations of Islam, using slogans like "Islam is the solution," while eschewing detailed descriptions of the measures that they intend to carry out. As they campaign to build up their constituencies,

> what reinstating the shari'a might involve in practice is often left vague . . . This vagueness is politically useful, since it allows Muslims who favor Islamization in the abstract to read into programs . . . the content that they would like them to have. Were the goals of an Islamization program specifically enumerated, Muslims who were committed to a different vision of Islamization could be alienated. Where left vague, "Islamization" could be espoused by Muslims hoping to achieve a wide variety of goals.[61]

In situations where governments are in place that are carrying out Islamization measures, the record has shown that they are not prepared to allow free and democratic elections to test whether the voters, after years of experience with what Islamization programs entail in practice, still endorse these. Unfortunately, even semi-free elections are infrequent in Middle Eastern Muslim countries, so there have been few tests of how voters would evaluate governmental Islamization programs after living under them. However, looking at patterns of holding and not holding elections in countries that have lived under Islamization for decades, one can draw some conclusions. In Pakistan and the Sudan, the official Islamization programs were undertaken by military fiat, not on the basis of any electoral mandate. They were indirectly repudiated by a majority of voters in brief interludes when the military dictatorships imposing them ended and relatively free national elections were held in which candidates associated with Islamization fared poorly. During the buildup to Iran's Islamic Revolution, Ayatollah Khomeini deliberately avoided specifying his plans to turn Iran into a theocracy imposing medieval Islamic rules. Since the clerical elite seized the reins of power, no candidates have been allowed to run for office unless they deferred to the official Islamic ideology, accepted theocratic rule, and were approved by Iran's clerical rulers, a policy that suggests that these rulers fear being voted out if ever candidates opposed to them are allowed to campaign in free elections. The fact that democratization has been consistently seen as a threat by regimes with long investments in Islamization suggests that these regimes doubt that their official Islamization measures enjoy widespread popular support.

This is not to say that if human rights were submitted to referenda in Muslim countries, voters would endorse all features of the International Bill of Human Rights; as in other parts of the world, democratic voting could open the door to curtailing some rights. It is possible that if Muslims were allowed to vote freely, segments of the Muslim population would endorse some Islamic criteria at odds with international human rights law. Moreover, there is no reason to assume that if given a chance freely to express their opinions, most Muslims would call for precisely the same human rights formulations that one finds in Western legal systems. Their priorities could well diverge, even as the views of the United States and Canada diverge on many rights issues, despite the fact that the two countries are closely linked in terms of their history and legal heritage. Westerners tend to overlook the significant differences in rights concepts and rights protections that exist in Western countries. This is true even within the European Union, which has adopted the concept of a "margin of appreciation" in order to accommodate different national approaches to human rights.[62]

Respect for international human rights law does not require that every culture take an identical approach, but it does require that human rights be defined and protected in a manner consonant with international principles. One Muslim scholar who has offered a thoughtful critique of typical misuses of cultural relativism has suggested that a proper respect for cultural relativism means that we should accept "the right of all people to choose among alternatives equally respectful of human rights," and that the latter must include the rights of life, liberty, and dignity for every person or group of people.[63]

The kind of cultural relativism that demands tolerance for dissimilar ways of resolving rights problems in different cultures seems legitimate. Likewise, the cultural relativism that calls for the West to forbear condemning intact traditional societies as defective because they fail to protect human rights according to modern international standards seems justifiable. There is little reason to disturb the already jeopardized equilibrium of the few communities that have so far managed to resist the inroads of globalization. The social orders in isolated mountain villages, the hierarchy in a remote oasis settlement, or the mores of a nomadic clan struggling to survive in inhospitable conditions and to preserve an ancient way of life may not conform to UDHR ideals, but these may offer their members a more humane environment than the larger state societies surrounding them. However, it does not seem defensible for cultural relativism to insulate the conduct and ideological apparatus of modern nation-states from critical scrutiny simply on the basis that the dictates of a religion or a culture override the duty to abide by international human rights law. The most serious and pervasive human rights problems afflicting the Middle East are not ones created by the increasingly rare survival of intact traditional cultures; they are ones created by governmental policies and laws inimical to rights and democratic freedoms—and in the case of Islamic human rights schemes examined here, by policies and laws that are designed by elites for implementation by modern state systems at the expense of the rights and freedoms of the individual. The way governments treat those they govern should not be ruled off-limits to critical scholarly inquiry, and evaluating Islamic schemes of human rights by the standards of the international human rights law that they seek to replace is entirely appropriate.

Summary

As the foregoing exposition has indicated, scholars writing on Islam and human rights have to be prepared to deal with a great deal of ambient "noise" that often interferes with attempts to communicate their analyses. Therefore, in this chapter I have explained how the political background impinges on discussions of this topic. In addition, this introduction has not only pointed out where some sources of confusion lie and warned against problematic tendencies in the secondary literature but also has addressed some common preconceptions that may impede readers' grasp of the nature and purpose of the kind of comparative legal analysis that is undertaken in subsequent chapters.

CHAPTER 2

Human Rights in International Law and Legal Systems in Muslim Countries

Sources and Contexts

International Human Rights: Sources

Even with a focus narrowed to civil and political rights, the range of potential sources is too vast to be covered in this book. For the comparisons undertaken here, the International Bill of Human Rights exemplifies the position of public international law on civil and political rights. The International Bill of Human Rights consists of the Universal Declaration of Human Rights (UDHR) of 1948, the International Covenant on Economic, Social, and Cultural Rights (ICESCR) of 1966, and the International Covenant on Civil and Political Rights (ICCPR), also of 1966, along with the ICCPR's Optional Protocol. The 1966 covenants entered into force in 1976. The Universal Declaration has, since its adoption by the UN General Assembly, achieved great international renown as an authoritative statement of the modern standards of human rights protections and is the single most influential international human rights document.

Acknowledging that there is not full academic or political consensus regarding the authority of aspects of the International Bill of Human Rights, one can nonetheless maintain that these rights are representative, if perhaps not ultimately definitive, statements of what a broad segment of the international opinion considers to be human rights. In addition, because of the general recognition of their validity in state practice—in which they are commonly treated as governing legal standards—many provisions of the bill have achieved the stature of customary international law and, as such, are binding on states regardless of whether they have ratified individual conventions.

Many countries have refused to ratify one or more of the two main covenants. Among the Middle Eastern Muslim countries that did not ratify the ICCPR and the ICESCR, one finds Pakistan, Saudi Arabia, and the United Arab Emirates (UAE). On the other hand, such diverse countries as Afghanistan, Algeria, Egypt, Iran (here it is undoubtedly significant that the issue of Iran's ratification came up prior to the Islamic Revolution), Iraq, Jordan, Kuwait, Libya, Morocco, the Sudan (during 1985–1989, the brief period of democracy between two military regimes committed to Islamization), Syria, and Tunisia have ratified the same covenants.[1]

Another reason for relying on these international human rights documents is that their formulations of human rights principles are succinct enough to allow easy comparisons with principles in Islamic human rights documents. Furthermore, the broad outlines of the Islamic documents in many instances are clearly inspired by provisions in the International Bill of Human Rights, even though they may differ from the latter in important respects.

Islamic Human Rights: Sources

The materials authored by Muslims purporting to define where Islam stands on human rights are extensive, and only a small fraction of the literature can be covered here. Due to space limitations and the fact that so much has been published on criminal law and procedure, the latter topics have been relegated to the margins. My survey focuses on selected provisions on civil and political rights in several Islamic human rights schemes and in Islamic constitutions. By "Islamic constitutions," I mean constitutions that purportedly adhere to Islamic principles, not merely constitutions of countries where the inhabitants are predominantly Muslim. The treatment of human rights in constitutions is critical, because international human rights law relies on national laws and institutions for its implementation. The international standards are meant to serve as models for the rights protected under the constitutions and other domestic laws in individual countries.[2]

The works to be examined have been composed by Muslims from both the Sunni and Shi'i traditions, from inside and outside governments, and from several countries. All are from the Middle East and North Africa, and the comparisons are limited to these regions. In selecting the material to be surveyed, I have emphasized Islamic approaches to human rights that have been presented by major Islamic institutions and influential figures as well as ones adopted by governments. The exception is the work of Sultanhussein Tabandeh, who, although a relatively minor figure, is interesting because of his candor and his detailed responses to various UDHR provisions. The range of material surveyed is, therefore, broad enough to permit some generalizations to be made.

A word is needed at this point about the way I characterize different rights positions. It is necessary to distinguish between the views of Muslims who favor and those who oppose adherence to international human rights standards. Since the aim is to contrast the views of Muslims who fall on one or the other side of the line in this dispute, for the purposes of this study, only two categories are utilized. Here and throughout the book, the terms *liberal* and *conservative* are used in their dictionary senses: "liberal" denotes views favoring reform and progress toward democracy, and "conservative" denotes views calling for the preservation of established institutions and opposing any changes in these. Here, liberal Muslims are those who favor adherence to democratic principles and human rights, and conservative Muslims are those who oppose democratization and resist human rights insofar as they appear to threaten established Islamic institutions. Obviously, many finer distinctions could be drawn, but they would only burden a work that is already heavily weighted down by discussions of very specific distinctions.

One of the documents I assess is *A Muslim Commentary on the Universal Declaration of Human Rights,* by Sultanhussein Tabandeh (occasionally transliterated as Sultan Hussain Tabanda). This pamphlet was originally published in Persian in 1966 and appeared in an English translation in 1970. Tabandeh, who was born in northeastern Iran in 1914, inherited the leadership of the Ni'matullahi Sufi order, a mystical brotherhood affiliated with Twelver Shi'i Islam. He was educated at Tehran University and Tehran Teachers' Training College and traveled widely in the Muslim world and also in Europe. He presented his commentary on human rights to the representatives of Muslim countries who attended the 1968 Tehran International Conference on Human Rights. His purpose was to advise them of the positions they should adopt vis-à-vis various provisions in the UDHR, which he had analyzed in terms of the requirements of Islamic law. In his comments, one sees the reactions of an Iranian Shi'i leader of a religious order. Apparently uninhibited by political considerations, he is much more outspoken in his criticisms of international human rights and his defenses of premodern doctrines than are many of his fellow conservatives.

A pamphlet titled *Human Rights in Islam,* by the internationally prominent Sunni religious leader from the subcontinent, Abu'l A'la Mawdudi, is also assessed. The centerpiece of the pamphlet, first published in 1976, is an English translation of a speech given by Mawdudi in 1975 in Lahore, Pakistan. In 1941 Mawdudi founded a political group, Jama'at-i-Islami, whose members are committed to the reinstatement of Islamic law and the establishment of an Islamic state in Pakistan; the group and allied factions have continued to be active in Pakistani politics over the past several decades. Before his death in 1979, Mawdudi wrote extensively on the application of Islam to contemporary problems, and his work was widely disseminated in translations. In recognition of what were said to be his outstanding services to Islam, he was accorded the King Faisal Prize by Saudi Arabia. Lacking the traditional religious education enjoyed by highly trained religious scholars, Mawdudi presented his ideas in a way that enabled him to reach a wide popular audience, and his words resonated with Muslims who shared his bitter resentment of Western power and the West's dismissal of Islamic civilization as backward. He adopted a combative stance vis-à-vis the West, castigating Western society and culture for decadence and materialism and arguing that Islamic civilization was far superior to its Western counterpart. His human rights pamphlet embodies the attitudes that informed his work generally.

The 1981 Universal Islamic Declaration of Human Rights (UIDHR) is discussed as well. This document was prepared by representatives from Egypt, Pakistan, Saudi Arabia, and other countries under the auspices of the Islamic Council, a private, London-based organization affiliated with the Muslim World League, an international nongovernmental organization headquartered in Saudi Arabia that tends to represent the interests and views of conservative Muslims. The declaration was presented with great public fanfare to the United Nations Educational, Scientific and Cultural Organization (UNESCO) in Paris. In a casual reading, the English version of the UIDHR seems to be closely modeled after the UDHR, but upon closer examination many of the similarities turn out to be misleading. In addition, the English version diverges from the Arabic version at many points. Both versions of the UIDHR are examined here. As I show, many of the formulations in the UIDHR are obscure or ambiguous. Although the UIDHR is generally representative of conservative Muslim opinion, the inconsistencies and equivocations in the UIDHR suggest that its authors may not have been able to achieve a consensus among themselves about how Islamic human rights should be formulated.

The rights provisions in the "Draft of the Islamic Constitution" are reviewed. These provisions were devised by the Islamic Research Academy of Cairo, which is affiliated with al-Azhar University, the most prestigious institution of higher education in Sunni Islam and a center of conservative Islamic thought. This draft constitution, published in 1979 in Volume 51 of the Azhar journal *Majallat al-Azhar,* appears to represent an official position of that institution as to what rights should be recognized in a political system based on Sunni Islamic principles. Published at the time that the Iranian constitution was receiving much attention and Iran's Shi'i leadership was attracting a following in the Sunni world, the Azhar draft may be seen as a Sunni response to the political repercussions of the Iranian Revolution and an effort to demonstrate that Sunni Islam was not bereft of resources to fashion a constitution for a modern government.

The rights provisions in the 1979 Iranian constitution, which, according to its preamble, "is based upon Islamic principles," is also assessed.[3] The Iranian constitution represents one attempt to resolve the question of what rights belong in a constitution tied to Twelver Shi'i Islam, and it may be usefully contrasted with the Azhar draft.

The 1979 Iranian constitution replaced Iran's first constitution, which was drawn up in 1906–1907. This first constitution had emerged out of a struggle between laypersons and clerics who supported the campaign to limit the powers of the shah by a constitution and laypersons and clerics who upheld a traditional autocratic system of government. That is, there were secular and clerical forces on both sides. The disputes were never resolved, and the constitution embodied compromises that left neither side satisfied.[4] The 1979 constitution did not signify a new beginning for constitutionalism but only an Islamic overlay resting on a constitutional tradition of many decades that was heavily indebted to French influences.

Although there were many elements in Iran's first constitution that seemed to recognize the supremacy of Islamic law, in actual practice, Iran's legal culture became increasingly secularized over subsequent decades. Objections by Iran's clerics to the displacement of *shari'a* law were largely ignored. After Iran's Islamic Revolution of 1978–1979, a draft constitution was prepared in spring 1979, a period in which leftist and secular forces still retained influence. Like the 1906–1907 constitution, this draft contained both secular and Islamic principles, but it showed far less deference to the ideas and wishes of conservative clerics than the constitution that was subsequently adopted. However, the balance of power soon shifted in favor of conservative clerics. The first draft was discarded, and in August 1979 elections that were denounced as unfair by secular political groups, a constituent assembly with a majority consisting of conservative Shi'i clerics was chosen to draft a new constitution. The new constitution, approved by a referendum in December 1979, reflected the consolidation of clerical control. It retained some features of the earlier draft but gave much greater scope for the application of Islamic law and significantly enhanced the power of the Shi'i clergy over the government and the legal system. Given the hostility of Ayatollah Khomeini to human rights, it is not surprising that the final text of the constitution, though referring to human rights in Article 20, did not include any endorsement of the UDHR, which secular groups had called for incorporating into the constitution.[5] The current Iranian constitution is, therefore, a product of a long history of struggle to define what role Islamic law and the clergy should play in the legal system and government. It perpetuates rather than resolves old tensions in this regard. Significant revisions were made in July 1989 in an attempt to establish a mechanism for resolving these tensions—without much prospect of ending them.[6]

Two recent documents are also considered. The Cairo Declaration on Human Rights in Islam was presented at the 1993 World Conference on Human Rights in Vienna by the Saudi foreign minister,[7] who asserted that it embodied the consensus of the world's Muslims on rights issues.[8] The declaration has assumed special importance because it continued the trends already established in previous

Islamic human rights schemes and because it was endorsed in August 1990 by the foreign ministers of the Organization of the Islamic Conference (OIC). It thus appeared, at least superficially, to embody a more general consensus—albeit only at the governmental level—on how Islam should affect rights. However, the appearance of consensus was belied by the actual stances on rights taken by OIC member states, which continued to diverge as widely after the issuance of the declaration as they had before.

The 1993 World Conference on Human Rights in Vienna provided impetus for Muslim countries to define their stance on human rights. The conflicts over whether human rights were inextricably linked to Western culture and whether they could or should be universal were central preoccupations of the conference.[9] In the period leading up to the conference, Saudi Arabia and Iran remained strong supporters of the 1990 Cairo Declaration. At one point, Iraq joined Iran in pressing the UN Commission on Human Rights for the acceptance of the Cairo Declaration as the Islamic alternative to international human rights.[10] That these regimes with their vastly diverging philosophies would promote any document on the basis of a commitment to shared Islamic values was highly improbable. Saudi Arabia's official Wahhabi Islam, which upheld the rule of an absolute monarchy and had a strong anti-Shi'i bias, was denounced by Iran. Saddam Hussein, Iraq's dictator, had been excoriated by Ayatollah Khomeini. A member of Iraq's Sunni minority, Saddam Hussein adhered to a secular Arab nationalist ideology and repressed and persecuted Iraq's restive Shi'i majority. However dissimilar their religious customs, all three regimes had a common practice of denying rights and freedoms to their citizens and resorting to drastic measures to repress and eliminate their opponents and critics, and all three apparently calculated that they stood to benefit from promoting an alternative to international human rights law that was supposedly based on Islam. On the occasion of the OIC meeting in Tehran in December 1997, Iran and various other OIC members continued to press the idea that the existing UN human rights system was excessively Western and needed to be adjusted to accommodate the culture and religious values of Muslim countries, a view rejected by UN Secretary General Kofi Annan, who insisted that human rights were universal.[11]

Also reviewed is the Basic Law of Saudi Arabia, which was issued on March 1, 1992.[12] Unlike Iran, Pakistan, or the Sudan, Saudi Arabia was not pursuing Islamization, having elected instead to retain premodern Islamic law as set forth in juristic treatises as the law of the land. Instead, Saudi Arabia was belatedly embarking on a program of tentative reforms of a kind that most nations had already undertaken by the early twentieth century. The 1992 Basic Law, although very rudimentary, was the closest thing to a constitution that Saudi Arabia had ever possessed. The provisions of the Basic Law purported to derive from Islam and to establish a government that likewise derived from Islam.[13] The disparity between the rights that the Basic Law affords and those in the Cairo Declaration, which Saudi Arabia had also publicly espoused, is yet another sign of the difficulties that Muslim states have in articulating a coherent policy on rights.

The new Afghan and Iraqi constitutions are briefly discussed in later chapters. Of course, these documents were prepared after the previous regimes had been overthrown by US military invasions, and therefore US advisors had significant input into the constitution-drafting process. Nevertheless, in both countries, the question of how to balance the competing claims of Islam and human rights has been a central bone of contention, just as it was in several other Muslim countries.

Aspects of a number of other publications dealing with how Islam relates to human rights are also discussed for the purpose of comparison. I stress throughout this critique that the fact that the Islamic human rights schemes presented here are referred to as "Islamic" does not imply that the principles involved represent definitive statements of where Islamic doctrine stands on rights issues, nor does it mean that all or even a majority of the world's more than 1 billion Muslims would endorse them. The question of how human rights protections relate to the Islamic tradition remains an intensely contested issue throughout the Muslim world.

The Islamic human rights documents reviewed here represent in many respects a middle ground between two sharply opposed positions. Muslims in the middle tend to advocate compromise positions, asserting that Islam does accept human rights—as long as those human rights are subordinated to Islamic criteria and incorporate Islamic values. The result is a mélange—and often a very awkward one—of international law principles with concepts that are taken from the Islamic legal heritage or that are presented as having Islamic pedigrees.

The literature corresponding to the compromise position offers the most interesting material for comparison with international legal standards. It provides a fascinating illustration of what happens when two very dissimilar legacies combine, producing a blend of legal principles with no historical antecedent. As it happens, the compromise view that Islam tolerates human rights in some form but imposes conditions and restrictions on them is also one that has enormous political significance. Over the past decades, regimes undertaking Islamization programs and states that derive their legitimacy from their application of Islamic law have increasingly exploited the notion that unfettered rights are incompatible with Islam to justify restrictions that they impose on rights and freedoms.

Controversies over Islam and Human Rights

As the burgeoning human rights movement in the Muslim world has demonstrated, many Muslims believe that Islam and human rights can be successfully integrated, denying that the two are incompatible and even taking the position that Islam reinforces human rights.[14] Even Muslims who do not use the terminology of modern human rights often display attitudes revealing their belief that justice and respect for human life and dignity are such central principles of Islam that a legal system that fails to honor these cannot be in conformity with Islamic requirements.

Muslims who are appalled by the rights violations perpetrated in the course of Islamization programs include prominent Islamic clerics who have denounced oppressive governmental measures and curbs on rights undertaken in the name of Islam. For example, viewing the deteriorating rights situation in the Sudan in the wake of Omar al-Bashir's harsh Islamization measures and despite the great dangers of speaking out, in 1997 an imam in his Friday sermon denounced governmental repression, publicly asserting, "Islam does not accept oppression and confiscation of the rights of the people and suppression of the freedom of expression."[15]

The vigorous debates about Islam and human rights in postrevolutionary Iran have exposed how strongly Iran's clerics disagree on how Islam relates to human rights. In 1980, immediately after the revolution, Ayatollah Taleghani, one of Iran's most distinguished clerics, denounced the climate of repression, protesting the fact that the Khomeini regime was invoking Islam as it sought to limit freedoms, when, in his view, the protection of freedom was a central concern of Islam.[16] Ayatollah Taleghani saw Islam as a vehicle of liberation that was inherently inimical to restrictions on personal freedoms. Far from concurring with the official view that the pursuit of Islamization justified curbs on freedom, Taleghani charged that the ruling classes in Iran were attempting to further their own interests by using a self-serving definition of "Islam" to justify enslaving and exploiting the poor. Although Taleghani did not use the language of human rights or appeal to international law in his denunciations of oppression, in appealing for observance of the values of Islam, he was effectively implying that Islam and civil and political rights are natural allies. As disillusionment with Iran's corrupt and oppressive theocracy has mounted, many of Iran's most popular and prestigious clerics have followed Taleghani's example. They have spoken out to demand expanded rights and freedoms and denounced the official practice of using Islam to ratify tyranny, despite the fact that the regime punishes clerical dissent with particular fury.[17]

The controversies about Islam and human rights were put to a political test in the 1997 and 2001 Iranian elections. After long excluding any prospective candidates who might pose a challenge to the establishment, Iran's clerical elite miscalculated in 1997 and permitted Mohammed Khatami, a liberal cleric, to run for president. Although he was expected to attract only token opposition to the officially approved candidate, Khatami, to the chagrin of Iran's hard-liners, won a broad popular mandate, a surprise result that was repeated in the 2001 elections. His victories were achieved with promises to advance the causes of human rights, democracy, and the rule of law and to end the use of Islam to justify oppression.[18] Iranians, especially young Iranians, responded enthusiastically to Khatami's promises of liberalization, and many clerics and intellectuals were prompted to speak out in support of human rights and to denounce the conservative clergy's use of Islam to crush freedom.[19] However, conservatives intent on maintaining their stranglehold on power were able to thwart his reform efforts and even began to escalate their repression. Khatami was not up to the task of curbing the entrenched hard-liners, and when in 2004 they engineered a victory of conservative candidates for parliament, a period of tentative liberalization came to an end. Tehran mayor Mahmoud Ahmadinejad, an acolyte of Ayatollah Khomeini who was inflamed with a similar kind of ideological zealotry, won the presidency in June 2005 after the Council of Guardians had drastically winnowed the candidate list to preclude the election of a charismatic reformer like Khatami. His victory led to further clampdowns on human rights in the name of Islam.

As this case illustrates, critical assessments of Islamic rationales for rights violations come not only from Western observers but also from Islamic clerics, who are deeply versed in the Islamic tradition, and from ordinary Muslims like the citizens of Iran, who have had a good deal of experience with the repression of human rights under Islamization. At the other end of the spectrum, one finds Muslims who are determined to see medieval jurisprudence upheld and who disparage human rights as reflecting alien, Western values that Muslims are obligated to reject. Thus, some Iranian clerics have offered scornful denunciations of human rights. Ayatollah Khomeini asserted, "What they call human rights is nothing but a collection of corrupt rules worked out by Zionists to destroy all true religions." Ali Khamene'i, then president of Iran and not yet elevated to the dignity of supreme jurist, stated: "When we want to find out what is right and what is wrong, we do not go to the United Nations; we go to the Holy Koran. For us the Universal Declaration of Human Rights is nothing but a collection of mumbo-jumbo by disciples of Satan."[20]

In summary, contemporary Muslim opinion is far too divided to provide a basis for making general pronouncements regarding where Islam stands on rights. It is not appropriate for an outsider to interfere in an internal doctrinal debate among Muslims. However, it is legitimate for an outside observer to investigate what the range of opinion among contemporary Muslims is, to present critical comparisons and appraisals of various Islamic versions of human rights, and to evaluate the significance of various positions that Muslims have taken. I undertake these tasks in the following chapters.

The Impact on Rights of Islamization
Programs in Iran, Pakistan, and the Sudan

A brief review of some patterns of governmental responses to demands for Islamization, as well as specific governmental Islamization measures, is in order. Measures to implement Islamic law and ideology in individual countries cannot realistically be severed from local politics. Thus, for example, the specifics of the Islamization programs in neighboring Iran and Pakistan differ considerably, and these two models in turn differ from the version of Islamization that was pursued in their neighbor Afghanistan under the Taliban. Islamization in the chaotic war-torn Sudan has had its own particularities. However, the official Islamization programs in all countries have tended to correlate with deteriorating human rights situations and a drastic weakening of institutions that could secure the rule of law.

The autocratic regime of the late shah of Iran pursued a course of rapid Westernization and only belatedly confronted the political potency of Islam as a means of mobilizing political protest. Iran's Islamic Revolution was originally a broad-based popular revolution, but a clerical faction ultimately wrested control over the government and crushed secular and liberal forces. Iran's Islamization program, following a major revolutionary upheaval and masterminded by conservative clerics, was naturally more radical and more representative of clerical attitudes than the versions of Islamization implemented by more secular leaders.

Strong countermeasures by undemocratic regimes in countries such as Algeria, Egypt, Iraq (before the US invasion), Syria, Libya, and Tunisia at least temporarily crushed opposition groups calling for Islamization. Other regimes tried to co-opt Islamization movements by making concessions to demands for reviving Islamic law. In 1979, two years after his coup overthrowing Pakistan's elected government, the military dictator General Muhammad Zia ul-Haq launched an official Islamization campaign, which he pursued until his death in 1988. The aftereffects of his Islamization measures continued to be felt long after his demise; Pakistan is an unstable polity, and even leaders not favoring Islamization have had to tread warily lest in rolling back Islamization measures they would further rile Pakistan's numerous, well-organized Islamist groups. Islamization was inaugurated in the Sudan in 1983–1985, during the last years of Ja'far al-Nimeiri's military dictatorship and again after the military coup of June 1989, led by Omar al-Bashir, overthrew the elected government.[21]

In these countries, Islamization was theoretically designed to bring the law and the administration of justice into conformity with the standards of the *shari'a,* or Islamic law. Many rules taken from the premodern *shari'a,* or at least ostensibly inspired by *shari'a* principles, were enacted into law, and the previous Western standards were abandoned. Not only substantive laws but also courts and enforcement practices were altered to reflect what were officially described as Islamic requirements. The Western-influenced bar and judiciary were regarded as roadblocks in the way of implementation of Islamic law. In all three countries there was a pattern of replacing judges who had Western-style legal training with Islamic clerics or persons with a traditional Islamic education. Members of the bar in these countries, who had the outlook of highly trained professionals and who were influenced by liberal values that supported human rights, often found it difficult, if not impossible, to fulfill their professional responsibilities in the changed circumstances. In Iran and the Sudan, Islamization had the most drastic impact on the legal profession. After sharply curtailing the powers of lawyers in reaction to their criticisms of mounting political repression and the increasingly arbitrary regime of justice, the Iranian authorities finally took measures in 1981–1982 to dismantle and altogether destroy Iran's bar association, and the Sudan followed suit under the Bashir regime.[22]

All in all, the systemic changes made under the rubric of Islamization in Pakistan, Iran, and the Sudan did much to erode the rule of law by highly politicizing the administration of justice and compromising judicial independence. The deterioration meant particularly severe setbacks in Pakistan and the Sudan, where the legal systems had previously upheld a higher standard of justice than was common in developing societies. The pursuit of Islamization in Iran, Pakistan, and the Sudan also coincided with shifts in the pattern of human rights violations, contributing to an upsurge in aggravated discrimination against women and more aggressive persecution of minorities and religious dissidents. The significance of the overall change in human rights violations that accompanied the Islamization programs has been extensively documented by many reputable observers and by international organizations and institutions concerned with the protection of human rights.[23]

A clarification is in order. Islamization programs in Iran, Pakistan, and the Sudan correlated with policies of dismantling rights protections, but this does not mean that the negative outcomes of these programs are attributable to factors inherent in the Islamic tradition. Discussing official Islamic rationalizations offered for governmental policies should be distinguished from presenting Islam as a causal factor. There is merit in the analysis of a prominent Moroccan human rights leader, who treats Islamic law as a mere epiphenomenon and points to the dominant political culture as the cause of human rights problems in the Arab world.[24]

In general, regimes pursuing Islamization have reacted defensively and angrily when accused of violating human rights, even when proffering Islam as a pretext for these. This suggests that, by and large, despite their assertions that Islamic law justifies breaching human rights, states regard international human rights as normative and fear criticism for violating them. In a few cases, however, information

on egregious human rights violations was proudly disseminated by the governments involved as an indication of the seriousness of their commitment to applying Islamic law. This was the case in January 1985 when the Nimeiri regime
convicted Mahmud Muhammad Taha of apostasy and chose to publicize both
the trial and his subsequent execution by hanging, and in February 1989 when
Khomeini called for the murder of author Salman Rushdie. Such instances of
flaunting human rights violations have been exceptional.

When pursuing Islamization, the governments of Iran, Pakistan, and the Sudan were concerned that the deteriorations in rights would lead to embarrassing
constitutional challenges. As a result, various strategies were devised for obviating such challenges, including rewriting constitutional provisions so as to evis-
cerate rights or simply suspending them. In all three countries, Islamization has
led to the dominance of philosophies antithetical to constitutionalism.

In Iran, the basic approach was to elevate Islamic law above the 1979 constitution and to add a number of vague Islamic qualifications to constitutional
rights provisions. These Islamic qualifications are discussed in greater detail in
Chapters 4–8. Although the addition of qualifications to rights provisions did
not entirely eliminate conflicts between the government's conduct and certain
provisions of the Iranian constitution, it provided sweeping justifications for infringing on rights. For example, Article 4 of the Iranian constitution set the stage
for using Islamization as a pretext for diluting rights. It provides: "All civil,
penal, financial, economic, administrative, cultural, military, political laws and
other laws or regulations, must be based on Islamic criteria. This principle applies absolutely and generally to all articles of the Constitution as well as to all
other laws and regulations, and the *fuqaha* [Islamic jurists] of the Guardian
Council are judges in this matter." These jurists are Islamic clerics who, according to Article 110, are to be appointed by Iran's supreme religious leader. The
clerics on the council have been given the ultimate power to decide what laws
are or are not in conformity with Islamic principles.

In consequence, even constitutional rights guarantees cannot have force
should clerics decide that those guarantees are not compatible with Islamic principles. Significantly, the specific legal impact of Islamic principles on constitutional rights has never been clarified with any precision. The clerical elite has
dismantled many elements of Iran's largely French-based legal order but has not
replaced them with a firm framework of effective legality using Islamic standards, leaving Iran in a kind of legal limbo. As one human rights report on Iran
asserts, Iran's clerics have seriously undermined the rule of law in the country by
monopolizing the interpretation of core ideological precepts.[25]

Rather than showing the scrupulous concern for legality that would be expected on the part of senior jurists, Iran's ruling clerics have often displayed a

thuggish character. An example of their mind-set was presented in 1997 when Ayatollah Yazdi, the head of Iran's judiciary, reacted to Ayatollah Montazeri's challenge to the authority of supreme jurist Ayatollah Khamene'i. Montazeri, once Khomeini's chosen successor but later a bold critic of the regime's abuses and advocate of democratization, was barred from the succession and placed under house arrest. To chasten Montazeri for questioning a pillar of Iran's system of clerical rule, agents of the regime launched violent attacks on his home, and menacing demonstrations were staged by a hostile rabble. Not being sure that the violence and threats had been sufficiently intimidating, Ayatollah Yazdi thought it well to warn publicly that Montazeri would face "an even stronger response" if he did not desist from speaking out.[26] That is, in responding to critical remarks by an eminent cleric, the head of Iran's judiciary, instead of addressing the points that had been raised, spoke like the head of a criminal syndicate accustomed to threatening violence to obtain acquiescence—hardly like a judicial official charged with upholding the law.

Iran's theocracy has afforded the country what should be called "political law," amounting to a system where laws and courts are subordinated to politics.[27] The imposition of Iran's official Islamic ideology has shaped features of the human rights violations perpetrated since the revolution, especially in Iran's treatment of political prisoners and the distinctive systems of torture utilized in Iran's prisons.[28] The extensive record of human rights violations that the regime has accumulated since 1979 makes it impossible to cover them here; they have been well chronicled in reports by Amnesty International and Human Rights Watch.

In the Sudan and Pakistan, a different approach was taken: Their constitutions were effectively suspended during most of their respective Islamization programs. Several aspects of the connection between Islamization and the human rights violations perpetrated by the Sudanese and Pakistani regimes are catalogued here.

President Ja'far al-Nimeiri, who had ruled the Sudan after seizing power in May 1969, decided in 1983 to try to consolidate his increasingly unpopular regime by cementing an alliance with the Sudanese contingent of the Muslim Brothers, who had long championed Islamization. He inaugurated an ambitious but haphazard Islamization program, which led to a renewed outbreak of civil war between the Arab and Muslim north and the mostly African animist or Christian South, a devastating conflict in which 2 million people may have died.[29] In 1984, Nimeiri sought to rewrite the Sudanese constitution to make himself the supreme political and religious leader but was thwarted by determined opposition. Instead, in order to press ahead with his Islamization program while avoiding charges that he was violating the constitution, he declared a state of emergency on April 29, 1984. Nimeiri expressly associated the state of emergency with the protection of

Islam, insisting that it was needed to preserve Islam from its enemies.[30] Although the state of emergency was officially lifted in autumn 1984 under US diplomatic pressure, in practice, constitutional rights remained suspended until Nimeiri's overthrow the following year. Obviously, Sudanese Islamization was closely associated with the suspension of the constitution.

Upon Nimeiri's overthrow by a popular revolution in 1985, there was a period of rule by a caretaker military regime, during which the 1973 Sudanese constitution was replaced by an interim constitution.[31] The Sudan reverted to a free, democratic system in April 1986. After plans were launched in spring 1989 to abrogate Nimeiri's Islamic laws, military leaders allied with Hassan al-Turabi's National Islamic Front (NIF) staged a coup, which resulted in the installation in July 1989 of a military dictatorship under General Omar al-Bashir, in which Turabi played the role of an éminence grise until a falling out with Bashir in 2001. With the 1989 coup, prospects for ending the ravages of the civil war collapsed. Zealously committed to Islamization, the Bashir regime promptly abrogated the interim constitution and suspended all the rights and freedoms that the Sudanese had enjoyed in the brief interlude of democracy. Mass arrests of politically active Sudanese ensued, political parties were suppressed, harsh censorship was imposed, and government employees who criticized the Islamization trend were dismissed from their jobs. Laws curbing women's freedoms were enacted, and ethnic and religious minorities were severely abused. The criminal justice system utilized harsh physical punishment, protracted incarceration without trial, and torture. Oppressive military dictatorship and systematic denials of rights and freedoms were associated with the pursuit of Islamization.[32] As the years went on, slaughters of civilians, the abduction and enslavement of children, and mass rapes were perpetrated.[33]

Bashir's regime promptly disbanded the independent Sudan Human Rights Organization, replacing it in 1991 with a docile, government-controlled organization by the same name with a mission to defend Khartoum from charges of human rights violations.[34] As it continued dismantling the institutions of civil society, the regime undertook various initiatives designed to enhance its image, such as staging sham elections in 1993 and issuing the Sudan Document of Human Rights, an attempt to convince outsiders that the Sudan protected human rights—albeit according to Islamic standards.[35] However, it was not until 1997 that the regime finally announced that a constitution would be promulgated and set up a committee to draft it.[36] That for eight years this regime did not even bother to start the process of establishing a formal constitutional basis for government was indicative of the disdain it had for constitutionalism.

Responses by Sudanese officialdom to independent human rights monitors, who continued to decry rights abuses, were revealing. Reacting to the critical 1994 UN Commission on Human Rights report by Caspar Biro, finding that

Sudanese law, including its Islamic laws, clashed with international law, the Sudanese delegate to the commission lashed out with charges that the findings constituted an attack on Islam.[37] The attorney general of the Sudan charged that Biro's report was "satanic," and he castigated Biro as "an enemy of Islam" guilty of "blasphemy" for criticizing the Sudan's Islamic laws.[38] That is, he resorted to thinly veiled death threats against the UN rapporteur—apparently assuming that the kind of terror employed by the regime to silence its domestic critics could be appropriately employed to intimidate critics in the international arena.

Human rights violations proliferated as the civil war continued and as Bashir embraced violence in his attempts to shore up his shaky control. One observer has aptly characterized the Bashir dictatorship as a totalitarian regime with a security obsession.[39] Another calls the outcome of his policies "a human rights disaster."[40] Much has been made of the regime's forced conversions to Islam in the Nuba region and in the South, but Bashir's oppression did not spare members of the Muslim majority.[41] By 2004, it was clear that a genocidal campaign backed by Khartoum was being waged against the Muslim Fur people in the province of Darfur in western Sudan, indicating that factors other than animus toward non-Muslims were driving policies that correlated with atrocious human rights violations.

As the Sudan suffered from being demoted to the status of a pariah state and as victory in the civil war proved elusive, the dictatorship chose to become more conciliatory. In 1998 a draft constitution was put forward that showed a willingness to compromise on the issue of Islamization. Under outside pressure, the Khartoum regime finally made a peace agreement with rebels in the South in January 2005, culminating in the adoption of a constitution signed on July 9, 2005. The new constitution rejects the features of Islamization that had prompted the civil war and embraces reconstruction and reconciliation through the recognition of Sudanese racial, religious, and cultural diversity. Whether the peace settlement will hold or the human rights picture will improve is hard to predict.[42]

There are intriguing similarities between the Sudan under Nimeiri and Pakistan in the period 1977–1988. President Muhammad Zia ul-Haq, after overthrowing the elected government of President Zulfikar Ali Bhutto, ruled Pakistan as a military dictator until his death in a plane crash in August 1988. President Zia declared martial law after seizing power, and it remained in force until December 1985. However, the formal termination of martial law in 1985 did not result in a full restoration of constitutional guarantees of fundamental rights, even though these were officially revived when martial law ended.

President Zia's reliance on a suspension of constitutional rights may be connected to the fact that in Pakistan, as in Nimeiri's Sudan, a project for drafting an Islamic constitution, which was to replace the existing 1973 constitution, eventually came to naught. It appears that Zia found the question of what constitutes an

Islamic constitution to be so divisive that he decided to abandon the project. Had it been pursued, given President Zia's dictatorial style, it is probable that Islamic qualifications would have been placed on constitutional rights provisions, substantially reducing the protections that they afforded. It would then have ceased to be necessary to suspend constitutional rights, since the rights themselves would have become eviscerated, as they were in the 1979 Iranian constitution.

Zia used his pursuit of Islamization as the justification for his retention of dictatorial powers and the suspension of constitutional rights. As in Nimeiri's Sudan, the major thrust of Islamization in Pakistan under Zia was in the area of criminal law and procedure, which means that many of the developments in Pakistan lie outside the scope of this book. In a major address given in 1983, while all fundamental constitutional rights were formally suspended, Zia analogized his position as chief martial law administrator to that of a traditional prince, or emir.[43] Like Nimeiri, Zia indicated that opposition would not be tolerated:

One basic point that emerges from a study of the Quranic verses and the Prophet's sayings is that as long as the Amir or the head of State abides by the injunctions of Allah and his Prophet (PBUH) ["peace and blessings upon him"] his obedience becomes mandatory for his subjects or the people, irrespective of the personal dislike that someone may harbor for the Amir or any of his actions. Not only in my opinion but also in the opinion of legal experts and scholars, my Government, too, is a constitutional Government, which has been acting upon the tenets of Islam. We are devout Muslims. I concede, and I am proud of it, that the present Government is a military Government.[44]

Zia's dedication to Islam was offered as the rationale for a military dictatorship. In fact, Zia's ideas came from premodern Islamic thought, in which there was considerable support for the proposition that Muslims should obey persons in authority as long as they were not being commanded to engage in conduct that was sinful; some Muslims still believe that a government that applies Islamic law must be obeyed. Still, for all his appeals to Islamic loyalties, Zia seems to have been concerned about possible charges that his overthrow of the previous, elected government and his rule by martial law violated the Pakistani constitution—hence his surprising assertion that his was a "constitutional" government. In this assertion, Zia relied on the fact that his government was acting "upon the tenets of Islam," which to his way of thinking legitimated a military seizure of power and a subsequent military dictatorship. Notwithstanding this claim, "legal experts and scholars" would be hard-pressed to cite a constitutional provision that supported Zia's position. In fact, later events proved that Zia was worried that, should he ever lose political control, he and his associates could be prosecuted for acts committed during martial law. In 1985 he had the constitution amended to validate and affirm all the acts and rules of the martial law regime so that he would have special immunity to escape civil and criminal liability once martial law had ended.

In that same year Zia again had the constitution amended to include Pakistan's Objectives Resolution, an aspirational statement that had not formerly been treated as part of the operative principles of the constitution. The resolution was inserted into the text as Article 2-A, and one segment provided the basis for further Islamization measures, indicating that Pakistan was a nation "Wherein the Muslims shall be enabled to order their lives in the individual and collective spheres in accordance with the teachings and requirements of Islam as set out in the Holy Quran and the Sunnah."

Zia tried to consolidate his alliance with those Islamic clerics who supported his regime by granting them the opportunity to serve as judges. As a result of this policy, many persons deficient in conventional professional qualifications, with solely religious educations, were appointed to the judiciary, leading to changes that compromised the integrity and independence of Pakistan's formerly distinguished judiciary.

Through legal initiatives and court rulings such as the *Zaheeruddin* decision, discussed in Chapter 8, Islamization continued to have an impact well after Zia's demise.[45] Pakistan's leading politicians were locked in a bitter rivalry that precluded much benefit ensuing from the return to democracy. Benazir Bhutto, Zia's most determined opponent, and Nawaz Sharif alternated terms as prime minister, using their time in office to pursue partisan advantage rather than working to advance the national welfare. In late 1997, Prime Minister Nawaz Sharif emerged victorious from a fierce political contest with the president and the supreme court, a victory that undermined the independence of the judiciary. As Zia's protégé, Sharif had voiced his support for Islamization, and in 1998 he seemed poised to expand Islamization measures. However, before having had the chance to take Zia's Islamization to the next stage, he was overthrown in October 1999 by General Pervez Musharraf. Musharraf proclaimed himself "president" in June 2001, a status that was formally confirmed in a dubious election in 2002.

Musharraf, effectively ruling as a military dictator, suspended the constitution for several years before restoring it in 2003. A basically secular military officer, he has been preoccupied with Pakistan's difficult international relations and serious domestic unrest, making him reluctant to confront Islamist forces. With the spillover of turmoil caused by the overthrow of the Taliban in neighboring Afghanistan, US demands for Pakistani cooperation in the US war on terrorism, simmering anti-American sentiment and intensifying militant Islamism, aggravated clashes between Sunnis and Shi'is, and other explosive problems, his hold on power has been threatened from many angles.

In previous decades, Pakistani factions that called for Islamization did poorly in the polls, but in 2001, a coalition of such factions known as the Muttahida Majlis-e Amal, or MMA, succeeded in winning local elections in the Northwest Frontier Province and also gained influence in Baluchistan. The MMA also made a strong showing in the 2002 national elections. Intensely anti-American, the MMA has been able to exploit widespread anger over Musharraf's alliance with the United States.[46] With Pakistan lurching from crisis to crisis and tensions in the region growing ever more acute, predicting the future of Islamization in that country is difficult.

The Taliban Takeover of Afghanistan and Its Aftermath

Afghanistan has suffered traumatic turmoil since the brutal Russian occupation and the protracted and devastating civil war, which culminated in an eventual Russian pullout in 1989.[47] The 1996 conquest of most of the country by the Taliban, a Pashtun faction of Islamist zealots, led to the implementation of an extraordinarily repressive version of Islamization. Afghanistan is an example of how distinctive the local versions of Islam can be. The Taliban's official Islam reflected the attitudes of a brutish Pashtun rabble influenced by the ideas of Deobandi Islam, a rigid purist version of Islam that seeks to return to a supposed model of the original Islamic community and to reject all Western influences.

In October 1997 the Taliban renamed the country the Islamic Emirate of Afghanistan. The emir was a Sunni cleric with a reactionary mentality, Mullah Mohammed Omar, who ruled the country without the benefit of institutions of modern governance such as a constitution. Under the Taliban's Islamization program, human rights violations assumed epic proportions. After they discarded Western-style laws on the pretext of returning to the *shari'a*, the rule of law, already shaky, was further undermined. Taliban abuses included the arbitrary murders of many men, women, and children, the unacknowledged detention of thousands of persons abducted by various armed political groups, the torture of civilians, the rape of women, the savage persecutions of Shi'is and non-Pashtun ethnic groups, and the routine ill treatment of persons suspected of belonging to rival political factions. Under the rubric of applying Islamic law, a highly retrograde version of gender apartheid was instituted.[48]

Although Afghans suffered grievously under Taliban rule and many celebrated their overthrow in late 2001 by the invading US forces, Afghans subsequently faced disarray and insecurity under a weak central government. Living in their shattered country, Afghans remain deeply divided on crucial issues, including the acceptability of being governed by a Kabul regime answerable to the

US embassy. Due to the anarchic violence that prevails, it is unclear whether the 2003 Afghan constitution, the provisions of which effectively repudiate the previous Islamization campaign, will remain in force.

Saudi Arabia Confronts Pressures for Reforms and Liberalization

Unlike countries that were pursuing Islamization and dismantling rights that had previously been afforded under their modern constitutions, Saudi Arabia, where medieval Islamic jurisprudence retained its authority and powerful Islamists decried any loosening of Islamic strictures, was experiencing pressures to open up the existing system. In the domains where commercial and economic interests had required adjustments and to qualify for WTO membership in 2005, Saudi Arabia had been willing to sideline some Islamic law and institutions. However, in other areas Islamic law remained entrenched.

Since the 1990s, Saudi Arabia has embarked on a program of modest reforms, which included promulgating the 1992 Basic Law.[49] The tentative moves to accommodate change came after both liberal and conservative sectors of Saudi society had indicated their impatience with the Saudi family's autocratic rule, the deficiencies of the legal system, and the failure to respect basic rights and freedoms.[50] The Basic Law did not improve the country's deplorable human rights situation, which, even in the relatively charitable assessment of allied governments like the United States, continued to be marked by pervasive violations of international human rights.

The Basic Law affirmed the absolute monarchy, treating it as if it were grounded in the Islamic sources.[51] King Fahd appealed to "Islamic beliefs" to defend the failure to guarantee Saudis any of the rights that constitutionalism normally affords citizens. He asserted:

> The democratic system that is predominant in the world is not a suitable system for the peoples of our region. Our people's makeup and unique qualities are different from those of the rest of the world. We cannot import the methods used by people in other countries and apply them to our people. We have our Islamic beliefs that constitute a complete and fully integrated system. In my view, Western democracies may be suitable in their own countries but they do not suit other countries.[52]

Notwithstanding the truculent stubbornness of the ruling house, mounting pressures on the monarchy after the September 11, 2001, terrorist attacks on the United States and spillover violence on Saudi territory unsettled the status quo.

In 2003 and 2004 several petitions calling for reforms and expanded rights were circulated. The monarchy occasionally lashed out at those demanding change—for example, arresting thirteen reformers who in March 2004 tried to circulate a petition calling for a constitutional monarchy with an elected parliament and proposing the establishment of an independent human rights group. In the first concrete instance of tentative democratization, elections were held at the municipal level in April 2005. However, women were neither allowed to vote nor permitted to stand for office, despite increasing signs that the Saudi system of gender apartheid was under severe strain.

The 2005 death of the ailing and inept King Fahd and the accession to the throne of King Abdullah raised the possibility that a more astute monarch might see it in the regime's interests to rethink the past use of Islamic rubrics to buttress absolute monarchy and reactionary social policies. Shaken by the spread of terrorist movements claiming Islamic authority and by manifestations of mounting popular clamor for reform and democratization, in December 2005 the Saudi regime gathered OIC members in Mecca for a summit meeting. In a sign that even this group, long wedded to conservative positions, had a sense that change was in order, the declaration proclaimed a unanimous conviction "that reform and development are the priority to which all efforts should be channeled within a framework that is intimately molded in our Islamic social make-up," and that the Muslim community should "drive to achieve good governance, widen political participation, establish the rule of law, protect human rights, apply social justice, transparency, and accountability, fight corruption, and build civil society institutions."[53]

Summary

The consequences of Islamization programs for human rights deserve to be carefully considered. The pursuit of Islamization—or in the Saudi case, the regime's attempts to placate conservatives wedded to premodern jurisprudence—has correlated with patterns of disregard for human rights and with policies inimical to the rule of law. To date, one cannot find governments that are purporting to accord supremacy to Islamic law that have shown solicitude for protecting human rights as embodied in local constitutions, much less human rights as established in international law. On the contrary, their policies correlate with curbs on human rights and setbacks for constitutionalism.

CHAPTER 3

Islamic Tradition and Muslim Reactions to Human Rights

The Contribution of Western Civilization

To understand the problems of accommodating human rights within an Islamic framework, it is necessary to review the development of international human rights concepts. The human rights formulations utilized in international law are relatively recent, although one can find ideas that anticipate human rights concepts in ancient times. Certainly, the development of the intellectual foundations of human rights was given an impetus by the Renaissance in Europe and by the associated growth of rationalist and humanistic thought, which led to an important turning point in Western intellectual history: the abandonment of the premodern doctrines of the duties of man and the adoption of the view that the rights of man should be central in political theory.[1] During the European Enlightenment, the rights of man became a preoccupation of political philosophy, and the intellectual groundwork for modern human rights theory was laid.

Eighteenth-century British and French thinkers put forward the precursors of modern human rights ideas and had great influence on the rights provisions in the American Declaration of Independence of 1776, the Virginia Declaration of Rights of 1776, and the Bill of Rights that was added to the US Constitution in 1791. The most important model from this era was the 1789 *Déclaration des droits de l'homme et du citoyen,* developed at the time of the French Revolution. The formulations used in these models have had great historical influence.

Common to the British and French philosophies that prefigured modern human rights was the idea that the rights of the individual are paramount. In a survey of the historical evolution of rights concepts, one scholar has said that the significance of the shift from concern for law to concern for rights "derives from the fact that the concept of rights is individualistic in the sense that it is a from-the-bottom-up view of morality rather than one from the top down, and from the related fact that it generally expresses claims of a part against the whole."[2]

Long before international human rights law emerged, constitutionalism had been viewed as a means of securing negative rights that placed limitations on the powers of government, and the US Constitution and later European constitutions became models that were widely copied elsewhere. Central to these constitutions are curbs on governmental power and safeguards for individual liberty, which is to be insulated from governmental intrusions. The rules establishing these curbs embody reactions to experiences of oppression and misrule and presciptions for correcting these ills. Recognizing that individual rights would sometimes need to be curtailed in the public interest or in extraordinary circumstances, the drafters of constitutions sought to define and restrict the justifications that states could invoke to curtail rights, because it was appreciated that without such limitations states could unduly exploit various rationales for infringing rights.

It was on these Western traditions of individualism, humanism, and rationalism and on legal principles protecting individual rights that twentieth-century international law on civil and political rights ultimately rested. Rejecting individualism, humanism, and rationalism is tantamount to rejecting the premises of modern human rights.

The Role of the United Nations

Proponents of international human rights espoused the idea that rights should be guaranteed not just in constitutional rights provisions but also by an international law, binding on all nations. After World War II, the United Nations, as the preeminent international organization, took a leading role in formulating rights that had previously been left to domestic legislation. The UN Charter in 1945 called for respect for human rights and fundamental freedoms but did not undertake the difficult task of specifying what these entailed. The Universal Declaration of Human Rights (UDHR), adopted by the General Assembly in 1948, in its Preamble called for members to seek to construct a new world order on a sounder basis, one in which "recognition of the inherent dignity and of the equal and inalienable rights of all members of the human family is the foundation of freedom, justice, and peace in the world." Borrowing ideas from the European socialist tradition of the nineteenth century, the declaration assumed that rights, in addition to securing individual freedoms, had to encompass affirmative rights, which require governments to provide for people's basic needs.

One way of looking at this UN initiative is to see it as intimately bound to the particular situation facing the world community in the aftermath of World

War II, when people around the globe contemplated the horrors of the war and proposed that respect for human rights should be ensured to preclude any repetition. The wording of the Preamble can be interpreted as spelling out "a political, sociological, and historical interpretation of the historical circumstances of world society in the aftermath of World War II."[3] That is, the UDHR may constitute UN members' responses to a shared historical experience, meaning that its inspiration was independent of any particular theological or metaphysical framework. Viewed from this perspective, international human rights, even if they appropriate formulations from the Western tradition, have a different starting point, being grounded in a situated geopolitical moral rationality.[4] If one accepts this assessment, the fact that substantive UDHR provisions have antecedents that were first clearly articulated in the context of Western civilization does not mean that the new system inaugurated by the UDHR expresses principles that belong uniquely to the West.

Many instruments codifying international human rights were subsequently issued under the auspices of the United Nations, vastly expanding the scope of human rights law. As UN membership expanded to encompass all the countries of the Global South, many crucial declarations and conventions were produced with input from around the world. Rights of particular concern to the countries in the Global South, such as the right to self-determination and the right to development, were established. Although the patterns of ratification of international human rights conventions have been uneven and there is much that remains controversial about international human rights law, there is sufficient consensus to justify the claim that many human rights have come to be part of customary international law and are therefore binding on all countries regardless of the status of their ratifications.

The Role of Islamic Law

The learned literature on international human rights produced by academic specialists has traditionally shown an indifference to the Islamic tradition. Until recently, Islamic law was only occasionally mentioned in scholarly writing on international human rights, and then it was treated as a marginal, exotic phenomenon. Behind this lay an assumption about the authority of international law and its associated institutions and a belief in the relative backwardness of any Islamic models with which international law might conflict. The critiques offered by Muslims who object to international human rights law on religious grounds did not provoke much consternation or interest on the part of Western scholars of international law, for the latter did not feel that the legitimacy of international law was in any way jeopardized by assertions that it clashed with Islamic rules.

Since the 1990s, the interest in the topic of Islamic beliefs and Islamic law as obstacles to international human rights law has intensified, resulting in a burgeoning literature written from a variety of authorial standpoints, ranging from apologetic writings seeking to justify upholding Islamic standards at the expense of human rights to writings of Islamophobes seeking to portray Islam as defective and Islamic law as irremediably incompatible with human rights. This literature often evinces not so much a desire to explore the Islamic legal heritage or the evolution of Islamic thought as a search for proof of the clash-of-civilizations paradigm that was posited by the eminent Harvard political scientist Samuel P. Huntington in a famous article in *Foreign Affairs* in 1993. There is a common preoccupation with how Islam factors into the tensions between the West on the one side and various Muslim countries and Islamist movements on the other.

The perspectives of legal scholarship in the area of international human rights law are developed in the context of the unequal positions of the West and the Muslim world today. Centuries ago there was a brilliant Islamic civilization from which a relatively backward Europe borrowed extensively. Today it is the Western world that has attained the model of civilization that other societies generally seek to emulate—or to which they are forced to adjust due to the dynamics of globalization.

To assert that today the West has a legal tradition that is more attuned to the needs of contemporary governments and the operations of a globalizing system than its Islamic counterpart is *not* to say that Western law is, by its nature, superior or that Islamic law is, by its nature, inferior. The impressive accomplishments of Islam's great premodern jurists are easily on a par with the work of their Western counterparts. The subsequent lag in Islamic legal development vis-à-vis that of the West was the result of a complicated interplay of political, economic, and cultural factors. Islamic doctrines often were influenced by their environment at the same time that they were forces shaping that environment. For many reasons, the Islamic legal tradition failed to make the necessary adjustments to the new circumstances that presented themselves in the nineteenth century. By the twentieth century it was increasingly displaced; rulers of Muslim countries resorted to extensive borrowings from codified Western legal systems as they belatedly sought to catch up with the economically dynamic and more powerful West. Once premodern Islamic law had been shelved by the governments of Muslim countries, there was little incentive to rework it to make it suitable for application.

This critique in no way aims to establish that human rights law could not have developed in Islamic milieus or to deny that one can find many concepts that prefigure human rights in the Islamic sources and in the work of premodern jurists. However, although the Islamic heritage provided the potential resources for articulating human rights, this potential long remained latent. The formulations of distinctively Islamic versions of human rights discussed in this book were proffered well after Western and international human rights models had already been produced. This lag must be taken into account. Without exploring some of the factors and circumstances that may have delayed the production of human rights within Islamic frameworks, one cannot account for many of the peculiar features of the Islamic human rights schemes to be reviewed here. In many instances, aspects of Western rights concepts associated with a different level of political and legal development have been superficially imitated without their underlying tenets being fully examined or assimilated, and these borrowed concepts are inserted into a matrix of discordant values appropriated from the premodern Islamic heritage.

Meanwhile, except in rare cases, such as the episode of Taliban rule in Afghanistan, the legal systems in place in Muslim countries mostly rely on borrowed Western models. Even conservative Saudi Arabia has been displacing Islamic law and courts in the interests of economic development; it has been willing to make major adjustments to Western legal models in the course of its campaign to qualify for WTO membership. In contrast, it professes an aversion to Western models when human rights are the issue. That is, arguments are being made by proponents of Islamic human rights on behalf of Islamic particularism at a time when the systems that would be deploying Islamized rights are increasingly looking like copies of their Western counterparts.

The Premodern Islamic Heritage

As we have seen, the individualism characteristic of Western civilization was a fundamental ingredient in the development of human rights concepts. Individualism, however, is not a characteristic feature of Muslim societies or of Islamic culture, even though Sufism, or mysticism, which is a major component of the Islamic tradition, does have elements of individualism.[5] Other features of the Islamic tradition likewise provide foundations for an individualistic approach to rights.[6]

Islamic doctrines were historically produced in traditional societies, where one would not expect the elaboration of individualism. Non-individualistic and even anti-individualistic attitudes are common in traditional societies, whether in the West or elsewhere, where individuals are situated in a given position in a social context and are seen as components of family or community structures rather than as autonomous, separate persons. When I say that individualism was not prized in Islamic doctrines elaborated by Muslim thinkers in the past, I am making an observation that relates more to the historical context in which these ideas were produced than to Islam as a religion. This background does not warrant assertions that Islam is inherently incapable of accommodating individualism or necessarily hostile to it. As Khaled Abou El Fadl has noted, "Premodern

Muslim jurists did not assert a collectivist vision of rights, just as they did not assert an individualistic vision of rights."[7] However, as many examples in this book illustrate, proponents of the Islamic human rights schemes examined here have tended to associate the defense of Islamic values with the rejection of individualism and have espoused principles—such as a ban on converting from Islam—that cannot be reconciled with philosophical premises of individualism.

The connection of Islamic thought with the values of traditional societies has not, however, meant that Islamic culture lacks features that in the West contributed to the development of human rights. The Islamic heritage offers many philosophical concepts, humanistic values, and moral principles that are well adapted for use in constructing human rights principles. Such values and principles abound even in the premodern Islamic intellectual heritage.[8] However, historical factors such as the political ascendancy of an orthodox philosophy and theology that were hostile to humanism and rationalism—and ultimately, hostile to the liberal ideals associated with human rights—kept the exponents of such values and principles in a generally weak and defensive position over much of the history of Islamic civilization. If the adherents of rationalist and humanistic currents had attained greater political power and influence, such thinkers might have oriented Islamic thought in ways that would have created a much more propitious climate for the early emergence of human rights ideas. Despite their minority position, the views of rationalist and humanistic Muslim thinkers are definitely anchored in the Islamic tradition.

One of the most important rationalist currents in Islamic thought was that of the group known as the Mu'tazila, whose members' influence in the Sunni world reached its zenith in the ninth century, after which they were largely suppressed.[9] The Mu'tazilites called for rational interpretations of the Islamic sources and claimed that Islam mandated justice in both the political and social spheres. The community was to control the government, not to defer blindly to authority, and it was free to revolt against governments that denied fundamental liberties.[10] Although rationalist thinkers have generally been on the defensive in Muslim milieus since the crushing of the Mu'tazila, rationalist currents were never entirely extirpated, and in Twelver Shi'i Islam these ideas have remained influential. However, Islamic thinkers who have adopted the Mu'tazilite approach, openly espousing the idea of the supremacy of reason over Revelation and calling for laws to conform to human notions of justice, have always risked being branded heretical by staunch adherents of the view that neither Islam nor its divine law can be evaluated by reference to the tenets of human reason.

The cases of Nasr Hamid Abu Zaid, discussed in Chapter 8, and of Abdolkarim Soroush illustrate the continuing relevance of the controversies set in motion by the Mu'tazilites' refusal to defer meekly to established orthodoxy.

Soroush, an Iranian professor of philosophy, offers visions of an Islam stripped of the restraints on freedoms that had characterized the reigning Islamic ideology, expressly endorsing Mu'tazilite positions.[11] Among other things, Soroush has dared to maintain publicly that justice preceded Islam and that Islamic law should conform to the criterion of justice. Although Iran's ruling clerics attacked him for espousing heretical views, in exalting the principle of justice, Soroush was endorsing a rationalist philosophy that had long roots in the Shi'i tradition. His assertions gave Shi'is grounds for challenging demands that they defer unquestioningly to what they were instructed was required by Islamic doctrine, regardless of whether reason would say that such doctrine entailed injustice. For making bold critiques of the official manipulation of Islam to circumscribe rights and freedoms, Soroush was subjected to harsh censorship and restrictions designed to silence him, and he became a target of violent physical assaults and threats, which has often forced him to flee to overseas havens.

Some eminent Islamic philosophers, such as al-Farabi (d. 950) and Ibn Rushd ("Averroes") (d. 1198), came close to saying that reason determines what is right and true and that religion must conform to reason's dictates.[12] However, orthodox theologians in Sunni Islam were generally suspicious of human reason, fearing that it would lead Muslims to stray from the truth of Revelation. There was an ongoing tension between the rationalist inclinations of Islamic philosophers, many of whom were influenced by Greek philosophy, and the tenets of the dominant philosophy of ethical voluntarism, which was the prevailing view in the Sunni world. Human reason, in the orthodox Sunni view, was incapable of ascertaining what was just. Instead, the orthodox view was that Muslims should unquestioningly defer to the wisdom of God as expressed in Islamic doctrines, which represented instructions derived from the divinely inspired sources.[13] The dominance of this mainstream Islamic view made it difficult to realize an Islamic version of the Age of Reason.

The ascendancy of ethical voluntarism and the relative weakness of rationalist currents in Sunni Islam had important consequences for Islamic thinkers' views of the relationship of ruler and ruled. Islamic thought tended to stress not the rights of human beings but, rather, their duties to obey God's perfect law, which, by its nature, would achieve the ideal balance in society. Since whatever God willed was ipso facto just, according to the orthodox Islamic view, perfect justice could be achieved if all God's creatures, both ruler and ruled, were obedient to God's commands as expressed in Islamic law. Today one still finds this emphasis on duties. For example, Ayatollah Khomeini insisted that man had no natural rights and that believers were to submit to God's commands.[14]

Since the pious Muslim was simply supposed to understand and obey the divine law, which entailed abiding by the limits that God had decreed, demands for individual freedoms could sound distinctly subversive to the orthodox mind. Such demands might be taken to suggest that individuals did not consider themselves strictly bound to submit to the dictates of Islamic law and the commands of the authorities charged with its execution or that they were presuming to use their own fallible human reasoning powers to challenge the supremacy of religious teachings.[15]

The aim of Islamic law was generally conceived to be ensuring the well-being of the Islamic community, or *umma,* as a whole, in a situation where both the ruler and the ruled were presumed to be motivated to follow the law in order to win divine favor and avoid punishment in Hell. In consequence, *shari'a* doctrines remained highly idealistic and were not elaborated with a view to providing institutional mechanisms to deal with actual situations where governments disregarded Islamic law and oppressed and exploited their subjects.[16] Scholars of Islamic law did not traditionally address issues such as what institutions and procedures were needed to constrain the ruler and curb oppression; rather, they tended to think in terms of an idealized scheme, in which rulers were conceived of as pious Muslims eager to follow God's mandate.[17] Provisions to protect the rights of the individual vis-à-vis society or the government were wanting—with the single exception of the area of property rights, where the *shari'a* did provide remedies for the individual wrongfully deprived of property by official action.[18]

These characteristics of Islamic thought inhibited the growth of concepts of individual rights that could be asserted against infringements by governments but never totally eclipsed other currents in Islamic thought that were hospitable to rights ideals. One can identify humanistic currents beginning in the early stages of Islamic thought and continuing to the present.[19] In addition, early Islamic thought includes precursors of the idea of political freedom.[20] Concepts of democracy very much like those in modern political systems can be found in the earliest period in Islamic history in the ideas of the Kharijite sect, which broke off from mainstream Islam in the seventh century over the latter's refusal to agree to the Kharijite tenet that the successors to the Prophet Muhammad must be elected by the community.[21] Kharijites have been castigated for their unorthodox views, and their literature is not familiar to most other Muslims; but it still might be said that the Islamic tradition from the outset has included ideas that anticipated some of the democratic principles that underlie modern human rights norms.[22]

The premodern Islamic heritage comprised many intellectual currents. The dominant currents did not provide a congenial setting for the early development of human rights concepts, but there were from the earliest stages of the Islamic tradition features that offered the potential for successful integration of the premises of modern human rights. Those who deploy Islam as a bulwark against democratization and human rights are therefore utilizing only one aspect of the multifaceted Islamic heritage. As a former member of the Egyptian Organization of Human Rights has observed: "Authoritarian and oppressive projects draw on the wealth of authoritarian traditions, images and symbols that are present in every human culture. Liberationist projects draw on the resistance and emancipatory traditions that are equally present in every human culture."[23] Muslims who are mining their tradition for guidance on how to deal with the human rights dimensions of contemporary problems find ample ground for rejecting the authority of interpretations that construct Islam as an obstacle to progress.[24] As I argue throughout this book, where interpretations of Islamic requirements constitute obstacles to human rights, they likely are tied to political preferences that discount those elements in the Islamic heritage that can accommodate and support human rights.

Muslim Reactions to Western Constitutionalism

Just as there is no unitary Islamic position on the merits of rationalism or humanism, so there is no unanimity on where Islam stands vis-à-vis constitutionalism, an institution closely tied to the development of legal protections for rights. The modern system of human rights set forth in international law requires translation into rights provisions in national constitutions in order to afford effective legal guarantees for those rights. The reactions of Muslims to modern constitutionalism, which clearly came to the Middle East from the West, have historically run the gamut from enthusiastic endorsement to hostile rejection.[25]

The hold of Islamic doctrines, which tended to buttress the existing order and to stress the duties of the believer rather than individual rights, started to weaken as Muslim elites became familiar with Western ideas of law and governance in the nineteenth century. When Muslims began seeking legal means for curbing despotic and oppressive rulers, they turned not to the Islamic tradition but to Europe for models. Constitutionalist movements in the Middle East— typically inaugurated by adherents of secular nationalist movements and led by Westernized elites and often by Western-trained lawyers—were formed.[26] These groups perceived the inadequacies of traditional institutions of government in the Middle East. The relative weakness of Middle Eastern countries, which proved incapable of standing up to European powers, became associated with the failure to establish and protect political freedoms. Early constitutionalists moved in the direction of dismantling legally imposed inequalities among citizens, and the nation rather than the religious community became the focus of political loyalty.[27]

Muslims who advocated constitutionalism frequently found that conservative *ulama,* or learned men of religion, were among their most determined foes. Often the *ulama* fought constitutionalism in the name of preserving Islam because they were convinced that constitutional principles conflicted with *shari'a* law.[28] The historical pattern of *ulama* resistance to constitutionalism endured longest in Saudi Arabia, the Muslim country where conservative *ulama* have retained the greatest political influence. Despite decades of efforts by liberal members of the Saudi elite to win acceptance for the notion of constitutionalism, a basic law was not adopted until 1992, and even then it fell far short of meeting the standards of modern constitutionalism.[29]

However, there have also been many *ulama* who worked closely with liberal and reformist movements that promoted Western-style constitutionalism. The influential Islamic reformer Muhammad 'Abduh (d. 1905), who served as grand mufti of Egypt, is a prime example. An Azhar graduate and Islamic legal scholar, 'Abduh was a strong supporter of Egyptian nationalism and constitutionalism. He and other like-minded reformist clerics saw no fatal conflict between constitutionalism and fidelity to Islam.

In sum, one can say that Islamic clerics were divided and have remained so on the merits of constitutionalism and whether the *shari'a* permits it. As current events show, Muslims continue to dispute whether elements of constitutionalism, an institution that is of central importance for the protection of human rights, are compatible with the *shari'a*.[30] Controversies in this area have been aggravated as contemporary Islamization programs have tended to correlate with the degradation of constitutionalism, the suspension of constitutions, or as in the case of the Taliban, a complete rejection of constitutionalism as an alien, Western idea.

Muslim Ambivalence on Rights

As has been noted, international human rights find a receptive audience in Muslim countries. Many Muslims find the values and priorities of international human rights congenial, which suggests that currents of Islamic thought must provide conditioning that is favorable for the reception of human rights. But what of those Muslims who accept human rights only warily and only with substantial modifications and restrictions? What influences from the Islamic tradition account for their attitudes?

The best evidence of the attitudes of the authors of Islamic human rights schemes examined here lies in the texts of the schemes and in comments that they and other persons associated with the production of Islamic human rights documents have made. These sources are analyzed in detail in Chapters 4–8. However, some general characterizations of typical attitudes of the authors of Islamic human rights schemes can be made. Their attitudes are fundamentally at variance with the values of international human rights law, but their failure to acknowledge this has often engendered confusion.

Unlike Western scholars concerned with international human rights law, who consider international rights models without worrying about conflicting Islamic rules, the authors of Islamic human rights schemes are referring to two conflicting models. Even while promoting Islamic versions of human rights, they seem to regard international human rights as the ultimate norm against which all rights schemes are inevitably measured, one from which they do not want to be seen as deviating. This accounts for the defensive or apologetic tone that pervades much of the literature that puts forward distinctive Islamic schemes of human rights. On the evidence of the schemes analyzed here, the authors of Islamic human rights principles must feel torn between a desire to protect and perpetuate principles that they associate with their own tradition—in many respects a premodern one—and anxiety lest that tradition be assessed as backward and deficient if Islam is shown not to possess the kinds of "advanced" institutions that have been developed in the West. They thus seek to accentuate the formal resemblance between their schemes and the international ones even where that resemblance is misleading in terms of the actual level of rights protections they intend to provide. Where there are deviations from international models that are likely to provoke the opprobrium of the international community, they seek to conceal these or to minimize their importance. As the following analyses of Islamic human rights schemes shows, in such areas, the discussion of rights protections is often kept at a level of idealistic abstraction and individual provisions are kept vague, equivocal, and evasive.

The desire to produce human rights schemes that appear to correspond to internationally accepted norms correlates with a lack of coherence in the thinking behind Islamic human rights schemes. This lack of coherence would not have arisen if the authors were deriving their rights schemes from Islamic models after having first identified the philosophical premises on which an Islamic approach to rights issues should be based and an appropriate methodology for interpreting the Islamic sources. Creating a human rights scheme in this fashion would entail genuine confidence in the viability of resources within the Islamic tradition on rights questions. These authors do not in fact possess that confidence.

As is illustrated by the analyses of Islamic human rights schemes in the following chapters, the authors have not bothered to work out any clear theory of what rights should mean in an Islamic context or methods for deriving their content from the Islamic sources in a consistent and reasoned manner. Instead, they merely assemble pastiches of ideas and terminology drawn from two very different cultures without determining a rationale justifying these combinations of Islamic and secular elements or a way to reconcile the conflicting premises underlying them. That is, the deficiencies in the substantive Islamic human rights principles are the inevitable by-products of methodological confusion and weaknesses.

It must be emphasized that neither these methodological inadequacies nor the problematic results are inevitable consequences of working within an Islamic context. With an approach informed by methodological clarity and rigor, elaborating human rights on Islamic foundations can be fruitful. One can see, for example, in the work of Abdullahi An-Na'im the recognition that methodological questions are central to resolving the problem of where Islamic law stands on human rights. Offering a methodology that allows a fresh approach to the Islamic sources, An-Na'im has been able to develop a coherent scheme of human rights principles that is, for those who accept the validity of the proposed methodology, also one that rests on Islamic principles.[31] Using a different methodological approach, the work of Khaled Abou El Fadl has shown how a Muslim with a deep understanding of the resources in the Islamic heritage can mine these to elaborate meaningful human rights on an Islamic foundation.[32]

The methodological shortcomings that afflict Islamic human rights literature are just another manifestation of problems that typify contemporary Islamic thought more generally and that have seriously hampered its ability to keep pace with modern intellectual and scientific developments. Valuable critiques of the deficient quality of contemporary Islamic thought have been provided by intellectuals such as Mohammed Arkoun and, from very different angles, by Sadiq Jalal al-'Azm and Muhammad Sa'id al-Ashmawy.[33] Seeking to remedy these deficiencies, contemporary Muslims are reviewing old methodologies with critical eyes and proposing new approaches to the Islamic sources.[34] Thus, the methodological defects decried here reflect a much bigger problem that presently preoccupies some of the most outstanding figures in the domain of Islamic thought.

Authors of the Islamic human rights schemes discussed here, who both borrow from secular models and try to deny such borrowings, seem to worry that their creations will be perceived as basically derivative, as the schemes examined here obviously are. When they address the issue of what came first, the authors insist, against the weight of historical evidence, that Islam invented human rights and that the international standards are, at best, belated attempts to codify rules that Islam introduced in the seventh century.[35] Examples of such assertions can be found in the literature under consideration here and are also discussed later in this chapter

In their attempts to support the contention that human rights originated in the Islamic tradition, the authors rely on strained readings of the Qur'an or the accounts of the custom, or *sunna,* of the Prophet Muhammad to establish the Islamic pedigrees of rights.[36] They cite passages that they claim demonstrate that from its origins Islam possessed the equivalents of modern human rights. By concentrating on the era of the Prophet and projecting human rights principles back to the start of Islamic history and then jumping more than a millennium to the present, they largely avoid referring to the history of Islamic jurisprudence.

However, if one is arguing that the Islamic tradition has a much older set of human rights principles than the West, it is important to show how Muslims have historically interpreted the Islamic sources.

Traditionally, the learned expositions of *shari'a* rules in the juristic treatises have been consulted as the definitive statements of how the Islamic sources should be interpreted. To answer the question of whether and when human rights concepts were produced in Islamic culture and to discover what Islamic jurists have traditionally believed Islam provided in the area of rights and freedoms, a legal historian would turn first to the great legal treatises and possibly also the writings on theology and philosophy that were produced in the premodern period of Islamic civilization—very approximately, from the ninth to the fourteenth century—and that are still widely consulted as the most prestigious statements of premodern Islamic doctrine. No documented Islamic authority dating from the premodern period has come to light that squarely addresses human rights issues as such or that directly anticipates modern rights formulations.

The authors of these Islamic human rights schemes largely ignore the many centuries of juristic elaborations of the Qur'an and *sunna,* which one would expect them to examine and assess before asserting that Islam has a longer tradition of human rights than does Western culture. Even if the principles of Islamic human rights did inhere in the original sources, for purposes of legal history, one would want to know when Muslims first started perceiving the human rights implications of the sources. This, the record shows, did not happen until very recently. Thus, Islamic human rights principles are newly coined, much newer than rights principles in the West, which can be traced back to the era of the Enlightenment and to a certain extent even before that.

When one abandons the search for express treatments of human rights issues and looks instead in the writings of the premodern jurists, theologians, and philosophers for the elaboration of ideas that would either tend to accommodate human rights principles or to create obstacles to their reception in the Islamic tradition, one finds voluminous relevant material. The problem then becomes an overabundance of authority that has conflicting implications for rights. After one surveys premodern Islamic intellectual history, one realizes that there was no settled Islamic doctrine on rights or protorights in that period, only currents of thought that would create either a more or a less propitious foundation for the assimilation of modern human rights concepts within an Islamic framework.

The production of Islamic human rights comes at a time of strong pressures for Islamization, along with calls for a return to Islamic models in the areas of government, law, social organization, and culture. A prominent feature of Islamization programs has been demands for decolonization in the legal sphere—a rejection of Western legal models that were imposed or borrowed in a period when Muslims were ruled or dominated by Western powers. This legal decolonization in theory should mean the reinstatement of indigenous Islamic models. However, the Islamization programs rest on a false premise: that there exist in all areas settled Islamic legal countermodels of the Western models that are being repudiated. Such countermodels may be developed in the future, but in many areas they are lacking, as even Iran's ruling clerics have had to acknowledge.[37]

Proponents of Islamization insist that Islam is a comprehensive ideology, for which purpose it must be seen as unitary. They do not acknowledge that it comprises a variety of competing strains or that there were major gaps in the shari'a.[38] Similarly, authors of Islamic human rights schemes want to promote the idea that Islam provides a uniform body of principles on rights. To concoct their Islamic human rights, they must simplify the Islamic tradition, paper over cracks, and deny evidence of disagreement.

Under these circumstances, provisions of Islamic human rights schemes, to serve the ends of Islamization programs, must be given Islamic pedigrees and enough distinctively Islamic characteristics to satisfy the demands for Islamic versions of rights. Simultaneously, the schemes must stick close enough to Western models in order to cover essentially the same terrain as these models, which are ostensibly being rejected. It is natural, therefore, that some authors of Islamic human rights schemes who have not developed an adequate methodology for constructing human rights on an Islamic foundation should feel tempted to rewrite the historical record of the development of human rights in the Muslim world in an attempt to cancel out in advance the intellectual debt that they owe to modern rights concepts and to defend their schemes against charges that they are borrowing heavily from secular models.

The Persistence of Traditional Priorities and Values

For reasons already discussed, proponents of Islamic human rights may not comprehend the problems involved in integrating borrowed provisions on individual rights and freedoms into a matrix of values found in traditional Muslim societies and premodern Islamic thought. The authors of the Islamic human rights schemes reviewed here cling to the ideas and attitudes of traditional orthodoxy, such as ethical voluntarism, the supremacy of divine Revelation, and hostility toward rationalism and humanism. They have thus elected to adhere to the same intellectual framework that historically impeded the development of human rights concepts, with consequences that are delineated in analyses of rights provisions in Chapters 4–8.

Ideally, one would want complete expositions of the authors' philosophies of human rights appended to each of the schemes, which would enable one to correlate those philosophies directly with the provisions of each scheme. Unfortunately, the authors have not provided such expositions. In default of such, there are still some grounds for characterizing their values and priorities.

Insofar as the schemes expressly indicate their priorities, they uphold the primacy of Revelation over reason; none endorse reason as a source of law. For example, when one examines the Preamble to the English version of the Universal Islamic Declaration of Human Rights (UIDHR), one sees that it takes the position that divine Revelation has provided the "legal and moral framework within which to establish and regulate human institutions and relationships." This idea is implicit throughout the text of the Arabic version, as passages from the Qur'an and the *sunna* of the Prophet are extensively quoted. It is thus clear that for the authors of the UIDHR, divinely inspired texts enjoy primacy as the source of law. The status of reason is correspondingly demoted. In a later passage in the Preamble of the UIDHR, the authors proclaim in the Arabic version that they believe that human reason *(al-'aql al-bashari),* independent of God's guidance and inspiration, is insufficient to provide the best plan for human life. In the corresponding part of the English version, after stating that "rationality by itself" cannot be "a sure guide in the affairs of mankind," they express their conviction that "the teachings of Islam represent the quintessence of Divine guidance in its final and perfect form."

In such a scheme, any challenges that might be made to Islamic law on the grounds that it denies basic rights guaranteed under constitutions or international law are ruled out ab initio; human reason is deemed inadequate to criticize what are treated as divine edicts. This affirms the traditional orthodox view that the tenets of the *shari'a* are perfect and just because they represent the will of the Creator, being derived from divinely inspired sources. In the Islamic human rights schemes proffered by Mawdudi and Tabandeh, there is also reliance on extensive quotations from the Islamic sources, which is an indication that they follow the traditional view that the texts of Revelation are the definitive guides for what law should be, not human reason.

The supremacy of Islamic law in Iran is confirmed in various provisions of the 1979 Iranian constitution in addition to Article 4, which has already been quoted. The primacy of Revelation is confirmed in Article 1, which calls for a government based on truth and Qur'anic justice, and in Article 2, which states that the Iranian Republic is based on belief in the acceptance of God's rule and the necessity of obeying his commands, affirming belief in "divine Revelation and its fundamental role in setting forth the laws" and the "justice of God in creation and legislation." Also according to Article 2, these aims are to be achieved by "continuous *ijtihad* [interpretation] of the *fuqaha* possessing necessary qualifications, exercised on the basis of the Qur'an and the *Sunnah* [traditions] of the

Ma'sumun [the divinely inspired imams of Twelver Shi'ism]." The Iranian constitution thus professes to be anchored in principles derived from divine Revelation.

In a similar vein, according to the Preamble of the Cairo Declaration on Human Rights in Islam: "Fundamental rights and universal freedoms in Islam are an integral part of the Islamic religion," and they "are contained in the Revealed Books of God and were sent through the message of the last of His Prophets." That is, Revelation is theoretically central to this scheme of human rights, as well. Moreover, after speaking of "basic human dignity" in Article 1(a), the Declaration states, "True faith is the guarantee for enhancing such dignity along the path to human perfection," indicating that faith—as opposed to reason—is to guide Muslims in this connection. In a similar vein, Article 7 of the Saudi Basic Law affirms that the Qur'an and the *sunna* of the Prophet reign supreme over the Basic Law and all other laws of the state, thereby clearly subordinating rights to Islamic Revelation and the custom of the Prophet.

In the Azhar draft Islamic constitution, the evidence is less clear. One can, however, infer a similar emphasis on divine Revelation and conclude that a command of religious texts is deemed central to knowledge from individual provisions that incorporate Qur'anic language and concepts, from the requirements in Articles 12 and 13 that call for the memorization of the Qur'an in schools and the teaching of the custom of the Prophet, and from the provision in Article 11 stating that religious instruction should be a main subject in education.

In addition to according Revelation a central role in their Islamic human rights schemes, the authors do not seem to accept the shift from an emphasis on human duties to the emphasis on individual human rights that characterizes modern thought on rights. In a passage in the English version of the Preamble to the UIDHR that has no obvious counterpart in the Arabic version, the authors indicate "that by the terms of our primeval covenant with God our duties and obligations have priority over our rights," thereby coming close to reaffirming the traditional idea that Islam prescribes duties, not individual rights. It is therefore obvious from the outset that the UIDHR will have the effect of denying rights in the guise of establishing Islamic duties. Should there be complaints about its denying rights afforded under international human rights law, the ready-made defense will be that Islam aims not to secure individual rights but to ensure obedience to divine commands.

In the Azhar draft constitution, one sees a similar concern for the fulfillment of Islamic duties. In Article 12 the government is required to teach Muslims their duties *(al-fara'id)*. In contrast, in Chapter 4, which deals with the individual's rights and freedoms (which turn out to be highly circumscribed), there is no mention of any need to teach Muslims about freedoms.

The Cairo Declaration refers to duties and obligations and stresses the inferiority of humans vis-à-vis their Creator. For example, Article 1 provides in section

(a) that all human beings "are united by submission to God" and "are equal in terms of basic human dignity and basic obligations and responsibilities," and states in section (b) that all human beings are God's children *('iyal)*. Similarly, having declared in Article 1 that the government is Islamic and in Article 5 that it is a monarchy in the Saudi family, the Saudi Basic Law in Article 6 treats the duty to obey the monarch as being religious in nature, asserting that citizens are to pay allegiance to the king, "in accordance with the Holy Qur'an and the *sunna* of the Prophet, in submission and obedience," thereby linking obedience to the king to obedience to God. Section 5, titled "rights and duties," contains precious few rights.

A former minister of law and religious affairs in Pakistan, A. K. Brohi, has written a number of pieces on human rights in Islam and puts forth a rights philosophy similar to the ones embodied in the schemes under review here. Brohi was prominent enough in this field to be selected to give the keynote address at a major international conference on human rights in Islam held in Kuwait in 1980 under the sponsorship of the International Commission of Jurists, Kuwait University, and the Union of Arab Lawyers.[39] Brohi's speech recapitulated points made in an earlier piece on Islam and human rights, published in the official Pakistani case law reporter in 1976—while Zulfikar Ali Bhutto, the prime minister executed by Zia after his coup, was still in power.[40] It is significant that the same points were incorporated in an article in the official Pakistani case law reporter in 1983, when President Zia's martial law regime and Islamization programs were in full force, showing that the regime found his perspective congenial.[41] Excerpts from the seminar and the article show how Brohi rejects the philosophical underpinnings of Western human rights:

> Human duties and rights have been vigorously defined and their orderly enforcement is the duty of the whole of organized communities and the task is specifically entrusted to the law enforcement organs of the state. The individual if necessary has to be sacrificed in order that the life of the organism be saved. Collectivity has a special sanctity attached to it in Islam.[42]

> The Western man's perspective may by and large be called anthropocentric in the sense that there man is regarded as constituting the measure of everything since he is to be regarded as the starting point of all thinking and action. The perspective of Islam, on the other hand, is theocentric, that is, God-consciousness, the Absolute here is paramount; man is here only to serve His Maker. . . . [In the West] rights of man are seen in a setting which has no reference to his relationship with God—they are somehow supposed to be his inalienable birthrights . . . . Each time the assertion of human rights is made, it

is done only to secure their recognition from some secular authority such as the state or some such regal power.[43]

[In Islam] there are no "human rights" or "freedoms" admissible to man in the sense in which modern man's thought, belief, and practice understand them: in essence, the believer owes obligation or duties to God if only because he is called upon to obey the Divine Law and such Human Rights as he is made to acknowledge seem to stem from his primary duty to obey God.[44]

Thus, it would appear, there is a sense in which Man has no rights within a theocentric perspective; he has only duties to His Maker. But these duties in their turn, give rise to all the rights, Human Rights in the modern sense included. . . . There can, in the strict theory of the Islamic law, be no conflict between the State Authority and the individual—since both have to obey the Divine Law.[45]

Human Rights conceived from the anthropocentric perspective are treated by Western thinkers as though they were no more than an expedient mode of protecting the individual from the assaults that are likely to be made upon him by the authority of the State's coercive power—by the unjust law that may be imposed by that authority to deny man the possibility of self-development through the law-making power of the brute majorities. Islam, on the other hand, formulates, defines and protects these very rights by inducing in the believers the disposition to obey the law of God . . . and showing obedience to those "constituted authorities" within the realm who themselves are bound to obey the law of God. . . . Furthermore, affirmation of these rights is to enable man not only to secure the establishment of those conditions in terms of which the development of man as an individual on earth may be possible, but also to enable man so to conduct himself, inwardly as well as outwardly, as to be able to obey the Divine Law. . . . By accepting to live in Bondage to this Divine Law, man learns to be free.[46]

The tenets of Western individualism are unacceptable in Brohi's scheme, where the emphasis is on duties. The need for human rights standards to protect the individual from oppression by the government is neglected, as it was in the idealistic visions of premodern Islamic thinkers that precluded the development of modern concepts of individual rights. Like the premodern theorists of Islamic government, Brohi assumes that governments will necessarily obey the dictates of the *shari'a*.

In Brohi's treatment of rights, one sees both a strong affirmation of the idea that the individual is bound by the duty of obedience and, withal, a carelessness regarding the issue of to whom or to what the individual owes obedience. One notes that Brohi is sometimes speaking of subordination to God and Islamic law, which is clearly required in the Islamic tradition, but that at other times he means the subordination of the individual to organized communities, a collectivity, political authorities, or the state. Regarding the latter, there is much less in the way of unequivocal Islamic authority justifying claims that obedience is owed. Brohi does not seem to perceive that the Islamic warrant establishing the duty of a believer to obey the commands of God should not necessarily be extended to cover the obligations of citizens of modern states to obey the commands of their governments.

Like many other Muslim conservatives who discuss rights, Brohi fails to appreciate that the model of communal solidarity that one finds in traditional societies in the Muslim world is in no way distinctively Islamic but reflects the features commonly found in societies that have not yet experienced the disruptions of industrialization and urbanization. Brohi apparently does not appreciate that the lack of individual rights and freedoms in traditional societies did not have the same nefarious consequences that the lack of protection for individual rights has had under the modern nation-state. From the fact that premodern Islamic thought was not anthropocentric, he leaps to the conclusion that an anthropocentric perspective would violate Islamic precepts. Brohi goes from a description of the subordination of the individual to group interests that was widely accepted in traditional societies—regardless of whether Islam was the dominant religion—to the unwarranted conclusion that Islamic doctrine requires the individual to accept such subordination in the radically different circumstances of modern state societies.[47]

That there will of necessity be conflicts between the competing interests of individuals and the government of a modern state is rejected by Brohi. His notion that in an Islamic system one cannot separate the individual and the government reflects adherence to the premodern jurists' views that the ruler and ruled stood together, united in their duties of obedience to the *shari'a*.[48] Where there is reliance on these anachronistic views, denials of individual rights and freedoms by governments are naturally not seen as a problem.

Mawdudi's main political concern with regard to duties seemed to be how to preserve the power of the state. In his book *The Islamic Law and Constitution*, Mawdudi inaccurately quoted the Prophet, who was telling Muslims to obey divine commands, as telling Muslims that "the state" (not referred to in the original account) "shall have to be obeyed, in adversity and in prosperity, and whether it is pleasant or unpleasant to do so," elaborating as follows:

In other words, the order of the State, be it palatable or unpalatable, easy or arduous, shall have to be obeyed under all circumstances [save when this means disobedience to God]. . . . [A] person should, truly and faithfully and with all his heart, wish and work for the good, prosperity and the betterment of the State, and should not tolerate anything likely to harm its interests. . . . It is also obligatory on the citizens of the Islamic State to cooperate wholeheartedly with the government and to make sacrifices of life and property for it, so much so that if any danger threatens the State, he who willfully refrains from making a sacrifice of his life and property to ward off that danger has been called a hypocrite in the Qur'an.[49]

This is obviously an attempt to provide an Islamic rationale for total subjugation of the individual to the state—although assuming that the Prophet was referring to the modern nation-state is anachronistic. One can see how Mawdudi's formulation of the individual's obligations to obey the government tracks that offered by President Zia in justifying his military dictatorship in Pakistan (Chapter 2). The only excuse for disobeying the government is in cases where obeying would entail violating Islamic law, thereby constituting disobedience to a command of God. Of course, a government that purports to follow Islamic law, as President Zia's did, would not concede that it was giving the citizenry any grounds whatsoever for disobedience. In fact, many members of the political group that Mawdudi founded were among the mainstays of support for President Zia's Islamization program, accepting the loss of rights and freedoms under Zia's military dictatorship.

The Basic Law of Saudi Arabia sounds a similar theme in Article 6, which includes a provision that citizens are to acknowledge the rule of the King in accordance with the Qur'an and *sunna,* doing so "in submission and obedience," codifying the premodern tenet that Muslims owe an unqualified duty to obey their monarch—here translated into a duty to submit to the autocracy of the Saudi rulers.

Such ideas betray a fundamental antipathy to human rights. If one accepts Ronald Dworkin's definition of a "right" as a claim that it would be wrong for the government to deny an individual, even though it would be in the general interest to do so, one could say that it would be impossible for authors with such attitudes to accept such rights, since they consistently accord priority to the interests of the collectivity, the community, or the state. In contrast, in international law, civil and political rights accord primacy to the rights of the individual, ensuring them against infringements, particularly by governments but also by society.[50] Given their position, one would expect authors wedded to philosophical positions at odds with rights to say that human rights cannot be accommodated within an Islamic framework and to assert that Muslims owe duties. Instead, one sees them trying to preserve traditional anti-individualistic, communitarian values and priorities while paradoxically trying to associate their projects with human rights.

A person unfamiliar with Islamic history might assume that special circumstances or unique institutions in Islamic civilization may have compensated for the lack of formal legal safeguards for individual rights and freedoms and that this lack had less nefarious consequences in the Muslim world than it had in Western societies prior to the imposition of legal restraints on governments' ability to infringe human rights. In fact, in the Middle East the absence of legal protections for human rights has correlated with patterns of misrule, oppression, and denials of rights by despotic rulers that are very similar to those historically experienced in the West. The idealized schemes of Muslim ruler and Muslim ruled both acting in concert and in common obedience to the divine law were not realized in practice. Although some Muslims would say that the feasibility of the Islamic model was illustrated by the harmonious collaboration of ruler and ruled in the era of the Prophet and under some of his immediate successors—to which the Shi'is would add the era in which they were ruled by divinely inspired imams—these reports of saintly rulers in the earliest period of Islamic history by no means signify that the dictates of Islamic piety have generally proved adequate to inhibit despotic regimes from oppressing their subjects. Although Muslim rulers had at their disposal the mechanisms to compel obedience, individual subjects had few ways other than the risky course of overt rebellion to challenge cruel and tyrannical misrule.

In reality, the individual and the state in the Muslim world have had conflicting interests that have most often been resolved at the expense of individual rights and freedoms. The authors of these Islamic human rights schemes must be aware that this pattern has continued in the Muslim world and now has more serious consequences, given the massive repressive apparatus wielded by today's governments. Nonetheless, such writers are disposed to ignore the significance of the vast disparity in power between the individual and the modern nation-state.

Consequences of Insecure Philosophical Foundations

Most current theorists of Islamic human rights persist in relying on an idealized vision of Islamic social harmony, even though the evidence of centuries, not to mention the acts of current governments, has manifestly demonstrated that this vision is unrealistic. Because of their otherworldly, idealistic focus, it is not surprising that the authors of Islamic human rights schemes produce provisions that seem grossly inadequate by the standards of international human rights law and that fail to afford protections from the patterns of human rights abuses most prevalent in contemporary Middle Eastern societies.

Lacking a coherent rights philosophy, authors of Islamic human rights schemes have in some instances simply appropriated ideas from texts on Islamic

law and ethics, treating them as if they offered statements on rights, irrespective
of whether these ideas involve principles that could remedy actual problems or
deserve the status of rights. The consequence is the inclusion of many frivolous
notions of entitlements, trivial or meaningless "rights" that in international law
would not rise to the level of human rights. The Iranian constitution is a noteworthy exception in this respect. It appears that Iran's established tradition of
constitutionalism inhibited its drafters from abandoning most of the familiar
categories that are normally used in formulations of rights.

Provision is made for a "right" not to have one's corpse mutilated,[51] which
seems to envisage that human rights protections should be extended to corpses,
even though human rights concerns ordinarily presuppose that the rights claimant
be living, not dead.[52] As a kind of corollary to the development of "rights" not to
be subjected to behavior censured in the Islamic sources, behavior that is treated as
good or proper in Islamic sources may create a related "right." "Rights" that fall
within this category include "the obligation of believers to see that a deceased person's body is treated with due solemnity,"[53] affording yet another right to corpses,
and the "right" to safety of life—meaning that people should come to the aid of a
person in distress or danger.[54] It seems here that rights are being confused with legal duties to ensure the proper handling of corpses or moral obligations incumbent on persons encountering others in distress or danger.

Other "rights" that have been derived from Islamic sources include the right
of women not to be surprised by male family members of the household walking
in on them unannounced.[55] When one thinks about the implications of protecting women from surprise intrusions, one realizes that, far from affording protection for freedoms, it contains implicit restrictions on women's rights. There is an
assumption that the world is sexually segregated and that women stay at home in
seclusion from men. This segregation is so extensive that even male family members should never intrude on women's quarters without giving women warning
so that they can cover themselves in a suitably modest manner. The provision
implies that even in the home there will be female seclusion and veiling, which
in turn is connected with a woman's duty to avoid indecency. Thus, the "right" is
linked not with any meaningful human right but with women's traditional duty
under the *shari'a* to stay segregated, secluded, and veiled.

Some "rights" provisions that are included in these Islamic human rights
schemes do not belong in compilations of human rights because they concern
offenses by private actors better dealt with by tort or criminal law. Some inadequate formulations seem to have resulted from an author gleaning from the Islamic sources the idea that certain conduct is censured or criminalized and
drawing the conclusion that human beings have "rights" not to be affected by
such conduct. Thus, Islamic human rights include the "right" not to be made
fun of or insulted by nicknames,[56] which is obviously taken from the Qur'an

44:11: "Let not a folk deride a folk who may be better than they . . . neither defame one another, nor insult one another by nicknames." One also encounters the "right" not to be tied up before being killed,[57] provisions that guarantee the "right" not to be burned alive,[58] and the "right" to life—which turns out in context to be a right not to be murdered.[59]

Generally, international human rights law, because it is concerned with governmental conduct, does not set rules for cases where injury or death is caused either by negligence or by the criminal conduct of a private individual.[60] Most legal systems consider sanctions through tort or criminal law as adequate for the purposes of compensation, retribution, and deterrence. In contrast, Islamic human rights schemes may stipulate a woman's "right" to have her chastity respected and protected at all times.[61] Although murder and rape do violate international human rights law if they are inflicted as a matter of state policy, these crimes are ordinarily left to domestic criminal law if perpetrated by a private actor. In contrast, these Islamic "rights" appear to be directed not against state policy but against the criminal. Furthermore, the woman's right to have her chastity respected is a very ambiguous one, since, in the context of the contemporary Middle East, the protection of women's chastity is often associated with regimes of sexual segregation and female seclusion and veiling, practices that are justified on the grounds that they are necessary to protect women's chastity. In other words, rather than offering meaningful protections for individual freedoms, these Islamic "rights" can be utilized to deprive women of freedoms.

A similarly insignificant "right" is the right of divorced individuals to strict confidentiality on the part of their former spouses with regard to information that could be detrimental to them.[62] This belongs to the realm of evidentiary privilege or private tort claims, which are not normally the concern of human rights law. Another "right" stipulated is that of unbelievers—a category that by itself is problematic—to recover the corpses of their fellows who have fallen in battle against the Muslims without having to pay for the privilege.[63] The question of whether a fee could be assessed from unbelievers in these circumstances is hardly one that any serious advocate of enhanced human rights protections in the Middle East would choose to place on an agenda of urgent human rights problems.

This category of rights that have no international counterparts also includes the "right" to cooperate (in the cause of virtue—presumably, Islamic virtue) and not to cooperate (in the cause of vice and aggression—presumably, as defined by Islam)[64] and the "right" to propagate Islam and its message.[65] These "rights" differ from international norms, where religious freedoms are protected regardless of one's religion; here it appears that only Muslims would benefit from these "rights."

After examining the vague and confused concepts that the authors of Islamic human rights include in their agendas, one sees that they have no sure grasp of what the concerns of human rights really are. They include provisions that would be totally out of place in a scheme that shared common philosophical premises with those of international human rights.

Islamic Human Rights and Cultural Nationalism

Campaigns for Islamization of law are based on the notion that the imposition of Western law was part of an imperialist plot both to undermine the independence of Muslim states and to demean the Islamic heritage, displacing Islamic law. Many would claim that a similar imperialist motivation lies behind contemporary Western charges that Muslim countries are violating international human rights. Claims by the current Bush administration that the US invasions of Afghanistan and Iraq were motivated by concerns to end the appalling human rights abuses by the Taliban and Saddam Hussein only encourage the existing tendency in the region to associate Western promotion of human rights with agendas to undermine the sovereignty of Muslim countries. In this connection, US attempts to reduce the role of Islamic law in the post-invasion constitutions of Afghanistan and Iraq, while pressing for acceptance of a narrow human rights agenda centered on a few civil and political rights, could have the effect of strengthening the hand of Muslims who argue that human rights threaten Islamic law.

The impetus behind the campaigns to uphold Islamic law and cast aside laws associated with the era of Western domination is rooted as much in nationalism as it is in religion. Campaigns to Islamize human rights are linked to the unease that is felt in the Muslim Middle East over the extent of the region's cultural dependency on the contemporary West. Resentment of this dependency can engender efforts to assert cultural autonomy, to defend institutions associated with Muslims' cultural heritage against charges of backwardness, and to offer countermodels to Western ideas and institutions.[66] Some of the features of the Islamic human rights schemes discussed here are directly shaped by resentment of the West. The authors' perspectives are influenced by cultural nationalism, and they also seek to appeal to sentiments of cultural nationalism in the wider population.

Cultural nationalists want to show that Islam and indigenous culture have institutions comparable to those in the West and that they are equally "advanced." But "advanced" is defined in modern, Western terms. Thus, in the course of reacting against Western law, proponents of Islamization do not necessarily achieve the goal of banishing the influence of the Western legal culture. This leads to cultural confusion in drawing up Islamic counterparts to Western legal models, because the Islamic counterparts are constructed with constant reference to the Western models that they are designed to replace. The *shari'a* is reformulated to fit borrowed Western categories, such as constitutional rights provisions.

The writings of two authors who energetically condemn the West exemplify this cultural confusion. Both Abu'l A'la Mawdudi and Sultanhussein Tabandeh have utilized Western examples and precedents to prop up the legitimacy of *shari'a* rules that restrict human rights. For example, in his book, when criticizing the Western model of emancipation for women and calling for its repudiation by Muslims, Mawdudi relied extensively on the findings of Western "scientists," "experts," and "authorities" to establish that Western freedoms have led to social and moral disaster—with the corollary that *shari'a* rules mandating female subjugation and seclusion are sound.[67] Tabandeh, despite claiming to believe in the superiority of *shari'a* law, found a clinching argument to support his assertion that under *shari'a* rules women should be excluded from politics in the fact that women were denied the vote in Switzerland, "one of the most civilized and most perfect societies of the world."[68] These arguments are revealing; the criticisms they fear are those that emanate from Muslims who are familiar with Western models and approaches to rights. Therefore, Mawdudi and Tabandeh felt compelled to devise rationales for *shari'a* rules based on Western science—or pseudo-science—and Western experience. However, such Western-inspired rationales are utterly irrelevant from the standpoint of Islamic jurisprudence and would play no role in any rights scheme that was actually based on Islamic sources.

Cultural nationalism also helps explain why authors of Islamic human rights schemes insist, despite the overwhelming historical evidence to the contrary, that human rights originated in Islam, asserting falsely that the Western and international principles from which they are heavily borrowing are the derivative ones. Because the sources of Islamic law date from the seventh century, and all Islamic law is in theory derived from these sources, the authors seem to have concluded that human rights must be shown to have been established from the outset of Islamic legal history. Thus, Islamic human rights principles have to be projected back into the seventh century—as they are in the preamble to the Cairo Declaration, which situates them in the Revelation to the Prophet Muhammad. There is an utter failure to deal with the historical reality that, although the Islamic sources may have foreshadowed ideas that were later developed into human rights principles, the study of Islamic civilization shows that the potential of the sources as statements of human rights principles was not developed until after modern human rights law emerged.

If one bears in mind the need to avoid acknowledging an intellectual debt to Western civilization, the claims for the Islamic origins of human rights become intelligible. What one sees in these Islamic human rights schemes is a manifestation of a broader phenomenon that has been commented on by French scholars observing contemporary developments in Islamic thought. Called *concordisme* or *concordisme pieux* (harmonization or pious harmonization), the practice involves strained attempts by Muslims to project modern intellectual developments that have emerged outside the Muslim world back into the Islamic past. The impetus behind this *concordisme* is a desire to show that Islam anticipated all valued achievements of modern civilization. It entails retroactively Islamizing these by inventing supposed Islamic antecedents. However, in this process, readings of Islam are being forced to conform to external models, at the same time that comparative intellectual history is being distorted.

A desire to establish that the West is indebted to Islam for advances that the West has wrongfully claimed as its own prompted the foreword to the UIDHR to assert that "Islam gave to mankind an ideal code of human rights fourteen centuries ago," this being calculated using the Islamic lunar calendar. In the 1980 Kuwait seminar on human rights in Islam, the conclusion was drawn that "Islam was the first to recognize basic human rights and almost 14 centuries ago it set up guarantees and safeguards that have only recently been incorporated in universal declarations of human rights."[69] In the keynote address at the same seminar, it was claimed: "To the student of the Qur'an not one word, in the preamble or in the objectives of the [UN] Charter and not a single article in the text of the 'Universal Declaration of Human Rights' will seem unfamiliar. . . . [T]he 'Universal Declaration of Human Rights' must follow as a basic corollary, or an extension of the Qur'anic programme."[70] Attending a 1997 Sarajevo seminar on the Qur'an and human rights, Iran's Ayatollah Jannati insisted that Islam had best defined all aspects of human rights and that the human rights proposed by the United Nations merely recapitulated rights propounded over a thousand years earlier.[71]

Tabandeh, for all of his professed disappointment with certain features of the Universal Declaration of Human Rights (UDHR), argued that Islam anticipated all the declaration's provisions and projected these back into the Islamic past, asserting that the UDHR "has not promulgated anything that was new nor inaugurated innovations. Every clause of it, indeed, every valuable regulation needed for the welfare of human society . . . already existed in a better and more perfect form in Islam."[72] Despite the fact that the details of Tabandeh's commentary on the UDHR reveal a deep philosophical antipathy toward the rights that it provides, Tabandeh obviously feels that Islam will be considered deficient if it cannot be shown to have anticipated the UDHR.

It is instructive to contrast the attitudes of authors of the Islamic human rights schemes, who anxiously assert the superiority of Islamic law in the human rights domain, with those of the authors of the International Bill of Human Rights, which betray none of the defensiveness of the former. As has been indicated earlier, many of the important contributors to the International Bill were delegates from Muslim countries, and these included Muslims who expressed confidence in the viability of the Islamic tradition while unapologetically supporting the international human rights project. Those who formulate international law do not feel a need to justify their work by asserting the superiority of international law over the *shari'a*—or over any religious law—because for them the authority of international law in the particular domains that it covers is a given.

Mawdudi, who espoused ideas that are in fundamental conflict with international human rights law, nonetheless sought to portray Islamic law as having an earlier and more perfect version of human rights than what was offered by international law. He attempted to defend the thesis that human rights originated in Islam, while castigating Westerners for their presumptions to have originated human rights. In keeping with his general concern for showing that Islam and Muslim societies are wrongly accused of being culturally backward and under-developed, he complained that "people in the West have the habit of attributing every beneficial development in the world to themselves."[73] After presenting his own list of human rights, Mawdudi asserted:

This is a brief sketch of those rights which 1400 years ago Islam gave to man. . . . It refreshes and strengthens our faith in Islam when we realize that even in this modern age, which makes such loud claims of progress and enlightenment, the world has not been able to produce more just and equitable laws than those given 1400 years ago. On the other hand, it is saddening to realize that Muslims nonetheless often look for guidance to the West.[74]

Mawdudi clearly meant to persuade Muslims that they should abandon all references to the allegedly derivative Western rights concepts and refer instead to the original models, which are Islamic rights.[75] His disappointment with Muslims who seek intellectual guidance in the West did not reflect the teachings of Islam, the doctrines of which are free of nationalist bias and which do not set any geographical limits on where Muslims may seek wisdom and enlightenment, but instead reflected a cultural nationalist perspective.

One sees that cultural nationalism lies behind some of the confusion in these Islamic human rights schemes. If one takes the position that Islam anticipated the most influential post–World War II human rights instruments, then Islamic human rights and constitutional rights provisions must somehow be shown to resemble those in the international documents and Western constitutions. Thus, instruments such as the UDHR effectively become the templates for presentations of the Islamic human rights that are designed to replace them, leading to the extensive borrowing from Western models and terminology. In such an endeavor, there is no room for critical examination of whether the rules and priorities of the premodern *shari'a* that the authors seek to preserve are compatible with human rights. Internal contradictions and inconsistencies are the inevitable result of the authors' casually appropriating the formulas and terminology of international human rights law without first assessing the intellectual foundations on which international human rights rest and comparing these philosophical premises with the underpinnings of premodern Islamic jurisprudence.

Another feature of Islamic human rights that indicates the influence of cultural nationalism is the frequent reference to practice in the West (from any period in the history of Western civilization) that deviated from modern human rights standards, along with a corresponding unwillingness to deal with actual rights problems in contemporary Muslim societies. Accounts of the golden age under the Prophet Muhammad and his immediate successors in the seventh century are treated as the model of how Islamic rights work in practice—as if all Muslim societies over the centuries had conformed to the perfections being ascribed to *shari'a* law in that remote period. The failure to examine critically the human rights situation in Muslim societies throughout history reflects this literature's apologetic, defensive function—to denigrate Western civilization and to exalt the heritage of Islamic civilization rather than to come to grips with the human rights problems faced by contemporary Muslims, as well as their historical origins.

Of course, historically, governments in both the West and the Muslim world have engaged in conduct that would constitute egregious violations of rights by the standards of the International Bill of Human Rights. However, despite many grievous lapses, Western countries since the nineteenth century have by and large been moving in the direction of affording greater protections for the human rights of their citizens and imposing limits on the ability of governments to trample on these rights. Today, the rights protections afforded in the laws of Western democracies, although far from perfect, are nonetheless better developed than elsewhere, with Scandinavian countries standing out as having exemplary rights records. In contrast, the current human rights situation in the Muslim world is generally a dismal one, even worse than it was under traditional, despotic regimes. The oppressive rule of the centralized, authoritarian or totalitarian regimes that predominate in the Middle East is stifling in its impact on freedom. The state has vastly increased its power and strengthened its security apparatus, and a variety of social and economic changes have weakened the ability of societies to resist governmental overreaching and coercion. Thus, rather than making progress in the direction of enhancing rights, with some exceptions, Middle Eastern countries have tended to move in the direction of expanding oppression.

The realities of rights violations by governments in the Muslim world are neglected by the authors of Islamic human rights schemes. Naturally, they have no wish to address how Islamization programs have further degraded rights. Instead, where these authors do treat real human rights problems, they tend to focus on Western human rights violations in an attempt to show that Western human rights protections are inadequate and ineffectual and that Westerners who criticize human rights abuses in the Middle East are hypocritical.[76] When one considers how improbable it would be for people in a Western society to try to deflect criticism of their government's violations of human rights by pointing out that serious violations of human rights had occurred in Muslim countries, one grasps that such tactics reveal which side feels beleaguered and defensive about its poor progress in the human rights domain.

By alluding to the violations of human rights that have been perpetrated by the West, the authors seem to think they are discrediting both the Western rights models and potential Western critics of their Islamic human rights schemes. Thus, the record of rights violations in the West, which was touched on in the Kuwait seminar, was somehow deemed relevant to understanding the comparative merits of Islamic human rights.[77] In contrast, the proponents of Islamic human rights at the 1980 Kuwait seminar on Islam and human rights expressly denied that Islamic human rights could be evaluated by reference to the historical record, saying, "It is unfair to judge Islamic law (Shari'a) by the political systems which prevailed in various periods of Islamic history."[78]

This last statement would be unexceptionable if it meant that one should distinguish between practice and theory and between the conduct of governments and the teachings of the Islamic religion, but it would be misguided if it suggested that the quality and efficacy of human rights guarantees could not be evaluated by the degree to which they protect rights in practice. The historical record of the centuries in which Islamic law was officially the governing standard indicates that protections for rights equivalent to the protections afforded by international human rights law were lacking. However, conceding this is difficult in a period when cultural nationalism is surging in response to circumstances that seem to confirm Western hegemony.

Summary

As the foregoing discussion has indicated, the Islamic tradition is but one factor among many that influence how Muslims react to human rights. At least as important is the history of the relationship between the West and the Muslim countries of the Middle East. Many Muslims—although certainly not all—associate human rights with Western attempts to dominate the Middle East at a time when the region is struggling to adjust to challenges that have destabilized old structures. Thus, some of what appears to be an Islamic reaction against human rights, perceived as an artifact of secular Western culture antithetical to Islam, may actually be part of a broader pattern of resistance to Western hegemony and to the unsettling transformations that Muslim societies are undergoing.

CHAPTER 4

Islamic Restrictions on Human Rights

One of the most striking and consistent features in all the Islamic human rights schemes is the use of Islamic criteria to restrict human rights. Provisions in the Islamic human rights schemes reflect the thesis that the rights afforded in international law are too generous and that these only become acceptable when they are subjected to Islamic restrictions. However, there is no explicit articulation of the thesis. Exactly what these restrictions on rights would entail is not clarified in the Islamic human rights schemes examined here. The resulting ambiguity in rights formulations, in which familiar rights are qualified by reference to vague "Islamic" limitations, turns out to be one of their distinguishing characteristics. The use of Islamic criteria to circumscribe otherwise applicable international human rights is evaluated in this chapter.

Permissible Qualifications of Rights and Freedoms

International law recognizes that many rights protections are not absolute and may be suspended or qualified in exceptional circumstances such as wars or public emergencies or even in normal circumstances in the interests of certain overriding considerations.[1] In international law, one expects these overriding considerations to fall within one of several established categories. Qualifications may be placed on human rights in the aggregate common interest and to serve particular, specified policies.[2] The latter might include the preservation of national security, public safety, public order, morals, the rights and freedom of others, the interests of justice, and the public interest in a democratic society.[3] To ensure that accommodations and derogations are made within structures of authority and to prevent arbitrariness in decisions, the measures imposing these limitations must be taken in accordance with the law.[4]

International law therefore seeks to balance the need to protect human rights against other needs; in some cases, rights may have to defer to other priorities. The international community recognizes that unless the circumstances in which curbs can be placed on human rights are sharply circumscribed, rights would become illusory. However, the extent to which curbs are permissible and exactly what grounds justify restricting rights remain contested questions in international human rights law. Despite the unsettled nature of international law in this area, the International Bill of Human Rights offers some guidelines regarding the qualifications that may be imposed on civil and political rights. These guidelines are relevant for evaluating the restrictions in Islamic rights provisions.

The Universal Declaration of Human Rights (UDHR) treats a number of rights as absolute or non-derogable rights, meaning that there could be no justification for curtailing them. Among these are the right to freedom and equality in dignity and rights; the right to equality before the law and to equal protection of the law; the right in full equality to a fair and public hearing by an independent and impartial tribunal; the right to marry and the right to equal rights in marriage and divorce;[5] freedom of thought, conscience, and religion, including the freedom to change one's religion;[6] and the right to work and to free choice of employment.[7] The UDHR would not accept any criteria that would deny these rights.

The UDHR includes a separate clause that defines the limits that may in general be placed on human rights. In Article 29.2 one finds the following provision: "In the exercise of his rights and freedoms, everyone shall be subject only to such limitations as are determined by law solely for the purpose of securing due recognition and respect for the rights and freedoms of others and of meeting the just requirements of morality, public order and the general welfare in a democratic society." In the drafting of the UDHR, the Soviet delegation tried to impose a derogation clause that would nullify the new rights being drafted by adding the words "and also [for the purpose of] the corresponding requirements of the democratic state," but the Philippine delegate objected to this on the grounds that the definition of the "corresponding requirements" would lie with the state and thereby potentially annul all the rights and freedoms in the declaration. The Soviet proposal for this sweeping derogation rule was rejected.[8]

The qualifications permitted in the general provision in Article 29.2 of the UDHR should be taken to apply only to those rights that are not among the absolute rights. The absolute character accorded to certain rights correlates with the values and priorities of societies that have adjusted to modern legal norms. In contrast, in traditional societies, hierarchy, inequality, and systems of control over individual behavior may be entrenched. In such societies, considerations analogous to ones of morality, public order, and the general welfare that are invoked in Article 29.2 might be construed expansively to justify denials of rights that would enjoy unqualified protection under international human rights law.

The limitations that could be applied to human rights were further clarified in subsequent international human rights documents, as specific qualifications were inserted in the texts of individual rights provisions. Provisions guarantee that rights that are derogable will be restricted only in specified ways. Thus, one sees rights with the following qualifications:

1. Freedom of expression: subject only to qualifications provided by law and necessary for respect of the rights and reputations of others and for the protection of national security or of public order *(ordre public)*, or of public health and morals

2. The right of peaceful assembly: subject only to restrictions "imposed in conformity with the law and which are necessary in a democratic society in the interests of national security or public safety, public order *(ordre public)*, the protection of public health or morals or the protection of the rights and freedoms of others"

3. Freedom of association: subject to the same qualifications as the right of peaceful assembly, above

4. The right to take part in the conduct of public affairs, to vote and be elected, and to have access, on general terms of equality, to public service "without unreasonable conditions"[9]

A number of other fundamental rights are qualified, including the right to life, which is qualified by the state's ability to impose a death penalty, but only for the most serious crimes and subject to a number of other conditions, and the right to liberty and security of person, which is qualified by the state's ability to deprive the person of these "on such grounds and in accordance with such procedure as are established by law."[10]

The International Covenant on Economic, Social, and Cultural Rights (ICESCR) has a general rule on how rights may be qualified, providing in Article 4 that governments "may subject such rights only to such limitations as are determined by law only insofar as this may be compatible with the nature of these rights and solely for the purpose of promoting the general welfare in a democratic society."

Thus, international human rights law offers definite standards regarding what constitutes permissible reasons for curbing human rights protections. The standards may not have been perfectly drafted, and the formulations of the qualifications are not so airtight as to preclude all efforts by states to manipulate them at the expense of the rights of the individual. However, the formulations are designed to shore up rights by delineating the circumstances in which states may curtail them. As discussed in the following examinations of Islamic human rights schemes, one of the most important differences between Islamic human rights schemes and international human rights law is that Islamic qualifications on rights have been deliberately left so vague that they allow states vast discretion in circumscribing rights.

Islamic Formulas Limiting Rights

A review of Islamic human rights schemes reveals a pattern of borrowing substantive rights from international human rights instruments while restricting the rights by providing that they can be enjoyed only within the limits of the *shari'a,* limits that are consistently left unspecified. As a result, states have discretion in defining the scope of the affected rights. In this respect, the Islamic limitations on rights resemble the qualifications that have been placed on human rights in the African Charter on Human and Peoples' Rights, similarly devised to dilute rights protections. These qualifications have been decried as "claw-back clauses" that allow the state "almost unbounded discretion" in using domestic legal standards to restrict internationally guaranteed human rights.[11]

International law does not accept that fundamental human rights may be restricted—much less permanently curtailed—by reference to the requirements of any particular religion.[12] International law provides no warrant for depriving Muslims of human rights by according primacy to Islamic criteria. Thus, to limit or dilute human rights in deference to the requirements of the *shari'a* is to qualify human rights established under international law by standards that are not recognized as legitimate bases for curtailing rights.

Limitations on rights that use terms like "the *shari'a,*" "Islamic precepts," or "the limits of Islam" to qualify human rights cannot be unambiguously defined by consulting the work of the premodern jurists, because this work is far too diverse. Premodern Islamic law included the doctrines of several sects and many law schools. Divergence of opinion among major law schools was historically tolerated in Islam, a situation acknowledged in the *shari'a* concept of *ikhtilaf al-madhahib,* or difference of law schools. In fact, even within one law school, doctrines and opinions could differ significantly on the interpretation of the Islamic sources.[13] Furthermore, there were many individual jurists whose opinions differed from the views of the major schools, but whose works, nonetheless, are part of the premodern *shari'a* legacy. With such a rich heritage, Muslims are faced with many conflicting views of Islamic requirements.

Despite the great diversity in Islamic doctrine, on certain points of premodern jurisprudence there is sufficient consensus to allow reasoned speculation on how the application of Islamic principles would affect rights. Reliance on rules of the premodern *shari'a* to determine the permissible scope of modern human rights could open the way to nullification of rights in areas where the *shari'a* calls for restrictions on rights and freedoms, such as the rules relegating women and non-Muslims to subordinate status or prohibiting conversion from Islam. Even on these topics, where there are extensive rules in the *shari'a,* there is enough complexity and diversity in the body of relevant legal doctrines to give the state considerable leeway in deciding what rules should apply.

On other topics relevant for civil rights and political freedoms, where the premodern jurisprudence is underdeveloped or the *shari'a* standards are very uncertain, resorting to Islamic criteria to qualify rights is also incompatible with the protection of the rights involved. Where no uncontested Islamic authority can be found in the doctrines of premodern jurisprudence, states enjoy wide leeway in constructing Islamic rationales to curb rights. They can always find some spokesman for Islam who will concur that the curbs have Islamic authority. The Saudi rule—ostensibly based on Islam–that women cannot drive cars is a perfect example. This deprives the affected rights of any substance.

Just as there is no definitive guidance in the premodern *shari'a* on human rights restrictions, there is no established doctrine in contemporary Islamic thought. The ambiguities that existed in the premodern tradition have multiplied with the diverging interpretations of the requirements of Islamic law. Understandings of Islamic law have changed under the impact of new intellectual currents. Reformist movements led to substantial departures from premodern models of Islamic thought around the turn of the century.[14] More recently, new strains in interpretation have emerged.[15] In addition to the literature that attempts a progressive rethinking of Islamic law and theology, one sees Islam ideologized to mobilize Muslims for the struggle against the West and Western culture in writings by figures such as Abu'l A'la Mawdudi and Ayatollah Khomeini.[16] The differences in contemporary approaches to understanding Islam have been compounded by the absence of any generally recognized central authority for resolving disputed points of *shari'a* doctrine.

It is natural that in the prevailing circumstances in the contemporary Middle East, all such ambiguities in rights formulations will be exploited by the state and resolved at the expense of those human rights. Thus, vague "Islamic" limitations on human rights have ominous implications.

Restrictions in the Iranian Constitution

Before examining the 1979 Iranian constitution to see how provisions qualified by Islamic principles laid the legal groundwork for the denial of basic freedoms, earlier Iranian formulations of civil and political rights provisions should be considered. Iranian constitutional history illustrates the difficulties in accommodating human rights within an Islamic framework.

Many of Iran's *ulama* were violently opposed to the adoption of Iran's 1906–1907 constitution, and one of the grounds for their objections was their opposition to the idea of freedom, which they considered dangerous and inimical to Islamic principles and values.[17] Clerical denunciations of freedom and constitutionalism as heretical were often vehement and uncompromising.[18]

However, Iranian nationalist sentiment and the popular determination to constrain the tyranny of Iran's Qajar shahs were ultimately strong enough to overcome clerical opposition to the proposed constitution. In addition, some clerics supported constitutionalism, believing that it was compatible with Islam. However, their support was in part attributable to the fact that they did not fully grasp the significance of constitutionalism and interpreted its concepts in ways that corresponded to *shari'a* categories and principles.[19] Thus, the first Iranian constitution emerged in an environment where the religious establishment was divided about the compatibility of constitutionalism and Islam.

The qualifications placed on civil and political rights in the Supplementary Constitutional Law of 1907 were largely secular. However, religious criteria were also invoked to restrict constitutional rights.[20] Article 20 qualified freedom of publication by stating that this freedom did not apply to heretical books or materials hurtful to Islam. Article 21 qualified the freedom to form societies and gatherings by stating that it applied where such societies or gatherings did not provoke religious disorder.[21]

After the 1978–1979 Iranian Revolution, the draft constitution of June 1979, devised before the clergy had fully asserted its dominance, likewise relied primarily on secular qualifications of civil and political rights, but there were exceptions. Article 25 of the proposed constitution on freedom of the press excepted the category of publications insulting to religious belief. In an ambiguous formulation, Article 26 included in the reasons for denying freedom of association the negation of "the basis of the Islamic Republic," which left room for religious qualifications. Article 28 qualified the freedom to choose a profession by stating that the profession should not be opposed to Islam or the public interest.

The draft constitution received criticism from many quarters. Among others, a group that involved the Iranian Lawyers Association and the Iranian Committee for the Defense of Freedom and Human Rights offered proposals for rewriting the draft. The concerns of this group included ensuring the independence of the judiciary and protecting individual rights and the rights of women. It proposed that the UDHR be incorporated in the constitution and that international human rights organizations and lawyers be enabled to intervene in Iranian courts on behalf of Iranian nationals.[22] In other words, the proposals, had they been accepted, would have meant that international human rights law would have been treated as part of Iran's domestic law and that international human rights advocates would have had the capacity to defend Iranian nationals against their own government. This implied a mistrust of the ability of Iran's domestic legal institutions to afford adequate protection for human rights.

However, the draft constitution was also challenged by a coalition of clerics and Islamic organizations demanding that it be rewritten in a way that would give it a more Islamic character.[23] Ayatollah Khomeini said that he wanted the draft reviewed from an Islamic perspective, so that it would result in an Islamic constitution, not one made by foreign-influenced intellectuals who had no faith in Islam.[24] Ultimately, the rewriting of the draft was entrusted to an assembly of experts, in which clerics had a large majority; the assembly completed its task in December 1979. This was after the occupation of the US embassy in November 1979 and the taking of hostages had signaled the onset of a shift in power from liberal nationalists to conservative clerics and their followers.

The revision of the draft reflected this political shift. Not only were the proposals to adopt the UDHR as part of Iran's law rejected, but Islamic qualifications were added to the rights provisions in the draft constitution to dilute them. Nonetheless, it is a significant token of the prestige enjoyed by human rights that, even with the ascendancy of a clerical faction opposed to human rights, references to human rights were not excised from the constitution. They appear in the Preamble and in Articles 14 and 20, and individual rights are mentioned in Article 3.14. However, to make them palatable to conservative clerics, human rights had to be expressly subordinated to Islamic criteria. The most important provision in this regard was Article 4, quoted above, providing that Islamic principles should prevail over those in the constitution, and the text of Article 20, which provides: "All citizens of the country, both men and women, equally enjoy the protection of the law [*qanun,* or secular law] and enjoy human, political, economic, social and cultural rights, *in conformity with Islamic criteria [mavazin-e eslami].*" This equal protection article is discussed later in greater detail, but here it should be noted that Article 20 constitutes a rejection of the position that international law determines human rights standards. Instead, this article expressly states that Islamic criteria govern human rights.

A brief clarification of the term *qanun* used in Article 20 and elsewhere needs to be offered at this point. In Islamic milieus, *qanun,* derived from the Greek *kanon,* is normally used to refer to secular laws as opposed to laws based on Islamic sources in the *shari'a.* However, given the principles set forth in Article 4 and the Article 20 provision that rights are enjoyed in Iran "in conformity with Islamic criteria," references to *qanun* in articles of the constitution imply not that secular law determines the applicable standards but only that secular law will provide the legal framework for implementing principles reflecting Islamic criteria, which are ultimately controlling in the area of human rights.

Other rights provisions similarly provide that Islamic standards determine rights, using qualifications that in the following quotations are italicized for emphasis.

Article 21

"The government must ensure the rights of women in all respects *in conformity with Islamic criteria [mavazin-e eslami]*."

Like Article 20, this article indicates that Islamic criteria are controlling, and therefore it might be considered redundant. However, the specification that women's rights are determined by Islamic standards is meaningful in the particular cultural context of modern Iran, where the application of secular law has been associated with women's emancipation and the application of *shari'a* law with the relegation of women to a subordinate status. In this context, it is significant that there is no provision subordinating men's rights to Islamic standards. By including a separate provision stipulating that women's rights would be determined by reference to Islamic standards, the government was indicating its intention to reinstate discriminatory *shari'a* rules. The consequences of this for women's rights are addressed in Chapter 6.

Article 24

"Publications and the press have freedom of expression *except when it is detrimental to the fundamental principles of Islam [mabani-ye eslam]* or the rights of the public. The details of this exception will be specified by law *[qanun]*."

Article 26

"The formation of parties, societies, political or professional associations, as well as religious societies, whether Islamic or pertaining to one of the recognized religious minorities, is permitted, provided they do not violate principles of independence, freedom, and national unity, or *the criteria of Islam [mavazin-e eslami] or the basis of the Islamic Republic.*"

The status of minorities is discussed in greater detail in Chapters 7 and 8, but it is worth stating here that this provision not only waters down protection for freedom of association by making it subject to Islamic criteria but allows the government to deny minority religious groups even these fragile freedoms simply by refusing to accord them the status of "recognized" minority religious associations.

Article 27

"Public gatherings and marches may be freely held, provided arms are not carried and that *they are not detrimental to the fundamental principles of Islam [mabani-ye eslam]*."

Article 28

"Everyone has the right to choose any occupation he wishes, *if it is not contrary to Islam [mokhalef-e eslam . . . nist],* to the public interests, and does not infringe the rights of others."

Article 168

"Political and press offences will be tried openly and in the presence of a jury, in courts of justice. The manner of selection of the jury, its powers, and the definition of political offences will be determined by law *[qanun] in accordance with Islamic criteria [bar asas-e qavanin-e eslami]."*[25]

Because Article 168 provides that it will be Islamic criteria that determine what constitutes a political crime, it thereby places religious restraints on political freedom.

One can see that in the above provisions, concepts of rights have been taken from Western constitutions and international law. Some include both secular and Islamic qualifications, but others have only Islamic qualifications. As these examples demonstrate, in the Iranian constitution, Islam is not envisaged as the basis for protecting rights but utilized solely as the basis for limiting or denying the rights afforded by international human rights law that are typically embodied in modern constitutions.

One might object to this conclusion by questioning the idea that the Islamic qualifications placed on these rights would necessarily restrict them more than secular qualifications would. Could it not be the case, one might ask, that the Islamic qualifications on rights might be narrower than those permitted under international law, that these clauses could be interpreted to mean that the government would have to produce much stronger justifications for curbing human rights than it would under secular criteria? In other words, perhaps the assumption that broad Islamic qualifications on rights imply the erosion of rights protections is only that—an assumption. Although in the abstract this question might seem justified, there are good reasons to conclude that these qualifications are designed to dilute rights.

First of all, one must consider the nature of the Iranian government itself. Iran's theocracy has demonstrated a consistent proclivity to deploy any rationale to justify clamping down on freedoms. Both the regime's conduct and its statements show that the official version of Islam is seen as a pretext for curtailing rights, a situation that liberal President Mohammed Khatami struggled futilely to correct during his two terms in office. Islam is used by the ruling hard-liners as a tool for combating social change and expanded freedoms, which are identified with corrupting Western influences. Iran's ruling clerics have repeatedly lambasted restive Iranians who call for democratization and protection for human rights as minions of Western and Zionist conspiracies, "anti-Islamic," "enemies of God and the Prophet Muhammad," "Satanic," or "heretical."

Second, the relationship between the individual and the state in contemporary Middle Eastern societies predisposes governments in the region to be hostile to claims on behalf of individual liberties and the rights of the citizen. It is generally characterized by deeply ingrained patterns of authoritarian, if not totalitarian, government. Despite some tentative progress toward democratization in the region, suppression of opposition, censorship of dissenting opinion, and intolerance of any kind of political or intellectual pluralism are common. Discrimination against women and disfavored groups is rampant. Given this background, it is reasonable to expect that any vague qualifications of rights will tend to be exploited to enhance the power of the state at the expense of the freedoms of the individual.

Third, there is no developed tradition of Islamic human rights protections, no solid jurisprudence restricting the abuse of Islamic pretexts to deny rights. This means that none of the various formulas that are used to set the Islamic qualifications of rights in the Iranian constitution has any established legal content. One of the best illustrations of the arbitrariness that has resulted from relying on these vague Islamic qualifications is in the area of censorship, where subjective, supposedly Islamic pretexts have been invoked to silence and punish dissident Iranians in a harsh but often arbitrary and inconsistent manner.[26]

The problematic character of Islamic restrictions on rights might be contrasted with the vast number of precedents that limit the qualifications that may be placed on rights in the US Bill of Rights. For example, legal precedents establish that there are very few limits that the government may impose on freedom of speech in the United States. In the United States, when individuals assert that the government has unconstitutionally infringed First Amendment guarantees of freedom of speech, they can rely on an elaborate system of principles that have been developed by independent courts and that sharply inhibit the ability of the government to curtail freedom of speech. The constraints on the government's ability to curb speech are so firmly entrenched that a heavy burden is placed on the government to justify conduct or laws restraining speech. If the government does not abide by the limits that the courts have set, it will be deemed to have violated the Constitution, and the speech in question will be protected by measures such as injunctions or nullifications of relevant laws. US freedom of speech guarantees are strong in part because of the framework of legal rules that define narrowly and specifically the grounds on which this right can be restricted or denied, but also because of the respect for laws and legal institutions that has constrained the US government.

In contrast, in Iran there are no firmly ingrained precedents set by an independent judiciary that narrowly limit the circumstances in which Islamic principles can be invoked to justify restricting or denying rights. On the contrary, the Iranian judiciary is politicized and subservient to the government, meaning that the Islamic qualifications on rights provisions will have whatever content that the government chooses to ascribe to them. Those qualifications leave the Iranian government and its agents free to engage in rights violations without fear that injured citizens will be able to invoke Islamic criteria to challenge the legality of governmental actions. Of course, the ability of the government to rely on Islam to insulate its conduct from effective judicial review is linked to the deterioration in the rule of law, reflected in the destruction of Iran's bar in the wake of the revolution and judges' fear of standing up to the powers that be.[27] Iranian courts cannot offer a neutral forum that could build up a jurisprudence protective of human rights.

President Mohammed Khatami appreciated that these serious deficiencies needed to be rectified. He articulated a modern vision of a constitution serving as an instrument for shoring up rights and freedoms, and he appeared determined to curb the misuse of Islamic pretexts to nullify human rights and undermine the rule of law.[28] He twice won office by virtue of promising Iranians that he would pursue a reformed and democratized system with effective protections for their rights. However, he and his reformist allies lacked the wherewithal to dislodge hard-line clerics from their grip on power, and the reform measures were stillborn.

Fourth, Iran's Islam is not the Islamic religion but the state ideology, an ideology that the ruling theocrats insist embodies God's divine plan for human society. Since the government professes to be carrying out this divine plan, there is a built-in tendency toward absolutism, intolerance, and harsh repression of dissent. A symptom of the inherent repressiveness of the official Islamic ideology can be seen in the scope and vigor of the persecutions and prosecutions of dissident Shi'i clerics, many of whom have experienced severe retaliation after questioning the official Islamic ideology.[29]

For example, Ayatollah Montazeri's liberal sympathies and comments evincing disagreement with the Iranian regime's policy of disregard for human rights prompted Khomeini to oust him as his designated successor in March 1989. Despite his disgrace and his being kept under protracted house arrest, Montazeri raised questions in 1997 about the undemocratic features of the system of rule by the supreme jurist, which prompted a harsh backlash by Iran's ruling hardliners. Montazeri questioned a cornerstone of the regime's Islamic ideology, the principle that Islam requires accepting rule by an unelected supreme jurist, and complained that this constituted an obstacle to the reform program for which the electorate had overwhelmingly voted in the 1997 presidential elections. After his criticism of political intervention by the supreme jurist Ali Khamene'i, a jurist with credentials inferior to his own, Ayatollah Montazeri was accused by the former of treason and threatened with prosecution for the capital offense of plotting against the regime.[30] He was excoriated in official statements and the pro-establishment media.[31] A cleric close to the supreme jurist Khamene'i warned that anyone who took a political stand against Khamene'i would be dealt with "severely," and those who dared "the slightest affirmation of Montazeri's faction will face a bitter future."[32] As long as an entrenched clerical elite with such adamant hostility to any kind of dissent or pluralism fights to quell challenges to its largely discredited Islamic ideology, Islamic qualifications on rights will assuredly undermine rights.

In summary, constitutional civil and political rights have been denied in Iran under the rubric of following Islamic criteria and defending Islam and the official ideology. The evidence is overwhelming that Islamic qualifications of rights have stripped rights of their substance.

A clarification seems in order at this point: Showing the correlation between the Islamic qualifications on rights in the Iranian constitution and the subsequent pattern of government conduct restricting and denying human rights is not the same as asserting that, but for the Islamic qualifications that were placed on rights in the Iranian Constitution, the rights would have been protected or that the regime in each instance when rights were being overridden relied formally on the Islamic qualifications in the constitution to justify its conduct. In other words, no attempt is being made to argue here that adding the Islamic qualifications to rights provisions in the constitution by itself caused the infringement of human rights or that the regime always followed Islamic criteria when undertaking measures aimed at curbing or denying rights.

Instead, the connection appears to have been a more subtle one. The addition of the Islamic criteria qualifying rights signaled a general disposition not to be bound by the standards of the UDHR, which, as noted, some Iranians had unsuccessfully tried to have incorporated in the 1979 constitution. In addition, the Islamic qualifications were representative of the general philosophy of the associates of Ayatollah Khomeini, who eventually consolidated their hold over the country and who, as the ruling clerical elite, deemed that the norms of "Islam" could override all secular legal norms.

However, the conduct of the regime revealed that it did not lay great store by principles of legality, irrespective of whether these were religious or secular, and that it was even quite prepared to engage in public violations of basic tenets of Islamic law when those legal principles stood in the way of its political objectives.[33] The Expediency Council that was set up through the 1989 amendments in Article 112 to mediate when legislation in the public interest was deemed to be in conflict with Islamic law was a sign that the regime was looking for a mechanism to get out of the awkward situations that had been caused by the Council of Guardians blocking politically desirable legislation on the grounds that it conflicted with Islamic law.[34] This amendment was one sign that this was not a regime that fastidiously adhered to Islamic law. Since the clerical takeover, the government has acted out of its own notions of political expediency, as if it were unconstrained by Islamic law, resorting to whatever measures were deemed essential to defend its own interests. In this, of course, it acted just like the many secular regimes in the Middle East that pay lip service to official ideologies of nationalism or socialism, which on closer inspection turn out to be mere window dressing for policies dictated by the elites' desire to retain power to pursue their own selfish objectives.

In summary, I want to avoid creating the impression that the Islamic qualifications on constitutional rights provisions created the human rights violations that ensued in Iran. Nonetheless, there is an important correlation between the rights violations and the official position that rights could be restricted or denied in the name of Islam.

Restrictions in the UIDHR

The Universal Islamic Declaration of Human Rights (UIDHR) relies more extensively and explicitly than the Iranian constitution on Islamic criteria to limit rights. It must be emphasized that this pattern of pervasive reliance on the *shari'a* to qualify rights is less readily apparent in the English version than it is in the Arabic version of the UIDHR, which seems to be the authoritative text. The Explanatory Notes section accompanying the English version of the UIDHR states that the Arabic text is "the original," which suggests that it should be treated as more definitive than the English translation. However, the relationship between the Arabic and English versions is a very problematic one, as there are inconsistencies between the two as well as vagueness and ambiguities in the Arabic version.[35]

The Explanatory Notes section includes the following assurance: "In the exercise and enjoyment of the rights referred to above every person shall be subject only to such limitations as are enjoined by the Law for the purpose of securing the due recognition of, and respect for, the rights and the freedom of others and of meeting the just requirements of morality, public order and the general welfare of the Community (Ummah)." Reading the English version, one could get the impression that many of the UIDHR provisions are subject to qualifications imposed by secular laws, since the wording of the qualifications is consistently "according to the Law." However, in reality there is no similarity between the qualifications placed on rights in the UIDHR and those found in international law. In the UIDHR the *shari'a* is the law that qualifies rights when the term "according to the Law" is used.

It is difficult but not impossible for the reader of the English version to discover that by "the Law" the UIDHR means the *shari'a.* The Explanatory Notes section states that the term *Law* in the text means the *shari'a,* which is defined as "the totality of ordinances derived from the Qur'an and Sunnah [the reports of what the Prophet Muhammad said and did] and any other laws that are deduced from these two sources by methods considered valid in Islamic jurisprudence."[36] This definition does not by any means settle how this term should be understood or what qualifications would thereby be placed on rights. At a minimum, "the *shari'a*" under this definition would seem to constitute the totality of premodern *shari'a* jurisprudence, which means that "*shari'a*" here is a term encompassing a vast range of diverging legal positions.[37] Depending on what methods are "considered valid in Islamic jurisprudence," this term might or might not also include many more recent interpretations as well. That is, given the enormous literature that this definition potentially encompasses, the legal standards entailed in the qualification are extremely vague.

Consider some examples of how the *shari'a* is used in the UIDHR to qualify basic rights. In the English version of the declaration, Section 12 of the Preamble includes the guarantee that "no one shall be deprived of the rights assured to him by the Law except by its authority and to the extent permitted by it." Unless one bears in mind the fact that "Law" means the *shari'a,* one might not appreciate the implications of this provision; that is, *shari'a* requirements determine what rights people ultimately have. Essentially, this implies that the *shari'a* both ensures rights and takes them away. The wording of Section 12 of the Preamble in the Arabic version confirms this. It provides that "each person is guaranteed security, freedom, dignity, and justice according to the dictates of what the *shari'a* of God has decreed in the way of rights for people."

In the specific provisions of the UIDHR (English) one finds that the *shari'a* (the Law) determines the scope of the following rights:

1. The right to inflict injury or death, in Article 1.a.
2. The right to liberty, in Article 2.a.
3. The right to justice, in Article 4.a.
4. The right to assume public office, in Article 11.a.
5. The right of expression, in Article 12.a.
6. The right "to protest and strive," in Article 12.c.

7. The right to disseminate information (also qualified by considerations of the security of the society or the state), in Article 12.d.
8. The right to earn a living, in Article 15.b.
9. The right to pursue given economic activities (also qualified by considerations of the interests of the community), in Article 15.g.
10. The rights of spouses in marriage, in Article 19.a.
11. A wife's right to divorce, in Article 20.c, and her right to inherit, in Article 20.d.

An example of a problematic article is Article 14. In English it appears to guarantee a right to freedom of association, with distinctive Islamic qualifications, but it has no counterpart in the Arabic original, so its status is questionable.[38] Article 11 provides for a right to participate in public life, but the provision is qualified in a way that ensures that it will have discriminatory impact on non-Muslims (discussed in more detail in Chapter 5).

To evaluate the strength of the human rights provisions in the UIDHR, one should put oneself in the position of a person being denied rights by the Iranian government in the name of Islam. Could one utilize the UIDHR to prove that Iran's rights violations constitute violations of Islamic human rights? It seems not. The UIDHR accepts the idea that all rights may be qualified by the *shari'a,* but it effectively leaves it to the authorities to determine the scope of Islamic qualifications of rights; that is, it defines the *shari'a* so broadly that governments can freely choose what "Islamic" principles to apply. Thus, if the UIDHR standards were applicable in Iran, they would permit the Iranian government to do exactly as it has done: consistently interpret Islamic law to legitimize government curbs on rights. In contrast, a person being denied civil or political rights in Iran could utilize international human rights law to establish that the Iranian government was violating his or her human rights.

Restrictions in Other Islamic Human Rights Schemes

Just as the Iranian constitution and the UIDHR provide for the use of vague Islamic criteria to restrict basic rights and freedoms, so other Islamic human rights schemes impose Islamic limitations on basic rights and freedoms. Some examples are included in this section, while others that specifically affect women, minorities, and religious freedom are treated in greater detail in later sections.

The Azhar draft Islamic constitution should be examined in both the Arabic version, which one presumes was the original, and the often awkward English translation that accompanies it. It embodies a rights philosophy that is similar to the one in the Iranian constitution and the UIDHR, where rights are subject to vague *shari'a* criteria. The Azhar draft constitution relies especially heavily on these Islamic restrictions.

The Azhar draft constitution uses a variety of Islamic formulas to qualify rights. Article 29 guarantees freedom of religious and intellectual belief, freedom to work, freedom of expression, freedom to form and join associations and unions, personal freedom *(al-hurriya al-shakhsiya),* freedom to travel,[39] and freedom to hold meetings, all within *shari'a* limits *(hudud al-shari'a al-islamiya).* Article 37 guarantees the right to work and gain a living within *shari'a* precepts *(ahkam al-shari'a al-islamiya).* Article 43 states that rights are enjoyed according to the objectives of the *shari'a (wafqan li maqasid al-shari'a).* With the exception of Article 42, which places additional secular conditions on rights, Islamic law is treated as the sole basis for restricting or denying rights.

Although all of these qualifications are left indefinite, one might be particularly curious as to what Islamic restrictions on the freedom of travel would entail. Article 13 of the UDHR guarantees everyone the freedom of movement within the borders of each state and the right to leave and return to one's own country without any qualifications, and it may not be immediately obvious why religious criteria would be relevant in the exercise of this freedom. However, Islamic conservatives tend to believe that women should not leave their homes save in case of necessity, and that, if they do leave their homes, they should be chaperoned.[40] Some conservative Muslims believe that it is "un-Islamic" for women to be allowed to drive, which is why Islam is invoked as the reason for not allowing women to drive cars in Saudi Arabia. The general treatment of women in the Azhar constitution, which is examined later, warrants the inference that the "*shari'a* limits" on freedom of travel would be used to justify restrictions on women's freedom of movement.

In the work of the Iranian Sufi Sultanhussein Tabandeh, one finds similar religious qualifications placed on human rights. However, Tabandeh coupled Islamic qualifications with others that indicate a bias in favor of preserving social order and harmony and enforcing respect for authority. The UDHR in Article 3 guarantees the general right to life, liberty, and security of person without qualification, but according to Tabandeh, those rights should be qualified by the requirement that they not be "contrary to the regulations of Islam [or] molest the peace of others."[41] It is striking to see that in Tabandeh's view, even the right to life itself is qualified by Islamic criteria. Apparently, he would allow the subjective reactions of persons who felt that their peace had been molested to deny another the right to live.[42] These standards deviate sharply from international norms, such as the principle in Article 6 of the International Covenant on Civil and Political Rights (ICCPR) that the right to life should be protected by law and that no one should be arbitrarily deprived of life. With regard to freedom of opinion and expression, Tabandeh said that freedom in these areas ceases to be a right where "it threatens public order or grows contumacious against government and religion."[43] Again, this view betokens a mentality light-years removed from the philosophy of international human rights law, which would never accept limitations that treat speech critical of government or religion as being subject to banning under such open-ended, subjective criteria.

As has already been noted, Mawdudi's discussion of Islamic human rights is sketchy and uneven and leaves the impression that he was avoiding a number of difficult problems. His presentation of Islamic qualifications on human rights is correspondingly short and incomplete. In his scheme he did limit freedom of expression and association by imposing the condition that such freedoms must conform to the Qur'anic command in 3:104 to order what is good and forbid that which is evil.[44] This indicates that Islamic standards of virtue would be used to determine what could be expressed and what associations would be allowed, but without giving the exact meaning of this qualification. On the basis of this example, one can say that Mawdudi was disposed to think of Islam as a curb on rights. However, there is much more evidence that he supported the use of Islamic law to deny rights, as discussed in Chapters 6–8.

The pattern of imposing vague Islamic limitations on rights continues in the Cairo Declaration, Article 24 of which provides that "[a]ll the rights and freedoms stipulated in this Declaration are subject to the Islamic *shari'a*." Article 25 follows with a circular and unhelpful definition of what these limits would entail, providing that "[t]he Islamic *shari'a* is the only source of reference for the explanation or clarification of any of the articles of this Declaration."

In the Cairo Declaration one finds various vague Islamic restrictions placed on specific provisions. Several of the provisions relevant for civil and political rights are mentioned in this chapter, with others to be discussed subsequently. Article 16 establishes the right to enjoy the fruit of one's scientific, literary, artistic, or technical production and the right to the interests therefrom, except where such production is contrary to the principles of the *shari'a*. Article 22 invites extensive censorship based on vague Islamic criteria and Islamic morality. Article 22(a) provides that there is a right to express opinions freely—but only in a manner not contrary to the principles of the *shari'a*. Article 22(b), reflecting the directive in the Qur'an (3:104) to do good and prohibit evil, provides that everyone shall have the right to advocate what is right and propagate what is good and warn against what is wrong and evil according to the norms of the Islamic *shari'a*. In Article 22(c), the declaration provides that information "may not be exploited or misused in such a way as may violate the sanctities and the dignity of prophets, undermine moral and ethical values or disintegrate, corrupt, or harm society or weaken its faith."

In a similar vein, the Saudi Basic Law, which had already provided in Article 7 that the Qur'an and *sunna* of the Prophet were the supreme law, also provides in Article 26 that the state will protect human rights according to the Islamic *shari'a (wafqa 'l-shari'a al-islamiya),* with no further definition of what restraints this could entail. There is little chance of Islamic restraints being narrowly defined under Article 6, which states that citizens are to submit to the rule of the King in accordance with the Qur'an and *sunna* and to obey him, essentially treating Saudi citizens as mere subjects. Furthermore, Article 23 asserts that the state shall respect and apply the Islamic *shari'a,* ordering the good and forbidding the evil, thereby providing an additional basis for using Islamic law and Islamic values to shape the scope of rights and freedoms.

Under the Omar al-Bashir dictatorship, the Sudan likewise explicitly subordinated rights to Islamic principles. A document on human rights in the Sudan published in Khartoum on July 17, 1993, proclaimed that the principles of Sudanese philosophy protected the dignity and rights of individuals in accordance with Islamic law.[45]

In Pakistan and Egypt, rulings in two significant court cases involving constitutional freedom of religion issues held that the scope of rights was to be determined in accordance with Islamic criteria. In the course of decision in *Zaheeruddin v. State,* discussed in Chapter 7, the Pakistan Supreme Court effectively raised "the Injunctions of Islam" to a status above the constitution and also above the fundamental rights set forth in the constitution. According to the court, "the Injunctions of Islam" had become "the real and the effective law" of the country.[46] Speaking as if unqualified human rights would offend Islam, the court asserted that "even the Fundamental Rights as given in the Constitution must not violate the norms of Islam."[47]

In the notorious Nasr Hamid Abu Zaid case of 1994–1996, discussed in Chapter 8, the Egyptian Court of Appeals and Court of Cassation both purported to uphold the constitutional guarantee of freedom of religion, but in ruling that Abu Zaid was an apostate and severing his marital tie, they treated freedom of religion as if it were subject to Islamic qualifications.[48] That is, even where there is no express constitutional provision or law explicitly stating that constitutional rights are subordinated to Islamic criteria, courts may act as if rights are qualified by Islamic restrictions. As one might expect, what these criteria entail is vague and uncertain.

Islam and Human Rights in the New Constitutions of Afghanistan and Iraq

The controversial relationship between Islam and human rights was dramatically illustrated by the intense wrangling over their respective roles in the Afghan and

Iraqi constitutions that were drafted in the aftermath of the US invasions. There was no unitary Islam in either Afghanistan or Iraq, since both countries comprised Muslims adhering to various versions of Islam. As a result, any constitutional references to Islam were sure to provoke controversy. In both countries there are strong proponents of Islamization—predominantly Sunni in Afghanistan and predominantly Shi'i in Iraq—who face off against proponents of more secular systems. Both are politically volatile, and both have records of appalling human rights violations. Afghanistan has been wracked by rival warlords competing for control of the capital and provinces; in Iraq the policies of the brutal dictator Saddam Hussein aggravated tensions between the Kurdish north, the Sunni center, and the Shi'i south. In Afghanistan, women were harshly oppressed under the Taliban, with feminist activists fighting back and demanding protections for women's rights; in Iraq, the relatively secular Ba'thist regime had offered expanded opportunities to women and imposed a reformed version of Islamic law that enhanced women's rights—and alienated religious conservatives.

As one might expect given this background, the constitution-drafting process was highly fractious in both countries. US officials in Kabul and Baghdad pressed the contending factions to reach agreement and influenced the crafting of the substantive provisions. They often advocated their positions publicly, trying to counterbalance the forces calling for the supremacy of Islamic law. Afghan and Iraqi groups advocating a strong role for Islam tended to support rules ensuring conformity with Islamic law at the expense of rights.

Not surprisingly, since both countries neighbor Iran, where Islam has been converted into a rationale for denying and circumscribing rights, the assumption was made by supporters of human rights that the greater the role accorded to Islam in the constitution, the more enfeebled rights would be. That is, Islam and human rights tended to be treated as if they were two conflicting value systems.

Resolving how to treat the respective roles of human rights and Islam was a central problem in the work leading up to the November 2003 Constitution of the Islamic Republic of Afghanistan and the March 2004 Iraqi Transitional Administrative Law, or TAL. The tortuous formulations of the relevant constitutional provisions indicated that disagreements were not resolved on how to weight the respective concerns of Islam and human rights.

In the Afghan constitution, the preamble opens with statements that effectively establish Islam and the Universal Declaration of Human Rights (UDHR) as pillars of the new system.[49] The first line proclaims that the constitution is written "with firm faith in God Almighty and relying on His mercy, and Believing in the Sacred religion of Islam." Four lines below, one finds: "Observing the United Nations Charter and respecting the Universal Declaration." In Section 8 of the preamble, human rights are stipulated as being among the goals of Afghan society—without any mention of Islamic qualifications. Article 7.1 reiterates the commitment to the UDHR, stipulating that the state shall abide by the UN Charter, international treaties, international conventions that Afghanistan has signed, and the UDHR.

However, in addition to referring to the Universal Declaration, the Afghan constitution in Article 3 also provides that no law shall contravene the beliefs and principles of the sacred religion of Islam. This provision seemingly establishes Islam as the criterion of legality, but it leaves the dimensions of this criterion undefined, there being no objective way of ascertaining what a category like Islamic "beliefs and principles" should mean in the Afghan context, where there was a vast gap between the Taliban's mentality and that of progressive Afghan believers. In any event, the door was opened to references to conservative interpretations at odds with human rights.

The 2004 Iraqi TAL was merely an interim document.[50] It asserted that the Iraqi people were "affirming today their respect for international law, especially having been amongst the founders of the United Nations, working to reclaim their legitimate place among nations."[51] Islam's privileged status was affirmed in Article 7.A, but in a manner that was confusing. Islam was to be considered *a* source—not *the* source—of legislation. No law that contradicted the universally agreed tenets of Islam, the principles of democracy, or the rights provisions of the TAL could be enacted. Thus, proposed laws had to be acceptable under (vague) Islamic criteria while conforming to provisions on rights and democracy—without any ranking of these criteria. This was tantamount to requiring that laws meet two sets of potentially conflicting criteria.

As work progressed during 2005 on the permanent Iraqi constitution, the US Commission on International Religious Freedom (USCIRF) wrote in July to US Ambassador Zalmay Khalilzad, protesting that the drafters were moving away from the TAL model. At that time, provisions under consideration would have allowed Islamic law to override human rights. The USCIRF announced that it wanted the constitution to afford an unqualified guarantee of the right to freedom of thought, conscience, and religion or belief; an unqualified provision of equality and nondiscrimination for members of all groups, including women; and a provision that no law should be contrary to the rights guaranteed in the bill of rights in the Iraqi constitution and international human rights standards.[52] As the Iraqi drafters complained that irreconcilable differences precluded them from completing their work, the United States increased pressure on the drafters to finalize the constitution.[53] A final draft was somehow patched together, and it was eventually approved in October 2005.[54]

Unable to devise a coherent statement of the relationship between Islam and human rights, the drafters opted for a scheme resembling the one in the TAL, listing an amalgam of potentially conflicting principles in Article 2 without indicating which should have priority. On the one hand, it established Islam as *a main* source—as opposed to *a* source or *the main* source—of legislation and provided that no law could violate the established rules of Islam. On the other hand, it provided that no law could violate the principles of democracy or the rights and basic freedoms outlined in the constitution—without making any reference to international human rights law. The impact of Article 2 will ultimately be decided by those interpreting what the rules of Islam require. Article 90 gives the Supreme Federal Court the task of interpreting the constitution, and Article 89 provides that the court is to comprise judges and experts in Islamic law—leaving it to parliament to decide their numbers and the method of selection. If powerful Shiʻi conservatives come to dominate the new system, any ambiguities will be resolved as they have been in Iran: Islamic law will override guarantees of democracy and human rights. Khalilzad called the constitution a balance between forces demanding Islamic laws and those calling for universal human rights.[55] In reality, it offers no balance; it represents another example of unresolved tensions between Islam and human rights.

Summary

Imposing Islamic qualifications on rights sets the stage not just for the diminution of these rights but potentially for denying them altogether. As the foregoing discussion illustrates, those who impose vague Islamic criteria on rights do not see the relationship of the individual and the state as being an adversarial one in which the weaker party, the individual, needs ironclad guarantees of civil and political rights to offset the tendencies of modern governments to assert their powers at the expense of the freedoms of the individual. Furthermore, they seem to believe that where the freedom of the individual and religious rules are in conflict, it is the former that should give way. The individual is barred from asserting excessive rights that could harm the authority of the state or undermine the moral order of society. Islam is viewed in these schemes as a device for keeping the individual in a subordinate place vis-à-vis the government and society. However, the *shariʻa* criteria that are employed to restrict rights are so uncertain that they set no line beyond which curtailments of rights would be deemed impermissible. That is, with these undefined Islamic criteria in place, Islamic human rights offer no protections against laws and policies violating international human rights law.

CHAPTER 5

Discrimination Against Women and Non-Muslims

Equality in the Islamic Legal Tradition

Accommodating the principle of equality in an Islamic human rights scheme involves dealing with two basic strains in the Islamic heritage, one egalitarian and the other hierarchical.[1] Much depends on which of these is taken to be more truly representative of Islamic values.

There is much in the sources of Islamic law that indicates a fundamentally egalitarian philosophy. For example, it is an important tenet of Islam that the best person is the person who is most pious. The accounts of the earliest rulers of the Islamic community, including stories of the life of the Prophet, are full of incidents indicating the rulers' humility, their egalitarian spirit, and their humane concern for the rights and welfare of all of their subjects.

Other passages in the Islamic sources can provide a warrant for upholding privilege and discrimination. The sources do distinguish in a number of areas between the rights of Muslims and non-Muslims, men and women, and free persons and slaves. Premodern jurisprudence ranking males above females, Muslims above non-Muslims, and free persons above slaves became an ingrained feature of *shari'a* law.[2] Going beyond these distinctions, some of the early shapers of Islamic doctrine endorsed hierarchical features of local social structures, treating them as if they were mandated by Islamic law. The implications of these distinctions for today's societies are sharply debated. Although few would uphold the merits of slavery in current circumstances, in other areas contemporary Muslims sharply differ on whether laws should respect the old juristic categories or reflect the idea that Islam was ultimately meant to afford equality to all human beings.

When it comes to deciding whether the principle of equality is compatible with Islam, one can distinguish between two different approaches on the part of those Muslims who wish to retain the premodern *shari'a* rules affecting women and non-Muslims. One is to affirm that the principle of equality violates *shari'a* law. Conservative Muslim clerics in the past have been outspoken in their condemnation of the principle of equality on the grounds that it makes equal those who under the *shari'a* must be treated differently.[3] The other approach is to pretend to accept equality but to offer reasons why the principle of equality is not violated by the retention of the discriminatory rules of the premodern *shari'a* assigning subordinate status to women and non-Muslims. Today the second approach is the prevalent one.

In seeking to understand the position of Muslims who assert that the retention of discriminatory rules of the premodern *shari'a* does not violate the principle of equality, one should bear in mind that "equality" may have a different connotation for many Muslims than it has for people who have grown up with the idea of the absolute equality of all human beings. Social conditioning plays a crucial role in how people think about the principle of equality, as is clear from the history of this principle in the United States. Although egalitarianism was a fundamental tenet of the political and legal order envisaged by the Declaration of Independence, few white males in the era of the Founding Fathers thought that the principle of equality was violated by denying equality to women and to black slaves, who were assumed to be created unequal. Thus, it was possible to affirm equality while at the same time supporting a regime of laws that discriminated based on sex and race. Not until the 1960s was the contradiction between the principle of equality and toleration of de jure discrimination effectively tackled by civil rights legislation, which prohibited discrimination based on sex and race.

Because of the cultural conditioning that prevails in the Middle East, it is easy for conservative Muslims to assume that the distinctions made between different groups of persons in Islamic law are part of the natural order of things and to believe that the retention of premodern Islamic rules does not in any way contravene the principle of equality. Thus, one finds Muslims who argue that Islam recognizes the principle of equality even while they uphold rules relegating women and non-Muslims to an inferior status.

From the perspective of Muslims who have been taught to think that such distinctions are natural and essential, Islam treats as equal all those who should be so treated. From this perspective, *shari'a*-based discrimination is compatible with the principle of equality. However, those Muslims have a problem when they try to address international human rights standards, which clearly state that the principle of equality is not compatible with a regime of discrimination against women and non-Muslims.[4]

Equality in Islamic Human Rights Schemes

Although the authors of Islamic human rights schemes intend to preclude equality as set out in international human rights law, they appear reluctant to acknowledge this intention. The authors attempt to disguise the extent of their disapproval of equality because they are aware that their endorsement of discriminatory *shari'a* rules clearly conflicts with a prestigious human rights tenet.

Authors of Islamic human rights schemes may attempt to evade the issue by simply omitting references to crucial rights. For example, the Saudi Basic Law avoids the topic of equality in rights altogether, thereby obviating the need to stipulate the kinds of inequalities and discriminatory treatment that the authors planned to retain. Another tactic is the use of misleading language and the omission of categories of persons to be affected by Islamic provisions. Although Abu'l A'la Mawdudi included "the equality of human beings" in his list of Islamic human rights,[5] his discussion of this principle revealed that this is a restrictive equality, as he went on to assert that Islam outlaws discrimination among "men"—not among "men and women"—based on color, race, nationality, or place of birth.[6] In his comments on the principle of equality before the law in Islam, he stated that Islam also outlaws discrimination based on class.[7] Completely absent is any reference to discrimination based on sex and religion. Since these are areas where discriminatory rules are entrenched in Muslim societies, Mawdudi was writing around a crucial issue. (As I discuss later, Mawdudi's formulation resembles the provision on equality in Article 3.a of the Universal Islamic Declaration of Human Rights.)

In any social context, a critical measure of the human rights protections that are afforded by the law is the extent to which the laws aim at redressing ingrained patterns of discrimination. Where laws have traditionally discriminated against certain categories, it is essential that provisions on equality mandate an end to such discrimination. Therefore, it would have been hypocritical for the United States to have outlawed discrimination based, say, on caste while ignoring discrimination based on race, just as it would be meaningless in a Hindu environment to outlaw discrimination based on race while ignoring discrimination based on caste. In each case, the actual patterns of discrimination in the local culture would have been ignored. In a scheme like Mawdudi's—designed to be implemented in the Muslim world—it is disingenuous to talk about equality before the law without addressing the problems posed by discriminatory *shari'a* rules denying women and non-Muslims the rights and freedoms enjoyed by Muslim men. By omitting these categories, Mawdudi was effectively condoning the perpetuation of discrimination against these groups.

Article 19 of the Iranian constitution uses a similarly evasive formula to deal with the principle of equality: "All people of Iran, whatever the ethnic group or tribe to which they belong, enjoy equal rights; and color, race, language, and the like, do not bestow any privilege."[8] Significantly, Article 19 does not address the issue of whether equality can be denied on the basis of sex or religion. The extensive discrimination practiced against women and non-Muslims in postrevolutionary Iran indicates that the omission of these categories was deliberate.

The Iranian constitution also has an equality provision that echoes one in the draft constitution. The draft constitution had provided in Article 22, the very first principle in the chapter on rights, that "all members of the people, both women and men, are equal before the law." In the section of the 1979 constitution setting forth the aims of the Islamic Republic, one finds in Article 3.14 that these aims include "securing the multifarious rights of all citizens, both women and men, and providing legal protection for all, as well as the equality of all before the law [qanun]." The fact that this liberal provision was retained, even though it expressed a philosophy of equality that was radically at odds both with the actual policies of the emerging theocratic regime and with other provisions in the constitution shows how much normative force international human rights concepts still possessed in political circles, at least in the immediate aftermath of the revolution.

Article l(a) of the Cairo Declaration avoids stipulating that people are entitled to equal rights, stating instead that all human beings "are equal in terms of basic human dignity and basic obligations and responsibilities, without any discrimination on the grounds of race, color, language, sex, religious belief, political affiliation, social status, or other considerations." Given the evasiveness typically found in the wording of Islamic human rights schemes, one is alerted to the fact that the failure to stipulate equality in "rights" is not accidental and that the equality in "dignity" and "obligations" is not intended to signify equality in "rights." The declaration further provides in Article 19(a): "All individuals are equal before the law, without distinction between the ruler and the ruled." Viewed in isolation, this might seem to be an affirmation of equal rights, but in the context of a document that carefully avoids guaranteeing equal rights or equal protection of the law for women and non-Muslims, it should be read as meaning only that the law applies equally to rulers and ruled—that is, that rulers are not above the law. Similarly, Article l(b) says that the persons most loved by God are those who are most useful to the rest of his subjects, and no one has superiority over another except on the basis of piety and good deeds. This last statement should, in context, be taken as an endorsement of the proposition that people are equal in God's eyes, which is not the same as affording a legal guarantee of equality. These weak provisions are not necessarily an advance over the Saudi Basic Law, which makes no provision whatsoever regarding equality in rights.

Sultanhussein Tabandeh expressed approval of Article 1 of the Universal Declaration of Human Rights (UDHR), which says that all human beings are born free and equal in dignity and rights, and declared that the UDHR reflects ideas in the Qur'an.[9] In discussing equality, however, he talked of prohibiting class-based or racially based discrimination only, omitting any mention of sex discrimination. He explicitly claimed that differences are recognized based on "religion, faith, or conviction," seemingly in the belief—unfounded—that the UDHR Article 1 equality provision allows such religious discrimination.[10]

In his discussion of Article 2, the general provision of the UDHR prohibiting discrimination, Tabandeh also avoided addressing the issue of sex but did indicate his approval of Islamic rules according Muslims a higher status than non-Muslims and free persons a higher status than slaves.[11] He concluded that Islam could not accept certain parts of Article 2, "for it cannot deny the difference between Muslim and non-Muslim."[12] One gathers from Tabandeh's failure to mention the status of women in connection with these articles that the idea of female equality struck him as so farfetched that he did not need to bother explaining that it was unacceptable under the *shari'a.*

The Azhar draft constitution circumvents the issue of equality by avoiding any specific discussion of categories on the basis of which it is impermissible to discriminate. Article 28 does say that justice and equality are the basis of rule, but this vague provision is far from a stipulation that all persons enjoy equality. One can speculate that the authors of the Azhar draft constitution may have been less comfortable than authors of some of the other Islamic human rights schemes with stipulating an equality that they deemed incompatible with Islamic law.

One sees in the contrasting treatment of equality in the Azhar draft constitution and the Iranian constitution the impact of the very different circumstances in which the two documents were produced. The Iranian model is an actual constitution, unlike the Azhar draft, which was no more than a hypothetical agenda of rights formulations produced by Islamic conservatives, who did not have to deal with the arguments of Muslims who wanted to follow modern rights models. In Iran, the forces of Islamic conservatism had to engage in a dialogue with a real political opposition, since, at the time of the drafting, Iran's liberal opposition had not yet been quelled. Iran's clerics also had to cope with a political reality in which spelling out their rejection of human rights concepts would have been unpopular. It is significant that in this real-world conflict involving differing views on human rights, conservative Muslims backed away from the more extreme positions they had traditionally advocated and agreed to accommodate—at least at the formal level—a number of fundamental human rights principles such as equality and equal protection.

In contrast, many other Islamic rights schemes lack an endorsement of equality or equal protection, highlighting the fact their authors did not have to respond either to popular pressures for such provisions or to the arguments of liberal jurists on behalf of established norms of constitutionalism. This is yet another reason for questioning whether the Islamic human rights schemes discussed here are representative of where Muslim opinion generally stands on rights issues. These rights schemes may merely reflect the ideas of conservative elements and repressive governments that are not answerable to public opinion.

Equal Protection in US and International Law

The principle of equality before the law is closely related to the principle of equal protection of the law, which merits consideration at this juncture. The most influential formulation of the principle of equal protection of the law was set forth in the 1868 Fourteenth Amendment to the US Constitution, which stipulates that "no State shall . . . deny to any person within its jurisdiction the equal protection of the laws."

The purpose of the US equal protection clause in the aftermath of the Civil War was to end the legal regime of discrimination against blacks in the South.[13] Its original reach has been extended by judicial interpretation to end discrimination on bases other than race. In general, one could say that classifications for the purpose of placing minorities at a disadvantage and classifications based on the idea that one group is inherently inferior to another group, or based on stereotypical views of classes of people who are traditional victims of societal discrimination, violate equal protection. That is, the US principle of equal protection is understood to afford remedies correcting actual patterns of discrimination that result in persons who are similarly situated being treated differently.

Although many features of US equal protection jurisprudence necessarily reflect the peculiarities of US history, the basic concept has been emulated in other laws, and the idea of equal protection of the law is also endorsed in international law. Article 7 of the UDHR stipulates: "All are equal before the law and are entitled without any discrimination to equal protection of the law. All are entitled to equal protection against any discrimination in violation of this Declaration and against any incitement to such discrimination."

One sees in Article 7 of the UDHR unequivocal endorsement of equality and equal protection, and Article 2 of the UDHR delineates the relevant categories, providing that it is impermissible to discriminate based on sex or religion, race, color, language, political or other opinion, national or social origin, property, or birth or other status. Any legal measures that discriminate among groups of people using these criteria violate the UDHR guarantee of equality and equal protection.[14] Thus, the UDHR envisages equal protection under a neutral law, a law that does not deny rights to members of weaker or disfavored categories of society, according all people equal treatment.

Equal Protection in Islamic Human Rights Schemes

Although in Islamic law one can discern elements that in some ways anticipate modern notions of equality, one does not find any counterpart of the principle of equal protection under the law. For those trained in Islamic law rather than Western law, the meaning of equal protection may be obscure. In the past, when Muslims were first attempting to come to grips with the constitutional principles of equality, some tended to assume that the principle of equality was not violated as long as *shari'a* law, with its discriminatory features intact, was applied equally to persons within the separate categories that it established.[15] Where differences in religion were at issue, they took the position that equality before the law meant that all Muslims should be treated equally under the *shari'a* and that all non-Muslims should also be treated equally under the *shari'a*—not that Muslims and non-Muslims should be treated alike or accorded the same rights under the law.[16] This original confusion about the meaning of the modern principle of equal protection of the law appears to persist among Muslims who want to uphold traditional hierarchies.

It comes as no surprise that the Azhar draft constitution, the Cairo Declaration, and the Saudi Basic Law offer no guarantee of equal protection of the law, nor does it come as a surprise that, when equal protection of the law is included in one of the Islamic human rights schemes examined here, it does not have the same significance as it does in international law. As will be seen, the idea of equal protection is modified to accommodate forms of discrimination mandated by tradition and by premodern rules of Islamic law. In other words, the assumption is made that it is possible to have equal protection under a law that itself mandates unequal treatment.

In the English version of the UIDHR, Article 3.a provides that "all persons are equal before the Law and are entitled to equal opportunities and protection of the Law," which could leave the impression that the authors of the UIDHR wanted to end the discrimination required by *shari'a* law in the treatment of women and non-Muslims. Although the uninitiated Western reader might think that the authors had espoused the principle of equal protection of the law, this is not the case.

To understand the significance of the terminology, one needs to consult the Arabic version of Article 3.a of the UIDHR, which states that people are equal before the *shari'a* and that no distinction is made in its application to them or in their protection under it. That is, people are not being guaranteed the equal protection of a neutral law but "equal protection" under a law that in its premodern formulations is inherently discriminatory and thereby in violation of international standards.[17] The misleading formulation of the English version of Article 3.a, which tends to disguise this difference, is only one of many aspects of the UIDHR suggesting that the authors know that their philosophy is incompatible with international norms and are trying to hide nonconforming aspects from international observers.

One might ask why the authors of the UIDHR, who obviously reject the principle of equal protection, would bother to make the claim in the Arabic version of Article 3.a that all people are to enjoy equal protection before the *shari'a*. As will be shown in the discussion of the corresponding Arabic text, there are specifications in the Arabic version revealing that the authors do not believe that the principle of equal protection is violated when the discrimination is based on sex or religion. In other words, sex and religion are not included in their list of categories on the basis of which it is impermissible to discriminate. According to this approach, it is as legitimate to use the *shari'a* to deny women and religious minorities the rights granted to Muslim males as it is in Western legal systems to deny noncitizens the rights accorded to citizens.

In the UIDHR, one finds the categories on the basis of which it is impermissible to discriminate in the Arabic version of Article 3.a. Following the statement that all persons enjoy equal protection of the *shari'a*, there are in the Arabic text of Article 3.a quotations from the Prophet and the caliph Abu Bakr, his first successor. These quotations support the notion that there should be no discrimination based on ethnic background, color, social standing, and political connections.[18] These are, in fact, categories on the basis of which *shari'a* rules do not ordinarily discriminate. It is noteworthy that the categories do not include sex or religion.

Some clarification of the true intent of the authors of the UIDHR can be obtained by comparing provisions of various articles. Such internal comparisons reinforce the conclusion that the guarantee of equality and equal protection in Article 3.a does not extend to discrimination based on sex and religion, since such discrimination is endorsed in other provisions. Some of these provisions are examined in Chapters 6 and 7, but a few are presented here to illustrate how the rights that women and minorities enjoy under international law fail to receive protection in the UIDHR.

Article 11 of the UIDHR provides for a right to participate in public life. However, conservative Muslims generally claim that the *shari'a* excludes women and non-Muslims from most, if not all, governmental positions. The Arabic version of Article 11 appears to confirm this position by qualifying the right, providing that all members of the *umma,* or community of believers in Islam, who are possessed of the requisite *shari'a* qualifications are eligible to serve in public employment and public office. Although the Arabic version specifically provides that race and class cannot be utilized as a basis for excluding people from such positions, the possibility is left open that discriminatory *shari'a* rules may exclude women and non-Muslims from public office and employment on the grounds that they are lacking "requisite qualifications." Moreover, by its terms, the article seems to exclude non-Muslims from its protections since they are not members of the *umma*.

Dealing with the specifics of equality seems to have presented great problems for the authors of the UIDHR, leading to the production of extremely convoluted and ambiguous formulations. Since it is very easy, if one actually endorses full equality, to provide for it using the international standards, the obscurity of the UIDHR provisions on equality suggests that the authors had difficulty in finding formulations that would offer token recognition of the principle while restricting equality to domains where the principle would not threaten the advantages enjoyed by Muslim males.

Turning to Article 3.c of the UIDHR, one finds that in the English version under the rubric "Right to Equality and Prohibition Against Impermissible Discrimination" there is the following guarantee: "No person shall be denied the opportunity to work or be discriminated against in any manner or exposed to greater physical risk by reason of religious belief, color, race, origin, sex or language."

This differs significantly from the wording of the corresponding Arabic provision. In the Arabic version under the rubric "Right of Equality," the corresponding section, in Article 3.b, says that all people are equal in terms of their human value *(al-qaima al-insaniya),* that they are distinguished in merit (in the afterlife by God) according to their works *(bi hasab 'amali him),* that no one is to be exposed to greater danger or harm than others are, and that any thought, law, or rule *(wad')* that permits discrimination between people on the basis of *jins* (which can mean nation, race, or sex), *'irq* (race or descent), color, language, or religion is in direct violation of this general Islamic principle *(hadha 'l-mabda al-islami al-'amm).*

As a result of the difference between the English and Arabic texts and the ambiguity in the Arabic, one cannot tell whether the intent was to abolish discrimination based on sex with regard to the areas covered.[19] In light of the pattern of evasiveness that one finds in the provisions in the UIDHR, one has reason to assume that the wording here has been deliberately made opaque. Moreover, the range of discriminatory laws and practices affected by the Arabic Article 3 is so narrow as to afford no valuable guarantees against discrimination for any categories of persons. The English version in Article 3.b does seem to bar discrimination in work opportunities, but there is no corresponding provision in the Arabic version of Article 3. The Arabic version does not say that no one should be discriminated against "in any manner" based on the categories mentioned. Instead, this convoluted provision appears to be more of an endorsement of the proposition that people should not be discriminated against in the sense of being exposed to greater danger or harm by reason of those categories. It is not clear what kind of discrimination this greater exposure to danger or harm would involve, but, regardless of the construction placed on these terms, it seems certain that it would cover a narrower area than is indicated in the English version.

Although the Arabic version of Article 3.b does not correspond to any tenet of international human rights law, it could herald a concern for advancing rights protections if it addressed an existing pattern of rights deprivations in Muslim countries. However, the principle that groups of people should not be exposed to greater danger or harm does not seem to address the problems of discrimination faced by women and non-Muslims in Muslim countries. Members of these groups complain that they suffer discrimination in the areas of education, employment, and political participation. To the extent that Islamic law is applied in the rules of evidence and in criminal law, members of these groups are also relegated to inferior status, which they find objectionable. Feminists condemn patterns of sex discrimination in personal status law and restrictions on women's freedoms, while non-Muslims protest the favored status accorded to Islam and complain of denials of religious freedoms.

Therefore, in context, the protections offered in Article 3.b seem quite trivial. There is every reason to assume that discriminatory rules relegating women and non-Muslims to a subordinate status could coexist with this provision. In fact, other provisions of the UIDHR indicate that such discriminatory rules are being retained. Furthermore, the lack of protection against discrimination afforded in the Arabic version of Article 3 is not mitigated by the initial stipulation that all persons have the same human value. In context, this seems to be an abstract moral proposition, not a principle designed to establish full equality before the law.

Given the disparity between the English and the Arabic versions of Article 3 of the UIDHR, it is noteworthy that the English, not the Arabic, version of Article 3 was invoked in a recent court case in Pakistan.[20] In the case, the petitioner charged that the appointment of women as judges in Pakistan was un-Islamic. Although the petitioner was unable to adduce any support from the Qur'an or *sunna* for his argument, he did manage to cite prestigious medieval jurists who had ruled that women could not be judges. The attorney general of Pakistan in turn found a medieval jurist who held the contrary view and also argued that the other jurists had drawn an overly broad conclusion from a statement by the Prophet on women's capacity to rule. The court found that the petitioner had been mistaken in his interpretations of many of the relevant requirements of Islamic law. Although the decision did not turn on the UIDHR, the court did refer to Article 3 of the English version to support its decision that Islamic law did not prohibit women from serving as judges. It characterized the article as follows: "It deals with the equality before Law, entitlement to equal opportunities and protection of the Law [and] also provides firstly that all persons shall be entitled to equal wage for equal work and secondly that no person shall be denied the opportunity to work or be discriminated against in any manner or exposed to greater physical risk by reason of religious belief, color, race, origin, sex, or language."[21] Obviously, had the court examined the Arabic version of the same article, it would have had much greater difficulty finding support for the proposition that under Islamic law women should not be discriminated against in employment or excluded from serving as judges. Women aspirants to the bench were fortunate that in Pakistan competence in the Arabic language was not more widespread.[22]

It is not only in the provisions of Islamic human rights that deal expressly with equality or discrimination that one finds Islamic rules being applied to restrict the rights of women and non-Muslims. Careful scrutiny may be needed to identify discriminatory biases in measures dealing with other rights issues. Frequently, attempts are made to disguise these discriminatory features. A number of such instances of hidden biases in seemingly neutral provisions are discussed in the next two chapters, but I provide one example here, where the objective is to deny to non-Muslims rights that are accorded to Muslims.

One might get the impression from a reading of the English version of Article 14 of the UIDHR that it endorses a right to freedom of association. In fact, on closer reading, the provision mandates inequality between Muslims and non-Muslims in terms of their rights of association and expression. The "Right of Free Association" in the heading of Article 14 of the English version of the UIDHR seems to be qualified by the requirement in Article 14.a that such associations enjoin the good and prohibit the evil. The UIDHR provision states: "Every person is entitled to participate individually and collectively in the religious, social, cultural and political life of his community and to establish institutions and agencies meant to enjoin what is right *(ma'roof)* and to prevent what is wrong *(munkar)*." This provision relates to the command to Muslims in the Qur'an (3:104) to enjoin the good and prohibit the evil.

No protection is afforded for the right to participate in institutions or agencies—which presumably mean "associations" in this context—other than ones enjoining the good and prohibiting the evil. Since the right to freedom of association as understood today was unknown in premodern Islamic law, there are no established guidelines for interpreting the Qur'anic command in 3:104 as a principle governing freedom of association—especially where the affected associations would be ones involving non-Muslims. It therefore is unclear what the limits set in Article 14.a would mean for that right.[23]

When one looks at the heading of the Arabic version of the same provision, it is evident that one is not even dealing with what would be considered a right to freedom of association in the sense current in international law. Instead, according to the Arabic heading of Article 14, the provision deals with *haqq al-da'wa wa'l-balagh,* or the right to propagate Islam and to disseminate the Islamic message. Among the Qur'anic passages cited in the Arabic version of Article 14 is part of 12:108: "Say, this is my way. I call on Allah with sure knowledge, I and whosoever follows me."

From this, one understands that the only freedom of association that is being guaranteed is one that protects activities connected with spreading Islam. It is highly unlikely that the right to spread religions other than Islam or to disseminate works tinged with secularism or atheism could be accommodated within the scope of this wording. The provision of this restricted freedom carries with it the implication that no broader freedom of association is allowed. The Arabic Article 14 therefore actually seems to result in a curb on the associational freedoms of non-Muslims and also on freedom of expression more generally.[24]

The drafters of the Iranian constitution, who, as noted in Chapter 4, included an equal protection clause in Article 20, were apparently aware that it was, at least from the standpoints of constitutional theory and international law, a contradiction in terms to guarantee equal protection under the *shari'a.* Thus, the first sentence in the article provides for equal protection under the *qanun,* or secular law. This makes the Iranian equal protection clause look more like the international standard set forth in Article 7 of the UDHR than Article 3.a of the UIDHR. The intent is not, however, to guarantee equality to all persons under the law; in the Iranian constitution, discrimination against women and non-Muslims is legitimated by other provisions. As we have seen, the critical second sentence of Article 20 provides that all human rights are determined by Islamic principles, and Article 4 provides that Islamic principles in general prevail over constitutional principles. These provisions indicate that discriminatory *shari'a* principles would prevail over the secular equal protection principle.

The inclusion of an equal protection clause in Article 20 suggests the enduring influence that Western and international ideas of equal protection have had. Today, an equal protection clause seems to have become part of the necessary apparatus of a nation's constitution, so it may be included even where the philosophical premises on which the concept of equal protection rests are rejected—as they are in the Iranian constitution. In any event, the incongruous inclusion of an equal protection clause in the Iranian constitution is perfectly emblematic of that document's awkward blend of Islamic principles and dissimilar and imperfectly integrated elements of international human rights.

The question remains: How do the authors of the Iranian constitution rationalize the conflicting provisions they have included in the text? It is interesting to consider the treatment of equality in an article by a Shi'i cleric and strong supporter of Ayatollah Khomeini, Ayatollah Yahya Nuri, who played a prominent and active role in the postrevolutionary regime.[25] Nuri attempted to adjust the idea of equality so that it could fit within a framework of premodern *shari'a* rules mandating inequality. He argued that the principle of equality is the basis of Islam and that Islam shuns the violation of human rights and grants freedom to all under the law.[26] However, in listing impermissible bases for discrimination, he enumerated only the categories of race, color, social class, "weakness," and poverty.[27] This pattern of omitting the critical categories, sex and religion, is by now familiar.

Ayatollah Nuri elaborated on his philosophy of equality. He said that Islam supports the idea that all men (here the omission of women is probably not accidental) should have equal political and social rights, but with the qualification that "equality must be established by the law and it must not transgress the law."[28] For Nuri, the law, by which he means the *shari'a,* serves as a necessary corrective to the principle of equality, which, if not adequately curbed, would have undesirable effects on society, whence his formula "equality must be established by the law" but "must not transgress the law." By holding that equality should be confined within legal limits so that excessive equality can be avoided, Nuri is effectively saying that some inequalities should be imposed by law. Ultimately, he is appropriating the ideal of equality while at the same time calling for upholding laws that favor some at the expense of others. Nuri's formula, which is designed to enforce legal inequality at the same time that it proclaims support for the ideal of equality, is essentially a cousin of the conceit of the elite pigs in George Orwell's *Animal Farm,* according to which all animals were equal but some were more equal than others.[29]

A comparison of Nuri's formula and the treatment of equality in the Islamic human rights schemes shows that they share a common assumption—that the right to equality is acceptable as long as people who should not be made equal are kept in their proper place by the retention of the rules of Islamic law. In contrast, in international law, as embodied in UDHR Articles 1 and 3, the rights to equality and equal protection of the law are not subject to any conditions. The UDHR assumes that there can be no legitimate societal or governmental interest in mandating inequality.

Equality in the New Afghan and Iraqi Constitutions

Article 22 of Afghanistan's 2003 constitution bars any kind of discrimination or privilege among the citizens of Afghanistan and provides also that citizens, whether men or women, have equal rights and duties before the law. However, as noted in Chapter 4, Article 3 of the Afghan constitution provides that no law shall contravene the beliefs and principles of the sacred religion of Islam. It is unclear at this stage whether the equality provision will be upheld according to the references to international human rights law in the preamble and Article 7 or whether it will be judged to violate Islamic law. Iraq's 2005 constitution afforded a strong equality guarantee in Article 14, which asserted that "Iraqis are equal before the law without discrimination based on gender, race, ethnicity, origin, color, religion, creed, belief or opinion, or economic and social status." However, as noted in Chapter 4, provisions on Islam elsewhere in the constitution, such as those in Article 2, provided a potential basis for superimposing Islamic criteria on human rights. Thus, one is left to speculate whether these guarantees will be interpreted in a manner that will give them real substance.

Summary

On the basis of these examinations, one can say that the Azhar draft constitution, the Cairo Declaration, the Saudi Basic Law, and the models endorsed by Mawdudi and Tabandeh—all of which fail to fully and unequivocally endorse the principles that all persons are equal and that discrimination based on religion or sex is impermissible—are less internally inconsistent than the Iranian constitution, which is an admixture of human rights principles concerning equality and conflicting assertions of the supremacy of Islamic law. It is more difficult to characterize the treatment of equality in the UIDHR because of the numerous ambiguities and inconsistencies in the provisions regarding equality and equal protection, as discussed above. However, in general the UIDHR treatment of equality more closely resembles that in the models of Mawdudi, Tabandeh, and the Azhar draft constitution than the treatment of equality in the Iranian constitution.

Taken together, these schemes reveal the profound ambivalence that conservative Muslims feel about the principle of equality, a principle that they are reluctant to condemn openly but that they seek to circumvent by a variety of subterfuges. In these circumstances, the principles of equality and equal protection of the law as mandated in international human rights law are unlikely to be replicated in human rights schemes whose authors maintain the superiority of Islamic criteria.

CHAPTER 6

Restrictions on the Rights and Freedoms of Women

With interpretations of Islamic rules affecting women being sharply contested, it is difficult to make general characterizations regarding the impact of Islamic law on women's rights. Islamic human rights schemes have elected to utilize Islamic criteria to restrict women's human rights, endorsing the views of medieval jurists, views that reflect older sociocultural milieus that were imbued with patriarchal values. Official Islamization programs and associated ideologies aim to demote women to second-class citizenship, invoking a calcified version of Islamic tradition to justify this. In so doing, they disregard the views of Islamic feminists and reformers who have been mining the Qur'an and the example of the Prophet, finding support for women's equality in the sources. At the same time, conservatives who seek to use Islam to curb women's rights and freedoms mostly seek to avoid advertising their hostility to the principle of equality that international law offers women, resorting to equivocations and obfuscations. Current debates on what Islamic law actually says regarding women's rights, the actual practice of various Muslim countries, and prevailing patterns of sex stereotyping are examined in this chapter with a view to indicating the variety of factors influencing how contemporary Muslims think about the rights of women under Islamic law.

Islamic Law and Women's Rights

Some basic features of premodern Islamic law affecting women's rights must first be outlined. To avoid repetitive qualifications, I have resorted to generalizations. It is impossible to catalogue here all the diverging positions of the various sects and schools of law. Although I cannot offer in this chapter a treatise on the Islamic law

113

of personal status, it should be borne in mind that generalizations about Islamic rules affecting women's status can be misleading, since even within a single school of law one often encounters diverging juristic interpretations.

The Qur'an, as divine Revelation, is obviously a central source of guidance, and much of the text concerns women. Qur'anic innovations tend in the direction of enhancing women's rights and elevating their status and dignity. In an environment where women were so devalued that female infanticide was a common and tolerated practice, the Qur'an introduced reforms that prohibited female infanticide, permitted women to inherit, restricted the practice of polygamy, curbed abuses of divorce by husbands, and gave women the ownership of the dower, which had previously been paid to the bride's father.[1] As the thrust of the Qur'anic reforms in women's status is an ameliorative one, it seems reasonable to conclude, as did eminent liberal scholar of Islam Fazlur Rahman, that "the principal aim of the Qur'an was the removal of certain abuses to which women were subjected."[2]

Not only did the Qur'an dismantle existing institutions that contributed to women's degraded and vulnerable status, but Islam conferred rights on women in the seventh century that women in the West were unable to obtain until relatively recent times. For example, Muslim women enjoyed full legal personality, could own and manage property, and according to some interpretations of the Qur'an, enjoyed the right to divorce on very liberal grounds. The historical accounts regarding the status of women in the first decades of the Islamic community under the Prophet Muhammad suggest that women were originally accorded considerable freedom, that within the family the rights given them by Islam enabled them to defend their interests, and that they participated in public and religious affairs on a footing of approximate equality with men.[3]

Given this background, contemporary Islamic reformers are naturally skeptical when assured that Islam, which initially aimed to remove the disabilities women had suffered in pre-Islamic Arabia, provides the rationale for keeping women in a subjugated, inferior status. They have tended to place the blame for what they see as distortions of the original, authentic Islam on male interpreters of the Islamic sources who had vested interests in the preservation of patriarchal privilege. Thus, the influential Islamologist Fazlur Rahman argued that the influence of social conditions and the interpenetration of many diverse cultural traditions led to the inferior status of women being written into Islamic law.[4] Feminists have charged that the medieval juristic mentality was infiltrated by male biases and influences from local cultures that ultimately distorted Qur'anic ideals, and therefore juristic opinions should be distinguished from the authentic teachings of Islam.[5] The notion that Muslims should be free to disregard medieval jurisprudence is controversial, because for centuries juristic treatises were viewed as authoritative statements of doctrine.

The premodern jurists generally treated women as needing male tutelage and control, imposing many disabilities on women, putting them in a distinctly subordinate role vis-à-vis men within the family, and largely relegating them to secluded domesticity. Jurists condoned the marriage of young girls, which in practice meant that girls could be married off against their will by male marriage guardians. According to the jurists, women were required to be monogamous, whereas men could have up to four wives at a time. Wives owed obedience to their husbands, who were entitled to keep them at home and to beat them and to withhold maintenance for disobedience. Husbands could terminate marriages at their discretion simply by uttering a divorce formula, whereas wives, according to many jurists, needed to overcome difficult hurdles to obtain a divorce over their husbands' objections. Men enjoyed great power as the guardians of minors, and after a divorce, men got custody of children once they passed the stage of infancy. In the scheme of succession, women got one-half the share of males who inherited in a similar capacity (meaning that they stood in the same relationship to the deceased).[6]

Medieval jurists were rarely unanimous on points of family law and inheritance affecting women—even though these are the areas where the Qur'an and *sunna* provide extensive guidance. The lack of explicit texts in the Islamic sources on other topics meant that many questions about women's rights and freedoms were hard for the jurists to answer conclusively, leading to tensions and ambiguities in the juristic tradition. Women were commanded to dress modestly, but what modesty entailed was disputed. In domains such as access to education, employment, and participation in public life, relevant textual authority was conflicting or wanting. Furthermore, there were unresolved questions about how to reconcile the rights granted to women by the *shari'a*, such as the right to manage their own property and to conduct business, with other *shari'a* rules that seemed to be in direct conflict with them, such as rules barring women from contact with men outside the family and allowing the husband to control his wife's activities and to keep her at home, isolated from all but close family members.

Since the late nineteenth century, members of the elite in Muslim societies have been gradually won over to the idea that the premodern *shari'a* rules need to be reformed. Except for Saudi Arabia, Middle Eastern countries have introduced reforms to improve women's status and remove many, if not all, of the disabilities formerly imposed under the *shari'a*.[7] Until the forces of Islamization became so powerful that they were able to reverse this trend, it seemed that changes in the legal status of women were moving in the direction of their achieving greater equality.

Liberal political forces have generally welcomed the expanded opportunities that have come with political, economic, and social changes, but Islamic clerics and established Islamic institutions have strongly opposed allowing the role of women to evolve apace with these changes. As feminist ideas circulated through urban milieus and among a population whose literacy was expanding, Muslim conservatives rallied to denounce the idea of expanded freedoms for women.[8] The case of Afghanistan, discussed below, is an example of how extreme clashes between evolved urban societies and arch-conservative village mores can lead to the adoption of retrograde interpretations of Islam that call for women to be demoted to the status of chattel. Indeed, as modernization has unsettled old patterns and presented new questions, conservatives have often tried to expand Islamic rationales for depriving women of rights. Islamic rationales have been concocted for forbidding women to drive cars, banning women from participating in sports, and excluding them from working in television, radio, and entertainment programs. As new contraceptive techniques and expanded medical care have increased the ability of women to control their fertility, conservatives have argued that Islam limits or precludes the use of contraceptives and forbids abortion, thereby disregarding the established views of Islamic jurists, who generally accepted contraceptive measures and approved of abortions in the early months of pregnancy.[9] With the adoption of modern political institutions, new questions about women's political role have been raised. Conservatives have argued that "Islam" bars women from participation in politics and precludes them from voting.

As salaried employment outside the home has become common and even necessary for many urban women, conservatives have asserted that "Islam" mandates that women not work outside the home and that any employment should be limited to jobs dealing with women and children. With the growth of public education, questions have arisen about the degree to which women should have access to schooling and opportunities for advanced study. Muslim conservatives argue that Islam calls for sexual segregation in education and that women should be allowed to study only those subjects suitable for females, which tend to be ones that prepare women for a life oriented toward the home and family.

Arrayed against the foes of women's emancipation are Muslims who have critically reappraised traditional doctrines and concluded that authentic Islam supports reforms designed to ensure women's equality. Fatima Mernissi, a Moroccan sociology professor who was one of the founding members of the Moroccan Organization for Human Rights, offers a prominent example of a feminist who has reexamined the sources and concluded that Islam calls for women's equality.[10] Just as feminist perspectives have challenged the gender biases in Christian and Jewish theology, so Islamic feminists are challenging the theological justifications that have been offered for restricting women's rights.[11] The kinds of restrictions that conservative Muslims wish to impose on women's rights tend to be dismissed by Muslim feminists as representing nothing more than male biases and cultural traditions disguised as religious precepts.

Conservative Muslims routinely attack Muslims who advocate equality for women as being servile imitators of the West—as in Iran, where women who object to Iran's restrictive version of Islamic morality are lambasted as "foreign dolls." Feminists are condemned as agents of Western cultural imperialism who aim to destroy sound customs and morality and to deviate from *shari'a* principles.[12] Abu'l A'la Mawdudi sneered at "Oriental Occidentals," his pejorative epithet for Muslim women who espouse Western-style philosophy, moral concepts, and social principles.[13] Mawdudi complained that in the works of Muslims who support feminist interpretations of the Islamic sources, "the limited and conditional freedom that women had been allowed by Islam in matters other than home science is being used as argument to encourage the Muslim women to abandon home life and its responsibilities like the European women and make their lives miserable by running after political, economic, social and other activities shoulder to shoulder with men."[14] Thus, he cloaks his determination to curb women's rights in the garb of concern for safeguarding their happiness, a happiness that women would supposedly forfeit by emulating the Western experience.

One also encounters Muslims who may not believe that full equality of the sexes is compatible with Islamic doctrine but who are nonetheless unsympathetic to the arguments of conservatives that Islam requires that women be kept utterly subordinated and secluded. A substantial portion of the Muslim community seems to espouse views on women's status that constitute a middle-ground position.[15]

Because of these competing trends in Islamic thought, one cannot predict what a faithful Muslim's position would be on issues of women's status. Given the intense controversies that have developed regarding women rights in the Islamic world, Muslims can no longer rely on settled doctrine in this area but must decide which of the great variety of competing views they find most persuasive.

The authors of the Islamic human rights schemes examined here aim to deprive women of the rights to which they are entitled under international law. However, just as the authors were loath to concede that *shari'a* norms conflicted with the principle of equality, so, with the exception of Sultanhussein Tabandeh, they avoid acknowledging that they want women to be subjugated. Since the details of their rights schemes and policies—or in Mawdudi's case, the principles set forth in writings outside his human rights pamphlet—amply demonstrate their intention to keep women in restricted roles, it is noteworthy that they deploy formulations that minimize or hide their discriminatory impact. One could reasonably conclude that they fear that any frank admission that women cannot be equal with men under Islamic law may result in their schemes being branded backward, reactionary, or unacceptable under international law. Thus, their evasive formulations appear to confirm the prestige of international law even as they advocate substantive rules that conflict with women's international human rights.

Muslim Countries' Reactions to the Women's Convention

The Convention on the Elimination of all Forms of Discrimination Against Women (CEDAW), also known as the Women's Convention, entered into force in 1981. Measured by the standards of this convention, the treatment of women in Islamic human rights schemes seems particularly deficient. Article 1 defines discrimination as including "any distinction, exclusion or restriction made on the basis of sex which has the effect or purpose of impairing or nullifying the recognition, enjoyment, or exercise by women, irrespective of their marital status, on a basis of equality of men and women, of human rights and fundamental freedoms in the political, economic, social, cultural, civil, or any other field." Article 2.f of the convention calls on states to take all measures necessary to eliminate all laws, regulations, customs, and practices discriminating against women. CEDAW lists many specific kinds of sex discrimination that are to be eliminated. For example, Article 16 requires eliminating all discrimination between men and women in the family and ensuring that men and women have the same rights and responsibilities during marriage and at its dissolution.

Many Muslim states have ratified CEDAW without reservation—implying that they found its principles unexceptionable. A few Muslim countries have failed to ratify CEDAW, including Iran and the Sudan. However, a large number of Muslim countries have ratified CEDAW subject to significant reservations that have qualified their adherence to the convention's provisions. Many non-Muslim countries have also entered reservations in ratifying CEDAW, but often these reservations deal with relatively peripheral matters. What stands out in the case of Muslim countries is that so many of their reservations amount to rejections of the most central CEDAW provisions, such as Articles 2 and 16, and that many of them specifically invoke Islamic law as the reason for making these reservations.[16] Like the Islamic human rights schemes examined here, these ratifications effectively pay lip service to international law while using Islamic reservations to qualify their adherence to the law.

By qualifying adherence to CEDAW with Islamic reservations, Muslim states treat Islamic law as if it were binding supranational religious law, whereas in reality, Islamic law, where it survives, exists in the form of widely varying, inconsistent laws enacted by various national governments and amended at will. Moreover, Muslim countries enter Islamic reservations to different provisions of CEDAW, indicating that they have dissimilar opinions regarding which CEDAW articles conflict with Islamic law. Furthermore, many reservations have been entered by Muslim countries to CEDAW provisions on the basis of discriminatory domestic laws that are in no way connected to Islamic law, indicating that the real reason for nonacceptance may be a desire to uphold existing regimes of sex discrimination.[17] That is, the gross disparities in Muslim countries' responses to CEDAW are evidence that factors other than the Islamic tradition define Muslim countries' positions on women's rights.

Tabandeh's Ideas

Sultanhussein Tabandeh is exceptional in his forthright assertion that Islam opposes the idea of male-female equality. His candor on this point may be a byproduct of his general lack of political sophistication, which is much in evidence in his commentary. He himself conceded: "I have never taken part in politics, and know nothing of any political aspects or implications which the Declaration [the Universal Declaration of Human Rights] may have. It is only from the religious angle, and in particular the relation to the sacred theology of Islam and of Shi'a beliefs, that I shall discuss the matter."[18] Not only did Tabandeh consider that the Islamic sources were authoritative, but he even proposed that, where there were discrepancies, it was the UDHR that should be rewritten to make it conform to Islam.[19] That is, he had much more confidence in the definitive and binding character of Islamic law than did the other authors, who often seem uncertain about whether Islamic law can be deemed viable if its rules fly in the face of international law.

Thus, Tabandeh was unusually candid in his reaction to Article 16 of the UDHR, which provides for equal rights for men and women in matters of marriage and divorce and guarantees the right to marry without any limitations due to race, nationality, or religion. He flatly stated that the declaration contained several points that are contrary to Islam,[20] roundly castigating the representatives of Muslim countries who were involved in the drafting of the UDHR for not rejecting this article and explaining at the United Nations what Islamic teachings had to say about the status of women.[21]

The Islamic rules that in his view are violated by Article 16 include the *shari'a* ban on Muslim women marrying non-Muslims[22] and the right to initiate a divorce being reserved to men.[23] Tabandeh also professed his opposition to the notion of male-female equality embodied in Article 16 if it meant "that a natural equality exists between men and women, fitting them to undertake identical tasks and to make equal decisions."[24] He said that a wife must obey her husband, consult his wishes, not go out of the house without his permission, take due care of the property, look after the household equipment, invite a guest only with the husband's agreement, uphold the family's good name, and maintain her husband's good standing whether he is present or absent.[25] In addition, Tabandeh stated that Islam forbids women from "interference in politics."[26] He also made much of women's obligation not to stir up male lust, charging that "liberty granted to women, contrary to all reason and religion, results in libertinism, license, lust, lechery, and libidinousness."[27] He supported the Islamic curbs on women's freedom that conservative interpreters of the *shari'a* call for as part of a woman's duty not to provoke male lust, asserting:

> Islam has taken measures to prohibit practices which would lead to stimulating of sensual passion or to deviation from chastity. Women are therefore ordered not to do what would titillate men's feelings of lust. She must therefore cover her body, and not show her adornments of beauty or of jewelry or makeup to the outside world or to strangers. She must not frequent, more than absolutely essential, public gatherings attended by men. She must spend much time at home.[28]

Tabandeh's mind-set is typical of Muslim conservatives. It is assumed that all women will marry, so the primary determinant of an adult woman's life is her relationship with her husband. In this relationship, she is considered to be a dependent who is required to submit to her husband's authority and follow his wishes. It is expected that her life will be passed at home fulfilling domestic duties, nurturing and serving others. There is no concern for protecting women's rights to develop as individual persons with distinct identities and abilities, to become educated in ways that fit their specific talents and interests and enable them to sustain themselves, or to ensure that they can play a part in the social, economic, or political institutions that shape their destinies. Furthermore, women are assigned the burden of preserving morality: It is their responsibility to stay secluded and enshrouded so that they do not sexually arouse men. Sexual importunities or advances on the part of men are attributed to the flouting of norms of modesty by women, not to any lack of morality or to any blameworthy, lascivious attitudes among the male population. Although other authors are less forthcoming than Tabandeh, when one scratches the surface, one finds that they have similar philosophies.

Mawdudi's Ideas

Abu'l A'la Mawdudi avoided the subject of women's rights in his human rights pamphlet. Unlike Tabandeh, Mawdudi was a canny politician who seems to have appreciated the damage it would do to the credibility of his human rights scheme if he admitted that he wanted to deny fundamental rights to one-half of the population. Like the authors of the Saudi Basic Law, he preferred to avoid even mentioning the topic of women's human rights. However, Mawdudi's views on women are on record in his other writings, and they are similar to Tabandeh's, with the exception that Mawdudi believed that women should be able to sue for divorce on liberal grounds.[29]

In his book defending purdah, the custom of keeping women veiled and secluded, Mawdudi listed as doctrines of Western society the principles of male-female equality, economic independence of women, and "free intermingling of the sexes";[30] he then went to considerable lengths to document his abhorrence of these principles and to argue that they lead to the undermining of the family, lower birthrates, immorality, promiscuity, perversion, and social decay.[31] According to Mawdudi, people in the West "perpetually remain in a feverish condition on account of nude pictures, cheap literature, exciting songs, emotionally erotic dances, romantic films, highly disturbing scenes of obscenity and ever-present chances of encountering members of the opposite sex."[32] He accused Muslims who advocate "Western" rights for women of abandoning "the sense of honor, chastity, moral purity, matrimonial loyalty, undefiled lineage, and the like virtues."[33]

Perhaps realizing that it would seem strange if he failed to provide any rights for women in his human rights pamphlet, Mawdudi did list as one of his "basic human rights" respect for the chastity of women.[34] However, as has been amply demonstrated in many Middle Eastern countries, most notably in Afghanistan under the Taliban, the obsession with preserving women's chastity can justify a policy of nullifying women's rights and freedoms. Mawdudi himself has indicated that he associates preserving chastity with confining women to the home. Thus, the only "right" Mawdudi stipulated for women, respect for their chastity, does not really qualify as a human right but is a principle that, in context, can be deployed to keep women enshrouded, cloistered, and helpless.

Furthermore, Mawdudi's stance raises doubts about whether he understands the meaning of civil and political rights. International human rights law is no more designed to protect chastity against violation than it is to protect people from robbery, murder, or arson. In the main, international civil and political rights are addressed to presumptively law-abiding officials and governmental institutions. Thus, Mawdudi's chastity right is not a human right as understood in international law. (However, international law may become concerned with related issues in the event of mass rapes when these are perpetrated as instruments of state policy, such as when they are used as a tool of ethnic cleansing.[35])

Mawdudi tried to implicate the West in patterns of crimes against women's chastity:

This concept of the sanctity of chastity and the protection of women can be found nowhere else except in Islam. The armies of the Western powers need the daughters of their own nations to satisfy their carnal appetites even in their own countries, and if they happen to occupy another country, the fate of its womenfolk can be better imagined than described.

But the history of the Muslims, apart from individual lapses, has been free from this crime against womanhood. It has never happened that after the conquest of a foreign country the Muslim army has gone about raping the women of the conquered people, or, in their own country, the government has arranged to provide prostitutes for them.[36]

Mawdudi's resentment of the West seems to have impelled him to make the patently false charge that no legal systems other than the *shari'a* protect a woman from sexual molestation and assault or rape.[37] Moreover, contrary to his boasts, there is no evidence that Muslim armies have historically acquitted themselves any better in their treatment of vulnerable women than their counterparts in other societies. One is prompted to inquire why this curious, contrary-to-fact assertion was included in Mawdudi's human rights pamphlet.

Mawdudi's comments came after a notorious mass rape that was carried out by the Pakistani army in the course of the 1971 civil war fought in East Pakistan, which culminated in the independence of Bangladesh.[38] In this context, Mawdudi's insistence that a Muslim army had never raped women served at least two functions. It was designed to comfort members of his audience who were still smarting from the international condemnation following the Bengali mass rapes by denying that rape by Muslim armies was even possible.[39] It was also designed to put the West on the defensive by accusing it of systematic sexual exploitation and mistreatment of women in wartime. This correlates with Mawdudi's general approach to Islamic law, which is infused with a polemical spirit and serves as a vehicle for anti-Western mobilization.

Given Mawdudi's refusal to engage in self-criticism, he could not be expected to appreciate how the patriarchal cast of an Islamization program and the attendant rhetoric about protecting women's chastity could not only coexist with but encourage a tolerance of rape in Pakistan, his home country. However, in the wake of Zia's Islamization, rapes have often been committed with impunity, sometimes even being employed systematically as a device to subordinate women and to reinforce the subjugation of disadvantaged groups.[40]

The UIDHR

Aiming to present Islamic human rights diplomatically, the Universal Islamic Declaration of Human Rights (UIDHR) deliberately obscures crucial issues.

The UIDHR does not admit that women are to be accorded second-class status, and it takes a careful reading of the UIDHR to uncover what is intended. However, many of the provisions assigning women to a subordinate role do so only indirectly and are written in such a convoluted style that their significance may not be obvious to readers—and especially not to readers of the English version of the document.

For example, in Article 19.a of the English version, a provision begins with the following tenet: "Every person is entitled to marry, to found a family, and to bring up children in conformity with his religion, tradition and culture." This should be compared carefully with the wording of its international counterpart in the Universal Declaration of Human Rights (UDHR) Article 16.1: "Men and women of full age, without any limitation due to race, nationality or religion, have the right to marry and to found a family."

In international law the freedom to marry is unqualified. In contrast, UIDHR Article 19.a qualifies the entitlement to marry; the qualification "in conformity with his religion" means that rules of the *shari'a* can impose restrictions, including one that bars Muslim women from marrying non-Muslims.[41] Furthermore, a Muslim man is allowed to marry only a woman who is either a Muslim or a member of the "people of the book." In addition, other Islamic rules could prohibit marriages, say, between persons related by suckling or between Muslims and apostates.[42] Therefore, this UIDHR provision runs directly counter to the principle in the UDHR that men and women should be allowed without any religious restrictions to choose their own spouses. The UIDHR provision is not designed to protect the right of the individual to choose a spouse freely but rather to deny that right by employing Islamic criteria.

Article 19.a of the English version of the UIDHR continues: "Every spouse is entitled to such rights and privileges and carries such obligations as are stipulated by the Law." This language should be contrasted with the international rule in UDHR Article 16.1: "They are entitled to equal rights as to marriage, during marriage and at its dissolution." In the international standards of the UDHR, there is unequivocal endorsement of equality of husband and wife. There is no mention of equal rights in the English version in the UIDHR—only rights "stipulated by the Law." In the UIDHR, "the Law" means the *shari'a;* thus all the discriminatory rules of the premodern *shari'a* can be upheld. Qur'anic verses referred to in the English version of Article 19.a are listed in the fine print of the references section in the back of the document, where Islamic sources are noted, but the texts of those verses are not reproduced anywhere in the document.[43]

In the Arabic version of UIDHR Article 19.a, the implications for rights in marriage and divorce are much clearer, since the Islamic sources are incorporated into the text. The citation of one of the Qur'anic verses implies that the inequality of the sexes is an underlying assumption of the UIDHR. The verse, 2:228, states that "[women] have rights similar to those [of men] over them in kindness, and men are a degree above them." This is one of the texts that is traditionally interpreted by conservatives to confirm that male superiority is mandated by Islam.[44] Given the conservative thrust of the UIDHR, this traditional interpretation is most likely intended.

It is also interesting to contrast the English and Arabic versions of Article 19.h. The English provision runs: "Within the family, men and women are to share in their obligations and responsibilities according to their sex, their natural endowments, talents and inclinations, bearing in mind their common responsibilities toward their progeny and their relatives." This English version suggests that men and women share family obligations and responsibilities, although it qualifies this sharing in problematic ways. Depending on what is read into these qualifications, the English-language provision might or might not be taken to mean that a fairly equal division of duties in the home between husband and wife is intended, particularly since factors other than sex are listed as determinants of the spouses' obligations and responsibilities.

The Arabic version of Article 19.h, presumably the authoritative one, deals with quite a different subject. It says that the responsibility for the family is a partnership *(sharika)* among its members, each contributing according to his capacity and the nature of his character, and that this responsibility goes beyond the circle of parents and children and extends to close relatives and distant kinsmen *(al-aqarib wa dhawi'l-arham)*. In contrast to the English version of the article, the Arabic version establishes a right to collect support from members of one's extended family—a right not recognized in international law. The article potentially places binding support obligations on persons only distantly related to each other in accordance with the system of mutual obligations among members of the extended family that is reinforced by premodern *shari'a* rules.[45]

The stark disparity between the English and Arabic versions suggests that the English version was redrafted to make it more attractive to the audience in the West, where nuclear families are the norm and where the financial burden of maintaining distant relatives would be onerous and unwelcome. For such an audience the principle stated in the Arabic Article 19.h would have little appeal, whereas the English version would sound impressive.

The UIDHR contemplates retaining the premodern *shari'a* rules that impose disabilities on women. The one major exception is the provision in Article 19.i providing that no one may be married against his or her will. Rules developed by some jurists, especially in the Maliki school of law, allowed a girl's marriage guardian to marry her off at any age and without her consent.[46] Girls in traditional Muslim society were frequently forced into marriages as soon as they reached puberty. Parents continue to compel their daughters to marry while still very young in many parts of the Middle East today, causing much heartbreak for young women made to wed men they dislike—and who are often much older than they are—and to give up their hopes of pursuing studies and employment.

Many Muslims consider the premodern rules of *jabr* or *ijbar,* "forced marriage," outdated and incompatible with the ideal of marriage as a union freely consented to by both parties, and legal reforms in most Middle Eastern countries have officially eliminated the marriage guardian's traditional right to compel his ward to marry.[47] Other Muslims confuse the ingrained patriarchal practice of fathers selecting husbands for their daughters, regardless of their daughters' wishes, with *shari'a* rules. Because the practice of forced marriage has not ceased, the UIDHR is performing a service by going on the record as supporting the idea that as a matter of Islamic principle no one should be compelled to enter a marriage. This stands out as an isolated instance in the literature under discussion, in which a real human rights problem in the Middle East is confronted, the premodern jurisprudence is rejected, and an enlightened interpretation of Islamic requirements is offered.

The most extensive UIDHR provision dealing with women is Article 20. The rubric for Article 20 in the English version of the UIDHR is "Rights of Married Women." It is significant that no provisions in the document are made for the rights of unmarried women—just as there is no provision on the rights of married men or unmarried men. Given the nature of the document, one can hypothesize several reasons for this: All Muslim men are expected to marry, so the status of a single male is not significant. Married men presumably enjoy the husband's rights and privileges, which are counterparts of the wife's duty to obey and serve the husband. Given the apologetic nature of this exercise, it is understandable that the authors would not have wanted to include a separate article detailing the rights of the Muslim husband. To do so would make it all too obvious that they were endorsing a traditional, patriarchal system in which the law supports a regime of male privilege in matters of marriage and divorce. For example, if the authors catalogued as rights of the husband his entitlements to beat his disobedient wife, to have four wives at a time, and to have sexual intercourse regardless of his wife's wishes unless she has religiously acceptable grounds for refusing him, this would give their whole scheme the retrograde appearance that they were seeking to avoid.

The existence of autonomous adult women who are not answerable to male authority is not envisaged in this scheme, so there is no need to specify the rights of unmarried women. In Muslim countries, all women are expected to marry. It is natural for the authors of the UIDHR to assume that the contours of an adult woman's life are primarily shaped by her domestic obligations to her husband as his wife and as the mother of his children. By speaking exclusively of the rights of married women, the authors of the UIDHR reveal that they do not envisage a system where women escape male tutelage. Instead, they share the perspective that is pervasive in traditional Muslim societies that a female child should be under the control of her father or other close male relative until she marries, at which time she is to submit to the control of her husband.

It is important to note the significant disparity here. In international human rights schemes, the focus is on the rights of individuals, irrespective of their marital status. Because spouses enjoy equal rights in international law, although there are specific rights provisions dealing with marriage, marital status cannot be a prime determinant of rights in the way it appears to be in the UIDHR.

What are the "Rights of Married Women" granted by the English version of the UIDHR? Article 20 provides that every married woman is entitled to:

A. live in the house in which her husband lives;
B. receive the means necessary for maintaining a standard of living which is not inferior to that of her spouse, and, in the event of divorce, receive during the statutory period of waiting (Iddah) means of maintenance commensurate with her husband's resources, for herself as well as for the children she nurses or keeps, irrespective of her own financial status, earnings, or property that she may hold in her own right;
C. seek and obtain dissolution of marriage (Khul'a) in accordance with the terms of the Law. This right is in addition to her right to seek divorce through the courts;
D. inherit from her husband, her parents, her children and other relatives according to the Law;
E. strict confidentiality from her spouse, or ex-spouse if divorced, with regard to any information that he may have obtained about her, the disclosure of which could prove detrimental to her interests. A similar responsibility rests upon her in respect of her spouse or ex-spouse.

A review of the provisions dealing with support and inheritance rights illustrates how this scheme reinforces women's disadvantages. The English version of Article 20.b actually limits her ability to claim support. The premodern jurists disagreed about exactly how much maintenance a husband owed his wife during marriage and in the *idda,* or waiting period, following divorce (either three months or, if the divorcee turned out to be pregnant, until the birth of the child), but they agreed that this was a unilateral obligation on the part of the husband— as was to be expected in a system where it was assumed that the women would be dependent. However, at the end of the *idda,* the husband's obligation to support the divorced wife ceased. The woman was then expected to be supported by her relations or by a subsequent husband.

This cutoff of support obligations can leave a divorced woman destitute. The economic predicament of divorced women who are not wealthy or gainfully employed has worsened in modern times as urbanization and economic changes have undermined the extended family and diminished a divorced woman's ability to secure support from relatives. The recent tendency in family law reform in the Middle East has been to extend the husband's support obligations beyond what they were in the premodern *shari'a*. It is therefore noteworthy that the UIDHR fails to address the financial hardships of the indigent divorced woman while limiting the husband's financial obligations to the period of the *'idda*. In context, this constitutes a rejection of the reformist position and a reaffirmation of the premodern rules sharply limiting the husband's support obligation to a divorced wife, which in contemporary circumstances can expose such women to acute economic hardship.

The English version of Article 20.b makes no mention of the Qur'anic verse 4:34, which is cited in the Arabic version of the same article. The cited verse connects male control over women to the maintenance that men pay for women: "Men are in charge of women, because Allah has made the one of them to excel the other, and because they [the men] spend of their property [for the support of women]." This verse is invoked by Muslim conservatives to justify according men superior rights.[48] It is significant that this very verse is quoted in the text of the Arabic version of Article 20.b, a subsection of an article purportedly concerned with the rights of married women. Its quotation in this context reinforces the idea that male superiority comes from the fact that men support women economically. Women's financial dependence on men is in turn the consequence of other *shari'a* rules that keep women housebound and excluded from remunerative activity. With the inclusion of this Qur'anic verse in the Arabic text, it conveys a different impression than the English version does.

Similarly, Article 20.d seems innocuous in its English version, stating that a married woman has a right to inherit from her husband and other relatives in accordance with the law. However, this is *shari'a* inheritance law, which discriminates against women generally, allowing them to take only half the share that males do, and against widows in particular. In the Arabic version of this article, the impact of the *shari'a* on a woman's ability to inherit is more obvious. The Qur'an 4:12, quoted in the text, assigns the widow (a maximum of) one-quarter of her husband's estate if there are no children and (a maximum of) one-eighth of the estate if there are children. These Qur'anic shares constitute the legal maximum that the widow may take because, according to prevailing opinion, Islamic law does not allow the spouse relict (widow or widower) to inherit more than the Qur'anic share.[49] Moreover, the *shari'a* allows the Muslim husband to have up to four wives simultaneously, and if the husband dies and leaves more than one widow, the widows have to divide the one-quarter or one-eighth share that otherwise would go to a sole wife, in which case their shares will be very much reduced. Meanwhile, a widowed husband takes one-half of the estate in the absence of children and one-fourth if there are children, a portion that he does not have to share with any other heir. Thus, in incorporating the Qur'anic standards for inheritance by the spouse relict, Article 20.d reaffirms discriminatory *shari'a* inheritance rules and restricts a wife's right to inherit from her husband in a way that is very much to her disadvantage. This article does not afford protection for any human right as understood in international law, nor does it make an attempt to adjust the inheritance scheme to take into account the erosion of the extended family network that the original Qur'anic scheme assumed would ensure a widow's livelihood if her share of her husband's estate was minimal.

Regarding divorce, the reader of the English version of Article 20.c, cited above, might interpret the language to mean that a woman who wanted to terminate her marriage could claim a divorce as a right. The article provides that the wife "is entitled to seek *and obtain* dissolution of marriage" (emphasis added), an entitlement that is said to be "in addition to her right to seek divorce through the courts." This suggests that women are being guaranteed a right to divorce, which is not actually the case. When one consults the authoritative Arabic version of Article 20.c, one sees that no such right is being offered. The Arabic version says that a woman may *ask* her husband to agree to dissolve their union through a consensual termination of marriage, known as a *khul'*, or may *ask* a judge for a dissolution within the scope of *shari'a* rules *(ft nitaq ahkam al-shari'a)*. When one considers the implications of this wording, one appreciates that it is not much of a "right" for a wife to be allowed to *ask* her husband to agree to terminate a marriage or to *ask* a court for a *shari'a* dissolution. According to the *shari'a,* the husband is under no obligation whatsoever to grant her request, and except in the doctrines of the Maliki school of law, a woman must meet difficult requirements before she can obtain a divorce from a judge over her husband's objections. The provisions in the Arabic version of the UIDHR were meant to reassure a largely Muslim audience that the *shari'a* regime of male privilege was being maintained, whereas the English version, the audience for which would be largely non-Muslim, was meant to hide the discriminatory rules restricting women's right to divorce.

The remaining "rights" that are provided to married women in Article 20 are simply frivolous or meaningless. For example, in Article 20.a, a woman is given the right to live in the house in which her husband lives. This would appear to be a solution to a nonexistent problem under present circumstances in the Middle East, particularly in the urban areas that have grown so quickly in the past few decades. Few men today can afford to maintain separate residences for their wives, even if they might wish to live separately from them. In countries like Egypt, where the population pressure is enormous and the stock of urban housing is woefully inadequate, it would be virtually impossible for the average husband to find and afford two residences so that he could house his wife separately. Indeed, so serious is the shortage of housing in some urban areas that even couples who are divorced may have to continue to live together in the same dwelling, because neither ex-spouse can find affordable alternative housing. Moreover, since the UIDHR does not abolish polygamy, this "right" might be interpreted to mean that co-wives could not demand that the husband provide separate residences, as they could under the premodern *shari'a* rules, but would have to live together in their common husband's home. The beneficiary of this "right" would be the husband, who would be spared the expense of maintaining his co-wives in separate residences.

Article 20.e purports to give a woman a right to have any potentially damaging information that her husband may have about her kept confidential, but it accords the same right to the husband regarding any confidential information that his wife may have about him. Thus, listing this right with the rights of married women is misleading. Here, there is no significant difference between the Arabic and the English versions, but in neither case does the principle embodied in the provision rise to the stature of a human right. A puzzling aspect of this article is that no Islamic legal rule prevents spouses from disclosing detrimental information about each other; on the contrary, the husband may need to do so to annul a marriage, and the wife may need to do so to obtain an annulment or a divorce under *shari'a* rules. Depending on circumstances, the ability to disclose evidence about her husband's defects, failings, and misconduct may be the only means a Muslim woman has at her disposal to terminate a marriage.[50] Therefore, such a rule could conceivably inhibit a woman's ability to terminate a marriage over her husband's objections by barring her testimony about relevant evidence. Since this provision offers no significant rights for married women, its inclusion may amount to an effort to pad the very limited list of rights afforded women in the UIDHR scheme.

Islamization in Iran and the Iranian Constitution

The 1979 Iranian constitution does not expressly relegate women to second-class status. There are even provisions in the constitution that, taken in isolation, might indicate that it was proposing equal rights for men and women. A section of the Preamble titled "Women and the Constitution" portrays the revolution as being sympathetic to women's rights, saying that after the overthrow of the shah, people will regain their original identities and human rights *(hoquq-e ensani)* and that, in consequence, women "should benefit from a particularly large augmentation of their rights."[51] Article 3.14 includes in a listing of the goals of the Islamic Republic "securing the multifarious rights of all citizens, both women and men, and providing . . . the equality of all before the law *[qanun].*" Article 21.1 calls for the creation of "a favorable environment for the growth of women's personality and the restoration of her rights, both material and intellectual."

However, one sees provisions of a very different sort as well, ones that are much more in keeping with the spirit of the Islamic human rights that are under discussion here. It has already been noted that the Iranian constitution provides in Article 20 that citizens' rights are qualified by Islamic standards and that women's rights in particular are so qualified in Article 21. The negative implications of such qualifications are by now familiar.

In the section of the Preamble on women and the constitution, one also sees that women's function is primarily to bear children committed to the regime's ideology. The Preamble states, in part:

> The family is the fundamental unit of society and the main centre for the growth and edification of human beings. Compatibility with respect to belief and ideal, which provides the primary basis for man's development and growth, is the main consideration in the establishment of a family. It is the duty of the Islamic government to provide the necessary facilities for the attainment of this goal. This view of the family unit delivers woman from being regarded as an object or as an instrument in the service of promoting consumerism and exploitation. Not only does woman recover thereby her momentous and precious function of motherhood, rearing of ideologically committed human beings *[ensanha-ye maktabi]*, she also assumes a pioneering social role and becomes the fellow struggler of man in all vital areas of life. Given the weighty responsibilities that woman thus assumes, she is accorded in Islam great value and nobility.

In the context of Iranian history, the emphasis on the family and women's role in raising children signaled that the aim was to return Iranian women to a domestic role after decades in which they had made progress in the areas of education, employment and the professions, and government service. Among Islamic conservatives, emphasizing the family has become a code for programs designed to confine women to child care and housework.

This family theme is repeated in Article 10, along with a claim that the framework for family structure should be taken from Islamic law and morality: "Since the family is the fundamental unit of Islamic society, all laws, regulations, and pertinent programs must tend to facilitate the formation of a family, and to safeguard its sanctity and the stability of family relations on the basis of the law and the ethics of Islam *[hoquq va akhlaq-e eslami]*."

One of the first measures that Khomeini took after coming to power was to nullify in February 1979 the Iranian Family Protection Act of 1967 as amended in 1975. The Family Protection Act was one of the two most progressive reforms of Islamic personal status law (the other being the Tunisian Code of Personal Status of 1956) enacted in the Middle East in the latter half of the twentieth century. The act included rules requiring that all divorce actions be brought before a court (thereby eliminating the husband's right of extrajudicial divorce by uttering a divorce formula), significantly broadening the grounds on which women could seek divorce, assigning custody based on the best interests of the child (instead of automatically giving custody to the father after age two for boys and age seven for girls), and requiring a married man to get a court's permission before taking a second wife, which would only be granted if he convinced the court of his ability to provide justly for both wives.[52] Claiming that these reforms violated *shari'a* law, Khomeini and other clerics condemned the Family Protection Act.

One might wonder how the idea in Article 10 of exalting women's role in the family fits with Article 28, which provides in part: "Everyone has the right to choose any occupation he wishes, if it is not contrary to Islam *[mokhalef-e eslam . . . nist]* and the public interest, and does not infringe the rights of others." To better understand the provisions of Articles 10 and 28, it is helpful to examine the record of many years of Iranian government praxis. The accumulated evidence indicates that postrevolutionary Iran at first tried hard to push women back into the role of caretaker of the home and children. To lock women into a maternal role at the earliest opportunity, the regime encouraged early marriages for girls by lowering the minimum age for marriage from eighteen to nine.[53] The ruling theocrats also promoted the peculiar Twelver Shi'i institution of temporary marriage, in which a man may contract for a woman's sexual services for a limited period of time.[54] This institution has been widely condemned by Iranian feminists as degrading to women and is regarded by most Sunni Muslims as a form of prostitution.

Pursuant to the goal of keeping women housebound, in the years following the revolution, women's educational opportunities were restricted by a variety of measures, women were fired and excluded from a wide spectrum of prestigious jobs and displaced from employment in the media and the entertainment industry, and women were practically eliminated from the world of politics and government. Women were barred from serving as attorneys in court and as judges and thus were excluded from having a say in the legal order that was seeking to confine women to the domestic sphere.[55] In another effort to relegate women to the domestic sphere, the regime adopted vigorous pro-natalist policies. However, unable to cope with the soaring population growth that resulted from these policies, the regime subsequently reversed course, relaxing many restrictions on women's participation in the workforce and energetically promoting birth control to reduce population growth to a manageable rate.[56]

Iran's clerical rulers have aggressively, albeit unevenly, enforced the rules on Islamic dress, which are tied to the official version of Islamic morality. Women have been pressured to wear all-enveloping chadors or similar covering in dark, dull colors and have been subjected to harsh criminal penalties for minor contraventions of the dress rules. Iranian women have resisted these rules, trying to get away with more revealing head coverings and injecting some variety and color in their attire—at the risk of being arrested and flogged for their acts of defiance. Morality police also engage in systematic intimidation and harassment designed to discourage women from appearing in public with unrelated males. In addition, women's ability to participate in sports was drastically curtailed by rules mandating that women not engage in athletic activities where men could observe them and that when in public women must wear cumbersome, baggy, concealing clothing—even while swimming or skiing. Angered by women's resistance, the regime expanded the punishments for noncompliance in 1996, adding imprisonment and fines as penalties for women caught in "un-Islamic" attire.[57]

Having instituted these reactionary policies, Iran nonetheless took care to convey a progressive stance on women's attire when in the international spotlight. After years of barring Iranian women from participating in the Olympic games and sending all-male teams, which had refused to march into Olympic stadiums behind women from the host country carrying the placards with Iran's name, Iran allowed a few women athletes to go to the 1996 Olympic games in Atlanta. Although Iran's women athletes could compete only in events where they could wear their cumbersome and concealing Islamic dress, an Iranian woman athlete dressed in a smart white coverall carried the flag and led the team into the stadium. The purpose of this display, Iran announced, was "to neutralize poisonous propaganda on the status of women in Iran."[58] That is, even while cracking down domestically, the ruling clerics decided that the hallowed rules of Islamic dress could be significantly compromised in situations where forcing women to stay enshrouded could expose Iran to international criticism and ridicule.

An incident occurred on January 21, 1986, that epitomized the official Iranian mind-set on women. Although the theocracy has attempted to portray Iran's official stance on women as one of asserting Islamic values against corrupting Western influences, in this instance, one could clearly see that the clerical leadership viewed women, in this case African women, as inferior beings. In the course of a trip to Zimbabwe, President Ali Khamene'i, later to become Khomeini's successor, refused to attend a state banquet in his honor, in part because wine was to be served, but also because women were to be seated at the head table. The Iranian delegation demanded that all women, including a woman cabinet member, be relegated to the table that was farthest away from the head table. The Zimbabwe leadership refused, saying that women were entitled to equal standing with men. The Zimbabweans understood that the Iranian demand that women be confined to the remotest table did not just indicate sexual segregation at the dinner but also signified consigning them to an inferior status. In the estimation of Khamene'i, women were not worthy of being seated with men at the head table, regardless of their status in the government. In rejecting the Iranian demand, the Zimbabwean foreign minister noted that the roles played by women in Zimbabwe's struggle for majority rule and for development "entitle them to an equal status and standing in every respect with their male counterparts."[59] The physical segregation of an "inferior" group is obviously akin to the institutionalized practices in the US South during the era of racial segregation.

The second-class status that the ruling clerics imposed on women provoked ongoing contention, because, far from meekly submitting to clerical diktat, Iranian women tenaciously fought to regain the ground they had lost. Despite their reactionary attitudes, the ruling theocrats were sufficiently pragmatic to consider revising certain discriminatory policies, especially those that clashed too sharply with popular opinion and threatened to seriously tarnish Iran's revolutionary credentials. Over time, the regime has allowed some positive reforms; the government removed the "Islamic" bar to women serving in the legal profession and the judiciary and overrode established Islamic rules to enhance the ability of divorced women to claim support from their ex-husbands.[60]

The ongoing clashes between the conservative clergy and advocates for expanded women's rights have created a complicated landscape.[61] The zigs and zags in policies on women's rights in Iran in the relatively short period since the revolution have shown that even a government that is supposedly committed to following a particular school of Islamic law can shift its interpretation of that law in response to changing circumstances.

Far from being confident that its Islamic rationales excuse its noncompliance with international law, Iran has often shown acute embarrassment over being exposed as a violator of women's rights, and the Iranian leadership has proffered strained arguments asserting that its policies on women's rights are consonant with international law.[62] Iran's theocratic rulers detested the Taliban, who were virulently anti-Shiʻi. In an effort to disassociate its official Islam from what was disparagingly called "gender apartheid" in international human rights parlance, Iran eagerly exploited the contrast between its relatively lenient policies on women and the extraordinarily retrograde policies of the Taliban in neighboring Afghanistan. In 1996, Ayatollah Jannati publicly denounced the Taliban: "What could be worse than committing violence, narrow-mindedness and limiting women's rights [thereby] defaming Islam?"[63] However, the regime did not budge on basic issues. As ruling *faqih*, Khameneʼi admonished Iranian women not to embrace Western feminist ideas, insisting that these ideas brought sexual promiscuity and that Iranian women had to follow "Islamic models" of sexual equality.[64]

The theocrats' mind-set was exemplified by their persecution and prosecution of Mehrangiz Kar, who with fellow attorney Shirin Ebadi—later to become a Nobel Laureate—was one of Iran's most prominent advocates of women's rights as set forth in international law. Outspokenly critical of the discriminatory laws affecting Iranian women, Kar was arrested in 2000 and tried in proceedings characterized by the usual absence of due process on a host of charges, including spreading anti-regime propaganda, rejecting the commands of the *shari'a,* and violating Iran's Islamic dress rules. She was eventually convicted in 2001.[65] Kar was able to get permission to leave Iran to obtain urgently needed cancer treatment and decided to stay in exile. Meanwhile, her husband, who had remained in Iran, was "disappeared" by the regime and later tried in 2002 and sentenced to eleven years imprisonment in a closed trial that was obviously intended to punish Kar for her challenges to clerical oppression of women. The severity of the regime's retaliation against Kar was significant; an attorney exposing the disparity between the rights afforded women in Iran's Islamic laws and those in international law was seen as a dire threat by a regime that simultaneously wanted to discriminate against women and to maintain the fiction that it was progressive.

Significantly, after Iran's parliament voted to ratify the Women's Convention, the proposed ratification was subsequently overridden by the Council of Guardians on August 12, 2003. The council ruled that ratification would violate both Islamic law and the Iranian constitution. Thus, an attempt by the elected representatives of the Iranian people to endorse women's international human rights law was thwarted by clerics using constitutional provisions upholding the primacy of Islamic law. In the aftermath, Iranian women's rights activists mobilized to demand changes in the constitution, charging that the terms of the constitution presented the major obstacle to improving women's rights.[66]

The Iranian constitution turned out to be one of the obstacles in the way of Iranian women seeking the presidency. Article 115 sets forth the qualifications for running for the presidency, stating that candidates must be from among "the well-known religious and political *rejal.*" In the original Arabic, *rijal,* the word corresponding to the Persianized *rejal,* means "men," but Iranians have often assumed that the term would encompass persons of both genders. However, on October 23, 2004, the spokesman for the Council of Guardians, Gholamhussein Ilham, indicated that the wording meant that only men could run for the presidency. Not surprisingly, when eighty-nine women sought to qualify for the 2005 presidential elections, the Council of Guardians blocked all of their candidacies. Iran's Nobel Laureate Shirin Ebadi objected that this constituted unjust discrimination against half the population.[67]

As part of its systematic oppression of women, the Islamic Republic has banned them from sitting in stadiums to watch sporting events. Not accepting this discriminatory treatment, Iranian women have repeatedly challenged the ban. With President Ahmadinejad in office, the ban was more aggressively enforced, and the first week of March 2006 saw two incidents signaling a clampdown. In one, security officers forcibly removed several hundred women spectators from a Tehran stadium where they were watching athletes performing in the 2006 Gymnastics World Cup Tournament. Even female translators working for the international teams competing in the event were forced out. In the second, dozens of young women who had bought tickets to attend an international football match pitting Iran against Costa Rica were barred from entering Tehran's Azadi Stadium. The women held a protest demonstration after being denied entry, which prompted the authorities to threaten the demonstrators that they would be arrested and sent to Tehran's notorious Evin prison if they did not disband.[68]

Another manifestation of the regime's hostility to Iranian women's aspirations for equality took place on March 8, 2006, when Iranian security forces charged a peaceful assembly of hundreds of women's rights activists in a Tehran park who had gathered to commemorate International Women's Day. Ordered to disperse, the participants staged a sit-in and started to sing the anthem of the women's rights movement. The security forces then dumped cans of garbage on the heads of the demonstrators before charging into the group and beating them with batons to compel them to leave the park. Among those harshly beaten by the security forces was Simin Behbahani, a blind poet in her seventies. Several foreign journalists were arrested, and their photographic equipment and video footage were confiscated.[69] In typical fashion, Iran's theocratic regime sought to wield violence against Iranian women who did not meekly submit to its retrograde policies and also to block international reporting on how Iranian women were being abused and degraded.

The Sudan Under Islamization

Women's rights were not the focus of the Islamization program undertaken in the Sudan by Ja'far al-Nimeiri in the period 1983–1985. However, in the course of the second Islamization campaign, undertaken by the military regime of General Omar al-Bashir in 1989, the imposition of Islamic law became associated with much the same kind of oppression that was instituted in Iran after the Islamic Revolution. According to Bashir, the ideal Sudanese woman was one who took care of her husband and children, did her household duties, attended to her reputation, and was a devout Muslim.[70] Women were dismissed from public service and discriminated against in hiring and promotion; women in the legal profession were particularly targeted for removal. Women, regardless of age, were prohibited from traveling unless chaperoned by a male relative, a prohibition that was not lifted until 1996. In that same year, a law was enacted, imposing many curbs on women's freedoms under the rubric of protecting Islamic morality. Measures were introduced such as mandatory segregation of the sexes in public places, the requirement that women be chaperoned by male relations in marketplaces at night, and the requirement that women's sports be conducted in private. Vague new crimes against morality were manufactured; women could be prosecuted for offenses against public order such as suspicion of intent to commit prostitution.[71] In the immediate aftermath of the concessions made to opponents in southern Sudan in 2005, which included a constitution that turned away from Islamization, it was unclear whether the position of women might improve.

The Azhar Draft Constitution

The Azhar draft constitution has some features that are very similar to those found in the Iranian constitution, although the former is a significantly briefer and less detailed document. Article 7 in the section on rules governing "Islamic Society" provides that the family is the basis of society and that the family's foundations are religion and morality *(al-din wa 'l-akhlaq)*, and Article 8 states that safeguarding the family is a state duty. As has been noted, "protecting the family" is a code phrase used by conservative Muslims to denote a system requiring the subordination of women to men and their confinement to the domestic sphere.

In the Azhar draft, Article 8 provides that the state should encourage early marriage and provide "the means according to which the wife would obey her husband and look after her children and consider keeping the family the first of her tasks." This shows how in these schemes the state winds up as the enforcer of supposedly traditional values at a time when the tradition itself has crumbled and ceased to have its former normative force. It reflects the Azhar sheikhs' abhorrence of the situation that has developed in contemporary Egypt, where many women are educated and work in full-time jobs. In Egypt, as in other countries that have undergone similar changes, women have been less inclined than they formerly were to view their domestic roles as the center of their lives. Women's earning power has weakened the control that their husbands formerly enjoyed as the sole providers and has facilitated wives' challenging their husbands' authority. The Azhar draft therefore envisages governmental initiatives to ensure that the wife will accord primacy to her duties as mother and housewife and will submit to her husband.

In addition to a provision offering a general guarantee of the right to work in Article 37 of the Azhar constitution, there is a separate provision in Article 38 that states that women have the right to work within the limits of the precepts of the *shari'a (hudud ahkam al-shari'a al-islamiya)*. It is significant in this regard that there are no Islamic qualifications imposed on men's right to work—implying that there is no possibility that a man's right to work could infringe *shari'a* principles. There is no further explanation of what the Islamic limits on a woman's right to work might be, but extrapolating from the general attitudes of Muslim conservatives, one can presume that women would need their husband's permission to work, that they would be allowed to work in only a limited range of jobs deemed suitable for women, and that they would be barred from work that would bring them into inappropriate proximity to men.

The most distinctive provision in the Azhar draft constitution is Article 14, which in the English version provides: "Bedizement [bedizenment, or gaudy dress] is forbidden and observing others' feelings is a duty. The government is to pass the laws and decisions to preserve the feelings of the public against profligacy according to the rules of the Islamic Sharia." Like portions of the English translation of the UIDHR, this English translation of Article 14 seems disingenuous. The reader of the article may not realize that this prohibition of bedizenment is a call for governments to take measures to force women to veil themselves in public and to discourage them from leaving their homes or associating with men from outside the family circle. The use of the term "profligacy" is misleading in this context, since it gives the impression that the concern is for the curbing of dissipation generally, when in reality it is only "shameless" conduct by women that is targeted.

In the Arabic version of Article 14, the word corresponding to what should be "bedizenment" in the English version is *tabarruj*. The reference is to the command in the Qur'an 33:33, which in an English translation that favors archaisms reads: "[B]edizen not yourselves with the bedizenment of the Time of Ignorance."[72] The verse is widely interpreted to mean that women must avoid immodest or provocative clothing and ornaments, and by Islamic conservatives to mean that heavy veiling and no makeup are de rigueur for women whenever they are exposed to the sight of men who are not members of their own family circles.[73] Prohibitions like the ban on "bedizenment" are rarely interpreted as having any bearing on how men dress, however, and Muslim men who abandon traditional Middle Eastern dress and adopt conventional Western styles of clothing are not considered to be committing any offense against public decency. (The policies of the Taliban, discussed below, are a major exception in this regard.) Thus, this provision sets the stage for government-imposed, uniform standards of dress for women but leaves men free to dress like Europeans. Their enshrinement of the ban on female "bedizenment" in the early fundamental provisions of the Azhar draft constitution reveals the authors' mentality, their social priorities, and their attitudes toward women's rights. In the Arabic version of Article 14, the ban on bedizenment is followed by statements that preserving female honor is a duty *(al-tasawun wajib)*. This could be interpreted as justifying the retention of Arab concepts of honor, which traditionally have been used to justify keeping women segregated and secluded and imposing harsh penalties on women (not men) for violating sexual taboos.[74] The Azhar draft also provides that the state must issue laws to prevent offenses to the public sense of decency according to the principles of the *shari'a (ahkam al-shari'a al-islamiya)*. Such measures might include the prosecution of women for going about without male chaperones or for dress that is deemed "immodest."

The Cairo Declaration and the Saudi Basic Law

As has been noted, the Cairo Declaration is carefully drafted so as to avoid providing for equality in rights regardless of gender—as one would expect in a document endorsed by countries such as Iran and Saudi Arabia, where sex-based discrimination is state policy. In an evasive formulation, Article 6 provides that women are equal to men in "human dignity"—but not equal in "rights." However, the term "rights" is used later in the same article, when it is stipulated that a woman "has rights to enjoy as well as duties to perform." The duties are left unspecified, and only three rights are enumerated as such: a woman's right to legal personality, to own and manage her property, and "to retain her name and lineage." The first two were among the important improvements in women's rights provided by Islam more than a millennium ago, but they are less significant today, as such minimal rights are now taken for granted. The third "right" does not advance women's position in Middle Eastern societies, where women have traditionally kept their family names after marriage. Article 6 also imposes on the husband the duty to pay maintenance and to care for the family, thereby perpetuating the traditional spousal relationship in which the husband is treated as both master and provider and the husband's rights over his wife flow from his duty to support her.

Furthermore, it seems that the Cairo Declaration envisages using Islamic criteria to restrict both women's freedom of movement and their ability to select employment. Article 12 provides that everyone shall have the right, within the framework of the *shari'a (fi utur al-shari'a)*, to freedom of movement. If reference were made to traditional *shari'a* rules, this seemingly neutral provision would accommodate restrictions on women's mobility, preventing women from leaving the home except with their husband's permission and from traveling except when accompanied by a male relative. Although Article 13 provides that men and women are entitled to fair wages for work without discrimination—a positive step—it does not prohibit restricting the fields in which women are permitted to work. Instead, it provides that everyone "shall be free to choose the work that suits him best and which serves his interests and those of society," and that a person "may not be assigned work beyond his capacity." These conditions would permit excluding women from work on the grounds that it was unsuitable for them, that the demands were beyond their capacity, or that the interests of society dictated such exclusion. This is in violation of UDHR Article 23.1, which guarantees that everyone has the right to work and to free choice of employment, and Article 6 of the International Covenant on Economic, Social, and Cultural Rights (ICESCR), which guarantees the right of "everyone to gain his living by work which he freely chooses or accepts." Article 23 of the Cairo Declaration stipulates that the *shari'a* determines the right to assume public office, which could be exploited by conservatives opposed to women's participation in government. In this regard, it is significant that in Iran all women who have tried to run for president have been disqualified by the Council of Guardians; although the reasons for disqualifying individual candidates were not reported, one can assume that the clerics decided that Islam barred women from this office.

The Cairo Declaration affords no guarantee for the right to marry the partner of one's choice, providing in Article 5 only that the right to marry should not have "restrictions stemming from race, color, or nationality," hereby leaving intact the old *shari'a* rules restricting the ability of Muslims to marry outside their faith, rules that are especially restrictive where women are involved. Not only can Muslim women not marry non-Muslims, but they may lose their Muslim husbands if and when their husbands run afoul of some would-be enforcers of Islamic orthodoxy who declare their husbands to be heretics or apostates. One is far, indeed, from the standards of the UDHR, which in Article 16.1 guarantees that both men and women have the right to marry without any limitations due to religion.

The Saudi Basic Law has no provision directly addressing women's rights. However, in Article 10 it provides that the state is to "aspire to strengthen family ties" and to maintain "Arab and Islamic values." There are also stipulations in Article 9 that the family shall be inculcated with the Islamic faith and with obedience to God, the Prophet, and those possessing authority, and also with respect for the law. Taken together, these suggest an intention to employ appeals to Saudi family values and premodern Islamic law in order to maintain the traditional patriarchal family structure and to keep women subordinated and cloistered within its confines. In other words, the Basic Law accommodates the Saudi system of gender apartheid. Not surprisingly, Saudi Arabia was one of only three nations willing to have full diplomatic relations with the Taliban government in Afghanistan, a regime that nearly all states refused to recognize due to its appalling rights abuses, especially its gender apartheid.[75] Paradoxically, Saudi Arabia decided in 2000 to ratify the Women's Convention, albeit with reservations that nullified any obligations to eliminate sex discrimination, indicating that the Saudi version of Islamic law would override the convention, stating: "In case of contradiction between any term of the Convention and the norms of islamic law [*sic*], the Kingdom is not under obligation to observe the contradictory terms of the Convention."[76]

Of course, Islamic law as enforced in Saudi Arabia locks women into a system of rigid segregation and subordination that is utterly incompatible with women's equality, rendering the ratification essentially meaningless. In March 2002, a tragic incident illustrated how women continue to be devalued in the Saudi system: Fourteen schoolgirls were incinerated when a fire broke out at their school and the religious police blocked the girls' escape, judging that they were not sufficiently enshrouded to be exposed to the view of male strangers.[77] Better to have schoolgirls burned alive, so the police reasoned, than to have them appear in public unveiled. The Saudi public reacted with outrage to this event, a sign that such arch-reactionary policies do not reflect popular opinion.

Women's Rights in Pakistan

The complicated and fluid situation in Pakistan defies easy characterization. Although Pakistan is one of the rare Muslim countries to have elected a woman as prime minister, powerful Islamist factions agitate constantly for restrictions on women's rights, and many support the Taliban model of subjugating women. Pakistan's assertive feminists, including the distinguished human rights lawyers Asma Jahangir and Hima Gilani, mobilize and litigate, seeking to thwart proposals for more Islamization and to roll back discriminatory rules and practices. At the same time, the authorities have a record of condoning rape, tolerating egregious incidents of domestic violence, abusing women held in detention, and failing to punish perpetrators of honor killings. However, it is important to note that many of the most notorious incidents of violence against women in Pakistan have no connection to Islam, stemming instead from retrograde local customs and primitive sexism.

Not surprisingly, there were contentious debates about whether Pakistan should ratify the Women's Convention.[78] Ultimately, a compromise was made; the 1995 ratification was said to be "subject to the provisions of the Constitution of Pakistan." Since, as previously noted, the constitution called for Muslims to be enabled to live in "accordance with the teachings and requirements of Islam," what appeared to be a "constitutional" reservation was potentially the equivalent of the Islamic reservations that had been entered by other Muslim countries.

After Zia's death, the federal government pulled back from initiatives to curtail women's rights, but the situation has been different in Pakistan's Northwest Frontier Province, which has been governed since 2002 by a faction of Taliban sympathizers, the Muttahida Majlis-e Amal (MMA). Hoping to establish a separate system of Islamic law enforcement that would escape the supervision of the courts, the MMA enacted the so-called Hisba Bill. This measure called for the appointment of a *muhtasib,* an Islamic official empowered to eliminate vice, to arrange for policing the province and punishing "un-Islamic" behavior. Such a system could lead to replicating the Taliban's systematic oppression of women. The Musharraf government appealed to the Supreme Court, asserting that the bill impinged on the "fundamental rights of the people as provided in the Constitution." In an August 2005 ruling that was welcomed by supporters of human rights, the Supreme Court ruled that the Hisba Bill was unconstitutional.[79] Pakistani supporters of women's rights took some comfort from the fact that, at least in this instance, the Supreme Court had stood up to advocates of Islamization, but they braced themselves for the next attempt to curb women's rights in the guise of implementing Islamic morality.

The New Afghan and Iraqi Constitutions

In the turbulent, war-torn years just before the Taliban takeover, various factions competed for supremacy in Afghanistan. During this period, women suffered from abduction, displacement, abuse, torture, rape, and slaughter.[80] All this was but a prelude to the even harsher crackdowns and more extensive abuses perpetrated under the Taliban, who succeeded in extending their rule over most of the country in 1996, with their emir ruling by fiat in default of modern institutions like a constitution. They unleashed fierce enforcers of their retrograde version of Islamic morality to terrorize the population into submission. Ironically, their Islamic dress rules were less clearly discriminatory than many others, as men, too, were required to don the approved "Islamic" uniform and to also leave their beards untrimmed. Women had to be completely swathed in the enveloping *burqa* any time they left their homes, and their mobility was sharply curbed, since women were not allowed go out without a male relative to escort them. The Taliban's policies amounted to a regime of gender apartheid, barring women from all education and virtually all employment outside the home and blocking women's access to health care.[81]

Seemingly chastened by the international chorus of condemnation and the refusal of most states to recognize their regime, Taliban officials denied charges that they were trampling on women's human rights.[82] Their denial proved that the prestige of human rights had grown to the point where even regimes pursuing the most retrograde Islamization programs felt obliged to deflect charges of violations.

Afghan women struggled against the Taliban's program and mobilized to support the opposition.[83] Many celebrated the Taliban's 2001 downfall and the adoption by the new government of policies more supportive of women's rights. Women pressed hard to have protections for their rights written into the 2003 Afghan constitution, but they came out of the difficult drafting process with only limited victories; the constitution had both worrisome and positive features. It advises in Article 3 that no law should contravene the beliefs and principles of the sacred religion of Islam, which could be used to bar laws advancing women's rights. At the same time, Article 22 provides that citizens, whether men or women, have equal rights and duties before the law, which would seem to ban discrimination against women. Moreover, the post-Taliban government ratified the Women's Convention in 2003 without imposing any Islamic reservations.

Meanwhile, Afghan women in the aftermath of the US invasion were forced to cope with enormous turmoil and violence, as a weak central government struggled unsuccessfully to assert control beyond the capital and to uproot vestiges of the Taliban in the war-ravaged, economically prostrate country.[84] In these circumstances, the promise of eliminating discrimination against women and improving their lives seemed little more than an idealistic illusion, and boasts about the US mission of "saving" Afghan women could be viewed as the hypocritical rhetoric of "the new colonial feminism."[85]

The situation in Iraq was equally chaotic. Although Saddam Hussein's despotism affected all Iraqis, women fared relatively well under his dictatorship when compared with their sisters in Iran and Afghanistan. A reformed version of Islamic law prevailed in the area of personal status, and many opportunities were open to women. The US invasion displaced Saddam's Baathist ruling clique and enabled long-suppressed Shi'i forces to assume power, creating a situation where Islamist extremists could exert pressures on women to veil themselves and retire to the domestic sphere. The huge increase in crime and terrorist violence, in the chaos that ensued after Saddam was toppled, created such perils for women that many felt compelled to stay locked inside their homes.

The United States publicly pressed the drafters of the Iraqi constitution to include an express guarantee of equality for women.[86] (Perhaps in part due to US pressures, the 2004 Iraqi Transitional Law in Article 12 had already barred discrimination "on the basis of gender.") Nevertheless, ambiguous provisions in the 2005 Iraqi constitution left women's rights in doubt. Although Article 14 provides that Iraqis are equal before the law without discrimination because of gender, and Article 20 gives male and female citizens political rights, including the right to vote and run for office, provisions in Article 2 state that no law may contradict the undisputed rules of Islam and that Islamic law is to be a main source of legislation. These provisions open the door to restrictive Islamic criteria. Furthermore, Article 39 contains a vague provision allowing Iraqis to be governed by religious law in matters of personal status. The freedom to be governed by religious law would allow men to use the courts to impose the patriarchal system of premodern Islamic jurisprudence, an outcome that angered Iraqi feminists. Taken together, these provisions suggest that Iraqi women's rights in personal status matters could be severely eroded under the new constitution.

Summary of Islamic Approaches

In the various Islamic human rights schemes examined in this chapter, women are not recognized as fully equal human beings who deserve the same rights and freedoms as men. However, the authors of these schemes are generally reluctant to spell out their discriminatory intentions. The vague invocations of *shari'a* law are very useful in this regard, since the *shari'a* qualifications on rights tend to look harmless to a casual observer, while opening the way to restricting women's rights using Islamic criteria.

The purpose of international human rights law is to afford protection for human rights. In contrast, Islamic human rights schemes, as illustrated in this chapter, afford the legal basis to restrict or deny rights, including women's right to equality and to equal treatment under the law.

The Influence of Sex Stereotyping

The Convention on the Elimination of all Forms of Discrimination Against Women (CEDAW) recognizes that sex stereotyping constitutes an obstacle to realizing full equality for women and calls on governments to attack the attitudes and practices that stereotype women as inferior beings whose nature disqualifies them from enjoying freedoms on a par with men. Article 5.a binds the parties "to modify the social and cultural patterns of conduct of men and women, with a view to achieving the elimination of prejudices and customary and all other practices which are based on the idea of the inferiority or the superiority of either of the sexes or on stereotyped roles for men and women."

One sees no concern for transcending or eliminating sex stereotyping in the Islamic human rights schemes reviewed here; on the contrary, such stereotyping is a central feature of the schemes, if sometimes only an implied one. They show evidence of being shaped by the belief that men and women have inherently different natures and thus have distinct rights and obligations. This belief is reflected in the formal reservations to CEDAW expressed by several Muslim countries, which combine references to Islam and assumptions that women and men must play different, complementary roles.[87]

Given Sultanhussein Tabandeh's outspokenness, it is not surprising that he freely and unselfconsciously expressed his stereotypical views of men and women in the course of explaining why the human rights accorded to women in the UDHR are incompatible with Islam. Women, according to Tabandeh, are touchy and hasty, volatile and imprudent. They are generally more gullible and credulous than men. Their sexual desire makes them easy prey for the blandishments of salacious individuals.[88] Tabandeh cited these inherent female weaknesses to justify Islamic restrictions on women's right to obtain a divorce, but, obviously, these same female shortcomings could justify restrictions on other rights as well. In Tabandeh's opinion, men and women were designed by nature to perform different tasks. Women were designed for "cooking, laundering, shopping, and washing up," as well as for taking care of children. Men, in contrast, were created for field work, warfare, and earning a living.[89] Women are deficient in the intelligence needed for "tackling big and important matters"; they are prone to making mistakes and lack long-term perspective. For this reason, he said, they must be excluded from politics.[90] Women cannot fight in war because they are "timorous-hearted," limited by physical weakness, and may become frightened and run away.[91]

Abu'l A'la Mawdudi took a similar line, although not in his publication on human rights. In his book on purdah he argued that nature has designed men and women for different roles, treating menstruation, pregnancy, and nursing as incapacitating disabilities.[92] Women, he asserted, are created to bear and rear children. They are tender, unusually sensitive, soft, submissive, impressionable, and timid. They lack firmness, authority, "cold-temperedness," strong willpower, and the ability to render unbiased, objective judgment.[93] Men have coarseness, vehemence, and aggressiveness, which make them suited to assume roles as generals, statesmen, and administrators. The education of men should, therefore, aim at training them so that they can support and protect the family, whereas a woman should be educated to bring up children, look after domestic affairs, and make home life "sweet, pleasant, and peaceful."[94]

Similar observations were made by Ayatollah Javad Bahonar, a cleric who briefly served as Iran's prime minister before being assassinated. Bahonar was one of Khomeini's closest aides, and his thinking may be taken as representative of many of the leading clerics in Khomeini's regime who fashioned or supported policies vis-à-vis women. In an article on Islam and women's rights in an English-language journal distributed in the West by the Iranian regime, Bahonar said that men are bigger and stronger and have larger brains, with a larger proportion of the brain "dealing with thought and deliberation."[95] A relatively larger proportion of the smaller female brain is "related to emotions," and women have more in the way of the affection and deep tender sentiments that suit them for child care and nursing. Women's sentiments and emotions make them ill equipped to cope with earning a livelihood, which calls for farsightedness, perseverance, strength, tolerance, coolness, planning ability, hard-heartedness, connivance, and the like—characteristics that women lack. Men are equipped by nature to deal with "the tumult of life," to fight on the battlefield, and to manage the affairs of government and society.[96] A note at the end of the article offers some statistics on female physical inferiority, including the comment that "a man's brain weighs 100 grams more than a woman's." Bahonar summed up his evidence by saying that the "differences in physical structure are reflected in the mental capacities of the two sexes."[97]

Notwithstanding this recital of women's natural deficiencies and infirmities, Bahonar asserted that "Islam considers men and women equal as far as the basic human rights are concerned."[98] However, one might predict that any human rights scheme that he might devise would relegate women to the subordinate status mandated by his stereotype of female weakness and physical and mental inferiority. Indeed, although Bahonar cited many ways that men and women share equal religious and moral *duties*—both are required to pray, to be faithful and obedient believers, to command the good and prohibit the evil, to keep their looks cast down, and to accept punishment for crimes—Bahonar cited only two *rights* that the two sexes share on an equal basis: the right to own and use property and the right to inherit.[99]

Because the Islamic legal tradition developed in traditional, patriarchal milieus and because the authoritative works on the legal status of women in Islam have been exclusively written by men, it is not surprising that men's stereotypes of women were incorporated by that tradition and that they have been retained as part of Islamic rights schemes. However, there is very little in the original Islamic sources that supports these stereotypes, and there is, moreover, nothing distinctively Islamic about the self-interested and biased appraisals of women's inherent traits that they offer. In fact, the sex stereotyping that one sees in the Islamic tradition is very similar to stereotypes found in other cultural and religious contexts. For example, the Saudi prohibition against women driving, which is associated with conservative Islamic precepts, has a historical counterpart in the United States of the early twentieth century, when sex stereotyping was used to justify prohibiting women from driving.[100]

The Catholic Church is only one of many denominations where sex stereotyping has been used to support the view of Church clergy—all males—that women must be kept subjugated due to their "natural" inferiority to men. It is not a coincidence that Catholic theologians, having stereotyped women in much the same way that Muslim jurists had, developed a similar set of rules discriminating against women and restricting their freedom and opportunities. One need only review aspects of the Christian tradition to be reminded that sex stereotyping can be projected into dissimilar religious traditions. Among the characteristics that the Church Fathers attributed to women were fickleness, shallowness, garrulousness, weakness, slowness of understanding, and instability of mind.[101] Saint Augustine asserted that compared to men, women were small of intellect.[102] In a 1966 book designed to persuade Catholic women that due to their sex, their "entire psychology is founded upon the primordial tendency to love," two priests asserted that a woman's brain "is generally lighter and simpler than man's."[103]

Pope Pius XII, speaking to an audience of women in 1945, described "the sensibility and delicacy of feeling peculiar to woman, which might tempt her to be swayed by emotions and thus blur the clearness and breadth of her view and be detrimental to the calm consideration of future consequences."[104] He maintained that as a result of their characteristics, women were suited for tasks in life that called for "tact, delicate feelings, and maternal instinct, rather than administrative rigidity."[105] A Jesuit theologian who offered an outline of a divine plan for women asserted in the course of his discussion on the nature of a woman: "She has not lost the dispositions of impressionability and mobility which Eve had manifested in the initial drama of humanity. She remains fragile, more subject to an unreflected impulse, and more accessible to seduction."[106]

As a major feminist critic of Catholic doctrine has pointed out, the sex-role stereotypes upheld and disseminated by men in the Church hierarchy became closely intertwined with the Catholic teachings calling for the subordination of women: "The very emancipation which would prove that women were not 'naturally' defective was denied them in the name of that defectiveness which was claimed to be natural and divinely ordained."[107]

One can see the same nexus between culture-bound presuppositions about inherent female characteristics and religious doctrine in both the Islamic and Christian traditions. The question that remains is whether the sex stereotypes associated with religious doctrine are supported by the original sources or whether they are simply being read into them by interpreters with patriarchal biases.

CHAPTER 7

Islamic Human Rights Schemes and Religious Minorities

The Treatment of Religious Minorities in Muslim Countries

The issue of the rights of non-Muslim minorities in the Middle East has a peculiar historical background that casts a shadow over any discussion by a Western observer. Critical assessments of the use of Islam as a rationale for discriminatory treatment of non-Muslims tend to be linked in people's minds with the pursuit of Western neo-imperialist agendas. Of course, the US projects of post-invasion reconstruction of Afghanistan and Iraq, officially aimed at bolstering human rights, tend to reinforce this linkage. Aspects of the historical background are summarized here in an attempt to differentiate between the heyday of European imperialism, when grand strategies aimed at extending domination of Muslim countries by exploiting the issue of their treatment of non-Muslim minorities, and the present, when calls by international human rights NGOs and other independent observers for consistent and even-handed application of and respect for international human rights law have—or should have—different connotations. These efforts by international and independent organizations are contrasted with the selective invocations of human rights used by the United States to justify its interventions in the Middle East.

For centuries, the status of non-Muslims in the Middle East was determined by *shari'a* law. At the time of the growth of European commercial connections with the Ottoman Empire, European powers were able to wrest concessions from the Ottomans for their own citizens, who were given extraterritorial status. In the nineteenth century, European powers with political ambitions in the Middle East appointed themselves the protectors of the various local Christian minorities, and

Europeans began to monitor aggressively the treatment of non-Muslims, using allegations of mistreatment of non-Muslims as pretexts for interfering in Middle Eastern politics. In response to European pressures, the Ottoman sultans promulgated special edicts in 1839 and 1856 that formally granted equality to their non-Muslim Ottoman subjects.[1]

The treatment of non-Muslims thus became a bone of contention between Middle Eastern governments and European countries with imperialist ambitions. In this context, European expressions of concern for the rights of non-Muslims were intimately bound with the political agendas of the European powers. Where Europeans dominated Middle Eastern societies, they inevitably favored non-Muslim minorities, the most important instance being Great Britain's use of its mandate over Palestine to foster the development of a Jewish homeland.[2] In addition to according privileged treatment to the non-Muslim segment of the population, Europeans invoked the need to protect non-Muslims from oppression by the Muslim majorities as a rationale for their rule.[3] Since European powers were notably lacking in sympathy for the aspirations for freedom on the part of Muslim Middle Easterners, European expressions of solicitude for non-Muslims naturally became associated with hypocrisy and selfish political ambitions. Christian missionary activities in the Middle East, which flourished when the region was under European domination, suggested that there was a plot to draw Muslims into the European orbit by converting them to Christianity.

Eventually, Middle Eastern countries became independent of European domination. In most cases this happened in the wake of World War II. Although many members of non-Muslim minority communities emigrated from the newly independent states, the old Christian communities of Egypt and the Fertile Crescent remained largely intact. Overall the proportion of non-Muslims in the Middle East dwindled, leaving a reduced population that today is affected by *shari'a* rules governing the treatment of non-Muslims.

Events since World War II, especially the strong Western support for Israel, have tended to exacerbate Muslim resentment and suspicion of Western policies concerning non-Muslim minorities. Muslims were outraged that Britain and France ignored the right of self-determination of the native Palestinian population in order to accommodate members of a Jewish community long persecuted by European Christians. Palestinian self-determination has become a central concern in the regional human rights domain, which is reflected in the text of the 1999 Casablanca Declaration adopted by the First International Conference of the Arab Human Rights Movement:

> The Conference declares its full support for the right of the Palestinian people
> to self-determination and to establish their independent state on their occu-

pied national soil . . . The rights of the Palestinian people are the proper standard to measure the consistency of international positions towards a just peace and human rights. The Arab human rights movement will apply this standard in its relations with the different international organizations and actors.[4]

Continuing disregard for the right of Palestinian self-determination and the strong US support for Israel have reinforced the perception that Western solicitude for religious minorities in the Middle East—here a Jewish community—is a front for imperialist designs, a pattern long familiar to Middle Easterners. Religious minorities are seen by many in the region as pawns in a US strategy that aims to oppress and exploit the largely Muslim population, goals that entail the dismantling of Islamic law.[5]

Muslims tend to view any discussion of the status of non-Muslims in the contemporary Middle East in relation to this particular historical background. Muslim resentment has been exacerbated by the callous indifference shown by the West to the atrocities and genocide in Bosnia, which decimated and martyred Bosnia's Muslim population. Given this background, any critical evaluations of *shari'a* standards for the treatment of religious minorities are bound to provoke negative reactions.

The tendency to associate such critical evaluations with neo-imperialist designs has also been aggravated by recent US political initiatives, including the passing of the US International Religious Freedom Act of 1998 and the establishment of the Office of International Religious Freedom in the US State Department.[6] These measures were spearheaded by a coalition of politicians and lobbyists apparently seeking to win support from Christian Evangelicals. Although the scope of the legislation was later widened to encompass minorities such as Baha'is and Buddhists—apparently with the aim of avoiding charges of sectarian bias—the original focus was on assisting Christians and converts to Christianity.[7] Under the law, violations of the rights of religious minorities could trigger US sanctions against offending countries. Persons knowledgeable about the Middle East who were genuinely concerned for the well-being of beleaguered Christian and other religious minorities in the Middle East understood that associating calls for improvement in the status of religious minorities with aggressive US intervention on their behalf would only heighten Muslims' inclination to view religious minorities as pawns of Western interests. To appraise the rights accorded to non-Muslims in Islamic human rights schemes, one must look beyond issues that have been politicized by US interventions and conduct a more objective analysis using international human rights law.

It is important to note that patterns of denying rights to non-Muslims and to Muslim minorities are now often linked. The disposition to treat Islam as the state ideology has altered the significance of *shari'a* rules for religious minorities. Islamization has serious implications for the rights of non-Muslims, but it also has extremely ominous implications for Muslim religious minorities. This was appreciated by Iraq's Sunni minority as they witnessed the ascendancy of Shi'i clerics after the 2003 overthrow of Saddam's secular Baathist regime and the displacement of the Sunni ruling elite, which had savagely persecuted Shi'is under Saddam. Throughout the constitution drafting process, Sunnis determinedly fought plans by the Shi'i majority for enshrining the role of Shi'ism and Shi'i clerics in the new constitution. They had only to look at the discriminatory treatment of Sunnis in neighboring Iran to be reminded how the combination of Islamization and Shi'i rule had correlated with oppression of a Sunni minority. Meanwhile, sectarian tensions in Iraq had been brought to a boiling point by lethal violence and counterviolence between the Sunni and Shi'i communities—a replication of an experience that Pakistan had earlier endured, although in a context where Shi'is were in the minority. That is, the rules for the treatment of religious minorities are relevant not only for persons who are avowedly non-Muslim but also for persons within the Muslim community who may suffer discrimination and abuse due to their sectarian affiliations. In the light of the importance of minority rights for Muslim sects, it is time to stop automatically associating all critiques of the treatment of religious minorities under *shari'a* rules with neo-imperialist objectives and attempts to secure privileges for non-Muslims.

International Standards Prohibiting Religious Discrimination

Under international human rights law it is not permissible to discriminate against people on the basis of religion. This principle is enshrined in the Universal Declaration of Human Rights (UDHR) in Article 2, and in the International Covenant on Civil and Political Rights (ICCPR) in Articles 2 and 26. The Declaration on the Elimination of All Forms of Intolerance and of Discrimination Based on Religion or Belief, proclaimed by the UN General Assembly on November 25, 1981, reaffirmed this principle in Article 2, elaborating on it in Article 2.2 to define impermissible discrimination as "any distinction, exclusion, restriction or preference based on religion or belief and having as its purpose or as its effect nullification or impairment of the recognition, enjoyment or exercise of human rights or fundamental freedoms on an equal basis." Article 4.1 requires all states to take effective measures to prevent and eliminate discrimination on the grounds of religion. Article 4.2 calls on governments to take affirmative steps to dismantle patterns of discrimination and eliminate religious prejudice: "All States shall make all efforts to enact or rescind legislation where necessary to prohibit any such discrimination, and to take all appropriate measures to combat intolerance on the grounds of religion or belief in this matter."

Shari'a Law and the Rights of Non-Muslims

The premodern *shari'a* rules affecting the status of non-Muslims were formulated by Islamic jurists at an early stage of the history of the Islamic community and reflect the circumstances of that era. The nascent community was weak and beleaguered, faced with the difficult task of absorbing non-Muslim communities in newly won territories while having to meet the military threat of powerful non-Muslim foes.[8] The *jihad,* or Islamic holy war, was undertaken both to expand the territory subject to Muslim control and to spread the Islamic religion.[9] However, contrary to Western images of Muslim conquerors presenting the conquered peoples with a choice of conversion to Islam or the sword, conquered Christians and Jews were allowed to persist in their beliefs. In Islam, Christians and Jews are regarded as the recipients of earlier divine revelations, which were deemed to have culminated in God's final Revelation to the Prophet Muhammad. Christians and Jews are known as *ahl al-kitab,* or people of the book, an indication of Islamic respect for their scriptures.

Although the premodern doctrines of *jihad* remain part of the Islamic cultural legacy and *jihad* may be proclaimed in a variety of military and political contexts by contemporary leaders—much as "crusade" is invoked by leaders of Western countries in time of war or conflict—governments of Muslim countries appreciate that under international law they cannot invoke religious doctrines to justify military campaigns to conquer the non-Muslim world. In practice, many of the premodern doctrines regarding *jihad* and treatment of non-Muslims have been discarded, having been recognized as anachronisms in present circumstances, in which the Muslim community has burgeoned to well over a billion adherents and its existence is no longer threatened.[10] A few aspects of the *shari'a* that do remain relevant for the status of non-Muslims are summarized here.

In the early Islamic conquests, a major concern of the leaders of the new Islamic community was how to treat the Christians and Jews who persisted in their old beliefs.[11] Jews and Christians ruled by Muslims had the political status of *dhimmis,* or those accorded toleration in return for submitting to Muslim rule and accepting a number of conditions governing their conduct.[12] *Dhimmis* had to pay a special capitation tax, known as the *jizya,* and were excluded from serving in the military, since, as non-Muslims, they could not be expected to fight in wars on behalf of Islam. Depending on the jurists' opinions, *dhimmis* were either excluded from serving in government altogether or excluded from high government positions. Although they were generally subject to *shari'a* law, *dhimmis* were allowed to follow their own rules of personal status, except in cases where persons of different faiths interacted, especially when one party was a Muslim.[13]

In theory, other faiths were not tolerated. In premodern *shari'a* doctrine, non-Muslims who were not Christian or Jewish were categorized as polytheists or unbelievers. When conquered by Muslims, they theoretically either had to embrace Islam or accept death.[14] In practice, as Islam expanded eastward, the premodern doctrines had to be adjusted, and Muslims had to learn to coexist with Hindus and other polytheists.[15]

Despite incidents of mistreatment of non-Muslims, it is fair to say that Muslim rulers, when judged by the standards of the day, generally showed far greater tolerance and humanity in their treatment of religious minorities than European rulers did.[16] In particular, the treatment of the Jewish minority in Muslim societies stands out as fair and enlightened when compared with the dismal record of European Christian persecution of Jews over the centuries.[17]

With the rise of secular nationalism in the Muslim world in the nineteenth century, it seemed that the significance of distinctions between Muslim and non-Muslim was destined to diminish.[18] Although the *shari'a* prohibitions affecting intermarriage persisted and most Muslim countries retained the legal requirement that the chief of state be Muslim, in many respects non-Muslims gained the status of citizenship on a par with Muslims. Muslim countries imported constitutional models from the West and adopted twentieth-century concepts of national citizenship. In these models, discrimination based on religion is prohibited.

Today, as the influence of secular nationalism has waned and the influence of Islam as a political ideology is mounting, issues surrounding the status of non-Muslims, which had seemed settled, have recently been reopened. Proponents of Islamization are calling for reinstating rules on *dhimmi* status in contemporary Middle Eastern societies. For example, a leader of the Egyptian Muslim Brotherhood announced in April 1997 that Egypt's Coptic Christians should be excluded from the army and posts related to national defense and that they should also pay the *jizya,* a symbol of subjugation to Muslim rule. Although Copts have a long history of patriotic commitment to Egyptian independence, the Muslim Brotherhood leader claimed they could become enemy agents if an Egyptian Islamic state were attacked.[19] So fierce were the attacks by other Egyptians on the author of these remarks that he felt obliged to back down and deny ever having made them. Proponents of Islamization who demand the imposition of laws discriminating against non-Muslims face strong internal opposition from political factions that favor respecting modern norms of citizenship and constitutional equality guarantees.

The kind of robust human rights advocacy that one finds in the promotion of Islamic feminism today is rarely matched in Muslims' discussions of equal rights for non-Muslims. Still, one finds Muslims representing a variety of currents of Islamic thought who have taken the position that Islam accommodates equal treatment for non-Muslims. For example, the Lebanese scholar Subhi Mahmassani argued in his work on Islam and human rights that there can be no discrimination based on religion in an Islamic system.[20] His approach essentially assumes that there must be harmony between Islam and international law, which entails tacitly suppressing or discarding any features of the *shari'a* that would be incompatible with international human rights. Mahmassani places great emphasis on aspects of the original sources and examples from early Islamic history that demonstrate the tolerant and egalitarian strains that have from the beginning constituted important components of the Islamic tradition.[21]

The conviction that there must be a natural affinity between Islam and the tenets of international human rights law has led other Muslims as well to embrace the principle that full equality for all citizens is compatible with Islam.[22] Unfortunately, arguments supporting this conclusion are not always fully developed. For example, the Egyptian political theorist Tariq al-Bishri, concerned with the status of Egypt's Copts and insisting that they should enjoy equality, called on specialists to reconcile this equality with Islamic law, expressing confidence that in a tradition as flexible and egalitarian as the Islamic one this should present no great problem.[23] However, he also examined the implications of the political changes in the Muslim world that are relevant for evaluating whether the premodern *shari'a* rules remain applicable. Al-Bishri noted that the nature of the modern state is so different from the kind of government envisaged by medieval Islamic theorists that the *shari'a* restrictions on non-Muslims holding high political office no longer logically apply.[24]

In contrast, the interpretations of Islamic law that have been offered by Abdullahi An-Na'im show much more concern than al-Bishri's for establishing the methodological basis for the belief that Islam allows absolute equality of Muslim and non-Muslim.[25] An-Na'im's system is based on the teaching of the late Mahmud Muhammad Taha, who said that the applicability of legal rules in various Qur'anic verses must be rethought. By distinguishing verses that were meant to govern the early Islamic community from those that were meant to have enduring validity, Taha was able to derive Islamic human rights principles that abolish the status of *dhimmis* and mandate an end to all discrimination on a religious basis.[26]

Opposed to these points of view are Muslim conservatives such as Sultanhussein Tabandeh and Abu'l A'la Mawdudi, who want either to preserve or revive discriminatory *shari'a* rules affecting non-Muslims. Even where the Islamic human rights schemes reviewed here do not expressly relegate non-Muslims to an inferior position, they have been deliberately drafted so as to accommodate the continued application of discriminatory rules from the premodern *shari'a*. Whereas Islamic human rights schemes envisage that non-Muslims will be governed by the *shari'a,* international human rights law assumes that a neutral, nondiscriminatory law will be applied to all citizens of a country, not accepting that a person's rights can be denied by reason of discriminatory religious laws.[27] With the exception of Tabandeh, the authors of these human rights schemes formulate their provisions regarding non-Muslims in such a manner that their intention to discriminate against non-Muslims is not obvious. That is, as with their evasive treatments of the status of women, they are reluctant to state forthrightly that they refuse to endorse the principle of equality as understood in international law.

Tabandeh's Ideas

Sultanhussein Tabandeh demonstrated more candor than others in his admission that, according to his conception, the *shari'a* precludes equality between Muslims and non-Muslims. In commenting on the UDHR Article 1 guarantee of equality, Tabandeh insisted that the principle of equality does not apply when it comes to differences of religion, faith, or conviction. This is because "nobility, excellence and virtue consist in true worship of the One God and obedience to the commandments of Heaven." According to Tabandeh, the *ahl al-kitab* deserve respect because of their belief, but "since their faith has not reached the highest level of spirituality, but obeys commands which we believe to have been abrogated, and puts other laws in place of these revealed through Islam by the means of the Prophet and most righteous Judge, therefore [the *shari'a*] makes certain difference between them and Muslims, treating them as not on the same level."[28]

For those non-Muslims who are not *ahl al-kitab,* Tabandeh has only contempt. Humanists, he said, are "the gangrenous members of the body politic,"[29] and those who have not accepted the one God are "outside the pale of humanity."[30] Given his attitudes, Tabandeh naturally cannot concede that persons in the latter categories are deserving of any human rights protections. The view that non-Muslims who are not among the *ahl al-kitab* are not entitled to the status of legal persons is common among Muslim conservatives. This idea corresponds to features of the premodern *shari'a,* but it sharply conflicts with international human rights law, which does not recognize that a person may be denied legal personality because of religion or belief. The ICCPR says in Article 16 that everyone has a right to recognition everywhere as a person before the law.

Tabandeh's contention that the polytheist must be treated as a nonperson also comes up in comments regarding the issue of intermarriage. He insisted on preserving the premodern *shari'a* rules that absolutely prohibit marriage with polytheists.[31] He is equally adamant about preserving the premodern *shari'a* rule that prevents a Muslim woman from marrying a Christian or Jew, while allowing a Muslim man to marry a woman from those faiths.[32] According to Tabandeh, a marriage between a Muslim woman and a non-Muslim man is invalid, and any child born of such a marriage is illegitimate; moreover, if the woman knew before her marriage that the man she was marrying was a non-Muslim, she must be punished.[33] It is at this point in Tabandeh's argument that one sees how the inferior status of women and the inferior status of non-Muslims are linked—a linkage that is made by many Muslim conservatives. Tabandeh argued:

> The scripture says: "Men are guardians of women and guarantors of their rights" [Qur'an 4:34]. The wife must obey her husband. But, if she weds a non-Muslim husband it means that she as a Muslim is subordinating herself: and Islam never allows a Muslim to come under the authority of a non-Muslim in any circumstance at all, as is made perfectly plain in "God will never make a way for infidels (to exercise lordship) over believers" [Qur'an 4:41]: and therefore He never granted permission that Muslims should by marriage voluntarily subordinate themselves to non-Muslims. . . . In Islam every distinction is abolished except the distinction of religion and faith; whence it follows that Islam and its peoples must be above infidels, and never permit non-Muslims to acquire lordship over them.[34]

The rights of the individual man and woman who wish to marry despite religious differences are totally absent from Tabandeh's concerns. Instead of the concern that one finds in international human rights law for the freedom of the individuals involved, the concern is for the prestige of the Muslim community, the honor of which is sullied if one of its members is subordinated to a member of the inferior group, the non-Muslims. The assumption is that, just as Muslims are placed above non-Muslims, so men are placed above women, meaning that wives are necessarily subordinated to their husbands. Therefore, the Muslim man who marries a female *dhimmi* does not infringe the hierarchy of status, since by virtue of her sex, the non-Muslim wife is subordinate to her husband, who as a Muslim and a male ranks above her on two counts. In contrast, the Muslim woman who marries a *dhimmi* violates the rules of status, since as a wife she has lower status than the man to whom she is married, even though by virtue of her adherence to the Islamic religion she should rank above him. These *shari'a* rules regarding marriage have the effect of allowing Muslim men to exercise the powers that they enjoy as husbands over both their own women and *dhimmi* women, while allowing *dhimmi* men to exercise their marital prerogatives solely over women who are likewise relegated to *dhimmi* status.

On the questions of political rights and freedom of expression, Tabandeh is opposed to according to non-Muslims rights that are guaranteed by international human rights standards. Non-Muslims, he said, must be entirely excluded from the judiciary, the legislature, and the cabinet.[35] Furthermore, no "propaganda" for any non-Muslim religion may be allowed.[36]

The UIDHR

The disposition of the authors of the Universal Islamic Declaration of Human Rights (UIDHR) to evade hard questions regarding the compatibility of *shari'a* rules with international human rights law has already been established. Where the status of non-Muslims is concerned, the authors of the UIDHR are much less forthright than Tabandeh in spelling out the specifics of the discriminatory rules they mean to apply.

The UIDHR addresses the situation of non-Muslims in Article 10. This article does not guarantee equal treatment for religious minorities or state that discrimination based on religion is impermissible. Article 10.a states that the religious rights of non-Muslim minorities are governed by the principle that there is no compulsion in religion, which is based on the Qur'an 2:256. The traditional interpretation of this verse is that *dhimmis* should not be forced to convert to Islam. However, it has not traditionally been interpreted to mean that the prohibition against compulsion in religion precludes *dhimmis* or other non-Muslims from being subjected to discrimination based on their religion.

What the UIDHR seems to suggest is the *millet* system that flourished under the Ottoman Empire. Under this system, members of the various non-Muslim communities were governed under their own religious laws in internal matters and lawsuits involving members of the same faith, but they were subject to the *shari'a* in mixed cases and in all other matters. In most Muslim countries today, remnants of this system persist, since the religious law of the parties involved generally governs personal-status matters.

In the English version of Article 10.b, "religious minorities" are given the right to be governed either by Islamic law or by their own laws on personal-status or civil matters. Not limited expressly to Christians and Jews, Article 10.b appears to go beyond the premodern *shari'a* rules, which gave only *dhimmis* the right to be judged under their own law, seemingly allowing all non-Muslims to follow their own laws in personal or civil matters. However, the Arabic version of the same provision resurrects the old distinction between Christians and Jews on the one hand and other non-Muslims on the other, suggesting that only members of the *ahl al-kitab* enjoy this right. In a peculiar formulation, the Arabic version of Article 10.b provides that non-Muslims may appeal to Muslims for judgment, but that if they do not do so, they must follow their own laws, provided that they (seemingly, the non-Muslims) believe that those laws are of divine origin. This would seem to mean that where non-Muslims did not elect to be governed by the *shari'a,* their subjective convictions that the laws of their own communities were divinely inspired would lead to their laws being controlling. However, the references in the same provision to the Qur'an 5:47, dealing with people of the Gospel, and 5:42, dealing with the followers of the Torah, give reason to believe that this right of religious minorities to be bound by their own religious rules actually pertains only to Christian and Jewish minorities. That is, as in the premodern *shari'a,* no provision is made allowing non-Muslims who are not Christians or Jews to follow their own religious law in civil and personal-status matters within their own communities. This leaves open the question as to what status is accorded to non-Muslims outside the category of *dhimmis,* who under the *shari'a* were considered nonpersons.

In another article, the UIDHR echoes an idea put forth by Mawdudi in his human rights pamphlet, stating that Muslims must show respect for the feelings of non-Muslims. Mawdudi stated that Islam does not allow Muslims to use abusive language that may injure the religious feelings of non-Muslims.[37] The UIDHR states in Article 12.e that no one shall hold in contempt or ridicule the religious beliefs of others. Both of these principles seem to be ethico-moral injunctions rather than enforceable legal rights. Again, we see that Islamic human rights schemes are not concerned with actual laws or governmental action, which are the cause of the most egregious infringements of liberty, but with the conduct of private individuals, which is likely to have a less significant impact on non-Muslims.

Article 12.e of the UIDHR elaborates on this idea, stating that "people" should not incite hostility toward non-Muslims. This is a laudable ethico-moral precept, and the Islamic Council is performing a valuable public service by taking a stance condemning such incitement, which, in the volatile Middle East, can easily become a prelude to violence. However, for this principle to have teeth—and legal force—further clarification of what constitutes such impermissible incitement to violence is necessary. No such clarification is afforded in the UIDHR in Article 12.a, which provides that all speech is allowed within the limits of the *shari'a,* a standard that is far too vague to determine what would rank as unacceptable incitement to public hostility toward non-Muslims.[38]

The Iranian Constitution

The article of the Iranian constitution dealing with religious minorities seems to contemplate a model similar to the *millet* system, where there are two categories of persons, Muslims and the *ahl al-kitab,* which, reflecting local tradition, Iran deems should also include Zoroastrians. With emphasis added, Article 13 provides: "Zoroastrian, Jewish, and Christian Iranians are the *only* recognized religious minorities, who, within the limits of the law *[dar hodud-e qanun],* are free to perform their religious rites and ceremonies, and to act according to their own canon in matters of personal affairs and religious education."[39]

That is, aside from acts of religious observance and personal-status matters, the *ahl al-kitab* are to be governed by Iranian laws. As has already been discussed, Iranian laws are subordinate to Islamic law, which, under Article 4 of the constitution, is treated as the norm to which all laws must conform. This means that the *ahl al-kitab* are subject to discriminatory laws. The nonrecognition of religious minorities other than the *ahl al-kitab* in this *shari'a*-based system means that these other minorities can claim no constitutional protections. The problems of non-Muslims who are not accorded the status of recognized minorities are discussed after a review of the implications of constitutional provisions for the rights of recognized minorities.

The disabilities imposed on non-Muslims under the postrevolutionary regime have been severe, in many instances going beyond those that would be required under the premodern *shari'a*. Since in the postrevolutionary Iranian environment Twelver Shi'ism is interpreted to be an ideology—much as communism was in the Eastern Bloc countries—the fact that non-Muslims are persons who by definition do not subscribe to the official Iranian ideology has provided additional grounds for discriminating against them. Iran has imposed tests of ideological purity on applicants for public employment that effectively exclude non-Muslims.[40] Moreover, Muslims who subscribe to sects other than the peculiar ideologized version of Islam that is sponsored by the regime have also been excluded.

Mawdudi, who believed that Islam must be the official ideology of Muslim countries, had a similar attitude. Although he did not discuss this in his human rights pamphlet, he indicated elsewhere that he considered discrimination against persons who did not share a state's official Islamic ideology to be perfectly reasonable.[41] However, as a committed Sunni, Mawdudi would hardly have been pleased by the consequences of Iran's ideologization of Shi'ism, which has led to a pattern of discrimination and even persecution directed against Sunni Muslims. Members of Iran's ethnic minorities are largely Sunnis, which means that they may suffer discrimination and abuse on both ethnic and religious grounds. Since the revolution, Iran has been castigated for mistreating its religious and ethnic minorities, and several prominent Sunni figures have been executed or have died in suspicious circumstances.[42] This pattern turns out to be a mirror image of trends in neighboring Pakistan in the wake of the Islamization program of Muhammad Zia ul-Haq, which had a strong pro-Sunni bias. Pakistan's large Shi'i minority has become increasingly beleaguered and subjected to threats and assaults, and lethal sectarian violence has frequently broken out. A militant Sunni group has campaigned for laws that would stigmatize Shi'is and has called for declaring Pakistan a Sunni state, just as Iran has been declared a

Shi'i state.[43] When a state imposes an ideologized version of Islam with a sectarian bias, Muslims who dissent from this version may be effectively relegated to a subcategory where they are subjected to mistreatment.

An example of the consequences of ideologization of Islam can be seen in the Iranian constitution. There is an ideological test for those who wish to serve in the Iranian military. A close reading of Article 144 reveals that non-Muslims are excluded from the military, just as *dhimmis* were in premodern Islamic civilization. The article provides: "The Army of the Islamic Republic of Iran must be an Islamic Army, i.e., committed to Islamic ideology and the people, and must recruit into its service individuals who have faith in the objectives of the Islamic Revolution and are devoted to the cause of realizing its goals." Obviously, Iran's non-Muslim minorities have no place in an Islamic army set up under these criteria.[44]

Article 14 of the Iranian constitution provides in part: "The government of the Islamic Republic of Iran and all Muslims are duty-bound to treat non-Muslims in conformity with ethical norms and the principles of Islamic justice and equity, and to respect their human rights *[hoquq-e ensani]*. This principle applies to all who refrain from engaging in conspiracy or activity against Islam and the Islamic Republic of Iran." Here, following "Islamic justice" entails qualifying non-Muslims' rights through the application of *shari'a* law. Far from granting non-Muslims protections for the rights to which they are entitled under international law, the constitution reinforces the principle that all rights are subject to *shari'a* qualifications.

In addition, Article 14 provides that the human rights that non-Muslims enjoy, which one may assume are very limited to begin with, are to be forfeited if the non-Muslims become involved in activity against the Islamic Republic, a vague standard affording a broad range of potential justifications for curbing their rights. It is interesting that this article provides special grounds for depriving non-Muslims of human rights, even though there is already a general provision in Article 26 that enables the government to curb the activities of groups, including "minority religious associations," if they are "contrary to the principles of Islam or the Islamic Republic." Article 14 opens the way to even more extensive deprivations of human rights than those involved in the curbs placed on the freedom of association by Article 26. Taken together, they reveal that the drafters presumed that non-Muslims are disposed to be disloyal and to oppose Iran's Islamic Republic. Of course, given the Islamic bias in the system, such opposition would only be natural. In November 2005, Ayatollah Ahmad Jannati, a close associate of Ayatollah Ali Khamene'i, remarked in a speech that non-Muslims were not human beings but merely animals roaming the earth and engaging in corruption, indicating that clerical animus toward non-Muslims has not diminished over the years.[45]

Although Iran denies Christians, Jews, and Zoroastrians many rights and subjects them to discrimination and persecution, these minorities are distinctly better off than other non-Muslims who do not qualify as *ahl al-kitab*. The exclusion from the status of "recognized minorities," as expressly defined in Article 13, was particularly ominous for Iran's Baha'is.

The Baha'i religion, sometimes called Babism, originated in Iran in the nineteenth century. It is named after Baha'ullah, who in 1863 announced that he was a messenger from God and espoused liberal and ecumenical teachings. Baha'ism teaches veneration for the founders of all the major world religions and insists on the brotherhood and equality of all persons, stressing that men and women are meant to be equal. Baha'ism denies that clerics are needed as intermediaries in understanding religion, calling instead for universal education so that individuals can pursue the path of enlightenment. It also supports the idea of a world government and world peace.[46] Baha'i doctrines appealed to many of Iran's Muslims and led them to convert from Islam to the new faith.

Baha'is are subject to harsh discrimination in many Muslim countries. In Iran, the position of the Baha'i community, by far the largest in the Middle East, has always been precarious, and its members have suffered from periodic waves of persecution. From the beginning, Baha'ism has been perceived as a threat by Iran's clerics, and many of them have been violently hostile toward the religion. Since the nineteenth century, Shi'i clerics have supported attempts to eliminate Baha'ism from Iran through massacre, torture, intimidation, and discrimination.[47] This clerical animus was based on several grounds: Baha'ism challenged the doctrine of the finality of God's Revelation to the Prophet Muhammad; it tried to win converts from Islam, in violation of the *shari'a* prohibition of any conversion away from Islam to another faith; its egalitarian doctrines challenged the hierarchy of privilege mandated by the *shari'a,* according to which men are superior to women and Muslims superior to non-Muslims; and its members showed no inclination to defer to the views of Iran's clerics.

Given this long history of animosity toward the Baha'i community, which by the time of the Iranian Revolution may have numbered 200,000–300,000, it was natural that when Shi'i clerics achieved political dominance in the postrevolutionary regime, they would seek to eliminate Baha'ism once and for all. The government, sometimes acting directly and at other times indirectly through allied groups, has carried out a fierce campaign of terror against Baha'is, who have been slaughtered in large numbers. Hundreds of Baha'is were arrested, imprisoned, and subjected to brutal torture, and Baha'i leaders were executed on a variety of trumped-up charges. In addition, their shrines and houses of worship were destroyed and desecrated, and all of their associations were forcibly disbanded. They were fired from jobs, their property was confiscated, and their homes were subject to invasion at any time by persons bent on harassment and plunder in the guise of investigating "crimes." The savage persecution of the Baha'is has been extensively documented by neutral observers and international human rights organizations.[48]

Embarrassed by the bad publicity that Iran's discriminatory and cruel treatment of religious minorities has received, Iranian officials have made intermittent attempts to improve the country's image. For example, in 1999, a foreign ministry spokesman claimed that, following Islam and its constitution, Iran accorded full freedom to followers of all divine religions.[49] However, those trying to portray Iran as having tolerant and civilized standards vis-à-vis religious minorities found their efforts undermined as the Iranian government continued to lash out against non-Muslims. In a peculiar case that dragged on from 1999 to 2000, thirteen Jews in Shiraz were arbitrarily imprisoned and prosecuted on far-fetched charges of spying. A patently unfair trial culminated in the defendants' convictions.[50] As has often been the case in Iran, persecution based on religion morphed into prosecution for collaborating with the regime's foreign enemies—a secular rationale that the ruling clerics apparently deemed would be more acceptable to its critics.

Mawdudi and Pakistan's Ahmadi Minority

Abu'l A'la Mawdudi's vague, ambiguous position on equality has been appraised in previous chapters but merits further examination in connection with his views on the rights of non-Muslims. Just as Mawdudi avoided detailing his views on women's rights in his human rights pamphlet, he also steered clear of any specifics on how the *shari'a* affects non-Muslims. He merely mentioned *dhimmis* in passing, saying that their lives and properties are as "sacred" as those of Muslims.[51]

However, Mawdudi's views on this subject are on record in other publications, and in fact, he advocated discrimination against non-Muslims. According to him, Muslims were to be accorded superiority over non-Muslims. He favored reinstating the *jizya* tax traditionally imposed on *dhimmis*,[52] excluding them from military service,[53] and eliminating them from high positions in government.[54] He asserted that Islam "does not permit them to meddle with the affairs of the State."[55] Because Mawdudi believed that Islamic law should control personal-status matters as long as one party is a Muslim,[56] he believed that the *shari'a* prohibitions regarding intermarriage should be retained. Thus, although Mawdudi did not follow Tabandeh in acknowledging in the course of his discussion of human rights in Islam that he supported a regime of discrimination against non-Muslims, his other publications prove that he shared Tabandeh's views.

Mawdudi's Jama'at-i-Islami party was among the instigators of the Pakistani campaigns against the country's Ahmadi minority, who were later negatively affected by Zia's Islamization program. The experience of the Ahmadi minority demonstrates that in an era in which governments are adopting official versions of Islamic requirements as the law of the land, it is not only those who formally adhere to religions other than Islam who need to be concerned about their status in society; Muslims who adhere to minority sects or schools of thought may be demoted by governmental policy to the category of "non-Muslims." The treatment of the Ahmadi Muslim minority in Pakistan, a group of about 1 million people, provides a good illustration of how this can happen.

The Ahmadi sect was founded by Mirza Ghulam Ahmad (d. 1908) in India. Ahmadis, their opponents charge, treat their founder as a prophet, thereby violating the Islamic doctrine of the finality of the Prophethood of Muhammad. Although Ahmadis fervently believe that they are Muslims, they are considered heretics by many other Muslims. For a variety of reasons, Mawdudi's followers in the Jama'at-i-Islami became bitter foes of the Ahmadis, and the Jama'at was implicated in the serious disturbances that resulted from their anti-Ahmadi agitation in the Punjab in 1953.[57] Mawdudi wrote an anti-Ahmadi tract and was even incarcerated after being convicted of playing a leading role in anti-Ahmadi agitation.

In a concession to anti-Ahmadi sentiment, Prime Minister Zulfikar Ali Bhutto amended the constitution in 1974 to define the Ahmadis as non-Muslims. President Zia, who was closely allied with the Jama'at, went further and in 1984 issued a decree, the "Anti-Islamic Activities of the Quadiani Group, Lahori Group and Ahmadis (Prohibition and Punishment) Ordinance XX of 1984," forbidding Ahmadis to "pose" as Muslims or to call their religion Islam, to use Islamic terminology, to use the Islamic call to prayer, to call their houses of worship mosques, or to preach or propagate their version of the faith—all prohibitions under sanction of criminal law.[58] Extensive criminal prosecutions of Ahmadis ensued.

There have been various challenges to Ordinance XX, the most important of which resulted in it being affirmed in 1993 in *Zaheeruddin v. State* when the Supreme Court rejected the Ahmadis' claim that the ordinance violated the constitutional guarantee of freedom of religion.[59] This case showed how using the legal system to endorse the persecution of a religious minority can lead to consequences that have ominous implications for rights and freedoms more generally. A 1991 bill, the Enforcement of Shari'ah Act, had already proclaimed that the Qur'an and *sunna* were the supreme law of Pakistan and that law should be interpreted in the light of the *shari'a,* but the Court had initially resisted applying this principle to fundamental rights.[60] In *Zaheeruddin* the Supreme Court decided that the reference to "the Injunctions of Islam" that had previously been incorporated in the text of the constitution implied that the constitution itself was subordinated to Islamic criteria, including its provisions on fundamental rights.[61] However, the Court never troubled to define how "the Injunctions of Islam" affected rights protections, leaving this vague term open to being construed so broadly that rights could be essentially nullified. That is, through this judicial precedent, the Court essentially adopted the same provision that one sees in Iran's constitution in Articles 4 and 20. Thus, Islamization resulted in Pakistanis having human rights that could be overridden by Islamic criteria. Breaking with precedents that had upheld the supremacy of the constitution and safeguarded fundamental rights, the Court proceeded to rule that under Islamic law, Ordinance XX did not violate the constitutional guarantee of freedom of religion.

In a troubling development, in March 2005, after previously agreeing to remove a line in Pakistani passports identifying the holder's religion—a line that under Zia's Islamization program had been added to passports—the government capitulated to demands for the reinsertion of the line. Eliminating religious affiliation in passports had been supported by human rights groups and minorities, but this had provoked loud protests by various Islamist groups. Clearly, these groups wanted Pakistanis to be classed by religious affiliations in order to facilitate discrimination based on religion.

The Cairo Declaration, the Saudi Basic Law, and the Azhar Draft Constitution

Against the background of the prior Islamic rights schemes, one would expect that the Cairo Declaration, which duplicates so many of the flaws of its precursors, would also fail to ensure equality for non-Muslims. As I have already noted, there is no provision for equality in rights in the Cairo Declaration, even though the guarantee of equality in "basic human dignity" and "basic obligations and responsibilities" in Article l(a) does prohibit discrimination in these respects on the grounds of religious belief. The Cairo Declaration does not protect the rights of religious minorities any more than it protected women from being denied rights established in international law, particularly in a system like the one that it envisages, in which all rights and freedoms are subject to the *shari'a*. There is a vague provision in Article 18(a) to the effect that everyone shall have the right to live in security for himself and his religion, his dependents, his honor, and his property. This provides no real protection for religious minorities against discrimination, as can be seen in Article 23(b), which imposes *shari'a* restrictions on the right to serve in public office, in effect allowing the use of religious criteria to exclude non-Muslims.

The Azhar draft constitution avoids dealing with the status of non-Muslims. In the context of a document that seems to support the general applicability of premodern *shari'a* rules, the failure to address the issue suggests that the intent was to retain discriminatory rules governing the status of non-Muslims.

Virtually all Saudi citizens are Muslim, and Article 34 of the Basic Law provides that the defense of the Islamic faith is a duty imposed on every citizen. The Saudi Basic Law offers no protections whatsoever for the rights of non-Muslims.

However, Muslims are not insulated from mistreatment. According to Saudi officialdom, Islam is Wahhabism, a rigid creed deeply hostile to Shi'ism, and members of the large Shi'i minority in Saudi Arabia are vulnerable to persecution and are often treated as heretics.[62]

Non-Muslims, who are largely expatriates and exposed to discriminatory treatment on the basis of alienage, continue to be bereft of legal protections in all domains, which means that they are subject to police harassment for acts like worship in private. Because of the absence of any requirement for arrest warrants and the secrecy in which Saudi criminal proceedings are conducted, it is hard to ascertain which jailings and prosecutions of expatriates are actually based on their alienage as opposed to their religious affiliations. Thus, focusing on deficient protections for the religious rights of non-Muslims to the exclusion of the much broader pattern of human rights abuses in the country would be to isolate a problem that is in reality inseparable from the context from which it emerged, which is a legal order where discrimination against religious minorities, cruel abuse and exploitation of migrant laborers, harsh punishment of nonconformity and dissent, and aggressive and arbitrary police practices are pervasive.

US Policies on Religious Minorities and Developments in Afghanistan and Iraq

In 2004, pursuant to pressures from the US Commission on International Religious Freedom, the US State Department broke with a tradition of according lenient treatment to Saudi Arabia, abandoning the past policy of overlooking rights violations that would have been vigorously condemned had they been committed by a hostile government like Iran's. Under pressure from Christian groups angered by Saudi treatment of Christians, the State Department castigated Saudi deficiencies in religious tolerance and respect for the rights of religious minorities. In 2004 Saudi Arabia was placed with Burma, China, Eritrea, Iran, North Korea, Sudan, and Vietnam in the list of egregious human rights violators called the "Countries of Particular Concern," or CPCs.[63] It is unclear how US demands for enhanced protections for the rights of religious minorities will affect relations with Saudi Arabia or whether US complaints have any realistic prospects of ameliorating the situation. However, since these demands came at a juncture when the United States was accused of waging a crusade against Islam and infringing the sovereignty of Muslim countries, this call for improving the lot of religious minorities—in actuality Christians—in Arabia could well provoke a backlash.

In the post-invasion Afghan constitution, Article 2, which establishes Islam as the state religion, guarantees that followers of other religions are free to exercise their faith and perform their religious rites within the limits of the provisions of law. However, it is not specified what law, secular or Islamic, applies in this provision. Since Article 3 advises that no law shall contravene the beliefs and principles of the sacred religion of Islam, traditional Islamic rules affecting religious minorities could potentially be deployed under this rubric.

The United States was heavily involved in shaping the 2005 Iraqi constitution, which in Article 14 provided for equality before the law without discrimination because of religion, creed, belief or opinion. Article 2 guaranteed "full religious rights of all individuals to freedom of religious belief and practice"—mentioning Christians, Yazidis, and Sabeans, which was in addition to the Article 41 provision declaring that the state guaranteed freedom of worship. However, given that Article 2 also provided that Islam was the state religion and was a basic source of legislation, this provision might be customized to fit Islamic criteria. In the meantime, the sectarian polarization and Islamist fervor that had been stirred up by the US invasion and occupation has resulted in intensified intercommunal antagonisms. Local Christians were terrorized, leading them to flee in large numbers, potentially portending the decimation of some of the world's most ancient Christian communities.

Summary

The Islamic human rights schemes discussed here do not respect the requirements of international law regarding protections for the rights of religious minorities. In fact, to the extent that they deal with the question of the rights of religious minorities, they seem to endorse premodern *shari'a* rules that call for non-Muslims to be relegated to an inferior status if they qualify as members of the *ahl al-kitab* and for them to be treated as nonpersons if they do not qualify for such inclusion.

Not only does the record of the treatment of religious minorities in countries undergoing Islamization show that policies are being implemented that relegate religious minorities to second-class status, but it also establishes that Middle Eastern regimes are in some instances ready to engage in campaigns of religious persecution directed at non-Muslims. Moreover, as indicated, regimes that discriminate against their non-Muslim citizens tend to be equally ready to mistreat Muslims who belong to minorities or who refuse to defer meekly to their versions of orthodoxy.

CHAPTER 8

Freedom of Religion in Islamic Human Rights Schemes

Controversies Regarding the *Shari'a* Rule on Apostasy

In the West, the concept of apostasy as a criminal offense seems outmoded, so people there do not tend to think of the freedom to change religion as a central concern of provisions guaranteeing religious freedom. In Muslim milieus, the perspective is different, since attitudes are influenced by the *shari'a* rule prohibiting conversion from Islam, and the issues surrounding the punishment of Muslims for leaving the faith remain contentious. The transformation of Islam into state ideology has led governments to equate the abandonment of Islam—or more accurately, the rejection of the official ideology—with treason. The traditional notion that apostates are to be executed has taken on new life after decades in which there was an inclination to let the premodern Islamic jurisprudence on this topic languish.

Under the interpretations of the premodern jurists, apostasy was a crime. Apostates were to be given an opportunity to repent and return to Islam, but if they refused, they were to be executed if they were male or imprisoned until they changed their minds if they were female. Premodern *shari'a* rules also provided that apostasy constituted civil death, meaning, among other things, that the apostate's marriage would be dissolved, and the apostate would become incapable of inheriting. Naturally, the *shari'a* imposed no penalty on conversion to Islam from other faiths. Given this background, when one evaluates Islamic versions of human rights, it is particularly important to determine whether the schemes contemplate the retention of the *shari'a* prohibition on apostasy.

Muslims who currently call for the execution of apostates can find some juristic authority for their position, but they are ignoring other plausible interpretations of the Islamic sources that are more in keeping with modern ideas of religious freedom. Muslims who have repudiated the penalty argue that the premodern juristic interpretations were unwarranted by the texts of the Islamic sources.[1] The principle of tolerance for religious difference, which figures prominently in the Islamic value system and tradition, can support the notion that religious adherence should be a matter of conscience. In the Qur'an 2:26 one reads a specific admonition that there must be no compulsion in religion. Progressive interpretations note that no verse in the Qur'an stipulates any earthly penalty for apostasy and that the premodern jurists' rules on apostasy were extrapolated from incidents in the Prophet's life and from historical events after his death that are open to a variety of constructions. Having drawn distinctions between the Qur'anic respect for freedom of conscience and the concerns of public order that historically led jurists to devise a rule that the apostate should be punished by death, a Muslim scholar has concluded that the Qur'anic principle of religious liberty shares common foundations with the Western concept of religious liberty.[2]

Contemporary scholars have found many reasons for rethinking the jurists' rule that the apostate must be killed. For example, the Lebanese scholar Subhi Mahmassani asserted that the circumstances in which the penalty was meant to apply were intended to be narrow ones. He pointed out that the Prophet never killed anyone merely for apostasy. Instead, the death penalty was applied when the act of apostasy from Islam was linked to an act of political betrayal of the community. This being the case, Mahmassani argued that the death penalty was not meant to apply to a simple change of faith but to punish acts such as treason, joining forces with the enemy, and sedition.[3] Another Muslim thinker understands the Qur'an to say that God wants submission to Islam "in full consciousness and freedom," indicating that religious liberty is fundamental to respect for God's plan for humanity. This plan includes the mysterious privilege of rejecting Islam's message of salvation, a privilege that precludes recourse to compulsion or killing in matters of faith.[4]

Muslim Countries Confront Freedom of Religion

International human rights law allows no constraints on a person's religious beliefs: Freedom of religion is an unqualified freedom. One of the most influential statements of this freedom is in Article 18 of the Universal Declaration of Human Rights (UDHR). Article 18 states: "Everyone has the right to freedom of thought, conscience and religion; this right includes freedom to change his religion or belief, and freedom, either alone or in community with others and in public or private, to manifest his religion or belief in teaching, practice, worship and observance." Freedom of religion is unqualified in the International Covenant on Civil and Political Rights (ICCPR) Article 18.1. Although the wording is similar to UDHR Article 18, the ICCPR provision does not specifically mention the freedom to change religion.

It is historically significant that the phrase guaranteeing the right to change religion was added to the UDHR at the behest of the delegate from Lebanon (a Christian). Lebanon in the 1940s and 1950s was an oasis of religious pluralism and toleration, where large Christian, Muslim, and Druze communities coexisted. It seemed incongruous to the Lebanese that Christians could convert to Islam but that Muslims were barred from converting to Christianity. Not surprisingly, when the Lebanese representative proposed that this language be added, he faced objections from some Muslim countries.

Similar objections were later raised in other contexts. Iran, in discussions of the 1981 Declaration on the Elimination of All Forms of Intolerance, asserted that Muslims were not allowed to convert from their religion and were to be executed if they did so.[5] The Convention on the Rights of the Child (CRC), the most widely ratified of all the human rights conventions, guarantees a child's freedom of religion in Article 14. Although some Muslim countries ratified the CRC without reservation, others ratified subject to the qualification that they would uphold Islamic law in cases of conflict, using a variety of formulations in their reservations. Whereas some expressly invoked Islamic law in reserving, others resorted to circumlocutions, invoking their constitutions, which incorporated Islamic principles. Afghanistan, Iran, and Saudi Arabia entered sweeping reservations when ratifying the CRC, indicating that they would not be bound by provisions contravening Islamic law, potentially encompassing Article 14. In the Middle Eastern region, Algeria, Iraq, Jordan, Kuwait, Morocco, Oman, Pakistan, Qatar, Syria, and the U.A.E. entered specific reservations to Article 14.[6] Perhaps these countries were more willing to register their nonacceptance of freedom of religion in a context where paternal control over children was at issue. After all, in Middle Eastern countries, family solidarity and paternal authority are sacrosanct, and it is assumed that children must adhere to the religion of their father. These public statements by Muslim governments indicated their continued estrangement from the principle of freedom of religion.

The Contemporary Significance of Apostasy

Since Islam is the world's fastest-growing religion and attempts to convert from Islam are uncommon, one might find the efforts to ban apostasy puzzling. Many may consider the issue of whether Muslims are free to convert to other religions to be an academic one rather than a practical one. After all, it seems fair to assume that the number of persons affected by the *shari'a* ban on apostasy would be minimal. However, the ban on conversion from Islam has broad ramifications and potentially limits the rights of a much larger segment of the populations of Muslim countries than one might initially surmise.

As interpreted, the ban can apply to people who are born into a non-Muslim religion but whose parents, grandparents, or even more distant ancestors converted from Islam. The notion that Baha'is started as renegades from Islam has been one basis for their persecution in Iran since the revolution. Although the targeted individuals had not changed their religion, they were affected by the Iranian belief that most Baha'is are descendants of Muslim converts. The record shows that Iranian Baha'is may be punished and persecuted as apostates by virtue of their ancestors' defections from Islam.

The ban can also affect Muslims who adhere to doctrines that are out of keeping with whatever standard of orthodoxy is currently being espoused by powerful Islamic institutions or governments pursuing Islamization. Although premodern Islamic culture was generally tolerant of diverging views on questions of Islamic theology and law, when contemporary Middle Eastern governments have adopted Islamization programs or have tried to accommodate pressures for Islamization, they have tended to demand adherence to a uniform national version of Islam. As the official orthodoxy becomes identified with the regime's own ideology and legitimacy, modern governments have been inclined to label Muslims who do not accept the official version of Islam as heretics and apostates. The circumstances under which the Ahmadi minority in Pakistan was legally designated "non-Muslim" and was made a target of discrimination and persecution under the official Islamization program have already been discussed. Likewise, the Sudanese Republicans officially became "apostates" from Islam under Ja'far al-Nimeiri, even though they never repudiated Islam and believed that they were following authentic Islamic teachings. Thus, the ban on apostasy has become a curb on the religious freedom of Muslims—not only on their freedom to convert from Islam but also on their freedom to follow a particular version of Islamic teachings.

In the climate of intolerance that has been fostered by official Islamization campaigns and Islamist activism, Muslims following a particular sect or line of interpretation may be singled out by other Muslims as apostates, thereby exposing them to discrimination, harassment, and even assassination. This trend has grown so destructive and menacing that in July 2005 a meeting of high-ranking Islamic clerics was convened in Jordan to produce a declaration that denounced the practice of one group of Muslims calling others apostates, asserting that this was an affront to Islamic values and demanding that it cease. Although the declaration affirmed that both Sunnis and Shi'is are true Muslims, it failed explicitly to call for an end to the persecutions of more heterodox groups as apostates.[7]

Furthermore, the prohibition against conversion from Islam has significant implications for the freedom of Muslim women, preventing them from escaping *shari'a* law. The choice-of-law rules that are in force in most Muslim countries mean that religious affiliation decides which law is applicable to personal-status issues. Only in rare instances, such as in Turkey and Tunisia, where far-reaching reforms have been enacted, have Muslim countries modernized their personal-status rules so that one national standard applies to all citizens. Elsewhere, *shari'a* law still applies to personal-status questions where one or both of the parties is Muslim.[8]

In such systems, if there were no ban on conversion, a Muslim woman could change the personal-status law applicable to her simply by abandoning Islam or converting to another religion. Such conversions might be undertaken for purely practical reasons—to avoid the strictures of an unfavorable law—rather than being inspired by theological considerations. In the Middle East, conversions from one religion to another—and sometimes switches from one Islamic sect or school of law to another—have long been used to change the applicable law in personal-status issues. These conversions are the equivalent of forum shopping in the United States, where litigants, by changing their domicile from one state to another, can alter the law applicable to their family law and inheritance issues—"shopping" for the forum that has a more favorable law.

Conversions—including conversions to Islam—potentially enable parties to accomplish objectives impossible to achieve under their original personal-status law. For example, in a Middle Eastern country, a Roman Catholic woman married to a Catholic man would be barred from divorcing, but if she wanted a divorce, she could sever her marital tie by converting to Islam. Then her marriage would become void, for she would gain the benefit of the *shari'a* rule that a Muslim woman cannot be validly married to a non-Muslim. A non-Muslim man might also convert to Islam to gain the benefit of a more favorable personal-status law, such as a lenient divorce rule. Penalizing conversion from Islam can be utilized to deter "conversions" undertaken out of expediency by preventing such opportunists from converting back to their original faiths after they achieve an objective made possible by their temporary status as Muslims.

One of the options, admittedly a drastic one, open to Muslim women who seek to sever their marital ties but are unable to obtain a divorce is that of apostasy. By virtue of becoming apostates, Muslims incur civil death, regardless of whether a criminal penalty is imposed, and the civil death of one party terminates a marriage. Thus, the Muslim woman who is willing to incur civil death can escape from her marriage and from the applicability of *shari'a* law.

In the past, many informal social and cultural factors inhibited Muslim women from taking such a radical course, but these inhibitions are crumbling under the impact of major social changes. In intact traditional communities, the ostracism incurred by apostasy from Islam would inhibit women from taking such a drastic action, but such communities are being undermined by rapid urbanization and economic transformations that make it possible for women to become mobile and self-supporting. Improved educational opportunities, exposure to different social models through the media, a more skeptical attitude toward the traditional subordination of women, and other factors may lead women to chafe under an onerous marital tie that formerly might have been tolerated. In these changed circumstances, the prospect of achieving freedom through apostasy may be alluring.

Thus, there is a connection between the refusal of Islamic human rights schemes to allow freedom to change religion and their authors' determination to uphold traditional personal-status rules. Because Muslim women are emerging from their traditional roles at a time when modern ideologies favoring equal rights for women are spreading, the authors of Islamic human rights schemes anticipate challenges from Muslim women. In such circumstances, where *shari'a* rules are converted into a scheme for controlling and subjugating one-half of the population, it becomes essential to block any means by which women can evade the applicability of the *shari'a* through the manipulation of choice-of-law rules.

That Muslim women may be tempted to abandon Islam concerned Sultan-hussein Tabandeh, who has identified a number of discreditable reasons for which Muslim men might convert, while positing a Muslim woman's desire "to exploit easier conditions for divorce obtaining under other religions" as the sole reason for apostasy in a woman's case.[9] He sensed that the temptation to escape a marriage by way of apostasy was a real threat and that, in the wake of societal changes, the state would have to intervene with a strong deterrent. This led him to propose a penalty that has no counterpart in the premodern *shari'a*: life imprisonment at hard labor for the female apostate.[10]

In Kuwait, where a Muslim woman's ability to opt out of the *shari'a* system has likewise been perceived as a threat, a different legal solution was found. There, a law was enacted discarding the premodern *shari'a* rule that a Muslim woman's marriage would be automatically dissolved by her apostasy. The reason for this change was offered in an explanatory memorandum accompanying the text of the reform: "Complaints have shown that the Devil makes the route of apostasy attractive to the Muslim woman so that she can break a conjugal tie that does not please her. For this reason, it was decided that apostasy would not lead to the dissolution of the marriage in order to close this dangerous door."[11] One sees that in Kuwait, fidelity to the *shari'a* takes second place to concerns for preserving the patriarchal order; the *shari'a* tradition of civil death for the apostate has been abandoned due to worries that this traditional penalty is insufficient to deter women from exploiting the apostasy rules to terminate their marriages. With the change in the law, Muslim women in Kuwait can no longer open "this dangerous door."

Given this background, one can see that in the Middle East the freedom to change religion constitutes a far more significant dimension of religious freedom than it does in the West. However, until recently, the progressive Westernization of Middle Eastern legal systems seemed to promise that the practical importance of *shari'a* restrictions on religious freedom would diminish. Because of the nineteenth- and twentieth-century reforms in the area of criminal law, the application of the *shari'a* death penalty for apostasy from Islam became a rarity. In this regard, the Islamization of Middle Eastern law has resulted in dramatic changes. What until recently seemed to be an anachronism has been revived in ways that have led to serious breaches of international human rights in the name of applying *shari'a* law.

Even where no rule mandating execution of apostates from Islam has been incorporated in the criminal code, governments that have undertaken Islamization programs may nonetheless execute people for apostasy from Islam—as if the *shari'a* rules were binding even in the absence of corresponding provisions in the criminal code. However, it seems that governments that readily execute apostates are often reluctant to proclaim publicly that they kill people for their religious beliefs or to enact laws that confirm that the death penalty applies to converts from Islam. For example, trying to counter damaging publicity about its executions of Baha'is, Iran has proclaimed that apostasy is not a crime under its codified laws, which is true, and in 1995 falsely assured a UN rapporteur that "conversion was not a crime and no one had been punished for converting."[12] Thus, not only do Iran's ruling theocrats avoid stipulating in law that apostates are to be executed, but they also deny their practice of killing Baha'is as apostates.

In Egypt since the 1970s there have been insistent demands for a revival of the death penalty for apostasy from Islam.[13] These demands have met energetic opposition on the part of Egypt's large Coptic population and have also been opposed by liberal and secular forces. Although the Egyptian government in 1980 changed the constitution to make the *shari'a* the main source of legislation, it resisted attempts to have the death penalty for apostasy from Islam incorporated in its criminal law. However, many instances of harassment and intimidation of Egyptian Muslims who convert to other religions have been reported.

The notorious 1994–1996 case of the Cairo University professor Nasr Hamid Abu Zaid, divorced against his will for his alleged apostasy, showed that Egypt's courts were prepared to penalize religious dissent by classifying it as apostasy.[14] Egypt's personal status laws allow recourse to Islamic law in default of an applicable code provision, meaning that, where there are gaps, judges can treat the works of the jurists of the Hanafi school of law as authority. A third party, totally unrelated to Abu Zaid, was allowed to bring a personal-status law claim asserting that, according to Hanafi jurisprudence, Abu Zaid's marriage to his Muslim wife had to be dissolved because his writings showed that he was an apostate. Ignoring the conventional view that a person who is a professing Muslim should be deemed a Muslim, the courts decided that Abu Zaid's religious faith had been placed in doubt. They reviewed Abu Zaid's writings, which called for revising conventional approaches to Qur'an interpretation, and agreed that his theories on how the Qur'an should be read made him an apostate. On this basis, the courts declared his marriage dissolved. They referred to the constitutional protection for freedom of religion but interpreted it within the context of the Islamic legal tradition.[15] That is, although the constitution did not expressly place Islamic qualifications on religious freedom, the courts acted as if such qualifications were implicit and found that they supported the decision to rule Abu Zaid an apostate.

The Abu Zaid case also illustrates how the human rights issues of religious freedom and women's status are interlinked. The upholders of the premodern *shari'a* insist that the wife must be subordinate to her husband, which makes it intolerable for her, if she is a Muslim, to be married to a non-Muslim, since Islam—the Muslim woman being a marker for Islam—must not be subordinated to another faith. They also refuse to accept the principle that both men and women should be allowed freely to choose their spouses, without any hindrances based on religion. One could say that the outcome of the Abu Zaid case could be as readily attributed to Egypt's failure to accord women equality as to Egypt's failure to uphold religious freedom.

Among other things, the Abu Zaid case proves that the quarrel of Sunni orthodoxy with Mu'tazilite ideas, which are discussed in Chapter 3, is far from over, since many of his controversial positions were closely linked to the rationalist approach to Islam advocated by the Mu'tazilites.[16] Abu Zaid took stances at odds with the notion, popular among contemporary proponents of Islam as an ideology, that the Qur'an possesses a univocal meaning, emphasizing instead the diversity in interpretations.[17] Moreover, he disputed the tenet that Islam covers all domains, arguing that areas such as human rights are based on developments outside the sphere of religion.[18] Like the Iranian philosophy professor Abdolkarim Soroush, who has been persecuted for uttering similar views, Abu Zaid critically appraised the consequences of the monopoly over Qur'anic interpretation exercised by state theologians dependent on local rulers, claiming that such a scenario leads to repressing new interpretations and critical questions.[19] As if anticipating his own fate, he charged that this results in the ideological exploitation of the Qur'an to legitimize reality and in the branding of Muslims who fight against this situation as unbelievers, atheists, and heretics.[20]

Although the actual implementation of the divorce ruling was ultimately stayed, and Egypt subsequently changed its laws to prevent private parties from bringing such suits in the future, these belated responses did not protect Abu Zaid and his wife from the religious zealots who were ready to enforce their own version of Islamic justice. They threatened to kill him for his supposed apostasy or to kill them both for living together in sin after they had been forcibly divorced. The couple was obliged to seek asylum in Europe, where they have remained. This outcome is a reminder that in the climate of intolerance prevailing in many Muslim countries, it is not necessary for the state to impose a death penalty for an "apostate" to be severely penalized.

The outcome of the case also shows why it is an oversimplification to ascribe such rulings to Islamic law. After all, the objective of the premodern jurists was to punish Muslims who abandoned their faith and to deter defections from the early Islamic community. In Abu Zaid's case, a committed, professing Muslim who had been a member in good standing of the Muslim community and who wished to revitalize Islamic scholarship through his study of the Qur'an was cast out of the community against his wishes and on the flimsy basis of a decision by a secular court that happened to find his challenges to received opinions offensive. From punishment for a willful act of abandonment of the faith, "apostasy" had been converted into an arbitrary sanction that courts representing national governments, not the Islamic community, could mete out to Muslim believers who elected to take different paths to understanding scripture. In consequence of the "apostasy" ruling, two Muslims became outcasts and were forced to uproot themselves from their Muslim homeland and move for their own safety to live as exiles in non-Muslim territory.

Ironically, the same Egyptian courts whose rulings showed flagrant disregard for freedom of religion devoted considerable effort to arguing that the forcible divorce of a couple on the grounds of the husband's allegedly heretical religious beliefs did not conflict with freedom of religion as set forth in Egypt's constitution.[21] Like the authors of the Islamic human rights schemes that are reviewed here, the judges did not want to acknowledge that their recourse to Islamic criteria led to denying religious freedom, effectively revealing that the principle of freedom of religion was one that they recognized as authoritative at the same time that they were flouting it.

As I have argued throughout this book, human rights violations that seem at first blush to be tied to the Islamic tradition often turn out upon closer inspection to be intertwined with local politics. Abu Zaid himself claims that he was targeted for persecution as an apostate for reasons that had nothing to do with his religious views; it was, he said, retaliation for his criticisms of an Islamic investment scheme in which a powerful personage had an interest. Given the religious fervor whipped up by Islamic demagogues, and given the government's disinclination to intervene to protect a controversial intellectual, the stage was set for the offended individual to exact his revenge by having Abu Zaid labeled an apostate.

However, even if the original impetus behind the lawsuit was revenge for embarrassment caused by his criticism of a financial scheme, Abu Zaid's liberal views and his arguments on behalf of a reformed understanding of the relationship of the believer to the Islamic sources had also made him a target of conservative ire. He was vulnerable to the same kinds of denunciations and assaults that have forced so many of Islam's distinguished thinkers into exile. With important Islamic reformers seeking refuge in Europe and North America, it is not surprising that Islamic thought within the Middle East is often so stale. As one author who has written about the Abu Zaid case laments, it is precisely the most creative, the brightest, and the most courageous spirits in the Muslim world who are slandered, attacked, persecuted, and killed by their own culture—this for trying to take up the challenge of preserving their culture and identity in a changing world.[22] One should bear this in mind when Islam is portrayed as a reactionary and oppressive religion: The Muslims who could transform Islam into a more open system and who offer an enlightened version of their faith are all too often deterred from challenging orthodoxy because of the risk of sharing the fate that befell Abu Zaid and others like him.

In any event, this grim case illustrates why protecting freedom of religion is at least as important for Muslims as it is for the non-Muslim populations in predominantly Muslim countries. It is an illusion to think that a system that persecutes members of the Muslim majority can protect the religious freedom of minorities.

Tabandeh's Ideas

Not surprisingly, Sultanhussein Tabandeh is the most candid of the authors in calling for the retention of premodern Islamic rules restricting religious freedom. As we have seen, in his view, *dhimmis* do enjoy the right to practice their own religions, but this is not the case for adherents of other religions. Because they are largely descended from Muslims who converted, members of the Baha'i faith are considered by Tabandeh to be defectors from Islam who must be forced to recant and return to the fold. In what appears to be a thinly veiled attack on the Baha'i faith, Tabandeh asserted that "followers of a religion of which the basis is contrary to Islam, like those who demand Islam's extirpation, have no official rights to freedom of religion in Islamic countries or under an Islamic government, nor can they claim respect through their religion, any more than in certain countries definite political parties which are contrary to the ideology of the regime can claim freedom since they are declared to be inimical to the welfare of the land and people."[23] This view relates to Tabandeh's assumption that under Islam, religion and politics are united; Islam is effectively ideologized and classed as a political philosophy, and thus the government cannot be divorced from the official religion.[24]

Tabandeh said that "propaganda" for any religion other than Islam must be prohibited.[25] His position on this is a consequence of his unyielding insistence that conversion from Islam should not be tolerated because there is no legitimate reason for abandoning the Islamic faith: "No man of sense, from the mere fact that he possesses intelligence, will ever turn down the better in favor of the inferior. Anyone who penetrates beneath the surface to the inner essence of Islam is bound to recognize its superiority over the other religions. A man, therefore, who deserts Islam, by that act betrays the fact that he must have played truant to its moral and spiritual truths earlier."[26]

The reasons why a person might desert Islam, according to a speech by the Egyptian UN representative cited by Tabandeh, include duress, bribes, and a woman's desire "to exploit easier conditions for divorce obtaining under some other religions."[27] As other possible inducements to abandon Islam, Tabandeh listed false promises by another religion, spite on the part of a Muslim who has been injured by another Muslim, and being led astray by carnal lusts that Islam forbids.[28] Believing that straying from Islam is never justified, he opines that conversions from Islam should not be given encouragement, "let alone by an international law." A person born in Islam who deserts after coming of age must be killed since he is "diseased . . . gangrenous, incurable, fit only for amputation."[29] A person who was not born Muslim but converted to Islam and then leaves it is given three days to reconsider his apostasy, after which, if he fails to return to the faith, he must be executed.[30] To illustrate the solicitude of Islam for women's welfare, Tabandeh proposes that the female apostate is not to be killed but is to be offered a more lenient fate, being condemned "to life imprisonment with hard labor."[31] In contrast, Tabandeh noted that "a person who gives up some religion other than Islam to accept Islam's sound faith is received and respected."[32]

For Tabandeh, there are only two categories—Islamic truth and error. Seemingly unaware that such an approach is incompatible with international norms, he assumes that it is feasible to project these categories into international law. He apparently imagines that once those who make international law are made to understand the reasons why Islam forbids conversion, international law will likewise decree that conversions from Islam should be banned.[33]

It is worth considering how Tabandeh's arguments for banning conversion from Islam contrast with a central premise of international human rights law— that individuals are the best judges of their own interests, because individuals ultimately have greater insight into what they need to be happy. International human rights law is based on the assumption that exercising the freedom to choose, a fundamental right, is part of what is involved in being human and achieving dignity and self-respect.[34] It is therefore disposed to afford strong protection for the individual's freedom of choice in a matter like religious belief. In contrast, Tabandeh absolutely rejects the right of individuals freely to follow their consciences in matters of faith.

The UIDHR

The Universal Islamic Declaration of Human Rights (UIDHR) purports to treat the "Right to Freedom of Belief, Thought and Speech" in Article 12.a, but, again, it uses formulations in the English and Arabic versions that convey very different impressions. In the English, Article 12.a states: "Every person has the right to express his thoughts and beliefs so long as he remains within the limits prescribed by the Law. No one, however, is entitled to disseminate falsehood or to circulate reports that may outrage public decency, or to indulge in slander, innuendo, or to cast defamatory aspersions on other persons."

At first glance this provision appears to impose neutral, secular restraints on freedom of expression, while sidestepping the issue of freedom of belief. The idea that slanderous, defamatory speech can be curbed by law seems unobjectionable. The standards for curbing freedom of expression in this article are left sufficiently broad to allow for government interpretations that might make serious inroads in the area of freedom of expression, but if one assumed that the qualifications would be interpreted narrowly, one might find this formulation in substantial conformity with international norms.

The Arabic version of Article 12.a conveys a very different message because it reveals that Islamic criteria limit freedom of expression. It states: "Everyone may think, believe and express his ideas and beliefs without interference or opposition from anyone as long as he obeys the limits [hudud] set by the shari'a. It is not permitted to spread falsehood [al-batil] or disseminate that which involves encouraging abomination [al-fahisha] or forsaking the Islamic community [takhdhil li'l-umma]."[35] Thus, shari'a rules set limits not just on freedom of expression but also on the freedoms of thought and belief. As has already been pointed out, using the criteria of one religion to set limits on rights is unacceptable under international human rights law.

One can surmise what specific rules in the shari'a would likely be employed to curtail these freedoms. For example, one would expect that in a system based on the shari'a, people would be prohibited from attempting to convert Muslims to other faiths and would be forbidden to speak disparagingly of the Prophet. However, since there are no specific standards delineating the shari'a limits on the freedoms involved here, the scope of the *shari'a* restraints that could be imposed under this provision is potentially very broad.

The significance of the second sentence is difficult to ascertain. The English version suggests that defamation and slander are categories of expression that are not protected, but the Arabic version appears to deny protection to quite different categories of expression. Falsehood, the encouragement of abomination, or the forsaking of the Islamic community could be banned, but since these vague, value-laden terms have no settled meanings as they apply to limiting human rights, one cannot predict how the authorities would interpret them. It is conceivable that any speech that might threaten to diminish loyalty to the local version of Islamic orthodoxy could be banned. The provision also seems to allow broad censorship in order to protect morality. Here, as in other instances, the open-ended nature of the qualifications has the potential to emasculate the very freedoms that the UIDHR makes a pretense of granting.

"Right to Freedom of Religion" is the (misleading) rubric for Article 13 of the UIDHR. This article states in the English version that everyone has the right to freedom of conscience and worship in accordance with his religious beliefs. The wording is different from the wording of comparable international human rights principles, but the difference is a relatively subtle one.[36]

The significance of the difference between Article 13 and the relevant international standards is more readily ascertained if one consults the Arabic version, which states that everyone has freedom of belief and freedom of worship according to the principle, "you have your religion, I have mine." This line is taken from the Qur'anic sura "*al-kafirun,*" 109:6. *Al-kafirun* can mean "unbelievers," "infidels," or "atheists"; in any case, it has strong negative connotations. The complete sura runs as follows, in Marmaduke Pickthall's flowery translation: "Say: O disbelievers [*al-kafirun*] I worship not that which ye worship; Nor worship ye that which I worship. And I shall not worship that which ye worship. Nor will ye worship that which I worship. Unto you your religion, and unto me my religion."[37] The sura contemplates a division between Islam and "unbelief." It lays the groundwork for coexistence but does not attempt to establish any principle of freedom of religion comparable to that found in international human rights documents. If there is a right implied in this provision, it is the right to follow one's own religion, which in a *shari'a*-based system would be a right accorded only to Muslims and, within limits, to the *ahl al-kitab*. As a consequence of being obliged to follow their own religion, Muslims would be bound by *shari'a* rules, meaning that they would not be allowed to convert from Islam and could be executed if they did so.

The Arabic version of Section 7 of the Preamble of the UIDHR is relevant for appreciating the religious bias in this system. The English version of this section seems quite neutral and innocuous, calling for a society in which "all worldly

power shall be considered as a sacred trust, to be exercised within the limits prescribed by the Law and in a manner approved by it, and with due regard for the
priorities fixed by it." In sharp contrast, the same section in the Arabic version is
an expression of a commitment to a society where all people believe that Allah
alone is the master of all creation. This is tantamount to a commitment to converting the world's population to Islam, a commitment that is not compatible
with the attitudes that shaped the international human rights norms regarding
freedom of religion.

The Azhar Draft Constitution

The Azhar draft of an Islamic constitution states in the English version of Article
29 that "within the limits of the Islamic *shari'a,* the Government provides for the
natural basic rights of religious and intellectual beliefs." In this obscure formulation, there is no mention of any freedom of religion. Given this omission, the article could provide the same kind of "right" to follow one's own religion—without
granting any right for Muslims to change religion—that was set forth in Article 13
of the UIDHR, which is discussed in a previous section. In contrast, the same article of the Azhar draft constitution expressly mentions "freedoms" of labor and expression and personal "freedom." The omission of the "freedom" *(hurriya)* of
religion is unlikely to be accidental, particularly given the fact that "the natural basic rights" set forth in the article are offered only "within the limits of the Islamic
shari'a." Any doubts about whether the application of these limits is intended to
restrict the freedom of religion in accordance with premodern *shari'a* rules are removed by Article 71 of the draft constitution, which provides for the application
of the death penalty for apostasy. Since the *shari'a* sets the governing standards,
this penalty can only apply to apostasy from Islam. The relative candor of the
Azhar draft with respect to the death penalty for apostasy from Islam is in striking
contrast to the evasiveness one normally encounters on the part of Muslims who
intend to retain the rule but seek to convey the impression that they respect human rights.

The willingness of al-Azhar to call openly for the execution of persons who
abandon Islam is probably the result of several factors. The al-Azhar University
is the oldest institution of higher learning in Islam and the most prestigious center for training in Sunni Islam—and a very conservative one. Given the emphasis on the study of traditional Islamic sciences and premodern jurisprudence in
the curriculum, Azhar clerics are unlikely to be conversant with modern liberal
democratic values or well versed in international human rights law. Moreover,
the relative candor of the Azharites may have been a natural outcome of circumstances in Cairo. At the time of the drafting of the Azhar constitution the question of whether to execute apostates was a very hotly contested issue on the

Cairo scene. Given the intensity of the controversy about the death penalty for apostasy, it would have been difficult for a Cairene institution like al-Azhar to sidestep the issue of punishment for apostasy even if the Azharites had been motivated to do so. Furthermore, the draft was merely a proposal for what Azharites would ideally like to see incorporated in a constitution. Because their exercise was an academic one, the authors of the Azhar draft were not forced to accede to political compromises with disaffected Egyptian Copts. Nor did the drafters have to accommodate those politicians and jurists who were abreast of modern trends in constitutionalism.

The Iranian Constitution

The rights provisions of the 1979 Iranian constitution also fail to address the issue of religious freedom as such. It is significant that a constitution that in many respects copies the French model should have eliminated any protection for religious freedom from its list of rights. However, Article 23 does forbid interrogating or attacking people because of their beliefs. This provision might be interpreted as meaning that religious persecution should be outlawed. Whatever the original intent or hopes of the drafters of this article may have been, the Iranian government has certainly not interpreted it as a guarantee of freedom of religion or as a protection for religious minorities.

The conduct of the Iranian government serves as a gloss on the meaning of the protections afforded by Article 23. The extensive persecutions of Iran's Baha'is unequivocally establish that the Iranian government does not believe that Article 23 prevents interrogating or attacking members of disfavored religious minorities because of their religious beliefs.[38] Baha'is have been put under enormous pressure to recant their beliefs and return to Islam. It is well established that Baha'is are persecuted on the basis of their religious beliefs, because trumped-up criminal charges leveled against them have been dropped when Baha'is have repented and proclaimed their adherence to Islam.[39] That they are deemed apostates can also be seen in the fact that Baha'is are treated as persons who have incurred civil death, the consequence of apostasy from Islam under *shari'a* law. Thus, for example, all Baha'i marriages have been declared invalid, sexual intercourse between the former spouses has been treated as fornication (punishable by death), and the children of the dissolved marriages have been declared illegitimate, thereby depriving their parents of any claim to them.[40]

Despite the extensive evidence that the persecution of the Baha'is is religiously motivated, in communications designed for international audiences, the Iranian government has gone to great lengths to justify executions of Baha'is on the grounds that those executed had been guilty of political crimes. Executed Baha'is are routinely alleged to be guilty of spying for Israel or the CIA. Reclassifying

Baha'is as "traitors," "spies," and "conspirators" enables Iran to pretend that its criminal justice system follows a more conventional model than it actually does. In international forums, the regime insists that Baha'is who are not guilty of anti-regime activities are not molested and asserts that Iran does not persecute Baha'is for religious reasons.[41]

A comment published by the Iranian attorney general intended to debunk charges that Baha'is were being persecuted for religious reasons is revealing of the regime's attitude:

> Now, if a Baha'i himself performs his religious acts in accordance with his own beliefs, such a man will not be bothered by us, provided he does not invite others to Baha'ism, does not teach, does not form assemblies, does not give news to others, and has nothing to do with the administration [of the Baha'i community]. Not only do we not execute such people, we do not even imprison them, and they can work within society. If, however, they decide to work within their administration, this is a criminal act and is forbidden, the reason being that such administration is considered to be hostile and conspiratorial and such people are conspirators.[42]

Even if one accepted this disavowal at face value, one would see that the regime had acknowledged its anti-Baha'i policies and its refusal to grant Baha'is religious freedom on a par with adherents of other faiths. The attorney general effectively admitted in this statement that the religion and its institutions were officially associated with treasonous, conspiratorial activities, making it impossible for Baha'is to worship or associate with each other without risking criminal prosecution.

In trying to argue to an international audience that the prosecution of the Baha'i population is political rather than religious in character, the Iranian government has pretended that a distinction is made in Iran between political and religious crimes. However, this is a distinction that by the terms of Article 168 of the Iranian constitution cannot, in fact, exist. The second sentence in Article 168 reads: "The definition of a political crime, the manner in which the jury will be selected, their qualifications and the limits of their authority shall be determined by law, based upon Islamic principles [mavazin-e eslami]."[43] One sees in this article that it is not the secular law that defines political crimes but law based on Islamic principles. As befits a government following a religious ideology, religious categories and rules determine the definitions of political crimes; thus, political crimes are, ultimately, also religious crimes.

The lack of candor on the part of the Iranian government in its official representations to the international community concerning its treatment of Baha'is correlates with the patterns of ambivalence and evasiveness that one sees in Islamic human rights schemes generally. Given the fact that in the Iranian constitution Islamic principles are treated as the supreme law of the land, one might have expected that the legality of the executions of the Baha'is in Islamic terms would be Iran's only concern, that it would publicly admit its policy of killing apostates, and that the government would confidently cite *shari'a* rules in response to any criticisms of its actions. The Iranian government might, therefore, be expected to take a position like that taken in the Azhar draft constitution, where there was forthright endorsement of the rule that apostates were to be killed. However, in reality, the Iranian government realizes that the persecutions and executions of Baha'is are violations of international human rights standards, and it is not convinced that invoking Islamic law will suffice to justify such violations. Iran's dissimulations reveal that it implicitly recognizes the authoritative, universal character of the international human rights standards—even as it continues to violate them.

One notes the irony of Iran's theocratic government, ruled by an Islamic jurist, trying to disguise its religious persecutions as secular political cases, whereas in the far more secular political order in Pakistan, laws specifically target a religious minority for criminal prosecution and elevate blasphemy, a religious offense, to the status of a capital crime. Pakistani officials are trying to convince a constituency sensitive to religious appeals that they are committed to defending Islam, whereas Iran's theocratic rulers are trying to deflect charges that their Islam is reactionary and intolerant. Obviously, strategic calculations tied to local politics play a major role in shaping how different regimes decide whether to assert openly that Islamic law requires the prosecution of people for religious crimes. Where political considerations shape manifestations of religious intolerance, outsiders need to appraise with skepticism all official rationales that are proffered for persecutions and punishments.

Some Iranian officials have acted as if their initiatives were to be judged according to international law. The veil that the more diplomatic members of the regime had sought to draw around policies antithetical to religious freedom was lifted in the Salman Rushdie case. Ayatollah Khomeini quite deliberately courted international notoriety in the Rushdie affair, seeking thereby to buttress his faltering prestige as the leader of militant Islam after his stature had been tarnished by his acceptance of a UN plan to end the Iran-Iraq War, a war that he had earlier sworn to pursue until a final victory was achieved.

After rioting broke out in Asia over the supposed sacrilege committed by Salman Rushdie in his novel *The Satanic Verses,* Khomeini issued his death edict for Rushdie on February 14, 1989, claiming—without presenting any justification—that the novel was an attack on Islam, the Qur'an, and the Prophet. Khomeini was undeterred by concerns about whether it was legitimate for an

Iranian Shi'i cleric to issue a death edict for a person of Sunni background who was a British citizen or whether it was just to condemn Rushdie without affording him a trial or a chance to defend himself. In these peculiar circumstances, the charges were based on the contents of a work of fiction written in English, which the Iranian clerics had not even read. No evidence was offered that would illuminate how any religious offense had been committed. On February 19, Khomeini added to the death sentence the order that, even if Rushdie were to repent of his offense, he would still have to be executed.[44]

Muslims' responses to Khomeini's death edict, which ranged from enthusiastic plaudits to outspoken condemnation, proved that they were deeply divided on whether Rushdie should be executed and whether Islamic law supported this edict.[45] Despite the risks, courageous Muslims raised their voices in protest over the death edict.[46] Not a single Muslim country opted to endorse Khomeini's call for killing Rushdie, even though on March 16, 1989, the Organization of the Islamic Conference, the organization behind the Cairo Declaration, did label the book blasphemous and did call Rushdie an apostate.

Iran's clerical leadership seemed in its subsequent propaganda to lack confidence in the legitimacy of killing Rushdie solely on the basis of a putative religious offense. As the regime attempted to justify Khomeini's call for Rushdie's execution, efforts were made to portray Rushdie, in actuality a leftist supporter of Third World causes, as an antirevolutionary agent of the forces of capitalism and Zionism, an agent of both the CIA and its Israeli counterpart, the Mossad, and a participant in a British imperialist plot to destroy Islam. That is, as time went on, instead of delineating exactly what in the novel was so offensive to Iran's religious laws that it warranted Rushdie's assassination, the Iranian regime decided to characterize Rushdie's offense as a political one, as if he had been serving forces inimical to Muslims.

After Khomeini's death in 1989, it appeared that many officials were open to rescinding the Rushdie death edict, and Iranian factions have subsequently quarreled over whether Iran remained religiously bound to carry out Khomeini's order.[47] In an apparent effort to disassociate the Iranian regime from the practice of killing people for their religious beliefs, Iranian officials have argued that it is essential to differentiate between the responsibilities of the Iranian government and a religious ruling[48]—a claim that is particularly strange coming from a government committed to the indivisibility of religion and state and to enshrining rule by Islamic jurists. Iran subsequently tried to turn the tables on its critics, arguing that Rushdie was an offender under international law and that European countries were violating international law in praising and welcoming Rushdie.[49] Khomeini's bold flouting of international law in issuing the Rushdie death edict was thus an exception to the standard Iranian practice of claiming that Iran did comply with international law and that all accusations that Iran grossly violated the principle of freedom of religion were baseless.[50]

The country's ruling clerics also wield "apostasy" as a strategic tool to stifle dissent within the clerical establishment. One example could be seen in August 2000, when Iran's hard-liners decided to prosecute a liberal, pro-reform cleric, Hojjatoleslam Hassan Youssefi Eshkevari.[51] He faced a variety of charges, which included apostasy and propaganda against the regime.[52] Hard-liners were motivated to punish Eshkevari for his vigorous advocacy of the principle that Islam is compatible with democracy—thereby challenging absolute clerical authority. Eshkevari was tried in closed proceedings by the special court established after the revolution for the specific purpose of trying clerics—and stifling clerical dissent. Although he was convicted and sentenced to death, the death sentence was revoked on appeal, and he was sent to prison instead.

Another example of how politics shapes apostasy cases is the recent prosecution of Hamid Pourmand, a former military officer who had converted from Islam to Christianity. He had already been incarcerated after being convicted of deceiving the Iranian army about his religion. (He had been a military officer, a profession from which non-Muslims are excluded.)[53] Although Pourmand was clearly an apostate, Iran's leaders apparently concluded that, at a time when Iran's relationship with the West was particularly tense, executing a Muslim who had converted to Christianity would be imprudent. They therefore deemed it preferable to have Pourmand punished solely on the lesser charge, and he was acquitted in May 2005 on charges of apostasy and proselytizing and returned to prison to serve his sentence from the previous conviction. At least some members of the theocracy seem ambivalent about publicly implementing the death penalty for apostasy—even as the regime continues in practice to impose sanctions on those it deems apostates.

The Sudan Under Islamization

Except for a brief democratic interlude, the Sudan has been the site of atrocious and pervasive violations of human rights under particularly savage dictatorships since the 1980s. Although my focus here is solely on human rights violations tied to the application of Islamic law, it should be borne in mind that these violations are merely one facet of a broader pattern of egregious rights abuses, which have included genocide and mass rapes.

In 1985, Mahmud Muhammad Taha, the leader of the Sudanese Republican movement, was executed as a heretic and apostate from Islam. Too little attention was originally paid to the Taha case, an apostasy case that presaged others as Islamization increased the pressures for ideological conformity.

Taha had led a liberal school of thought in the Sudan known variously as the Republicans or the Republican Brothers. The Republicans viewed Islam as establishing an egalitarian order compatible with human rights. Taha offered a controversial interpretation of the history and aims of the Revelation of the Qur'anic verses, according to which much of what had come to be regarded as timeless *shari'a* rules was actually legislation that had been intended only to guide the early Muslim community in Medina. Using this interpretation, Taha was able to justify discarding various *shari'a* rules that violated human rights law, maintaining that these rules were never meant to be permanently binding on Muslims. Taha held that Islam, correctly interpreted, supported complete equality between men and women and Muslims and non-Muslims.[54] Taha's liberal, reformist views were anathema to many Muslim conservatives—so much so that, in 1976, al-Azhar officially declared him to be an apostate.[55] His views were also attacked by the Ikhwan, or Muslim Brothers, an Islamist movement. One faction of this movement collaborated with the Nimeiri and Bashir regimes in spreading repression in the name of Islam.

The Republicans criticized the human rights violations that were propagated as a result of Nimeiri's Islamization campaign of 1983–1985 and brought several unsuccessful suits claiming that the imposition of the premodern *shari'a* rules violated the constitution by discriminating against non-Muslims and women.[56] Taha was arrested along with a group of his followers and tried in January 1985. He boycotted as illegal and unconstitutional his original trial for offenses against the Sudan Penal Code of 1983 and the State Security Act of 1973. The trial court's judgment, which did not address the issue of apostasy, was overridden on appeal by a ruling convicting Taha of the additional offense of apostasy from Islam and condemning him to die—this despite the fact that there was no Sudanese law in force in 1985 establishing that apostasy from Islam constituted a crime. The Nimeiri regime may have been inhibited from formally reinstating the death penalty for apostasy by the same concerns that had deterred Iran from doing so, but the regime was also worried about aggravating the conflict with the South. Restive southern Sudanese, who were largely animist and Christian, saw Islamization as a policy that relegated them to second-class status, and formally reviving the apostasy penalty would only have further alienated the South.

As has been indicated elsewhere, under Islamization programs, the rule of law tends to implode, and the Taha case exemplifies this. To establish Taha's apostasy, the court referred to an ex parte civil proceeding that had been brought in Khartoum in 1968 by private plaintiffs offended by Taha's opinions, which had resulted in a ruling that he was an apostate. Declarations by al-Azhar and the Muslim World League to the effect that Taha was an apostate were also cited.[57] Taha was convicted of a capital crime on the basis of such secondhand evidence and in proceedings lacking any semblance of due process. When the judgment

calling for Taha's execution was referred to Nimeiri, he said that he was upholding it "on the basis of *Shari'ah* law to protect the nation from the danger of Mahmud Muhammad Taha and his slander of God and his insolence towards Him
[God] and to protect this homeland from heresy."[58] In reality, of course, Nimeiri
wanted him killed for criticizing the human rights abuses caused by Nimeiri's
Islamization campaign.

Taha's followers, although not condemned to die, were also declared apostates
from Islam. This meant that, like the Baha'is in Iran, they incurred civil death in
accordance with the premodern *shari'a* rules regarding apostasy. As a result, the
Republicans' marriages were dissolved, sexual intercourse between the erstwhile
spouses became punishable as a capital offense under the then-prevailing Islamic
criminal laws, and their children became illegitimate.

Taha was publicly hanged on January 18, 1985, in a prison courtyard in
Khartoum. According to reports, he conducted himself in his last moments with
the utmost dignity and calm while surrounded by a taunting mob of members of
the Ikhwan and other supporters of Nimeiri, who hailed his execution as a great
victory for Islam. The regime calculated that Taha's execution would bring it
credit for its zealous defense of Islam, but this calculation turned out to be a serious error in terms of the reaction of the average Sudanese. The revulsion over the
execution of the peaceable, elderly religious leader provided a strong impetus for
mobilizing the popular coalition against Nimeiri, which succeeded in toppling
him on April 6, 1985. Owing to the policies of Nimeiri, Islam became associated
with an act of medieval barbarism. At the same time, many Muslims considered
Taha's execution to be a violation of the fundamental values of their religion.
Killing Taha as a heretic converted him into a martyr for the cause of freedom.
Arab human rights activists selected the anniversary of Taha's execution as the
day on which Arab Human Rights Day is to be annually commemorated—a
sign that in his opposition to human rights violations perpetrated in the name of
Islam, Taha did not stand alone.

Mawdudi and Pakistani Law Affecting Religious Freedom

Abu'l A'la Mawdudi was not willing to confess in the text of his human rights
pamphlet that he supported killing those who convert from Islam. As was his
habit, when he realized that his views were so far out of keeping with international human rights standards that they would undermine the credibility of his
human rights scheme, he simply avoided the issue of apostasy. Thus, there is no
discussion of freedom of religion in his human rights pamphlet. However, Mawdudi is on the record elsewhere as supporting the death penalty for conversion
from Islam.[59] Mawdudi did not live long enough to see the enactment in Pakistan

of Ordinance XX, discussed in Chapter 7, which provided a legal warrant for persecuting Ahmadis, but this ordinance can be seen as the culmination of the anti-Ahmadi campaign that he and his followers waged.

Whereas prosecution for apostasy looms as a major threat to religious freedom in several countries in the Middle East, in Pakistan, prosecution for blasphemy is the major threat. President Zia ul-Haq modified blasphemy laws to facilitate prosecution for insults to Islam, and blasphemy was made a capital offense in 1991. Blasphemy law has been extensively used to initiate prosecutions that are often politically motivated or the result of grudges, mostly targeting Ahmadis and Christians but sometimes Muslims. Viewing the abuses of Pakistan's blasphemy law, in its 1992 report, "The 'Blasphemy' Episodes," the Human Rights Commission of Pakistan concluded: "[Religious intolerance] finds acquiescence, if not active encouragement, in the recent governments' voluble invocations of Islam. Intolerance is becoming holy, a distinguishing badge of devotion to Islam."[60] The same commission found that in Pakistan "the Islamic laws of religious offense are defined with reference to certain sacred 'truths' that may not be contradicted, challenged, satirized or ridiculed—it is the affront to the ideas themselves that is seen as threatening to the very fabric of Islamic society."[61]

An example of the far-fetched theories underlying blasphemy cases can be seen in the August 2001 conviction of Muslim medical professor Mohammed Younas Sheikh, who was sentenced to death for blasphemy. Members of a local Islamic organization charged that Sheikh, a progressive thinker, had made derogatory remarks about the Prophet in a lecture—one that they had not attended. His blasphemies had supposedly included statements asserting that prior to receiving the Islamic Revelation, the Prophet had not been a Muslim and that his parents, who had died before the Revelation, had not been Muslims. The courts agreed that Sheikh's alleged comments constituted a capital crime, and Sheikh endured a long period of incarceration, only narrowly escaping execution after sustained international protest led to a last-minute judicial intervention to acquit him in November 2003.[62]

In this climate, it is not only apostates and non-Muslim minorities who need to fear becoming the targets of prosecutions or extrajudicial killings for what are ostensibly religious offenses; Muslims of a variety of persuasions may find their freedom constrained and their lives jeopardized as well. In an especially ominous development, a Muslim judge who had courageously acquitted two Christians of blasphemy charges in a high-profile case was assassinated in October 1997, apparently by angry members of the Sunni extremist group that had originally brought the blasphemy charges.[63] The defense attorney in the case was also terrorized. Such events were emblematic of the degradation of the rule of law that followed the Islamization of criminal justice. As a human rights monitor aptly observed in a discussion of Pakistan's deteriorating legal environment, "when politics invades religion, legality becomes merely emblematic."[64]

The Cairo Declaration and the Saudi Basic Law

Not surprisingly, neither the Cairo Declaration nor the Saudi Basic Law offers any guarantee of freedom of religion, and both documents declare that the state should propagate Islam.

Article 10 of the Cairo Declaration provides that Islam is "the religion of unspoiled nature," prohibiting any form of compulsion or exploitation of a person's poverty or ignorance in order to convert him to another religion or to atheism. Given the biases in the declaration, one assumes that all conversions from Islam would be deemed to have resulted from "compulsion" or "exploitation," whereas presumably any technique that was applied to convert people *to* Islam would be acceptable.

Article 23 of the Saudi Basic Law calls on the state to propagate the faith, which in context means Wahhabism, the puritanical strain of Sunni Islam endorsed by the Saudi monarchy. As in other Muslim countries where there is no protection for freedom of religion and where the state endorses one version of Islamic orthodoxy, both non-Muslims and Muslim minorities were exposed to religious persecution. In Saudi Arabia, the Shi'i minority is characterized as heretical by clerics associated with the monarchy, and members of this sect have been harshly persecuted.[65] As already noted in Chapter 7, determining whether the mistreatment of non-Muslims is linked with their religious affiliation is complicated by the fact that non-Muslims in Saudi Arabia are almost exclusively aliens, and as such, they are particularly vulnerable to abuse within the Saudi system. A further complication lies in the fact that personal vendettas may play a role in who is targeted for prosecution.

The 1996 prosecution and execution of a Syrian national, 'Abd al-Karim al-Mara'i al-Naqshabandi, illustrates how arbitrary Saudi prosecutions for religious offenses can be. The Saudi style of administering justice is not constrained by principles such as the requirement that there be a law in force defining conduct as criminal before any criminal prosecution can be brought, leaving Saudi authorities unfettered discretion in defining what conduct constitutes a crime. Human Rights Watch concluded that this case was a prime example of how the absence of any written penal code in Saudi Arabia both encourages and disguises human rights abuses.[66]

Naqshabandi's alleged offense was witchcraft, "the practice of works of magic and spells and possession of a collection of polytheistic and superstitious books."[67] Although Saudi authorities do occasionally arrest people for activities like conjuring, Naqshabandi was apparently unaware that his possession of amulets, horoscopes, and suspect religious books could expose him to criminal prosecution for witchcraft. Once he was caught in the maw of the Saudi legal system, Naqshabandi was apparently isolated, severely mistreated, and prevented from obtaining a lawyer. In December 1996 the authorities executed Naqshabandi, whose case had been handled in such a manner that he was apparently not even aware that he had been found guilty of a crime, much less guilty of a capital crime. That "witchcraft" should be punished by death after such a travesty of justice speaks volumes about the caliber of the Saudi system.

People are exposed to persecution and prosecution on religious grounds in Saudi Arabia if they run afoul of powerful interests or provoke the ire of influential personages. Just as the accusation that Nasr Hamid Abu Zaid was an apostate seems to have been originally prompted by a personal vendetta, according to Human Rights Watch, the prosecution of Naqshabandi came about after he inadvertently provoked the ire of his mercurial and vindictive Saudi employer.[68] Again, it seems that the inaptitude of the Saudi system of criminal justice to secure an impartial administration of justice or to afford the accused the basis for mounting a proper defense deserves the blame for the outcome, not Islam per se.

The Afghan and Iraqi Constitutions

Although it was prepared under US supervision, the 2003 Afghan constitution did not deal squarely with freedom of religion. Article 2 establishes Islam as the state religion, while providing that followers of other religions are free to exercise their faith and perform their religious rites within the limits of the provisions of law. This offers some protection for freedom of worship for non-Muslims but falls short of guaranteeing freedom of religion. In an ominous development, a prosecution for apostasy soon surfaced.

The case that ensued illustrates how fragile the Afghan constitutional protections for religious freedoms are. In October 2005, Ali Mohaqiq Nasab, a liberal Afghan from the Hazara minority who edited a women's rights magazine, was convicted of "disrespecting Islamic law," after the prosecutor charged that he had committed apostasy. His crime had been publishing articles supporting Islamic feminist ideas and opposing the notion that Islam treated apostasy as a crime.[69] Outraged conservatives called for him to be executed as an apostate, and it seemed possible that Nasab would eventually be executed merely because he had challenged some medieval interpretations of the Islamic sources. Probably due to Western diplomatic intervention, Nasab was released from prison in December 2005 after agreeing to apologize publicly for his controversial writings.[70]

In the wake of US pressure, Article 2 of the 2005 Iraqi constitution guaranteed "the full religious rights of all individuals to freedom of religious belief and practice," which was in addition to provisions on freedom of worship in Article 41. Article 35 afforded a guarantee of protection from "religious coercion." However, given that Article 2 also barred laws violating established Islamic rules and made Islam a main source of legislation, the stage was set for religious freedoms being limited by Islamic criteria. Because US officials pressed the drafters of the constitution to roll back proposed Islamic provisions and to buttress religious freedom, religious freedom has become associated with the US political agenda. The stage was thereby set for a potential backlash against religious freedom, creating a worrisome situation for any Iraqis not supporting the Shi'i establishment that gained power after the December 2005 elections.

US Interventions in the Domain of Religious Freedom

As mentioned in Chapter 7, since the late 1990s Christian activists have been exerting pressure on the US government to use its resources to persuade Muslim countries to improve the treatment of Christian minorities and to remove obstacles to missionary activity. This resulted in the enactment of the International Religious Freedom Act of 1998 and the establishment of the US Commission on International Religious Freedom, entrusted with the task of dealing with religious freedom around the word.[71] Among other things, the commission publishes annual reports with very detailed information on the status of religious freedom in several countries, with reports on Muslim countries as well as reports on countries such as Cuba and China.[72] However, certain features suggest a specific preoccupation with religious freedom in Muslim countries; for example, a particularly detailed report on the treatment of religious freedom in the constitutions of Muslim countries has been compiled and made available in both English and Arabic.[73] Not surprisingly, Muslim countries figured prominently in the 2004 list of "Countries of Particular Concern," or CPCs, which included Burma, China, Eritrea, Iran, North Korea, Saudi Arabia, Sudan, and Vietnam.[74]

In theory, the commission's purpose is to promote respect for rights as set forth in the UDHR and ICCPR, but, in fact, it reflects a US policy of privileging religious freedom over other human rights, a distortion of the international human rights system.[75] The unilateral US initiative to expand religious freedom overseas coincides with a period of heightened anger over US intervention in the Middle East. In these circumstances, initiatives that are theoretically designed to advance the cause of religious freedom could play into the hands of those portraying this human rights agenda as a weapon of Western imperialism.

Summary

The lack of protections for freedom of religion in the Islamic human rights schemes is one of the factors that most sharply distinguishes them from the International Bill of Human Rights, which treats freedom of religion as an unqualified right. This omission reveals the enormous gap between their authors' mentalities and the modern philosophy of human rights. However, this does not mean that proponents of Islamic versions of rights want to be seen as advocates of persecuting others because of their religious beliefs. Astute politicians can calculate more accurately than Nimeiri and Khomeini the political costs of openly calling for executing people for apostasy. Showing some self-consciousness about being judged deficient by international standards, these schemes are mostly evasive or uninformative regarding their authors' hostility to freedom of religion and their intentions to apply the *shari'a* rules on apostasy.

Although a disturbing record of assaults on the principle of religious freedom has been accumulated by countries such as Egypt, Iran, Pakistan, Saudi Arabia, and the Sudan, it would be simplistic to blame Islam per se for these outcomes. After all, these countries' policies are so inimical to religious freedom that believing Muslims may be prosecuted as heretics or blasphemers for what is actually political or theological dissent or for having offended powerful, well-connected figures. Such outcomes have little to do with mandates of Islamic law. It seems fairer to assess these serious violations of religious freedom as the result of official policies that have exacerbated religious tensions and polarized religious communities and the lack of systemic protections for civil and political rights.

CHAPTER 9

An Assessment of Islamic Human Rights Schemes

The Significance of Islamic Human Rights Schemes

Islamic human rights schemes like the ones reviewed here, which use Islamic criteria to restrict rights, represent only one of the ways that contemporary Muslims have responded to the question of how their Islamic heritage relates to the human rights issues facing contemporary Muslim societies. The attitudes and values of the authors of these Islamic human rights schemes are not intrinsically more Islamic in the sense of corresponding to any definitive Islamic model of rights than are the attitudes and values of Muslims who reject all aspects of the Universal Declaration or those who enthusiastically embrace international human rights as fully compatible with their religious tradition. However, state practice and the impact of Islamization have augmented the practical significance of the idea that Muslims do have human rights, but only subject to significant "Islamic" qualifications.

These Islamic human rights schemes have a format and a terminology designed to convince people that they constitute valid counterparts of international human rights law, when they actually have an objective inimical to rights—reducing rights protections. This is why it makes sense to call them "schemes"—combinations of elements connected by design. Comparisons with international documents inevitably reveal the deficiencies of the Islamic schemes even where they superficially emulate international models. Where the Islamic human rights provisions diverge, it turns out that they dilute, if not altogether eliminate, civil and political rights afforded by international law. The authors of these schemes accord priority to rationalizing governmental repression, protecting and promoting social and religious conformity, and perpetuating traditional hierarchies, which include discriminatory treatment of women and non-Muslims. They assert the supremacy of

Islamic principles in all areas relevant for the protection of human rights, but these Islamic principles are left so vague and elastic that they can accommodate the nullification of human rights by those in power.

The authors do not seem to have approached their task with methodological rigor, as the many inconsistencies and deficiencies in their work indicate. There is no evidence of any serious inquiry into the reasons why human rights principles were not articulated as such in the framework of the premodern Islamic tradition. Grasping at elements of this tradition, the authors seem to have no interest in working through the jurisprudential adjustments that are needed to accommodate human rights. Instead, they rely on traditional values and rules developed by premodern Islamic jurists without examination of the historical context in which these arose and without critical assessment of the degree to which these may no longer be appropriate for the radically altered political, economic, and social circumstances of Muslim societies today.

One would expect professedly "Islamic" human rights schemes to rest on methods that would ensure that they would set forth pure, undiluted Islamic principles on the subject, but these Islamic human rights schemes are something other than efforts to mine the Islamic heritage for guidance. They amount to awkward hybrids of Islamic elements and concepts patently appropriated from Western constitutions and international human rights law. The authors borrow extensively from alien models, which is puzzling in terms of Islamic jurisprudence, because rules established without respect for Islamic methods and criteria are generally considered irrelevant. The resulting hybridity, which is never acknowledged, suggests that even conservative Muslims who are ostensibly dedicated to setting forth authentic Islamic teachings are disposed to borrow from Western and international models when they deal with human rights. Since the authors are not prepared to confess to borrowing from outside the Islamic tradition, they naturally fail to propose adequate theories for integrating the borrowed elements with Islamic ones. Not surprisingly, the resulting admixtures of undigested legal transplants and incompatible Islamic elements lack coherence.

What should one make of this awkward transitional stage? Viewing the incompleteness of their assimilation of international law, one could nonetheless argue that Islamic human rights do constitute a step forward. After all, they suggest that even Muslim conservatives have become persuaded that human rights can and should be integrated into Islamic culture—albeit only tentatively and superficially. One might speculate that drafters of the Universal Islamic Declaration of Human Rights (UIDHR) or the Cairo Declaration may have believed that, even if these did not measure up to international standards, their promulgation would nonetheless enhance the legitimacy of human rights in the eyes of some Muslims by associating Islam with human rights.

That is, one might see the phenomenon of Islamization of human rights as representing a temporary and transitional phase in the process of assimilating international human rights principles. One might propose that the indigenization of international human rights requires—at least for many Muslims who are still attached to aspects of traditional culture—that human rights concepts initially pass through a stage in which international human rights are disassembled and reconstructed to coincide with familiar categories and readjusted to fit conservative values and mores. The merit of such transitional rights formulations could be that rights, introduced gradually and conditionally, might avoid excessive clashes with familiar Islamic strictures.

In this regard, one might speculate that some of the obfuscation that one sees in these schemes could facilitate the reception of human rights by avoiding specifics that might highlight inherent conflicts. One might hypothesize that by using evasive tactics and intentionally ambiguous formulations, some authors may have intended to avoid a premature break with the heritage of premodern *shari'a* rules and associated cultural traditions, a break that could be exploited by adamant opponents of human rights eager to show that they are fatally at odds with Islamic law. If one took an optimistic stance, seeing in Islamic human rights a basically benign, transitional phenomenon, one might hope that the Islamic features that have been grafted onto imported human rights precepts would be eventually discarded when further social and economic development made the international standards more palatable.

Alternatively, one could adopt a more pessimistic view, predicting that the deficiencies of the Islamic human rights schemes that have been backed by governments and influential institutions would harm the prospects for realizing human rights. According to this perspective, these schemes might stand in the way of developing the kinds of human rights that are guaranteed in the International Bill of Human Rights and that are needed to enable people in the Middle East to mount effective challenges to patterns of rights abuses—particularly any human rights abuses perpetrated in the name of "Islam." Since Islamization pressures seem likely to continue, a skeptic might predict that any models that give governments grounds for claiming that they have an Islamic warrant for denying the rights afforded under international law could be exploited to impede the cause of human rights. Recent history appears to support this skeptical position.

Once embodied in law, Islamic criteria limiting rights protections present obstacles to reforms that would advance human rights. For example, by incorporating Islamic limitations on human rights into the text of the 1979 Iranian constitution, what were previously *informal* obstacles to realizing international human rights protections were elevated to the stature of *formal* constitutional norms affirming Islamic restrictions on rights, which will be difficult for subsequent generations of Iranians to dismantle. Many Iranian reformers now contend that the provisions affirming the supremacy of Islamic law in Iran's constitution need to be removed, precisely because they stand in the way of improved human rights protections.

One could speculate that these Islamic schemes of human rights might have broad popular appeal by virtue of their simultaneous associations with both Islam and human rights. However, there is little evidence to suggest that putting Islamic labels on enfeebled rights provisions make them attractive to Muslims who are familiar with the stronger rights guarantees found in the International Bill of Human Rights. In reality, these schemes appeal to social conservatives who are opposed to rights. Muslim advocates for human rights and the burgeoning human rights associations that have altered the political landscape in Muslim countries have campaigned to realize the human rights set forth in international law, not watered-down "Islamic" alternatives like the ones examined here. This commitment is forthrightly expressed in the April 1999 Casablanca Declaration, issued from the First International Conference of the Arab Human Rights Movement in Casablanca, Morocco, which specifically rejected "any attempt to use civilizational or religious specificity to contest the universality of human rights."[1]

As the world is brought closer together by modern communications, it becomes more difficult for even the most repressive regimes to block the penetration of ideas of democracy and human rights, which since the 1980s have resoundingly demonstrated their popular appeal and their capacity to undermine the legitimacy of despotic governments around the globe. Precisely because Muslim countries have human rights records that range from the mediocre to the atrocious, they provide fertile soil for conversions to the ideals of international human rights, which address the problems faced by contemporary Muslims.

Proponents of the idea that Islamic criteria should override international human rights principles, leaving people in Muslim societies with rights inferior to those guaranteed to the rest of humanity, have not been willing to submit this proposition to public referenda. However, when Muslims who have lived under regimes committed to Islamization have been allowed to vote, their disenchantment has been patent. For example, when Iran briefly loosened its strictures on candidates running for president and allowed a reform candidate, Mohammed Khatami, to run in 1997 and 2001, his vigorous attacks on the deployment of Islamic rationales to deny human rights twice gave him large majorities. Disillusioned after experiencing what Islamization entails in practice, the Iranian electorate showed itself hungry for democratization.

To identify what is at stake in the contest between Islamic and international human rights, one needs to ask who would benefit and who would lose if international human rights provisions were enacted into law and effective mechanisms to ensure their observance were set in place. The benefits of implementing international human rights would be felt by the population as a whole, which would be spared the pervasive rights abuses that have plagued Middle Eastern societies. With international human rights guarantees in place, instead of being terrorized and oppressed by brutal rulers, the population would have the means to hold rulers accountable for their misdeeds and to build up the institutions of civil society. Instead of living in intellectual prisons, they would be free to enjoy access to cultures from around the world and could express their ideas without fear of dire consequences lest they offend some cultural commissar or reactionary cleric. Muslims would no longer be menaced with punishment for heresy and apostasy if they questioned old verities or official lines on religious orthodoxy; with expanded freedoms, Islamic thought might be revitalized and flourish as it did centuries ago. Rather than being compelled to live like children under the tutelage of governments that equate upholding morality with repression, they could live like adults, free to make their own choices regarding how to live meaningful and rewarding lives. Upholding the international norms would lead to enhanced rights for women and religious minorities, who would be freed of the discrimination that relegates them to a vulnerable and inferior status.

The losers would include unpopular, tyrannical rulers and groups whose interests are closely linked to the preservation of privilege and inequality and the repression of dissident voices. Muslim men's reactions might be equivocal. They would forfeit many privileges both within the family and, to a lesser extent, in society at large, but many might find that the benefits offered by an open society and an accountable government outweigh the loss of such privileges.

Ambivalence in Islamic Human Rights Schemes

The authors of the Islamic human rights schemes reviewed here display a remarkable ambivalence regarding international human rights law. While speaking in terms of cultural particularism and exploiting features of the Islamic heritage to make a case for derogating from international law, the authors of these schemes have striven to disguise as much as possible disparities between their Islamic rights schemes and the international standards. Their determination to hide the differences between their schemes and international rights standards seems incongruous. Since the authors consistently maintain that Islamic law is superior to all secular legal principles, they might be expected to dismiss other conflicting rights principles as incorrect. In fact, Sultanhussein Tabandeh took this position, as noted earlier. He argued that Islam should be the universal model, replacing the rights set forth in international law:

> Why do we not simply put into practice our own Islamic laws? Indeed, why
> do we not put them forward at the United Nations Assembly and at its various
> Commissions and Conferences? Why do we not orientate the compasses of

the nations of the world by the pole-star of Islam, and publicly glory in our possession of laws that so exactly fit the human condition? Why do we not demonstrate the value of these laws, and illustrate their excellence in our words and in our practice? Why do we not invite the United Nations to express their Conventions in the terms already laid down in the Islamic Canon?[2]

Other proponents of Islamic human rights have more ambivalent feelings about the system of international law and do not have a relationship to the Islamic heritage that is as simple and straightforward as Tabandeh's. Tabandeh is exceptional in his open and proud acknowledgment that following Islamic criteria necessitates departures from international law.

One can see the ambivalence in the stances of Iran and Saudi Arabia, which approached the World Conference on Human Rights of June 1993 disposed to press the case for Islamic particularism. In their domestic policies, they have consistently relied on Islam to bar the application of international human rights norms. However, when the conference convened, both presented Islamic human rights as if they were compatible with adherence to international law. Both urged the acceptance of Islamic versions of human rights in lieu of the international ones, but without acknowledging, as Raja'i Khorasani had done a decade earlier, that this entailed violating international norms. Indeed, rather than insisting on distinctive Islamic standards, they proposed a kind of vague, qualified universalism.

For example, the Saudi foreign minister, in speaking at the conference, maintained that Islamic law afforded "a comprehensive system for universal human rights." He professed to concur that the principles and objectives of human rights were "of a universal nature," merely adding the modest caveat that in their application it was necessary to show "consideration for the diversity of societies, taking into account their various historical, cultural, and religious backgrounds and legal systems."[3] He did not attempt to defend the actual Saudi position, which claimed that Islam endorsed monarchical absolutism and various retrograde features, such as gender apartheid.

The head of Iran's delegation at the conference gave rhetorical support to the principle of universality and denied that rights based on religious teachings sacrificed the value of the individual for the well-being of the community. He also asserted that a multidimensional approach to rights—that is, one that would take into account Islamic rights—could "provide a better background for the full realization of human rights," arguing that "drawing from the richness and experience of all cultures, and particularly those based on divine religions, would only logically serve to enrich human rights concepts."[4] Thus, the Iranian delegation claimed that the incorporation of Islamic principles would enhance human rights.

After debates over the universality of rights, the Vienna Declaration and Program of Action issued at the end of the conference asserted: "The universal nature of these rights and freedoms is beyond question." However, the declaration injected a note of ambiguity by also advising that "the significance of national and regional particularities and various historical, cultural and religious backgrounds must be borne in mind." The ambiguity in the final declaration must have pleased Iran and Saudi Arabia, which had apparently decided that international human rights had garnered so much legitimacy that, at least when faced with international audiences, they would have to mute their hostility to the values of human rights. They found it expedient to present Islam as complementing human rights universality, obfuscating the incompatibility of contemporary Islamic human rights schemes and international human rights law.

Human Rights Concerns in the Middle East

As has been noted, the Islamic human rights literature avoids dealing with human rights problems in the Middle East, but human rights activists in the Middle East are engaged in struggles to identify the causes of these problems and to devise concrete, practical solutions that offer realistic prospects for ending rights violations. A deep cleavage has resulted between the idealistic focus of proponents of Islamization, who tend to envisage Islamic law as the utopian solution to all problems, and the focus of Muslim human rights activists, who are concerned with the practical obstacles to democratization and the institutional deficiencies that must be addressed to secure human rights protections. Reports of a debate between Islamists and human rights activists confirm how Islamists stress the virtues of Islamic principles in the abstract, whereas Muslim human rights activists stress the need to attend to details of process and institutional frameworks.[5]

In striking contrast to the silence of Islamic human rights schemes regarding human rights abuses, a thoughtful and exceptionally outspoken critique of the human rights situation in the Arab world was publicly issued by a group of Arab intellectuals after a meeting in Tunis in 1983. This turned out to be one of a series of critical appraisals of the ills besetting Arab societies issued by Arab intellectuals who saw all too clearly the negative consequences of the lack of freedom pervading their region. Portions of the 1983 critique, which also applies, mutatis mutandis, to many aspects of the rights predicaments in non-Arab countries in the region, is summarized here and paraphrased to show how Middle Easterners who are not swept up in the politics of cultural nationalism and who are not engaged in apologetic enterprises vis-à-vis the West appraise the situation.

The critique asserts that under various pretexts—such as the needs of socialism, development, realization of pan-Arab unity, protecting national sovereignty, and fighting Israel—demands for democracy have been denied. It claims that freedom, aside from its social usefulness, is a value in and of itself, one that all Arabs long for and all regimes deny. Not only are Arabs prevented from free expression and from participating in the determination of their fate, but they are also constantly exposed to repression. Fear of imprisonment, murder, mass murder, and torture dominates their lives. Arab individuals are so humiliated, their spheres of personal freedom so restricted, and their voices so crushed into silence and subjugation that they are prone to despair and become incapacitated. This critique condemns such repressive measures, as well as emergency courts and police-state tactics, and demands that trials be conducted according to law. It calls on Arab governments to respect civil rights and to refrain from infringing personal freedoms guaranteed by the UDHR. The first priority is affirmed to be equal treatment for all citizens regardless of belief, descent, or sex. In most Arab countries, the critique asserts, authority is based on the subjugation of citizens. The consequences are confusion in values and norms and the absence of critical thought. A monolithically structured, hermetically closed system of authority dominates the scene, leaving no room for political or intellectual pluralism or for the development of genuine culture. The participants called for guarantees for certain freedoms, especially freedom of belief, freedom of opinion and expression, freedom to participate, freedom of assembly, and freedom to form political organizations and unions. They also demanded guarantees for the rights of women and minorities and an independent judiciary.[6]

This critique and others that were to follow prove that intellectuals who genuinely aspire to advance human rights in the Middle East are prepared to speak out to denounce actual patterns of human rights violations and that they do not hesitate to invoke international human rights in their criticisms. In the face of such indigenous critiques, most ruling cliques have resisted democratization. However, the occasional case, such as Morocco, which has expanded human rights protections and democratized under King Muhammad VI, has shown that reforms are both possible and popular.

More recently, participants in a June 2004 conference of more than one hundred Arab intellectuals and politicians issued the Doha Declaration for Democracy and Reforms, which decried the specific patterns of undemocratic governance prevailing in the Arab world and dismissed the pretexts that regimes have used to defer democratic reforms.[7] Such instances of outspoken denunciation of ingrained patterns of despotism are growing more frequent and confirm that despotic Middle Eastern regimes are not just objectionable by Western standards but are also so perceived by people within these societies, especially their educated members. They show that the local rationales to justify tyranny and discrimination are not persuasive for those living in these societies and that people do not consider participatory democracy an exotic, Western luxury; instead, they attribute many of the problems afflicting their societies to its absence.

In 2002, Arab experts working for the UN Development Program presented a highly negative assessment of development problems in the Arab world and the reasons for its lag behind the more dynamic emerging economies. In this, the first of a series of reports, they found that the Arab region, one of seven world regions, had the lowest freedom ranking. Using indicators measuring the dimensions of the political process, civil liberties, political rights, and independence of the media, the authors depicted a gaping freedom deficit. Furthermore, the report highlighted the severe discrimination that Arab women face, ranking their political and economic participation lowest in the world.[8] The thoroughness and transparency of this critique was applauded by Arab advocates of human rights and democratization.[9]

In significant contrast to the kinds of critiques just mentioned, the Islamic human rights schemes examined in this book insist on the absolute perfection of abstract Islamic ideals while ignoring altogether the grim human rights records of Muslim countries. The schemes portray Islamic human rights as though such rights enjoyed unquestioned authority and automatic efficaciousness by reason of their divine provenance, owing to which no government would dare to tamper with them. For example, in its Preamble, the UIDHR says of Islamic human rights that "by virtue of their Divine source and sanction these rights can neither be curtailed, abrogated or disregarded by authorities, assemblies or other institutions, nor can they be surrendered or alienated."[10] In presenting the Cairo Declaration at the 1993 World Conference on Human Rights in Vienna as the authoritative statement of Islamic rights, the Saudi foreign minister insisted that in Islamic law, human rights are not mere moral exhortations but "legislative orders," containing "all the legal texts necessary for ensuring their implementation and enforcement."[11] He thereby portrayed Islamic law and the Cairo Declaration as affording efficacious rights protections. A recent study that endorses the Cairo Declaration and Islamic human rights more generally has elaborated on the Saudi position, making the argument that relying on Islamic precepts is sufficient to ensure a regime of virtue, harmony, and benevolence.[12]

Those who adopt such positions must ignore the grim reality of the human rights situation in the Middle East, because to admit its dimensions and the lack of respect that governments have routinely shown for the law, including Islamic law, would require confronting the fact that the religious pedigrees of Islamic rules are not by themselves sufficient to guarantee that they will be respected in practice. Muslims who are genuinely committed to advancing human rights and who understand the prerequisites for establishing a democratic order respectful of rights realize that reforms in the prevailing political cultures are required and that drastic systemic changes need to be undertaken. Thus, the utopian ideas of the Islamic human rights schemes that have been reviewed here are designed not to solve the human rights problems facing Muslim societies but rather to gloss over these problems and to provide justifications for retaining existing hierarchies.

Summary

As this assessment has indicated, the Islamic human rights schemes discussed in the foregoing chapter are products of the political contexts in which they emerged. Their Islamic pedigrees are dubious, and the principles that they contain do not represent the result of rigorous, scholarly analyses of the Islamic sources or a coherent approach to Islamic jurisprudence. Instead, they appear to be shaped by their conservative authors' negative reactions to the model of freedom in Western societies and the scope of rights protections afforded by the International Bill of Human Rights. Resentment of the West and cultural nationalism have also shaped the authors' approach to human rights.

Given their reactive character, it is not surprising that in producing their Islamic human rights schemes, the authors used material from the Islamic heritage, often confused with the values found in traditional societies, in a highly selective manner, resulting in a one-sided representation of Islamic teachings relating to rights. They have been disinclined to seek a synthesis of Islamic and international human rights that could alter the status quo or serve the cause of curbing the existing patterns of human rights violations prevailing in Middle Eastern countries.

The Islamic human rights schemes reviewed here do not simply replicate principles stated in the Islamic sources, even though they often incorporate references to Islamic sources. The consequences of turning to the Islamic sources for designing schemes of rights rest on the interpretations of the sources, which, depending on the philosophical orientation of the interpreters, may or may not be favorable to human rights.

These Islamic human rights schemes reflect their authors' own preferences for antirationalist, antihumanistic currents in Islamic thought. Thus, from an array of options afforded by Islamic civilization, the schemes deliberately incorporate those elements that present obstacles to the accommodation of modern human rights principles—obstacles that are then attributed to Islam. If the authors' aim had been to advance protection for human rights in Muslim milieus, they could have acknowledged that the Islamic heritage comprises rationalist and humanistic currents and that it is replete with values that complement modern human rights, such as concern for human welfare, social justice, tolerance, and egalitarianism. These could provide the basis for constructing a viable synthesis of Islamic principles and international human rights, as the work of Muslim proponents of democratization and reforms demonstrates.

All this leads to the conclusion that the characteristics of the Islamic human rights schemes examined here should not be ascribed to peculiar features of Islam or its inherent incompatibility with human rights. Instead, these should be seen as part of a broader phenomenon of attempts by elites—the beneficiaries of undemocratic and hierarchical systems—to legitimize their opposition to human rights by appealing to supposedly distinctive cultural traditions. All indications are that these elites will increasingly be forced to contend with fellow Muslims who aspire to enjoy human rights and who see such appeals to Islam to justify curbing rights and freedoms as reflecting political self-interest rather than the authentic teachings of the Islamic sources.

Excerpts from the Constitution of the Islamic Republic of Iran of 24 October 1979 As Amended to 28 July 1989

In the Name of Allah, the Compassionate, the Merciful
We sent aforetime Our apostles with clear signs, and sent down with them
the Book and the Balance that men may uphold justice . . .
—Qur'an 57:25

Preamble

The Constitution of the Islamic Republic of Iran sets forth the cultural, social, political, and economic institutions of Iranian society on the basis of Islamic principles and norms, which represent the earnest aspiration of the Islamic *Ummah* [community]. . . .

The Form of Government in Islam

In the view of Islam, government does not derive from the interests of a class, nor does it serve the domination of an individual or a group. It represents rather the crystallization of the political ideal of a people who bear a common faith and common outlook, taking an organized form in order to initiate the process of intellectual

---

Excerpted from Albert Blaustein and Gisbert Flanz, eds., *Constitutions of the Countries of the World* (Dobbs Ferry, N.Y.: Oceana, 1992). Various passages corresponding to Arabic quotations in the Persian original have been omitted.

and ideological evolution towards the final goal, i.e., movement towards *Allah*. Our nation, in the course of its revolutionary developments, has cleansed itself of the dust and impurities that accumulated during the *taghuti* [heathenish] past and purged itself of foreign ideological influences, returning to authentic intellectual standpoints and world-view of Islam. It now intends to establish an ideal and model society on the basis of Islamic norms. The mission of the Constitution is to realize the ideological objectives of the movement and to create conditions conducive to the development of man in accordance with the noble and universal values of Islam. . . .

Legislation setting forth regulations for the administration of society will revolve around the Qur'an and the *Sunnah*. Accordingly, the exercise of meticulous and earnest supervision by just, pious, and committed scholars of Islam *(al-fuqaha al-'udul)* is an absolute necessity. . . .

Women in the Constitution

Through the creation of Islamic social infrastructures, all the elements of humanity that hitherto served the multifaceted foreign exploitation shall regain their true identity and human rights. As part of this process, it is only natural that women should benefit from a particularly large augmentation of their rights, because of the greater oppression that they suffered under the *taghuti* regime.

The family is the fundamental unit of society and the main centre for the growth and edification of human being[s]. Compatibility with respect to belief and ideal, which provides the primary basis for man's development and growth, is the main consideration in the establishment of a family. It is the duty of the Islamic government to provide the necessary facilities for the attainment of this goal. This view of the family unit delivers woman from being regarded as an object or as an instrument in the service of promoting consumerism and exploitation. Not only does woman recover thereby her momentous and precious function of motherhood, rearing of ideologically committed human beings, she also assumes a pioneering social role and becomes the fellow struggler of man in all vital areas of life. Given the weighty responsibilities that woman thus assumes, she is accorded in Islam great value and nobility.

An Ideological Army

In the formation and equipping of the country's defense forces, due attention must be paid to faith and ideology as the basic criteria. Accordingly, the Army of the Islamic Republic of Iran and the Islamic Revolutionary Guards Corps are to be organized in conformity with this goal, and they will be responsible not only for guarding and preserving the frontiers of the country, but also for fulfilling the ideological mission of *jihad* in God's way; that is, extending the sovereignty of God's law throughout the world. . . .

General Principles

Article 1

The form of government of Iran is that of an Islamic Republic, endorsed by the people of Iran on the basis of their long-standing belief in the sovereignty of truth and Qur'anic justice, in the referendum of . . . [March 29 and 30, 1979], through the affirmative vote of a majority of 98.2% of eligible voters, held after the victorious Islamic Revolution led by the eminent *marji' al-taqlid* [source of emulation], Ayatollah al-'Uzma Imam Khumayni.

Article 2

The Islamic Republic is a system based on belief in:

1. the One God (as stated in the phrase "There is no god except Allah"), His exclusive sovereignty and the right to legislate, and the necessity of submission to His commands;
2. Divine revelation and its fundamental role in setting forth the laws;
3. the return to God in the Hereafter, and the constructive role of this belief in the course of man's ascent towards God;
4. the justice of God in creation and legislation;
5. continuous leadership *(imamah)* and perpetual guidance, and its fundamental role in ensuring the uninterrupted process of the revolution of Islam;
6. the exalted dignity and value of man, and his freedom coupled with responsibility before God; in which equity, justice, political, economic, social, and cultural independence, and national solidarity are secured by recourse to:
    A. continuous *ijtihad* [interpretation] of the *fuqaha* possessing necessary qualifications, exercised on the basis of the Qur'an and the *Sunnah* of the *Ma'sumun* [the Prophet, his daughter Fatima, the Shi'i Imams], upon all of whom be peace;
    B. sciences and arts and the most advanced results of human experience, together with the effort to advance them further;
    C. negation of all forms of oppression, both the infliction of and the submission to it, and of dominance, both its imposition and its acceptance.

Article 3

In order to attain the objectives specified in Article 2, the government of the Islamic Republic of Iran has the duty of directing all its resources to the following goals:

1. the creation of a favorable environment for the growth of moral virtues based on faith and piety and the struggle against all forms of vice and corruption;

2. raising the level of public awareness in all areas, through the proper use of the press, mass media, and other means;
3. free education and physical training for everyone at all levels, and the facilitation and expansion of higher education;
4. strengthening the spirit of inquiry, investigation, and innovation in all areas of science, technology, and culture, as well as Islamic studies, by establishing research centers and encouraging researchers;
5. the complete elimination of imperialism and the prevention of foreign influence;
6. the elimination of all forms of despotism and autocracy and all attempts to monopolize power;
7. ensuring political and social freedoms within the framework of the law;
8. the participation of the entire people in determining their political, economic, social, and cultural destiny;
9. the abolition of all forms of undesirable discrimination and the provision of equitable opportunities for all, in both the material and intellectual spheres;
10. the creation of a correct administrative system and elimination of superfluous government organizations;
11. all round strengthening of the foundations of national defense to the utmost degree by means of universal military training for the sake of safeguarding the independence, territorial integrity, and the Islamic order of the country;
12. the planning of a correct and just economic system, in accordance with Islamic criteria, in order to create welfare, eliminate poverty, and abolish all forms of deprivation with respect to food, housing, work, health care, and the provision of social insurance for all;
13. the attainment of self-sufficiency in scientific, technological, industrial, agricultural, and military domains, and other similar spheres;
14. securing the multifarious rights of all citizens, both women and men, and providing legal protection for all, as well as the equality of all before the law;
15. the expansion and strengthening of Islamic brotherhood and public cooperation among all the people;
16. framing the foreign policy of the country on the basis of Islamic criteria, fraternal commitment to all Muslims, and unsparing support to the *mus-tad'afun* [oppressed] of the world.

Article 4

All civil, penal, financial, economic, administrative, cultural, military, political, and other laws and regulations must be based on Islamic criteria. This principle applies absolutely and generally to all articles of the Constitution as well as to all other laws and regulations, and the *fuqaha* of the Guardian Council are judges in this matter.

Article 5

During the Occultation of the *Wali al-'Asr* [Shi'i Imam] (may God hasten his reappearance), the *wilayah* [governance] and leadership of the Ummah devolve upon the just *('adil)* and pious *(muttaqi) faqih* [jurist], who is fully aware of the circumstances of his age; courageous, resourceful, and possessed of administrative ability, [he] will assume the responsibilities of this office in accordance with Article 107.

Article 7

In the Islamic Republic of Iran, the affairs of the country must be administered on the basis of public opinion expressed by the means of elections, including the election of the President, the representatives of the Islamic Consultative Assembly, and the members of councils, or by means of referenda in matters specified in other articles of this Constitution . . .

Article 8

In the Islamic Republic of Iran, *al-'amr bi'l-ma'ruf wa al-nahy 'an al-munkar* [commanding the good and forbidding the evil] is a universal and reciprocal duty that must be fulfilled by the people with respect to one another, by the government with respect to the people, and by the people with respect to the government. The conditions, limits, and nature of this duty will be specified by law. (This is in accordance with the Qur'anic verse: "The believers, men and women, are guardians of one another; they enjoin the good and forbid the evil" [9:71]). . . .

Article 9

In the Islamic Republic of Iran, the freedom, independence, unity, and territorial integrity of the country are inseparable from one another, and their preservation is the duty of the government and all individual citizens. No individual, group, or authority, has the right to infringe in the slightest way upon the political, cultural, economic, and military independence or the territorial integrity of Iran under the pretext of exercising freedom. Similarly, no authority has the right to abrogate legitimate freedoms, not even by enacting laws and regulations for that purpose, under the pretext of preserving the independence and territorial integrity of the country.

Article 10

Since the family is the fundamental unit of Islamic society, all laws, regulations, and pertinent programs must tend to facilitate the formation of a family, and to safeguard its sanctity and the stability of family relations on the basis of the law and the ethics of Islam.

Article 12

The official religion of Iran is Islam and the Twelver Ja'fari school . . . and this principle will remain eternally immutable. Other Islamic schools, including the Hanafi, Shafi'i, Maliki, Hanbali, and Zaydi, are to be accorded full respect, and their followers are free to act in accordance with their own jurisprudence in performing their religious rites. These schools enjoy official status in matters pertaining to religious education, affairs of personal status (marriage, divorce, inheritance, and wills) and related litigation in courts of law. In regions of the country where Muslims following any one of these schools of *fiqh* [jurisprudence] constitute the majority, local regulations, within the bounds of the jurisdiction of local councils, are to be in accordance with the respective school of *fiqh*, without infringing upon the rights of the followers of other schools.

Article 13

Zoroastrian, Jewish, and Christian Iranians are the only recognized religious minorities, who, within the limits of the law, are free to perform their religious rites and ceremonies, and to act according to their own canon in matters of personal affairs and religious education.

Article 14

In accordance with the sacred verse ("God does not forbid you to deal kindly and justly with those who have not fought against you because of your religion and who have not expelled you from your homes" [60:8]), the government of the Islamic Republic of Iran and all Muslims are duty-bound to treat non-Muslims in conformity with ethical norms and the principles of Islamic justice and equity, and to respect their human rights. This principle applies to all who refrain from engaging in conspiracy or activity against Islam and the Islamic Republic of Iran. . . .

The Rights of the People

Article 19

All people of Iran, whatever the ethnic group or tribe to which they belong, enjoy equal rights; and color, race, language, and the like, do not bestow any privilege.

Article 20

All citizens of the country, both men and women, equally enjoy the protection of the law and enjoy all human, political, economic, social, and cultural rights, in conformity with Islamic criteria.

Article 21

The government must ensure the rights of women in all respects, in conformity with Islamic criteria, and accomplish the following goals:

1. create a favorable environment for the growth of woman's personality and the restoration of her rights, both the material and intellectual;
2. the protection of mothers, particularly during pregnancy and childrearing, and the protection of children without guardians;
3. establishing competent courts to protect and preserve the family;
4. the provision of special insurance for widows, and aged women and women without support;
5. the awarding of guardianship of children to worthy mothers, in order to protect the interests of the children, in the absence of a legal guardian.

Article 22

The dignity, life, property, rights, residence, and occupation of the individual are inviolate, except in cases sanctioned by law.

Article 23

The investigation of individuals' beliefs is forbidden, and no one may be molested or taken to task simply for holding a certain belief.

Article 24

Publications and the press have freedom of expression except when it is detrimental to the fundamental principles of Islam or the rights of the public. The details of this exception will be specified by law.

Article 25

The inspection of letters and the failure to deliver them, the recording and disclosure of telephone conversations, the disclosure of telegraphic and telex communications, censorship, or the willful failure to transmit them, eavesdropping, and all forms of covert investigation are forbidden, except as provided by law.

Article 26

The formation of parties, societies, political or professional associations, as well as religious societies, whether Islamic or pertaining to one of the recognized religious minorities, is permitted provided they do not violate the principles of independence, freedom, national unity, the criteria of Islam, or the basis of the Islamic Republic. No one may be prevented from participating in the aforementioned groups, or be compelled to participate in them.

Article 27

Public gatherings and marches may be freely held, provided arms are not carried and that they are not detrimental to the fundamental principles of Islam.

Article 28

Everyone has the right to choose any occupation he wishes, if it is not contrary to Islam and the public interests, and does not infringe the rights of others. The government has the duty, with due consideration of the need of society for different kinds of work, to provide every citizen with the opportunity to work, and to create equal conditions for obtaining it. . . .

Article 32

No one may be arrested except by the order and in accordance with the procedure laid down by law. In case of arrest, charges with the reasons for accusation must, without delay, be communicated and explained to the accused in writing, and a provisional dossier must be forwarded to the competent judicial authorities within a maximum of twenty-four hours so that the preliminaries to the trial can be completed as swiftly as possible. The violation of this article will be liable to punishment in accordance with the law. . . .

Article 37

Innocence is to be presumed, and no one is to be held guilty of a charge unless his or her guilt has been established by a competent court.

Article 38

All forms of torture for the purpose of extracting confession or acquiring information are forbidden. Compulsion of individuals to testify, confess, or take an oath is not permissible; and any testimony, confession, or oath obtained under duress is devoid of value and credence. Violation of this article is liable to punishment in accordance with the law.

Article 39

All affronts to the dignity and repute of persons arrested, detained, imprisoned, or banished in accordance with the law, whatever form they may take, are forbidden and liable to punishment.

Article 40

No one is entitled to exercise his rights in a way injurious to others or detrimental to public interests. . . .

The Right of National Sovereignty and the Powers Deriving Therefrom

Article 56

Absolute sovereignty over the world and man belongs to God, and it is He Who has made man master of his own social destiny. No one can deprive man of this divine right, nor subordinate it to the vested interests of a particular individual or group. The people are to exercise this divine right in the manner specified in the following articles. . . .

Powers and Authority of the Islamic Consultative Assembly

Article 72

The Islamic Consultative Assembly cannot enact laws contrary to the *usul* and *ahkam* [sources and rules] of the official religion of the country or to the Constitution. It is the duty of the Guardian Council to determine whether a violation has occurred, in accordance with Article 96. . . .

Article 91

With a view to safeguard the Islamic ordinances and the Constitution, in order to examine the compatibility of the legislations passed by the Islamic Consultative Assembly with Islam, a council to be known as the Guardian Council is to be constituted with the following composition:

1. six *'adil fuqaha,* conscious of the present needs and the issues of the day, to be selected by the Leader, and
2. six jurists, specializing in different areas of law, to be elected by the Islamic Consultative Assembly from among the Muslim jurists nominated by the Head of the Judicial Power. . . .

Article 96

The determination of compatibility of the legislation passed by the Islamic Consultative Assembly with the laws of Islam rests with the majority vote of the *fuqaha* on the Guardian Council; and the determination of its compatibility with the Constitution rests with the majority of all the members of the Guardian Council. . . .

The Leader or Leadership Council

Article 107

After the demise of the eminent *marji al-taqlid* and great leader of the universal Islamic revolution, and founder of the Islamic Republic of Iran, Ayatollah al-Uzma Imam Khumayni . . . who was recognized and accepted as *marji'* and Leader by a decisive majority of the people, the task of appointing the Leader shall be vested with the experts elected by the people. The experts will review and consult among themselves concerning all the *fuqaha* possessing the qualifications specified in Articles 5 and 109. In the event they find one of them better versed in Islamic regulations, the subjects of the *fiqh,* or in political and social issues, or possessing general popularity or special prominence for any of the qualifications mentioned in Article 109, they shall elect him as the Leader. Otherwise, in the absence of such a superiority, they shall elect and declare one of them as the Leader. The Leader thus elected by the Assembly of Experts shall assume all the powers of the *wilayat al-amr* [command] and all the responsibilities arising therefrom.

The Leader is equal with the rest of the people of the country in the eyes of law. . . .

Article 112

Upon the order of the Leader, the Nation's Exigency Council shall meet at any time the Guardian Council judges a proposed bill of the Islamic Consultative Assembly to be against the principles of *Shari'ah* or the Constitution, and the Assembly is unable to meet the expectations of the Guardian Council. Also, the Council shall meet for consideration on any issue forwarded to it by the Leader and shall carry out any other responsibility as mentioned in this Constitution.

The permanent and changeable members of the Council shall be appointed by the Leader. The rules for the Council shall be formulated and approved by the Council members subject to the confirmation by the Leader. . . .

The Presidency

Article 115

The President must be elected from among religious and political personalities possessing the following qualifications:

Iranian origin; Iranian nationality; administrative capacity and resourcefulness; a good past record; trustworthiness and piety; convinced belief in the fundamental principles of the Islamic Republic of Iran and the official *madhhab* [school of law] of the country.

The Army and the Islamic Revolution Guard Corps

Article 144

The Army of the Islamic Republic of Iran must be an Islamic Army, i.e., committed to Islamic ideology and the people, and must recruit into its service individuals who have faith in the objectives of the Islamic Revolution and are devoted to the cause of realizing its goals.

The Cairo Declaration on Human Rights in Islam

The Member States of the Organization of the Islamic Conference,

Reaffirming the civilizing and historical role of the Islamic Ummah which God made the best nation that has given mankind a universal and well-balanced civilization in which harmony is established between this life and the hereafter and knowledge is combined with faith; and the role that this Ummah should play to guide a humanity confused by competing trends and ideologies and to provide solutions to the chronic problems of this materialistic civilization;

Wishing to contribute to the efforts of mankind to assert human rights, to protect man from exploitation and persecution, and to affirm his freedom and right to a dignified life in accordance with the Islamic Shari'ah;

Convinced that mankind which has reached an advanced stage in materialistic science is still, and shall remain, in dire need of faith to support its civilization and of a self motivating force to guard its rights;

Believing that fundamental rights and universal freedoms in Islam are an integral part of the Islamic religion and that no one as a matter of principle has the right to suspend them in whole or in part or violate or ignore them in as much as they are binding divine commandments, which are contained in the Revealed Books of God

---

United Nations General Assembly, A/CONF.157/PC/62/Add.l8, June 9, 1993. Submitted to the World Conference on Human Rights, Preparatory Committee, Fourth session. Geneva, April 19–May 7, 1993. Item 5 on the provisional agenda. Annex to res. no. 49/19-P.

and were sent through the last of His Prophets to complete the preceding divine messages thereby making their observance an act of worship and their neglect or violation an abominable sin, and accordingly every person is individually responsible—and the Ummah collectively responsible—for their safeguard;

Proceeding from the above-mentioned principles,

Declare the following:

Article 1

A. All human beings form one family whose members are united by submission to God and descent from Adam. All men are equal in terms of basic human dignity and basic obligations and responsibilities, without any discrimination on the grounds of race, color, language, sex, religious belief, political affiliation, social status or other considerations. True faith is the guarantee for enhancing such dignity along the path to human perfection.

B. All human beings are God's subjects, and the most loved by Him are those who are most useful to the rest of His subjects, and no one has superiority over another except on the basis of piety and good deeds.

Article 2

A. Life is a God-given gift and the right to life is guaranteed to every human being. It is the duty of individuals, societies and states to protect this right from any violation, and it is prohibited to take away life except for a Shari'ah prescribed reason.

B. It is forbidden to resort to such means as may result in the genocidal annihilation of mankind.

C. The preservation of human life throughout the term of time willed by God is a duty prescribed by Shari'ah.

D. Safety from bodily harm is a guaranteed right. It is the duty of the state to safeguard it, and it is prohibited to breach it without a Shari'ah-prescribed reason.

Article 3

A. In the event of the use of force and in case of armed conflict, it is not permissible to kill non-belligerents such as old men, women and children. The wounded and the sick shall have the right to medical treatment; and prisoners of war shall have the right to be fed, sheltered and clothed. It is prohibited to mutilate dead bodies. It is a duty to exchange prisoners of war and to arrange visits or reunions of the families separated by the circumstances of war.

B. It is prohibited to fell trees, to damage crops or livestock, and to destroy the enemy's civilian buildings and installations by shelling, blasting or any other means.

Article 4

Every human being is entitled to inviolability and the protection of his good name and honor during his life and after his death. The state and society shall protect his remains and burial place.

Article 5

A. The family is the foundation of society, and marriage is the basis of its formation. Men and women have the right to marriage, and no restrictions stemming from race, color or nationality shall prevent them from enjoying this right.
B. Society and the State shall remove all obstacles to marriage and shall facilitate marital procedure. They shall ensure family protection and welfare.

Article 6

A. Woman is equal to man in human dignity, and has rights to enjoy as well as duties to perform; she has her own civil entity and financial independence, and the right to retain her name and lineage.
B. The husband is responsible for the support and welfare of the family.

Article 7

A. As of the moment of birth, every child has rights due from the parents, society and the state to be accorded proper nursing, education and material, hygienic and moral care. Both the fetus and the mother must be protected and accorded special care.
B. Parents and those in such like capacity have the right to choose the type of education they desire for their children, provided they take into consideration the interest and future of the children in accordance with ethical values and the principles of the Shari'ah.
C. Both parents are entitled to certain rights from their children, and relatives are entitled to rights from their kin, in accordance with the tenets of the Shari'ah.

Article 8

Every human being has the right to enjoy his legal capacity in terms of both obligation and commitment, [and] should this capacity be lost or impaired, he shall be represented by his guardian.

Article 9

A. The question [*sic*] for knowledge is an obligation and the provision of education is a duty for society and the State. The State shall ensure the availability of ways and means to acquire education and shall guarantee educational diversity in the interest of society so as to enable man to be acquainted with the religion of Islam and the facts of the Universe for the benefit of mankind.

B. Every human being has the right to receive both religious and worldly education from the various institutions of education and guidance, including the family, the school, the university, the media, etc., and in such an integrated and balanced manner as to develop his personality, strengthen his faith in God and promote his respect for and defense of both rights and obligations.

Article 10

Islam is the religion of unspoiled nature. It is prohibited to exercise any form of compulsion on man or to exploit his poverty or ignorance in order to convert him to another religion or to atheism.

Article 11

A. Human beings are born free, and no one has the right to enslave, humiliate, oppress or exploit them, and there can be no subjugation but to God the Most-High.

B. Colonialism of all types being one of the most evil forms of enslavement is totally prohibited. Peoples suffering from colonialism have the full right to freedom and self-determination. It is the duty of all States and peoples to support the struggle of colonized peoples for the liquidation of all forms of colonialism and occupation, and all States and peoples have the right to preserve their independent identity and exercise control over their wealth and natural resources.

Article 12

Every man shall have the right, within the framework of Shari'ah, to free movement and to select his place of residence whether inside or outside his country and if persecuted is entitled to seek asylum in another country. The country of refuge shall ensure his protection until he reaches safety, unless asylum is motivated by an act which Shari'ah regards as a crime.

Article 13

Work is a right guaranteed by the State and Society for each person able to work. Everyone shall be free to choose the work that suits him best and which serves his interests and those of society. The employee shall have the right to safety and security as well as to all other social guarantees. He may neither be assigned work beyond his capacity nor be subjected to compulsion or exploited or harmed in any way. He shall be entitled—without any discrimination between males and females—to fair wages for his work without delay, as well as to the holidays allowances and promotions which he deserves. For his part, he shall be required to be dedicated and meticulous in his work. Should workers and employers disagree on any matter, the State shall intervene to settle the dispute and have the grievances redressed, the rights confirmed and justice enforced without bias.

Article 14

Everyone shall have the right to legitimate gains without monopolization, deceit or harm to oneself or to others. Usury *(riba)* is absolutely prohibited.

Article 15

A. Everyone shall have the right to own property acquired in a legitimate way, and shall be entitled to the rights of ownership, without prejudice to oneself, others or to society in general. Expropriation is not permissible except for the requirements of public interest and upon payment of immediate and fair compensation.
B. Confiscation and seizure of property is prohibited except for a necessity dictated by law.

Article 16

Everyone shall have the right to enjoy the fruits of his scientific, literary, artistic or technical production and the right to protect the moral and material interests stemming therefrom, provided that such production is not contrary to the principles of Shari'ah.

Article 17

A. Everyone shall have the right to live in a clean environment, away from vice and moral corruption, an environment that would foster his self-development and it is incumbent upon the State and society in general to afford that right.
B. Everyone shall have the right to medical and social care, and to all public amenities provided by society and the State within the limits of their available resources.
C. The State shall ensure the right of the individual to a decent living which will enable him to meet all his requirements and those of his dependents, including food, clothing, housing, education, medical care and all other basic needs.

Article 18

  A. Everyone shall have the right to live in security for himself, his religion, his dependents, his honor and his property.
  B. Everyone shall have the right to privacy in the conduct of his private affairs, in his home, among his family, with regard to his property and his relationships. It is not permitted to spy on him, to place him under surveillance or to besmirch his good name. The State shall protect him from arbitrary interference.
  C. A private residence is inviolable in all cases. It will not be entered without permission from its inhabitants or in any unlawful manner, nor shall it be demolished or confiscated and its dwellers evicted.

Article 19

  A. All individuals are equal before the law, without distinction between the ruler and the ruled.
  B. The right to resort to justice is guaranteed to everyone.
  C. Liability is in essence personal.
  D. There shall be no crime or punishment except as provided for in the Shari‘ah.
  E. A defendant is innocent until his guilt is proven in a fair trial in which he shall be given all the guarantees of defense.

Article 20

It is not permitted without legitimate reason to arrest an individual, or restrict his freedom, to exile or to punish him. It is not permitted to subject him to physical or psychological torture or to any form of humiliation, cruelty or indignity. Nor is it permitted to subject an individual to medical or scientific experimentation without his consent or at the risk of his health or of his life. Nor is it permitted to promulgate emergency laws that would provide executive authority for such actions.

Article 21

Taking hostages under any form or for any purpose is expressly forbidden.

Article 22

  A. Everyone shall have the right to express his opinion freely in such manner as would not be contrary to the principles of the Shari‘ah.
  B. Everyone shall have the right to advocate what is right, and propagate what is good, and warn against what is wrong and evil according to the norms of Islamic Shari‘ah.

C. Information is a vital necessity to society. It may not be exploited or misused in such a way as may violate sanctities and the dignity of Prophets, undermine moral and ethical values or disintegrate, corrupt or harm society or weaken its faith.
D. It is not permitted to arouse nationalistic or doctrinal hatred or to do anything that may be an incitement to any form of racial discrimination.

Article 23

A. Authority is a trust; and abuse or malicious exploitation thereof is absolutely prohibited, so that fundamental human rights may be guaranteed.
B. Everyone shall have the right to participate, directly or indirectly, in the administration of his country's public affairs. He shall also have the right to assume public office in accordance with the provisions of Shari'ah.

Article 24

All the rights and freedoms stipulated in this Declaration are subject to the Islamic Shari'ah.

Article 25

The Islamic Shari'ah is the only source of reference for the explanation or clarification of any of the articles of this Declaration.

Cairo, 14 Muharram 1411H
5 August 1990

Glossary

ahl al-kitab People of the book. In Islamic law, the term for Jews and Christians, who are deemed to share the scriptural tradition that culminated in Islam. Some also include Zoroastrians and Sabeans in this category.

Ahmadi Pertaining to the sect founded by Mirza Ghulam Ahmad (d.1908) in India. Depending on interpretations, he is either to be considered as a new Prophet or as an Islamic reformer. Ahmadis have been accused of heresy for accepting a prophet after the Prophet Muhammad, and Pakistan officially treats them as non-Muslims.

Baha'i Pertaining to a religion established in Iran by Baha Ullah, known as the Bab, and promulgated by his son, Abdul Baha (1844–1921). It honors a line of prophets who include Abraham, Moses, Jesus, Muhammad, the Bab, and Baha Allah, which opens them to charges of apostasy from Islam. Iran's Shi'i clerics long denounced this religion, and since the Islamic Revolution, Baha'is have been the targets of particularly harsh persecution.

burqa A concealing, tentlike covering with a patch of netting in front of the eyes that permits the wearer to peer out. Required of women by social and religious pressures in many conservative areas of Afghanistan and Pakistan.

chador A large semicircle of cloth, today typically black, wrapped in such a way as to conceal all but a woman's face and hands. Commonly worn by lower class urban women in Iran, it became imposed as the form of Islamic dress favored by officialdom after Iran's Islamic Revolution.

concordisme In the context of the apologetic literature discussed in this book, the retroactive projection of prestigious modern developments in Western civilization into a putative Islamic past in efforts to demonstrate that Islam anticipated these developments.

Copts Depending on the context: the Coptic-speaking, Christian inhabitants of Egypt at the time of the Arab conquest or the remnants of this group. Copts have adopted the Arabic language but retain their Christian affiliation. Their community has been reduced by extensive conversions to Islam and is now a beleaguered minority in Egypt.

cultural relativism The rejection of the idea that universal standards can be validly used to judge individual cultures, based on the assumption that cultures can only be fairly judged in terms of their own internal value systems.

dhimmi A non-Muslim subject living under Muslim rule who enjoys protection in return for paying a special tax to the Muslim ruler and accepting a subjugated status governed by Islamic rules.

Druze Pertaining to a sect that was originally an offshoot of Isma'ili Islam but that is regarded as having broken away from Islam, now concentrated in the Levant, especially in Lebanon.

faqih **(plural,** *fuqaha)* An Islamic scholar possessed of advanced training in Islamic jurisprudence.

hijab **(Arabic)/***hejab* **(Persian)** A highly ambiguous term used to refer to various versions of Islamic modest dress for women. Potentially signifying everything from very concealing attire like a *chador* to a head scarf worn with otherwise conventional contemporary clothing.

Islamization The goal of many programs that have been put forward to reverse the Westernization of governments and legal systems in Muslim countries. Treating Islam as an ideology, Islamization programs typically assume that reviving Islamic law and strengthening Islamic morality will cure the ills of Muslim countries, enable them to block Western predations, and usher in an era of justice, prosperity, and social harmony.

jihad A term with a variety of connotations, but essentially connoting a struggle on behalf of Islamic causes. It potentially could include actual warfare against infidels but could also signify the individual believer's struggle to follow the teachings of Islam and to serve the faith.

jizya A tax amounting to a form of tribute required of non-Muslim subjects and paid to their Muslim rulers.

madhhab (plural, *madhahib*) Pertaining to the distinctive strains in jurisprudence that congealed into what are treated as separate schools with their own methodologies and rules.

millet The Ottoman term for the organization of society in which the Sunni rulers allowed separate communities to persist based on religious adherence (Armenians, Catholics, Greek Orthodox, Jews, and the like). These non-Muslim communities could enjoy a modicum of autonomy and self-government as long as they remained loyal to the Ottoman Sultan and paid the requisite taxes.

Muslim Brotherhood/*Ikhwan* One of the most influential of all the groups calling for Islamization. Founded in Egypt in 1928, this Sunni group has continued to press its program of remaking government, law, and society along Islamic lines in order to establish the ideal Islamic community. Members of the brotherhood, such as Hassan al-Banna and Sayyid Qutb, have spawned many emulators.

muhtasib In traditional Muslim societies, a kind of market and public safety inspector, also tasked with enforcing Islamic morality. In the contemporary context, more likely to be an official charged with the task of identifying and punishing infractions of conservative mores.

Mu'tazila A medieval rationalist current in Islamic thought that has always had some echoes in Shi'i thought and that recently seems to be spreading in influence among Islamic reformers and proponents of progressive positions.

Orientalism Since the 1978 publication of Edward Said's provocative study, *Orientalism*, this term has become associated with his critique of Western scholarship that he claimed was designed to portray Middle Eastern Muslims as enmeshed in an exotic and primitive culture. This portrayal was one that could be utilized by European powers to justify imperialist ventures, depicted as ways to bring progress and enlightenment to a benighted civilization.

purdah A system of keeping women in seclusion and segregated from men to whom they are not related and ensuring that, if they leave their homes, they are veiled and escorted by male family members. This system is often associated with the Indian Subcontinent.

qanun A term derived from the Greek that is used to denote secular law, especially codified laws. (All Islamic legal terminology derives from Arabic.)

shari'a The body of Islamic law, which is derived using approved methodologies from the Islamic sources, the Qur'an and the *sunna*.

Shi'i Pertaining to a branch of Islam whose adherents split from the Sunnis on the basis that the Prophet's divine inspiration had been inherited through his bloodline. Shi'is believe that Ali, the Prophet's son-in-law, was his rightful successor and that only the Prophet's descendants, known as Imams, should rule over the Muslim community.

Sufi Pertaining to the mystical tradition in Islam, in which the believer seeks oneness with God through mystical experiences.

sunna Roughly, the custom of the Prophet Muhammad, which is regarded as normative. Contained in accounts known individually as *hadith*, the sayings and actions of the Prophet Muhammad serve as an important source of guidance for Muslims. The accounts are contained in various collections, the contents of which can differ considerably.

Sunni Pertaining to the majority sect of Islam. The original Sunnis accepted the authority of the Caliphs who succeeded the Prophet Muhammad, rejecting the Shi'i position that his son-in-law Ali was the rightful successor. Over the centuries, Sunnis developed a jurisprudence that differed significantly from the Shi'i tradition, and within their own tradition, four separate schools of jurisprudence congealed.

Twelver Shi'ism The largest branch of Shi'ism. Adherents believe that the last of the divinely inspired Imams was the twelfth. After his disappearance, bereft of leadership, these Shi'is have turned to eminent Islamic clerics for guidance as they await his return. The geographical regions where Twelver Shi'is are concentrated have changed over the centuries. Today they constitute a majority in Azerbaijan, Bahrain, Iran, Iraq, and Lebanon.

'ulama Collective term for Islamic scholars and jurists.

umma The Muslim community, often entailing a reference to the early period of Islamic history when Muslims were united in a single religious and political community, which remains an ideal for many.

Wahhabi Pertaining to a puritanical sect of Islam that is dominant in Saudi Arabia and that takes its name from its founder Muhammad ibn 'Abd al-Wahhab (1703–1792).

Bibliography

Given the burgeoning literature and proliferating Web sites relating to Islam and human rights, this bibliography can offer only a small and selective sampling. An attempt has been made to list materials covering various topics, without any implication that the works cited are more meritorious than works not mentioned.

The Origins and Premises of the UN Human Rights System

Glendon, Mary Ann. *A World Made New: Eleanor Roosevelt and the Universal Declaration of Human Rights.* New York: Random House, 2001. A valuable account of the genesis of the UDHR.

_____. "Foundations of Human Rights: The Unfinished Business." *American Journal of Jurisprudence* 44 (1999): 1–14. An expert assessment of the UDHR.

Lindholm, Tore. "Prospects for Research on the Cultural Legitimacy of Human Rights: The Cases of Liberalism and Marxism." In *Human Rights in Cross-Cultural Perspectives: A Quest for Consensus,* ed. Abdullahi An-Na'im. Philadelphia: University of Pennsylvania Press, 1992, 387–426. A significant, original examination of the philosophical basis for the UDHR.

Morsink, Johannes. *The Universal Declaration of Human Rights: Origins, Drafting, and Intent.* Philadelphia: University of Pennsylvania Press, 1999. A valuable, detailed history of the process culminating in the production of the UDHR.

Waltz, Susan E. "Universal Human Rights: The Contribution of Muslim States." *Human Rights Quarterly* 26 (November 2004): 799–844. A review of the significant input from delegates of Muslim countries in the drafting of the human rights instruments.

_____. "Universalizing Human Rights: The Role of Small States in the Construction of the Universal Declaration of Human Rights." *Human Rights Quarterly* 23 (2001): 44–72. An important examination of how crucial UN human rights instruments were shaped by delegates from smaller countries.

The Islamic Heritage and Human Rights

Abou El Fadl, Khaled. "The Human Rights Commitment in Modern Islam." In *Human Rights and Responsibilities in the World Religions,* ed. Joseph Runzo, Nancy M. Martin, and Arvind Sharma. Oxford: Oneworld, 2003, 331–340. Reflections on how Muslims can rethink their religious heritage, identifying Islamic values consonant with human rights.

———. *Speaking in God's Name: Islamic Law, Authority, and Women.* Oxford: Oneworld, 2003. A vigorous challenge to authoritarian approaches to Islamic law and a lacerating critique of the methods underlying readings of the Islamic sources that call for subjugating Muslim women to male authority.

An-Na'im, Abdullahi Ahmed. *Toward an Islamic Reformation: Civil Liberties, Human Rights, and International Law.* Syracuse: Syracuse University Press, 1990. Representing the ideas of the martyred Mahmud Muhammad Taha, an explanation of how his system of Qur'an interpretation aimed at harmonizing Islam and human rights.

Baderin, Mashood A. *International Human Rights and Islamic Law.* Oxford: Oxford University Press, 2003. An extensively documented comparison of Islamic law and human rights written from the standpoint of a conservative Muslim who defends the Cairo Declaration and the stances of Iran and Saudi Arabia, arguing that deviations from the international human rights system are not significant.

Cohen, Joshua, and Ian Lague, eds. *The Place of Tolerance in Islam.* Boston: Beacon Press, 2002. Khaled Abou El Fadl examines tolerance; others respond and critique his stance.

Goodman, Lenn. *Islamic Humanism.* Oxford: Oxford University Press, 2003. A study of the humanistic elements that inhere in the Islamic heritage.

Hunter, Shireen T., ed. *Islam and Human Rights: Advancing a US Muslim Dialogue.* Washington, D.C.: CSIS Press, 2005. A collection of essays by Muslim and non-Muslim scholars discussing the relationship of the Islamic tradition to human rights and considering relevant US human rights policies.

Kurzman, Charles, ed. *Liberal Islam: A Sourcebook.* Oxford: Oxford University Press, 1998. Writings by a wide range of liberal Muslim intellectuals on subjects including democracy, the rights of women and non-Muslims, and freedom of thought.

Lawyers Committee for Human Rights. *Islam and Equality: Debating the Future of Women's and Minority Rights in the Middle East and North Africa.* New York: Lawyers Committee for Human Rights, 1999. Exchanges among participants at a conference on international law, human rights, and Islam, disputing whether equality can be accommodated within an Islamic framework.

———. *Islam and Justice: Debating the Future of Human Rights in the Middle East and North Africa.* New York: Lawyers Committee for Human Rights, 1997. A record of a debate about human rights between Islamists and Middle Eastern human rights activists.

Mayer, Ann Elizabeth. Review of *International Human Rights and Islamic Law*, by Mashood A. Baderin. *American Journal of International Law* 99 (2005): 302–306. My critical review of Baderin's book.

Mernissi, Fatima. *Islam and Democracy: Fear of the Modern World*, trans. Mary Jo Lakeland. Reading, Mass.: Addison-Wesley, 1992. An argument by a prominent Moroccan advocate of human rights and democracy challenging the barriers that Islam supposedly presents to democracy.

Sadri, Mahmoud, and Ahmad Sadri, eds. *Reason, Freedom, and Democracy in Islam: Essential Writings of Abdolkarim Soroush*. Oxford: Oxford University Press, 2000. See also the Web site of Soroush, http://www.drsoroush.com/English.htm. Proposals for enlightened, rationalist approaches to understanding Islam by one of Iran's leading philosophers, originally a supporter of the Islamic Revolution and now one of the country's most famous dissidents.

Safi, Omid, ed. *Progressive Muslims: On Justice, Gender, and Pluralism*. Oxford: Oneworld, 2005. A collection of essays by Muslims arguing for progressive interpretations of Islam on a variety of subjects.

Taji-Farouki, Suha, ed. *Modern Muslim Intellectuals and the Qur'an*. Oxford: Oxford University Press, 2004. Essays presenting a variety of current trends in Qur'an interpretation by liberal Muslims, demonstrating the importance of interpretive methodologies for drawing out the implications of the text.

Human Rights and Culture

Abu-Lughod, Lila. "Do Muslim Women Really Need Saving? Anthropological Reflections on Cultural Relativism and Its Others." *American Anthropologist* 104 (2002): 783–790. A tough assessment of the way people in the West and especially US feminists position themselves as disinterested humanitarians rescuing Muslim women from oppressive Islamic culture, effectively replicating the stances of former European colonial powers.

Engle, Karen. "Culture and Human Rights: The Asian Values Debate in Context." *New York Journal of International Law and Politics* 32 (2000): 291–333. A particularly interesting dissection of the Asian values debate and analysis of how "cultural" objections to international human rights can actually be proxies for other concerns.

Howard, Rhoda E. *Human Rights and the Search for Community*. Boulder: Westview Press, 1995. A study of how Western nostalgia for community can shape and distort Western perceptions of human rights issues.

Howland, Courtney W., ed. *Religious Fundamentalisms and the Human Rights of Women*. New York: St. Martin's Press, 1999. A collection of essays wrestling with the implications of various fundamentalisms for women's human rights.

Mayer, Ann Elizabeth. "Shifting Grounds for Challenging the Authority of International Human Rights Law: Religion as a Malleable and Politicized Pretext for Governmental Noncompliance with Human Rights." In *Human Rights with*

Modesty: The Problem of Universalism, ed. Andras Sajo. Leiden: Martinus Nijhoff, 2004, 349–374. An analysis of Iran's dramatically shifting stances on human rights universality over several decades, demonstrating the political contingency of "Islamic" objections to international human rights law.

_____. "Universal versus Islamic Human Rights: A Clash of Cultures or a Clash with a Construct?" *Michigan Journal of International Law* 15 (1994): 307–404. A dissection of how Huntington's clash of civilizations model misrepresents Muslims' reactions to human rights, relating Huntington's thesis to debates at the 1993 Vienna human rights conference.

"Women in Iran: An Online Discussion," *Middle East Policy* 8 (December 2001): 128–143. Excerpts from an online debate over women's rights in Iran, in which academics with dissimilar political and disciplinary perspectives appraise the situation.

Feminism and Islamic Feminism

Afkhami, Mahnaz, ed. *Faith and Freedom: Women's Human Rights in the Muslim World.* New York: I. B. Tauris, 1995. A collection of essays on various aspects of women's human rights in Muslim countries.

Afkhami, Mahnaz, and Haleh Vaziri. *Claiming Our Rights: A Manual for Women's Human Rights Education in Muslim Societies.* Bethesda, Md.: Sisterhood Is Global, 1996. A pioneering work providing real-life human rights dilemmas for Muslim women to study, discuss in group settings, and resolve.

Ali, Shaheen Sardar. *Gender and Human Rights in Islam and International Law.* The Hague: Kluwer Law International, 2000. Extensively documented discussions of Islam and women's human rights, with many references to women's rights in Pakistan.

Mernissi, Fatima. *The Veil and the Male Elite: A Feminist Interpretation of Women's Rights in Islam.* Reading, Mass.: Addison-Wesley, 1991. Reinterpretations of the Islamic heritage from an Arab feminist's perspective.

Mir-Hosseini, Ziba. *Islam and Gender: The Religious Debate in Contemporary Iran.* Princeton: Princeton University Press, 1999. An important account of competing Iranian feminist and conservative readings of the Islamic sources, with attention to the important feminist work of the cleric Mohsen Saidzadeh.

Moghadam, Val. "Islamic Feminism and Its Discontents: Toward a Resolution of the Debates." *SIGNS: Journal of Women in Culture and Society* 27 (2002): 1136–1171. An insightful comparison of Islamic feminism and its secular counterpart.

Human Rights Issues in the Islamic Republic of Iran

Abrahamian, Ervand. *Tortured Confessions.* Berkeley: University of California Press, 1999. An in-depth assessment of how the practice of torture under the Islamic Republic reflects Iran's Islamic ideology.

Afshari, Reza. *Human Rights in Iran: The Abuse of Cultural Relativism.* Philadelphia: University of Pennsylvania Press, 2001. A vigorous critique of the human rights record of the Islamic Republic and analysis of how Iran's religious ideology correlates with patterns in human rights violations.

Mack, Arien, ed. "Iran Since the Revolution." Special Issue, *Social Research* 67 (Summer 2000). A collection of articles assessing twenty years of the Islamic Republic from a variety of standpoints.

Mir-Hosseini, Ziba, and Richard Tapper. *Islam and Democracy in Iran: Eshkevari and the Quest for Reform.* London: I. B. Tauris, 2006. An important examination of the political context in which Iran's reformers press for democracy, with assessments of the writings and activities of one of Iran's most eminent dissident clerics.

Schirazi, Asghar. *The Constitution of Iran: Politics and the State in the Islamic Republic.* New York: I. B. Tauris, 1997. A thorough account of Iran's constitution and its political and legal context.

Shahidian, Hammed. *Women in Iran,* 2 vols. Westport, Conn.: Greenwood, 2002. A comprehensive assessment of gender politics under the Islamic Republic and an examination of women's mobilization to challenge the regime's curbs on rights.

The Rushdie Affair

Abdallah, Anouar, ed. *For Rushdie: Essays by Arab and Muslim Writers in Defense of Free Speech.* New York: George Braziller, 1994. A collection of Arab intellectuals' reactions to and evaluations of the Rushdie case.

al-'Azm, Sadiq Jalal. "The Importance of Being Earnest About Salman Rushdie." *Die Welt des Islams* 31 (1991): 1–49. An examination of the context and significance of the Rushdie case by an eminent Arab philosopher.

The Politics of Human Rights

Bennoune, Karima. "Toward a Human Rights Approach to Armed Conflict: Iraq 2003." *U.C.–Davis Journal of International Law and Policy* 11 (2004): 171–228. An inquiry into how international human rights law as well as international humanitarian law should apply to the US invasion and occupation of Iraq.

Chase, Anthony Tirado, and Amr Hamzawy, eds. *Human Rights in the Arab World: Independent Voices.* Philadelphia: University of Pennsylvania Press, 2006. Essays by both Arab and Western authors on a variety of current controversies about the struggle to advance human rights in Arab societies, including both Islamic and secular dimensions.

Danchin, Peter G. "US Unilateralism and the International Protection of Religious Freedom: The Multilateral Alternative." *Columbia Journal of Transnational Law* 41 (2002): 33–135. A dissection of the US pattern of privileging freedom of religion over other human rights and the unilateralist approach of the US International Religious Freedom Act.

Franks, Mary Ann. "Obscene Undersides: Women and Evil Between the Taliban and the United States." *HYPATIA* 18 (2003): 135–155. An examination of the oppression of Afghan women, finding fault in the policies of both the Taliban and the United States.

Mehdi, Rubya. *The Islamization of the Law in Pakistan.* Richmond, Surrey: Nordic Institute of Asian Studies, 1994. A critical assessment of Islamization in Pakistan, presenting it as a tool for legitimizing dictatorship.

Mendez, Juan E., and Javier Mariezcurrena. "Prospects for Human Rights Advocacy in the Wake of September 11, 2001." *Law and Inequality Journal* 22 (2004): 223–263. Appraisals of problematic US policies and actions in the war on terrorism, examining the repercussions of these on the human rights movement.

Nesiah, Vasuki. "From Berlin to Bonn to Baghdad: A Space for Infinite Justice." *Harvard Human Rights Journal* 17 (2004): 75–98. A study of the "crisis of cosmopolitan humanitarianism" in the wake of the US invasion and occupation of Iraq with analysis of the arguments for and against humanitarian intervention.

Proulx, Vincent-Joel. "If the Hat Fits, Wear It, If the Turban Fits, Run for your Life: Reflections on the Indefinite Detention and Targeted Killing of Suspected Terrorists." *Hastings Law Journal* 56 (2005): 801–900. An assessment of some of the human rights consequences of the way that the United States has conducted the war on terrorism

Risse, Thomas, Stephen Ropp, and Kathryn Sikkink, eds. *The Power of Human Rights: International Norms and Domestic Change.* Cambridge: Cambridge University Press, 1999. Proposal for a schematization of the stages through which international human rights law penetrates into domestic legal systems.

Roberts, L. Kathleen. "The United States and the World: Changing Approaches to Human Rights Diplomacy Under the Bush Administration." *Berkeley Journal of International Law* 21 (2003): 631–661. An assessment of the highly politicized and selective way human rights have been deployed in US foreign policy under the Bush administration.

Rone, Jemera. *Sudan, Oil, and Human Rights.* New York: Human Rights Watch, 2003. Also available at http://www.hrw.org/reports/2003/sudan1103/index.htm. A comprehensive overview of how the struggle to control the Sudan's oil resources has correlated with the government's policies and its egregious human rights abuses.

Waltz, Susan E. *Human Rights and Reform: Changing the Face of North African Politics.* Berkeley: University of California, 1995. Based on extensive research, a discussion of how human rights activism developed in North Africa and how it affected the political landscape.

Weissman, Deborah M. "The Human Rights Dilemma: Rethinking the Humanitarian Project." *Columbia Human Rights Law Review* 35 (2004): 259–336. An appraisal of the US deployment of human rights as an ideological rationale for neocolonial expansionism, showing parallels between the rationalizations for US intervention in Iraq and much earlier US interventions in Cuba and elsewhere.

Wickham, Carrie. "The Problem with Coercive Democratization: The Islamist Response to the US Democracy Reform Initiative." *Muslim World Journal of Human Rights* 1 (2004). Available at http://www.bepress.com/cgi/viewcontent.cgi?article=1018&context=mwjhr. An insightful analysis of how US initiatives to spread democracy in Arab countries have provoked a backlash among Islamists, who find these initiatives culturally offensive and fraught with double standards.

Internet Sites with Useful Information and Links

UN Human Rights Treaties, with texts of the instruments and information on ratifications and reservations:
http://www.un.org/rights/

Islam and Human Rights, School of Law, Emory University. Web site dedicated to the topic of Islam and human rights with extensive links to publications, bibliographies, materials for human rights activism, and other useful resources:
http://www.law.emory.edu/IHR/

al-bab (Arab Gateway)—Human Rights, with links to relevant declarations on human rights, including the UIDHR, human rights reports by NGOs and governments, and reports on specific Arab countries:
http://www.al-bab.com/arab/human.htm

Qantara.de Dialogue with the Islamic World, with many links to human rights institutions and NGOs, human rights documents and reports, including the UIDHR, the Cairo Declaration, and similar documents:
http://www.qantara.de/webcom/show_link.php/_c–449/i.html

Human Rights Index in the Arab Countries, offering extensive links to UN human rights committees, country human rights reports submitted to the UN, ratifications of human rights treaties, and some human rights organizations:
http://www.arabhumanrights.org/english/hrorgs/

University of Minnesota Human Rights Library—Islam and human rights links, including the UIDHR:
http://www1.umn.edu/humanrts/links/islam.html

University of Minnesota Human Rights Library—Middle East links, some of which relate to Islam and human rights:
http://www.umn.edu/humanrts/links/mideast.html

The Center of Islamic and Middle Eastern Law, SOAS, with links to writings on a
wide variety of Middle Eastern and Islamic legal topics and many source materials, including the Qur'an and *sunna:*
http://www.soas.ac.uk/Centres/IslamicLaw/Materials.html

Muslim World Journal of Human Rights published by the Berkeley Electronic Press,
with scholarly articles on human rights issues in Muslim societies:
http://www.bepress.com/mwjhr/

United Nations Development Program, Regional Bureau for Arab States, with links
to the Arab Human Development Reports that have been published since 2002
and that provide assessments of the development problems afflicting Arab societies and useful context for understanding the conflicts over human rights issues:
http://www.rbas.undp.org/ahdr.cfm

Internet Sites of Major International Human Rights NGOs

Amnesty International

http://www.amnesty.org/

Site offering many specific Amnesty reports on human rights issues in Afghanistan:
http://web.amnesty.org/library/eng-afg/index

Site offering many specific Amnesty reports on human rights issues in Iran:
http://web.amnesty.org/library/eng-irn/index

Site offering many specific Amnesty reports on human rights issues in Iraq:
http://web.amnesty.org/library/eng-irq/index

Site offering many specific Amnesty reports on human rights issues in Pakistan:
http://web.amnesty.org/library/eng-pak/index

Site offering many links for human rights issues in Saudi Arabia:
http://www.amnesty.org/ailib/intcam/saudi/issues/main.html

Site offering many specific Amnesty reports on human rights issues in the Sudan:
http://web.amnesty.org/library/eng-sdn/index

Human Rights Watch

http://www.hrw.org/

Site offering many links to reports on human rights issues in Afghanistan:
http://hrw.org/doc/?t=asia_pub&c=afghan

Site offering many links to reports on human rights issues in Iran:
http://hrw.org/doc/?t=mideast_pub&c=iran

Site offering many links to reports on human rights issues in Saddam's Iraq, relating
to the US invasion of Iraq, and in post-Saddam Iraq:
http://www.hrw.org/campaigns/iraq/

Site offering many links to reports on human rights issues in Pakistan:
http://hrw.org/doc/?t=asia_pub&c=pakist

Site offering many links to reports on human rights issues in Sudan:
http://www.hrw.org/doc?t=africa&c=sudan

Internet Sites for Women's Rights

Site of the UN Division for the Advancement of Women with many links and resources, including reports on the meetings of the Committee on the Elimination of Discrimination Against Women, where Muslim countries' defenses of
their stances on women's rights can be found:
http://www.un.org/womenwatch/daw/

Women's Human Rights Resources, Bora Laskin Law Library, University of Toronto,
with extensive materials and links for all dimensions of women's human rights,
relevant international law, and literature on the topic of women's rights:
http://www.law-lib.utoronto.ca/diana/

Bad Jens, an Iranian feminist Web site that offers a feminist online magazine mainly
addressing readers outside Iran:
http://www.badjens.com

Women Living Under Muslim Laws, a feminist NGO studying the rights of women
in Muslim countries, with many links:
http://www.wluml.org/

Women Living Under Muslim Laws publications and studies:
http://www.wluml.org/english/publications/engdossiers.htm

Women's Learning Partnership, aiming to empower women and girls in the Global
South through leadership training, capacity building, and helping women use
new technologies to generate and receive information and knowledge:
http://www.learningpartnership.org/

Notes

Chapter 1. Comparisons of Rights Across Cultures: Background Issues

1. Aspects of these adjustments and reformulations are discussed in Bassam Tibi, *The Crisis of Modern Islam: A Preindustrial Culture in the Scientific Technological Age*, trans. Judith von Silvers (Salt Lake City: University of Utah Press, 1988); Bassam Tibi, *Islam and the Cultural Accommodation of Social Change*, trans. Clare Krojzl (Boulder: Westview Press, 1990); Olivier Roy, *Globalised Islam: The Search for a New Ummah* (London: Hurst, 2004); and Gilles Kepel, *The Revenge of God: The Resurgence of Islam, Christianity, and Judaism in the Modern World* (Malden, Mass.: Polity Press, 2004).

2. A useful survey of early stages of human rights activism can be found in the articles assembled in *MERIP Middle East Report*, November-December 1987. See also Virginia Sherry, "The Human Rights Movement in the Arab World: An Active and Diverse Community of Human Rights Advocates Exists in Several Countries of the Region," Special Middle East Watch Issue, *Human Rights Watch* 4 (Fall 1990): 6–7; Kevin Dwyer, *Arab Voices: The Human Rights Debate in the Middle East* (Berkeley: University of California Press, 1991); Ann Elizabeth Mayer, "Moroccans: Citizens or Subjects? A People at the Crossroads," *New York University Journal of International Law and Politics* 26 (1993): 63–105; Hanny Megally, "Amnesty International and Human Rights in the Arab World: A Summary of the Last Decade," in *Democracia y Derechos Humanos en el Mundo Árabe*, ed. Gema Martin Muñoz (Madrid: Agencia Española de Cooperacion Internaciónal, 1993), 163–176; Susan Waltz, *Human Rights and Reform: Changing the Face of North African Politics* (Berkeley: University of California Press, 1995); *Cairo Papers in Social Science. Human Rights: Egypt and the Arab World* 17 (Fall 1994); and Nancy Gallagher, "Middle East and North African Human Rights Activism in Cyberspace," *Middle East Studies Association Bulletin* 31 (July 1997): 17–19. More recent accounts can be found in sources like Anthony Tirado Chase and Amr

Hamzawy, eds., *Human Rights in the Arab World: Independent Voices* (Philadelphia: University of Pennsylvania Press, 2006); The Arab Organization for Human Rights, http://aohr.org/; The Egyptian Organization for Human Rights, http://www .eohr.org/; The Ibn Khaldun Center for Development Studies, http://www.eicds.org/; The Human Rights Commission of Pakistan, http://www.hrcp-web.org/; and Bad Jens—Iranian Feminist Newsletter, http://www.badjens.com/.

3. See Alan Watson, *Legal Transplants: An Approach to Comparative Law* (Edinburgh: Scottish-Academic Press, 1974), 6–9.

4. Perverse mischaracterizations that are deployed by persons who are determined to discredit critical examinations of this topic are exemplified by the unfounded accusations that hostile reviewers have hurled at earlier editions of this book. These include charges that the book presents Islam as a monolithic model, that it suggests that Islam is static and inherently opposed to rights, that it argues for the superiority of Western law, and that it asserts that "contemporary Muslims do not possess the culture that entitles them to be concerned with human rights." See, for example, the extremely misleading reviews by Ahmad Dallal, *Middle East Studies Association Bulletin* 26 (1992): 245–246; Ridwan al-Sayyid, "Contemporary Muslim Thought and Human Rights," *IslamoChristiana* 21 (1995): 27–41; and Shamsheer Ali, "Review Article: Misguided Theorizing and Application," *Journal of Muslim Minority Affairs* 19 (1999): 299–320, to which I responded in Ann Elizabeth Mayer, "Misguided Interpretation: Ann Elizabeth Mayer's Response to Shamsheer Ali's Review Article," *Journal of Muslim Minority Affairs* 20 (2000): 181–184. See especially the wildly inaccurate charges in John Strawson, "A Western Question to the Middle East: 'Is There a Human Rights Discourse in Islam?'" *Arab Studies Quarterly* 19 (Winter 1997): 31–58, to which I responded in Ann Elizabeth Mayer, "A Rebuttal," *Arab Studies Quarterly* 20 (Winter 1998): 95–97, available at http://www.findarticles.com/ p/articles/mi_m2501/is_n1_v20/ai_20791170. See also an article on my Web site dissecting the canons of pseudo-scholarship in this area, "*Not* Taking Rights Seriously: Hallmarks of the Frivolous Human Rights 'Critique,'" available at http://lgst.wharton.upenn.edu/mayera/. A partisan of this movement to discredit critical appraisals of Islamic human rights schemes, Mashood Baderin, makes the outlandish claim that this book asserts that "Western culture should serve as the universal normative model for the content of international human rights law." See Mashood A. Baderin, *International Human Rights and Islamic Law* (Oxford: Oxford University Press, 2003), 10. Elsewhere, Baderin concocts an accusation that I have written that supporting "universalism"—*his* term, one not used in the passage referred to—entails agreeing that "Islamic law has no normative value and enjoys little prestige." See ibid., 12. Discussions of what I have actually written have been deliberately—and most conveniently—disregarded by these authors, whose political agendas dictate their recourse to misrepresentations of work supporting Muslims' entitlement to human rights, pretending that all such work aims to denigrate Islam.

5. There are important exceptions to the uncritical approach that dominated until recently. See, for example, Abdullahi An-Na'im, *Toward an Islamic Reformation:*

Civil Liberties, Human Rights, and International Law (Syracuse, N.Y.: Syracuse University Press, 1990); Sami Aldeeb Abu Sahlieh, *Les Musulmans face aux droits de l'homme: Religion et droit et politique. Etude et documents* (Bochum, Germany: Verlag Dr. Dieter Winkler, 1994); Jack Donnelly, "Human Rights and Human Dignity: An Analytic Critique of Non-Western Conception of Human Rights," *American Political Science Review* 76 (1982): 306–316; Bassam Tibi, *Der Schatten Allahs: Islam und Menschenrechte* (Munich: Piper Press, 1994); and Tore Lindholm and Kari Vogt, eds., *Islamic Law Reform and Human Rights: Challenges and Rejoinders* (Copenhagen: Nordic Human Rights Publications, 1993).

6. One of the influential voices expressing the critical mind-set that is becoming more common is that of Khaled Abou El Fadl. See Khaled Abou El Fadl, *Speaking in God's Name: Islamic Law, Authority and Women* (Oxford: Oneworld, 2003), and "The Human Rights Commitment in Modern Islam," in *Human Rights and Responsibilities in the World Religions,* ed. Joseph Runzo, Nancy M. Martin, and Arvind Sharma (Oxford: Oneworld, 2003), 331–340.

7. See, for example, Ann Gearan, "US Held Meetings with Taliban in 2000," *The Guardian*, August 19, 2005, available at http://www.guardian.co.uk/worldlatest/story/0,1280,-5220141,00.html.

8. Edward Said, *Orientalism* (London: Routledge and Kegan Paul, 1978).

9. Some implications of Said's work for legal scholarship are considered in William Lafi Youmans, "Edward Said and Legal Scholarship," *UCLA Journal of Islamic and Near Eastern Law* 3 (2003–2004): 107–116.

10. The Cairo Declaration is available at http://www.al-bab.com/arab/docs/international/hr1999.htm.

11. Said's analyses of Orientalist stereotypes have counterparts in assessments made in Sadiq Jalal al-'Azm, "Orientalism and Orientalism in Reverse," in *Forbidden Agendas: Intolerance and Defiance in the Middle East,* ed. Jon Rothschild (London: Al-Saqi Books, 1984), 349–381. See also "The Importance of Being Earnest about Salman Rushdie," *Die Welt des Islams* 31 (1991): 1–49, by the same author.

12. An important essay by Said's colleague Tony Judt has reminded us of Said's actual views on issues of human rights. See Tony Judt, "The Rootless Cosmopolitan," *The Nation,* July 19, 2004, available at http://www.thenation.com/doc/20040719/judt.

13. A good illustration of this position can be found in Adamantia Pollis and Peter Schwab, *"Human Rights: A Western Construct with Limited Applicability,"* in *Human Rights: Cultural and Ideological Perspectives,* ed. Adamantia Pollis and Peter Schwab (New York: Praeger, 1979), 1–18.

14. Ibid., 14. Pollis has come to acknowledge that the state may exploit the language of cultural relativism to rationalize its own repression. See Adamantia Pollis, "Cultural Relativism Revisited: Through a State Prism," *Human Rights Quarterly* 18 (1996): 316–344. Strangely, the author argues that universalists' conceptual framework blinds them to non-Western states' violations of the values and notions of justice and humanity that are established in their own cultures. In reality, as this book demonstrates, espousing the universality of human rights encourages inquiry into whether supposedly

cultural rationales for deviating from international law may in reality be prompted by state policy and political interests that should be distinguished from the local culture(s).

15. United Nations General Assembly. Thirty-Ninth Session. Third Committee. Sixty-fifth meeting, held on Friday, December 7, 1984, at 3 P.M., New York. A/C.3/ 39/SR.65. In a book that seeks to present Iran's stances on human rights in the most favorable light, the quote has been altered, and the statement that Iran would not hesitate to violate human rights has been excised. See Baderin, *International Human Rights,* 30.

16. See Ann Elizabeth Mayer, "Universal Versus Islamic Human Rights: A Clash of Cultures or a Clash with a Construct?" *Michigan Journal of International Law* 15 (1994): 317–320, 371–377, 392.

17. Fernando Teson, "International Human Rights and Cultural Relativism," *Virginia Journal of International Law* 25 (1985): 875.

18. Jack Donnelly, *Universal Human Rights in Theory and Practice* (Ithaca: Cornell University Press, 1989), 114.

19. For a critical evaluation of cultural relativists' tendency to totalize and reify Islamic culture, see Mayer, "Universal Versus Islamic Human Rights," 379–402; and Reza Afshari, "An Essay on Islamic Cultural Relativism in the Discourse on Human Rights," *Human Rights Quarterly* 16 (1994): 235–276. The need to differentiate between the ideologized Islam sponsored by Iran's national government and Islamic religion and culture as these persist in a village is shown by the observations in Reinhold Loeffler, *Islam in Practice: Religious Beliefs in a Persian Village* (Albany: State University of New York Press, 1988); and Erika Loeffler Friedl, *Women of Deh Koh: Lives in an Iranian Village* (Washington, D.C.: Smithsonian Institution, 1989).

20. "Women in Iran: An Online Discussion," *Middle East Policy* 8 (December 2001): 128–143.

21. See, for example, Susan Waltz, "Universalizing Human Rights: The Role of Small States in the Construction of the Universal Declaration of Human Rights," *Human Rights Quarterly* 23 (2001): 59–60; Mary Ann Glendon, "Foundations of Human Rights: The Unfinished Business," *American Journal of Jurisprudence* 44 (1999): 4.

22. Mary Ann Glendon, *A World Made New: Eleanor Roosevelt and the Universal Declaration of Human Rights* (New York: Random House, 2001), 185.

23. Glendon, "Foundations of Human Rights," 6.

24. Fereydoun Hoveyda, "The Universal Declaration and 50 Years of Human Rights," *Transnational Law and Contemporary Problems* 8 (1998): 432.

25. Susan E. Waltz, "Universal Human Rights: The Contribution of Muslim States" *Human Rights Quarterly* 26 (November 2004): 799–844.

26. See, for example, Michael Ignatieff, "Human Rights as Idolatry," in *Human Rights as Politics and Idolatry,* ed. Amy Gutman (Princeton: Princeton University Press, 2001), 58–60, 183.

27. Johannes Morsink, *The Universal Declaration of Human Rights: Origins, Drafting, and Intent* (Philadelphia: University of Pennsylvania Press, 1999), 25–26.

28. Ibid., 25.

29. Waltz, "Universal Human Rights," 815.

30. Ibid., 822.

31. Ibid., 820.

32. Ibid.

33. Ibid., 821.

34. Morsink, *The Universal Declaration,* 25.

35. Waltz, "Universal Human Rights," 823.

36. Ibid., 841.

37. Morsink, *The Universal Declaration,* 26.

38. Waltz, "Universal Human Rights," 839.

39. Ibid., 822–823.

40. Ibid., 824.

41. Ibid., 828–833.

42. Ibid., 840.

43. Ibid., 826–828.

44. Ann Elizabeth Mayer, "Rhetorical Strategies and Official Policies on Women's Rights: The Merits and Drawbacks of the New World Hypocrisy," in *Faith and Freedom: Women's Human Rights in the Muslim World,* ed. Mahnaz Afkami (New York: I. B. Tauris, 1995), 104–132, and "The Internationalization of Religiously Based Resistance to International Human Rights Law," in *Global Justice and the Bulwarks of Localism: Human Rights in Context,* ed. Christopher L. Eisgruber and Andras Sajo (Boston: Martinus Nijhoff, 2005), 223–255.

45. The human rights treaty ratifications can be researched on the UN Web site on the Status of Treaties Deposited with the Secretary General, available at http:// untreaty.un.org/ENGLISH/bible/englishinternetbible/partI/chapterIV/chapterIV.as.

46. For a critical appraisal of how Muslim countries allied with China on this issue, see Mayer, "Universal Versus Islamic Human Rights," 307–404.

47. Karen Engle, "Culture and Human Rights: The Asian Values Debate in Context," *New York University Journal of International Law and Politics* 32 (2000): 291–332.

48. Beirut Declaration on the Regional Protection of Human Rights in the Arab World available at http://www.cihrs.org/focus/almethaq/beirut-declaration.htm.

49. Amitabh Pal, "Shirin Ebadi," *The Progressive,* September 2004, available at http://www.progressive.org/sept04/intv0904.html.

50. Thus, for example, a recent study supporting the stances of countries such as Iran and Saudi Arabia and calling for "Islamic" curbs on women's rights and other human rights claims that international law is infected with "a strict and exclusive Western perspective." See Baderin, *International Human Rights,* 27.

51. Pal, "Shirin Ebadi."

52. Regarding the Western tendency to consider it incongruous for "Orientals" to have modern ideas, see Rhoda E. Howard, "Cultural Absolutism and the Nostalgia for Community," *Human Rights Quarterly* 15 (1993): 315–338.

53. Teson, "International Human Rights," 895.

54. This trend has been dissected in Rhoda E. Howard, *Human Rights and the Search for Community* (Boulder: Westview Press, 1995).

55. Louis Muñoz, "The Rationality of Tradition," *Archiv für Rechts und Sozial-philosphie* 68 (1981): 212.

56. Jack Donnelly, "Cultural Relativism and Universal Human Rights," *Human Rights Quarterly* 6 (1984): 411.

57. Rachad Antonius, "Human Rights and Cultural Specificity: Some Reflections," *Cairo Papers in Social Science. Human Rights: Egypt and the Arab World* 17 (Fall 1994): 22.

58. See Ann Elizabeth Mayer, "Qadhafi's Retreat from Revolutionary Legalism," in *Qadhafi's Revolution, 1969–1994,* ed. Dirk Vanderwalle (New York: St. Martin's press, 1995), 113–137.

59. See, for example, the discussions among Islamists and human rights activists in Lawyers Committee for Human Rights, *Islam and Justice: Debating the Future of Human Rights in the Middle East and North Africa* (New York: Lawyers Committee for Human Rights, 1997), showing how Islamists seek to associate their goals with human rights. In some cases, Islamists' programs sound much like the appeals of human rights NGOs. See Khaled Elgindy, "The Rhetoric of Rashid Ghannouchi," *Arab Studies Quarterly* (Spring 1995): 101–119.

60. Ann Elizabeth Mayer, "The Fundamentalist Impact on Law, Politics, and Constitutions in Iran, Pakistan and the Sudan," in *Fundamentalisms and the State: Remaking Polities, Economics, and Militance,* ed. Martin Marty and Scott Appleby (Chicago: University of Chicago, 1993), 110.

61. Ibid.

62. According to the margin of appreciation doctrine, instead of requiring uniform application of the European Convention on Human Rights throughout the European Union, national differences are accommodated. Through the margin of appreciation, national authorities are accorded a certain leeway and flexibility in deciding on the definition, interpretation, and application of the basic human rights guarantees contained in the treaty. See, for example, Howard Charles Yourow, *The Margin of Appreciation Doctrine in the Dynamics of European Human Rights Jurisprudence* (The Hague: Martinus Nijhoff, 1996).

63. Abdullahi An-Na'im, "Religious Minorities Under Islamic Law and the Limits of Cultural Relativism," *Human Rights Quarterly* 9 (1987): 5.

Chapter 2. Human Rights in International Law and Legal Systems in Muslim Countries: Sources and Contexts

1. Detailed information on the status of ratifications and reservations entered can be found for the ICESCR at http://untreaty.un.org/ENGLISH/bible/english internetbible/partI/chapterIV/treaty6.asp, and for the ICCPR at http://untreaty .un.org/ENGLISH/bible/englishinternetbible/partI/chapterIV/treaty5.asp.

After some delay, the relevant information also appears in hard copy adjacent to the respective human rights treaties in the annual volumes of the United Nations publication *Multilateral Treaties Deposited with the Secretary-General.*

2. Louis Henkin, "International Human Rights as Rights," in *Human Rights: NOMOS XXIII,* ed. J. Roland Pennock and John W. Chapman (New York: New York University Press, 1981), 258–259.

3. The translation in this edition is taken from "Constitution of the Islamic Republic of Iran of 24 October 1979 as amended to 28 July 1989," *Constitutions of the Countries of the World,* ed. Albert Blaustein and Gisbert Flanz (Dobbs Ferry, N.Y.: Oceana, 1992).

4. The problems of establishing constitutional government in Iran are discussed in Yann Richard, *Le Shi'isme en Iran: Imam et Révolution* (Paris: Maisonneuve, 1980); Abdul-Hadi Hairi, *Shi'ism and Constitutionalism in Iran* (Leiden: Brill, 1977); Said Arjomand, ed., *Authority and Political Culture in Shi'ism* (Albany: State University of New York Press, 1988); and Janet Afary, *The Iranian Constitutional Revolution, 1906–1911: Grassroots Democracy, Social Democracy, and the Origins of Feminism* (New York: Columbia University Press, 1996).

5. Shaul Bakhash, *The Reign of the Ayatollahs* (New York: Basic Books, 1984).

6. The amendments are discussed in Asghar Schirazi, *The Constitution of Iran: Politics and the State in the Islamic Republic,* trans. John O'Kane (London: I. B. Tauris, 1997), 95, 110–111, 234–237.

7. Both English and Arabic versions of the Cairo Declaration were submitted to the United Nations by the Organization of the Islamic Conference (OIC) prior to the World Conference on Human Rights in Vienna. See UN GAOR, World Conference on Human Rights, 4th Session, Agenda Item 5, UN Doc. A/CONF.157/PC/62/Add.18 (1993).

8. Ann Elizabeth Mayer, "Universal Versus Islamic Human Rights: A Clash of Cultures or a Clash with a Construct?" *Michigan Journal of International Law* 15 (1994): 375.

9. Ibid., 371–379.

10. See Isabelle Vichniac, "La Commission internationale de juristes dénonce un projet de 'déclaration des droits de l'homme en Islam,'" *Le Monde,* February 13, 1992. In response to a subsequent critical report by the International Commission of Jurists on the rule of law in Iraq, Iraq argued for a cultural relativist approach, defending its political order by asserting that democracy was affected by the "social, religious, and local characteristics of a nation" and that liberal democracy succeeded in the West because it suited the characteristics of Western societies—implying that it was unsuitable for Iraq. See International Commission of Jurists, *Iraq and the Rule of Law. Draft. A Study by the International Commission of Jurists* (February 1994).

11. "Closing Session of Teheran's Islamic Summit Delayed," *Deutsche Presse-Agentur,* December 11, 1997, available in LEXIS, Nexis Library, ALLWLD File.

12. An English translation of the Saudi Basic Law can be found in "Saudi Arabia: The New Constitution," *Arab Law Quarterly* 8 (1993): 258–270. The reforms are discussed in Rashed Aba-Namay, "The Recent Constitutional Reforms in Saudi Arabia," *International and Comparative Law Quarterly* 42 (1993): 295–331.

13. Article 7 of the law said that the government derived its power from the Islamic sources, the Qur'an and the custom of the Prophet, which constituted law superior to the Basic Law and other laws, and Article 1 asserted that Saudi Arabia was an Islamic state.

14. For examples of how Muslims are meshing human rights ideas with the Islamic tradition, see Abdullahi An-Na'im, *Toward an Islamic Reformation: Civil Liberties, Human Rights, and International Law* (Syracuse, N.Y.: Syracuse University Press, 1990); Tore Lindholm and Kari Vogt, eds., *Islamic Law Reform and Human Rights: Challenges and Rejoinders* (Copenhagen: Nordic Human Rights Publications, 1993); Fatima Mernissi, *Islam and Democracy: Fear of the Modern World,* trans. Mary Jo Lakeland (Reading, Mass.: Addison-Wesley, 1992); Lawyers Committee for Human Rights, *Islam and Justice: Debating the Future of Human Rights in the Middle East and North Africa* (New York: Lawyers Committee for Human Rights, 1997); Khaled Abou El Fadl, "The Human Rights Commitment in Modern Islam," in *Human Rights and Responsibilities in the World Religions,* ed. Joseph Runzo, Nancy M. Martin, and Arvind Shama (Oxford: Oneworld, 2003), 301–364; and Abdolkarim Soroush, *Reason, Freedom, and Democracy in Islam: Essential Writings of Abdolkarim Soroush,* trans. and ed. Mahmoud Sadri and Ahmad Sadri (Oxford: Oxford University Press, 2000). Works of Soroush are available at http://www.drsoroush.com/English.htm. The rethinking by contemporary Muslim feminists of the premodern norms of *shari'a* law affecting women, which is discussed in Chapter 6, is another example of the trend toward harmonization of Islamic precepts with international rights.

15. "Sudan Moslem Prayer Leaders Criticize Government," *Agence France Presse,* November 22, 1997, available in LEXIS, Nexis Library, ALLWLD File.

16. Suroosh Irfani, *Revolutionary Islam in Iran: Popular Liberation or Religious Dictatorship?* (London: Zed Books, 1983), on unnumbered page preceding the dedication page.

17. On the subject of clerical dissent, see, for example, Charles Kurzman, "Critics Within: Islamic Scholars' Protests Against the Islamic State in Iran," *International Journal of Politics, Culture and Society* 15 (2001): 341–359; Ziba Mir-Hosseini and Richard Tapper, *Islam and Democracy in Iran: Eshkevari and the Quest for Reform* (London: I. B. Tauris, 2006).

18. Ann Elizabeth Mayer, "Islamic Law as a Cure for Political Law: The Withering of an Islamist Illusion," *Mediterranean Politics* 7 (Autumn 2002): 117–142.

19. See Ladan Boroumand and Roya Boroumand, "Illusion and Reality of Civil Society in Iran: An Ideological Debate," in "Iran Since the Revolution," special issue, *Social Research* 67 (Summer 2000): 303–344.

20. Quoted by Edward Mortimer, "Islam and Human Rights," *Index on Censorship* 12 (October 1983): 5.

21. Bashir's military clique, which overthrew the elected government and seized power in Sudan in 1989, had a different perspective from Nimeiri's. By the time Bashir came to power, the Sudanese had already become disenchanted with Nimeiri's Islamization program, and Islamization had forfeited its mystique. Thus, rather than

catering to popular sentiment favoring Islamization, the Bashir regime was simply following its own ideological and political inclinations in disregard of the democratically expressed will of the voters, of whom only a minority had supported candidates committed to Islamization in the preceding democratic interlude.

22. See Lawyers Committee for Human Rights, *The Justice System of the Islamic Republic of Iran* (May 1993), 47–50; and Africa Watch, *Sudan: Sudanese Human Rights Organizations* (November 4, 1991), 2–5.

23. The reports reviewing the human rights situations in these countries have increased to the point that it is impractical to attempt a comprehensive listing. For specific assessments, consult the relevant country or regional sections in *Amnesty International Report, Human Rights Watch World Report,* and *US State Department Country Reports on Human Rights Practices,* all issued annually. See also topical reports prepared by the Africa, Asia, and Middle East regional sections of Human Rights Watch and also by Amnesty International, the Lawyers Committee for Human Rights (renamed Human Rights First), the International Commission of Jurists, and the Fédération Internationale des Droits de l'Homme. Reports prepared for the UN Commission on Human Rights are often informative. Excellent reports have been produced by local human rights groups, but one must be very careful to distinguish independent human rights groups from local organizations set up to disseminate pro-government propaganda. Relevant documentation can also be found in publications like *Index on Censorship* and *Human Rights Quarterly.* See also Ann Elizabeth Mayer, "The Fundamentalist Impact on Law, Politics, and Constitutions in Iran, Pakistan, and the Sudan," in *Fundamentalisms and the State: Remaking Polities, Economics, and Militance,* ed. Martin Marty and Scott Appleby (Chicago: University of Chicago Press, 1993), 110–151.

24. See the comments of Ali Oumlil, in Lawyers Committee for Human Rights, *Islam and Justice,* 72.

25. Human Rights Watch/Middle East, *Iran: Power Versus Choice. Human Rights and Parliamentary Elections in the Islamic Republic of Iran* (March 1996).

26. "Ayatollah Yazdi Denounces 'Conspiracy' Aimed at Undermining Country," *BBC Summary of World Broadcasts,* November 24, 1997, available in LEXIS, Nexis Library, ALLWLD File.

27. Mayer, "Islamic Law as a Cure for Political Law: The Withering of an Islamist Illusion," 117–142.

28. Reza Afshari, *Human Rights in Iran: The Abuse of Cultural Relativism* (Philadelphia: University of Pennsylvania Press, 2001); Ervand Abrahamian, *Tortured Confessions* (Berkeley: University of California Press, 1999).

29. Useful background is provided in J. Millard Burr and Robert O. Collins, *Requiem for the Sudan: War, Drought, and Disaster on the Nile* (Boulder: Westview Press, 1995); Human Rights Watch/Africa, *Civilian Devastation: Abuses by All Parties in the War in Southern Sudan* (New York: Human Rights Watch, 1994); and Ann Lesch, *The Sudan: Contested National Identities* (Bloomington: Indiana University Press, 1998); Human Rights Watch, *Sudan, Oil, and Human Rights* (New York: Human Rights Watch, 2003).

30. *BBC Summary of World Broadcasts,* May 1, 1984, ME/7631/A/8.

31. "The Transitional Constitution of the Republic of the Sudan, 1985," in *Constitutions of the Countries of the World,* ed. Albert Blaustein and Gisbert Flanz (Dobbs Ferry, N.Y.: Oceana, 1989). Article 3 made constitutional principles supreme so that they would prevail over other laws; Article 5 said that the state shall strive to "eradicate racial and religious fanaticism"; Article 11, that the state and each person "shall be subject to the rule of law as applied by the courts"; and Article 17, that all persons would be equal before the law.

32. Regarding rights violations in Sudan, see Africa Watch, *Denying "the Honor of Living." Sudan: A Human Rights Disaster* (March 1990). Other Africa Watch reports include *Sudan: Destruction of the Independent Secular Judiciary. Military Government Clamps Down on Press Freedom* (September 25, 1989); *Threat to Women's Status from Fundamentalist Regime* (March 1990); *Sudan: Sudanese Human Rights Organizations* (November 4, 1991); *New Islamic Penal Code Violates Basic Human Rights* (April 1991); *Inside al-Bashir's Prisons* (February 1991); *The Ghosts Remain: One Year After an Amnesty Is Declared, Detention and Torture Continue Unabated* (February 1991); and *Eradicating the Nuba* (September 1992). See also Amnesty International, *Sudan: What Future for Human Rights?* AI Index, AFR/54/01/95; Human Rights Watch/ Africa, *Behind the Red Line: Political Repression in Sudan* (New York: Human Rights Watch, 1996); and Lawyers Committee for Human Rights, *Beset by Contradictions: Islamization, Legal Reform and Human Rights in the Sudan* (July 1996).

33. See the accounts in Burr and Collins, *Requiem for the Sudan;* and Human Rights Watch/Africa, *Civilian Devastation.* See also Africa Watch, *Eradicating the Nuba.* A protest letter catalogues the extreme misery of the Nuba people, besieged and abused by the Bashir regime and its local militias. Forced conversions to Islam and executions of alleged apostates figure side by side with slave traffic in women and children, forced labor, orchestrated famines, pauperization, murder, rape, and genocide. Africa Policy Information Center, "Sudan: Women's Group Reports 'Genocidal Abuses' in Sudan," *Africa News,* October 26, 1997, available in LEXIS, Nexis Library, ALLWLD File.

34. Africa Watch, *Sudan: Sudanese Human Rights Organizations.*

35. "Transitional National Assembly Committee Completes Study of Draft Human Rights Document," *BBC Summary of World Broadcasts,* May 10, 1993, available in LEXIS, Nexis Library, ALLWLD File.

36. On the various pseudo-constitutionalist initiatives taken by Bashir's government, see Peter Nyot Kok, "Codifying Islamic Absolutism in the Sudan: A Study in Constitution-Making under al-Bashir," *Orient* 36 (1995): 673–706.

37. "Sudan Says UN Human Rights Text Offends Islam," *Agence France Presse,* February 23, 1994, available in LEXIS, Nexis Library, ALLWLD File.

38. "Sudan Calls UN Official a Blasphemer," *International Herald Tribune,* March 9, 1994, available in LEXIS, Nexis Library, ALLWLD File.

39. Haydar Ibrahim Ali, "Le Front National Islamique," *Politique Africaine* 66 (June 1997): 20.

40. Africa Watch, *Denying "the Honor of Living."*

41. Human Rights Watch/Africa, *Behind the Red Line: Political Repression in the Sudan* (New York: Human Rights Watch, 1996).

42. See Amnesty International, *Sudan: North-South Peace Deal Leaves Future of Human Rights Uncertain,* AI Index: AFR 54/002/2005 (Public) News Service No. 003, January 7, 2005.

43. As noted, President Zia was allied with such groups as Mawdudi's Jama'at-i-Islami. "Emir" is the term Mawdudi advocated for the leader of an Islamic government, which does not seem a coincidence in this context.

44. "Political Plan Announced, Seventh Session of Federal Council. Address by President General Muhammad Zia ul-Haq, Islamabad, August 12, 1983. Supplement to the Constitution of the Islamic Republic of Pakistan," in Blaustein and Flanz, eds., *Constitutions,* 182.

45. See Rubya Mehdi, *The Islamization of the Law in Pakistan* (Chippenham, England: Nordic Institute of Asian Studies, 1994).

46. See the discussion in Farooq Tanwir, "Religious Parties and Politics in Pakistan, " *International Journal of Comparative Sociology* 43 (2002): 250–268.

47. Relevant analyses include Olivier Roy, *Afghanistan: From Holy War to Civil War* (Princeton: Darwin Press, 1995); Ahmed Rashid, *Taliban: Militant Islam, Oil, and Fundamentalism in Central Asia* (New Haven: Yale Nota Bene, 2001).

48. Ossai Miazad, "Transitional Justice in Post-War Afghanistan," *Human Rights Brief* 9 (2002): 3–24; Mary Ann Franks, "Obscene Undersides: Women and Evil Between the Taliban and the United States," *HYPATIA* 18 (2003): 138–144.

49. This topic is discussed in Aba-Namay, "Recent Constitutional Reforms," 295–331, and is critically evaluated in Middle East Watch, *Empty Reforms: Saudi Arabia's New Basic Laws* (May 1992).

50. For discussions of the petitions that had preceded the Basic Law, see Middle East Watch, *Empty Reforms,* 59–62.

51. Ann Elizabeth Mayer, "Conundrums in Constitutionalism: Islamic Monarchies in an Era of Transition," *UCLA Journal of Islamic and Near Eastern Law* 1 (2002): 190–204.

52. Middle East Watch, *Empty Reforms,* 2.

53. "The Makkah Declaration of the OIC Summit Conference," *Arab News,* December 10, 2005, available at http://www.arabnews.com/services/print/print.asp?artid=74469&d=10&m=12&y=2005&hl=The%20Makkah%20Declaration%20of%20the%20OIC%20Summit%20Conference.

Chapter 3. Islamic Tradition and Muslim Reactions to Human Rights

1. Leo Strauss, *Natural Right and History* (Chicago: University of Chicago Press, 1953), 181–182.

2. J. Roland Pennock, "Rights, Natural Rights, and Human Rights: A General View," in *Human Rights: NOMOS XXIII,* ed. J. Roland Pennock and John W. Chapman (New York: New York University Press, 1981), 1.

3. This provocative interpretation has been put forward in Tore Lindholm, "Prospects for Research on the Cultural Legitimacy of Human Rights: The Cases of Liberalism and Marx," in *Human Rights in Cross-Cultural Perspectives: A Quest for Consensus,* ed. Abdullahi An-Na'im (Philadelphia: University of Pennsylvania Press, 1992), 397.

4. Ibid., 396–397.

5. For a general account, see A. J. Arberry, *Sufism: An Account of the Mystics of Islam* (New York: Macmillan, 1950). Notwithstanding Sufis' concentration on dissolving the individual and achieving spiritual oneness with God, their focus on the perfection of the individual soul and their common disregard for Islamic law and ritual does tend to link them with currents of thought that challenge state authority in religious matters.

6. Khaled Abou El Fadl, "The Human Rights Commitment in Modern Islam," in *Human Rights and Responsibilities in the World Religions*, ed. Joseph Runzo, Nancy M. Martin, and Arvind Sharma (Oxford: Oneworld, 2003), 331–340.

7. Ibid., 336.

8. Ibid., 301–364; Lenn Goodman, *Islamic Humanism* (Oxford: Oxford University Press, 2003).

9. The ideas of the Mu'tazila are discussed in George Hourani, *Islamic Rationalism: The Ethics of 'Abd al-Jabbar* (Oxford: Clarendon Press, 1971); Majid Khadduri, *The Islamic Conception of Justice* (Baltimore: Johns Hopkins University Press, 1984), 41–53; and Chikh Bouamrane, *Le problème de la liberté humaine dans la pensée musulmane: Solution mu'tazilite* (Paris: J. Vrin, 1978).

10. Bouamrane, *Le problème de la liberté humaine,* 344–345.

11. For an introduction to his ideas, see *Reason, Freedom, and Democracy in Islam: Essential Writings of Abdolkarim Soroush,* ed. and trans. Mahmoud Sadri and Ahmad Sadri (Oxford: Oxford University Press, 2000) and his Web site, http://www.drsoroush.com/.

12. Khadduri, *The Islamic Conception of Justice,* 78–105.

13. The struggles between proponents of reason and Revelation in Islamic intellectual history are described in A. J. Arberry, *Revelation and Reason in Islam* (London: Allen and Unwin, 1957); Khadduri, *The Islamic Conception of Justice,* 39–58, 64–70; and Mohamed El-Shakankiri, "Loi divine et loi humaine et droit dans l'histoire juridique de Islam," *Studia Islamica* 59 (1981): 161–182.

14. Khomeini's views are presented in Farhang Rajaee, *Islamic Values and World View: Khomeyni on Man, the State, and International Politics* (Lanham, Md.: University Press of America, 1983): 42–45.

15. These points are made in Noel Coulson, "The State and the Individual in Islamic Law," *International and Comparative Law Quarterly* 6 (1957): 49–60.

16. In this, Islamic legal thought resembles aspects of the natural law approach to rights in Western civilization. See Myres McDougal, Harold Lasswell, and Lung-chu

Chen, *Human Rights and World Order: The Basic Policies of an International Law of Dignity* (New Haven: Yale University Press, 1980), 68–71.

17. Background on this is offered in Erwin J. Rosenthal, *Political Thought in Medieval Islam: An Introductory Outline* (Cambridge: Cambridge University Press, 1962).

18. Coulson, "The State and the Individual," 50.

19. Examples of works that document the humanism that was and continues to be part of the Islamic tradition are Mohammed Arkoun, *L'humanisme Arabe au ive/ve siècle: Miskawayh, philosophe et historien* (Paris: J. Vrin, 1970), and *Rethinking Islam: Common Questions, Uncommon Answers* (Boulder: Westview Press, 1994); Marcel Boisard, *L'humanisme de l'Islam* (Paris: Albin Michel, 1979); Hisham Djait, *La Personnalité et le devenir arabo-islamiques* (Paris: Albin Michel, 1974); Joel Kraemer, *Humanism in the Renaissance of Islam: The Cultural Revival During the Buyid Age* (Leiden: Brill, 1986); Fazlur Rahman, *Islam and Modernity: Transformation of an Intellectual Tradition* (Chicago: University of Chicago Press, 1982); and Goodman, *Islamic Humanism.*

20. Some examples are given in Franz Rosenthal, *The Muslim Concept of Freedom Prior to the Nineteenth Century* (Leiden: Brill, 1960), 100–101, 105, 144.

21. Elie Adib Salem, *Political Theory and Institutions of the Khawarij* (Baltimore: Johns Hopkins University Press, 1965); Khadduri, *The Islamic Conception of Justice,* 20–23.

22. The general ignorance of Kharijite doctrines is partly linked to the fact that the remnants of the original community fled under persecution to remote parts of the Muslim world. Thus, one finds them in places like Oman and the mountains or isolated settlements in Algeria. Because so much of the writing by Kharijites was destroyed by their foes, the source materials on their ideas are quite limited.

23. Hani Shukrallah, "Human Rights in Egypt: The Cause, the Movement and the Dilemma," *Cairo Papers in Social Science. Human Rights: Egypt and the Arab World. Fourth Annual Symposium* 17 (Fall 1994): 55. For a discussion of the tensions between these value systems as they are embodied in the current political struggles in Morocco, see Fatima Mernissi, *Islam and Democracy: Fear of the Modern World,* trans. Mary Jo Lakeland (Reading, Mass.: Addison-Wesley, 1992); and Ann Elizabeth Mayer, "Moroccans: Citizens or Subjects? A People at the Crossroads," *New York University Journal of International Law and Politics* 26 (1993): 63–105.

24. See, for example, Omid Safi, ed., *Progressive Muslims: On Justice, Gender, and Pluralism* (Oxford: Oneworld Publications, 2005); Joshua Cohen and Ian Lague, eds., *The Place of Tolerance in Islam* (Boston: Beacon Press, 2002).

25. For background, see Said Amir Arjomand, "Constitutions and the Struggle for Political Order: A Study in the Modernization of Political Traditions," *European Journal of Sociology* 33 (1992): 39–82.

26. For an examination of the case of Egypt, see Farhat Ziadeh, *Lawyers, the Rule of Law, and Liberalism in Modern Egypt* (Stanford: Hoover Institution, 1968); Nathan Brown, *The Rule of Law in the Arab World: Courts in Egypt and the Arab States of the Gulf* (Cambridge: Cambridge University Press, 1997).

27. A classic account of the changing political views of the Arab elite at the time that constitutionalist ideas were percolating through Muslim societies is in Albert Hourani, *Arabic Thought in the Liberal Age, 1798–1939* (Oxford: Oxford University Press, 1967).

28. Examples can be found in Abdol Karim Lahidji, "Constitutionalism and Clerical Authority," in *Authority and Political Culture in Shi'ism,* ed. Said Arjomand (Albany: State University of New York Press, 1988), 133–158; and Abdul-Hadi Hairi, *Shi'ism and Constitutionalism in Iran* (Leiden: Brill, 1977).

29. I have compared the Saudi Basic Law with the far more developed Moroccan constitutional model in Ann Elizabeth Mayer, "Conundrums in Constitutionalism: Islamic Monarchies in an Era of Transition," *UCLA Journal of Islamic and Near Eastern Law* 1 (Spring/Summer 2002): 183–228.

30. An example of the uncertain status of constitutionalism is the fact that, to avoid offending Muslims who believe that constitutions are un-Islamic, the 1992 Saudi Basic Law, within its text, disavows any intention to be a constitution. Instead, it modestly calls itself *al-nizam al-asasi li'l-hukm,* or "basic regulation for government." Article 1 of the Basic Law reaffirms the primacy of the Islamic sources, maintaining that the country's "constitution," or *dustur,* is the Qur'an and the *sunna* of the Prophet Muhammad, on the theory that Saudi Arabia has a divine constitution—as opposed to a man-made one.

31. Examples of Professor An-Na'im's work can be found in his study of the religious reformer Mahmud Muhammad Taha, along with the translation of Taha's major work, *The Second Message of Islam* (Syracuse, N.Y.: Syracuse University Press, 1987); and his *Toward an Islamic Reformation: Civil Liberties, Human Rights, and International Law* (Syracuse, N.Y.: Syracuse University Press, 1990).

32. See, for example, Khaled Abou El Fadl, "A Distinctly Islamic View of Human Rights—Does It Exist and Is It Compatible with the Universal Declaration of Human Rights?" in *Islam and Human Rights: Advancing a US-Muslim Dialogue,* ed. Shireen Hunter (Washington, D.C.: CSIS Press, 2005), 27–42.

33. See Arkoun, *Rethinking Islam;* and the famous critique of religious thought by Sadiq Jalal al-'Azm, *Naqd al-fikr al-dini* (Beirut: Dar al-tali'a, 1972); and Muhammad Sa'id al-Ashmawy, *Against Islamic Extremism,* ed. Carolyn Fluehr-Lobban (Gainesville: University Press of Florida, 2001).

34. See, for example, Suha Taji-Farouki, ed., *Modern Muslim Intellectuals and the Qur'an* (Oxford: Oxford University Press, 2004).

35. See, for example, Abu'l A'la Mawdudi, *Human Rights in Islam* (Leicester, England: Islamic Foundation, 1980), 39; Sultanhussein Tabandeh, *A Muslim Commentary on the Universal Declaration of Human Rights,* trans. F. J. Goulding (Guildford, England: F. J. Goulding, 1970), 1, 85; and the first page of the English-language pamphlet version of the Universal Islamic Declaration of Human Rights (UIDHR).

36. This is particularly true in the case of the UIDHR, Tabandeh, and Mawdudi. They cite sources without attempting to show how the rights they purport to see in the text have been derived. Examples are offered in subsequent chapters.

37. See, for example, Asghar Schirazi, *The Constitution of Iran: Politics and the State in the Islamic Republic* (New York: I. B. Tauris, 1997), 162–72.

38. The writings of Mawdudi epitomize these characteristics.

39. A. K. Brohi, "The Nature of Islamic Law and the Concept of Human Rights," in International Commission of Jurists, Kuwait University, and Union of Arab Lawyers, *Human Rights in Islam: Report of a Seminar Held in Kuwait, December 1980* (International Commission of Jurists, 1982), 43–60.

40. A. K. Brohi, "Islam and Human Rights," *PLD Lahore* 28 (1976): 148–160.

41. A. K. Brohi, "The Nature of Islamic Law and the Concept of Human Rights," *PLD Journal* (1983): 143–176.

42. Brohi, "The Nature of Islamic Law" (Kuwait seminar), 48.

43. Brohi, "Islam and Human Rights," 150.

44. Ibid., 151.

45. Ibid., 152.

46. Ibid., 159.

47. For other perspectives resembling Brohi's, see Abdul Aziz Said, "Precept and Practice of Human Rights in Islam," *Universal Human Rights* 1 (1979): 73–74, 77; M. F. al-Nabhan, "The Learned Academy of Islamic Jurisprudence," *Arab Law Quarterly* 1 (1986): 391–392; Taymour Kamel, "The Principle of Legality and Its Application in Islamic Criminal Justice," in *The Islamic Criminal Justice System*, ed. Cherif Bassiouni (New York: Praeger, 1982), 169; and Cherif Bassiouni, "Sources of Islamic Law and the Protection of Human Rights," in *The Islamic Criminal Justice System*, ed. Cherif Bassiouni (New York: Praeger, 1982), 13–14, 23.

48. This failure to accord significance to the question of the rights of the individual vis-à-vis the state has a counterpart in the *shari'a* classification of rights into only two categories, the rights of God (to obedience from Muslims), *huquq Allah,* and the rights of the slaves (of God), *huquq 'ibad.* The latter are the rights that give individuals legal claims against other individuals. Coulson, "The State and the Individual," 50.

49. Abu'l A'la Mawdudi, *The Islamic Law and Constitution* (Lahore: Islamic Publications, 1980), 252. The original, in a more accurate translation, reads: "Hearing and obeying are the duty of a Muslim man both regarding what he likes and what he dislikes." Ibn al-Farra' al-Baghawi, *Mishkat Al-Masabih,* vol. 2, trans. James Tobson (Lahore: Muhammad Ashraf, 1963), 780.

50. Jack Donnelly, "Human Rights as Natural Rights," *Human Rights Quarterly* 4 (1982): 391.

51. Mawdudi, *Human Rights,* 37.

52. It is not unheard of, but highly unusual, to claim that the dead have human rights. If one adopted the view, based on a coherent philosophical approach, that the dead have human rights, one would be likely to propose other rights for the dead as well. See Raymond Belliotti, "Do Dead Human Beings Have Rights?" *Personalist* 60 (1979): 201–210.

53. Universal Islamic Declaration of Human Rights (UIDHR), Article 1.b.

54. Mawdudi, *Human Rights,* 18.

55. Ibid., 24–25.

56. Ibid., 24.

57. Ibid., 36.

58. Ibid.

59. Ibid., 17.

60. In the 1990s, efforts began to expand international human rights law to cover conduct in the private sphere, such as violence against women in the family. See, for example, Celina Romany, "State Responsibility Goes Private: A Feminist Critique of the Public/Private Distinction in International Human Rights Law," in *Human Rights of Women: National and International Perspectives,* ed. Rebecca J. Cook (Philadelphia: University of Pennsylvania Press, 1994), 85–115. Given the way that they treat women's rights, discussed in Chapter 6, the authors of the Islamic human rights schemes would not welcome such expansion of women's international human rights.

61. Mawdudi, *Human Rights,* 18.

62. UIDHR, Article 20.e.

63. Mawdudi, *Human Rights,* 38.

64. Ibid., 22.

65. UIDHR, Arabic version, Article 14.

66. The issues discussed here are not, of course, unique to the Muslim world. They relate to the search for cultural identity that is occurring in many formerly colonized societies. For a valuable analysis of the problems of establishing cultural identity in these societies, see Borhan Ghalioun, "Identité, culture et politique culturelle dans les pays dépendants," *Peuples Méditerranéens* 16 (1981): 31–50.

67. Abu'l A'la Mawdudi, *Purdah and the Status of Women in Islam* (Lahore: Islamic Publications, 1979), 45. Cited are figures such as "Judge Ben Lindsey, President of the Juvenile Court of Denver" (59), "Dr. Kraft Ebing [sic]" (116), and "Wester Marck [sic]" (127) to show that there was a scientific justification for *shari'a* rules. Even statements in the popular US monthly *Reader's Digest* were deemed worthy of citation to establish that *shari'a* rules are correct.

68. Tabandeh, *A Muslim Commentary,* 51.

69. International Commission of Jurists, Kuwait University, and Union of Arab Lawyers, *Human Rights in Islam: Report of a Seminar Held in Kuwait, December 1980* (International Commission of Jurists, 1982), 9. See also remarks on pages 11 and 34.

70. A. K. Brohi, "The Nature of Islamic Law and the Concept of Human Rights," in ibid., 54.

71. "Islam a Champion of Human Rights, Official Says," *Compass Newswire,* October 28, 1997, available in LEXIS, Nexis Library, ALLWLD File.

72. Tabandeh, *A Muslim Commentary,* 85.

73. Mawdudi, *Human Rights,* 15.

74. Ibid., 39.

75. Presumably, these are meant to resemble the ones in the scheme of drastically circumscribed and watered-down rights that he set forth in his human rights pamphlet.

76. For example, see Mawdudi, *Human Rights,* 15, 17–22.

77. International Commission of Jurists, *Human Rights in Islam, 7.*

78. Ibid., 49–55.

Chapter 4. Islamic Restrictions on Human Rights

1. Rosalyn Higgins, "Derogations Under Human Rights Treaties," *British Yearbook of International Law* 48 (1976–1977): 281.

2. Myres McDougal, Harold Lasswell, and Lung-chu Chen, "The Aggregate Interest in Shared Respect and Human Rights: The Harmonization of Public Order and Civic Order," *New York Law School Law Review* 23 (1977–1978): 183.

3. Ibid., 201–202.

4. Ibid., 202.

5. Universal Declaration of Human Rights (UDHR), Articles 1, 7, 10, and 16, respectively.

6. UDHR, Article 18, and International Covenant on Civil and Political Rights (ICCPR), Article 18.

7. UDHR, Article 23, and International Covenant on Economic, Social, and Cultural Rights (ICESCR), Article 6.

8. Johannes Morsink, "The Philosophy of the Universal Declaration," *Human Rights Quarterly* 6 (1984): 318.

9. UDHR, Articles 19, 20, and 21, respectively.

10. ICCPR, Articles 6 and 9, respectively.

11. Ebow Bondzie-Simpson, "A Critique of the African Charter on Human and Peoples' Rights," *Howard Law Journal* 31 (1988): 660–661.

12. See Courtney W. Howland, "The Challenge of Religious Fundamentalism to the Liberty and Equality Rights of Women: An Analysis Under the United Nations Charter," *Columbia Journal of Transnational Law* 35 (1997): 327–331.

13. Yves Linant de Bellefonds, *Traité de droit musulman comparé,* vol. 1, *Théorie de l'acte juridique* (Paris: Mouton, 1965), 18–50; and Noel Coulson, *A History of Islamic Law* (Edinburgh: Edinburgh University Press, 1964), 21–119. There is a vast literature on this subject written by Islamic jurists over many centuries.

14. The results of Islamic reformist thought are assessed in many studies, including Malcolm Kerr, *Islamic Reform* (Berkeley: University of California Press, 1966); Charles Adams, *Islam and Modernism in Egypt: A Study of the Modern Reform Movement Inaugurated by Muhammad Abduh* (New York: Russell and Russell, 1968); and Aziz Ahmad, *Islamic Modernism in India and Pakistan, 1857–1964* (London: Oxford University Press, 1967).

15. See, for example, Abdolkarim Soroush, *Reason, Freedom, and Democracy in Islam: Essential Writings of Abdolkarim Soroush,* trans. and ed. Mahmoud Sadri and Ahmad Sadri (Oxford: Oxford University Press, 2000); Mohammed Arkoun, *The Unthought in Contemporary Islamic Thought* (London: Saqi Books, 2002); Khaled Abou El Fadl, *Speaking in God's Name: Islamic Law, Authority and Women* (Oxford:

Oneworld 2003); and Omid Safi, ed., *Progressive Muslims: On Justice, Gender, and Pluralism* (Oxford: Oneworld Publications, 2005).

16. See Ervand Abrahamian, *Khomeinism* (Berkeley: University of California Press, 1993).

17. See Abdul-Hadi Hairi, *Shi'ism and Constitutionalism in Iran* (Leiden: Brill, 1977), which gives many examples of the objections raised by the *ulama* to the proposed constitution.

18. One eyewitness to a religious demonstration against the proposed constitution reported that religious students chanted "We do not want liberty" and "We do not want a constitution," while a mullah proclaimed that merciful Allah could pardon drinking wine, gambling, adultery, murder, and every form of crime, but constitutionalists were to be killed in as great numbers as possible, egging on his followers to beat two constitutionalists to death. The naked mangled bodies of the constitutionalists were then displayed. Ibid., 218.

19. The phenomenon of the *ulama* misconstruing the purport of Western freedoms is examined in many parts of Hairi's book. A good example is the explanation that one religious scholar gave for his support of freedom of speech and freedom of the press, which he understood to mean that writers and religious orators would be allowed to teach the truth regarding freedom according to the Qur'an and *sunna*. Ibid., 219.

20. Article 15 allowed persons to be dispossessed of property in cases where religious law authorized it. Although this could be read as a religious restriction on the right of private ownership, the traditional clerical interpretations of the *shari'a* afforded great protections for private property. Here, the "Islamic" grounds for interfering with the right would have been interpreted very narrowly, probably more narrowly than in many secular legal systems.

21. Abid Al-Marayati, *Middle Eastern Constitutions and Electoral Laws* (New York: Praeger, 1968), 17–20.

22. Shaul Bakhash, *The Reign of the Ayatollahs* (New York: Basic Books, 1984), 77.

23. Ibid., 78.

24. Ibid.

25. *Qavanin* (pl. of *qanun*) would normally refer to secular laws. However, with the modifications by the adjective "Islamic," as here, *qavanin* seems to mean "Islamic principles." This application of the term contrasts with the use of *qavanin* in Article 4, where the reference can only be to secular law, since there it is stated that laws, *qavanin*, should be based on (and qualified by) "Islamic principles," *mavazin-e eslami*. In the context of Article 4, *qavanin* must logically refer to secular laws, since interpreting *qavanin* in that article to refer to Islamic law would result in the provision saying that Islamic principles should be based on Islamic principles.

26. The arbitrariness of the censorship process is documented in Middle East Watch, *Guardians of Thought: Limits on Freedom of Expression in Iran* (New York: Human Rights Watch, August 1993).

27. For a review of the deficiencies of Iran's justice system, see Lawyers Committee for Human Rights, *The Justice System of the Islamic Republic of Iran* (New York: Lawyers Committee for Human Rights, 1993).

28. I have examined the significance of Khatami's ultimately futile campaigns for the rule of law and against the politicization of justice in Ann Elizabeth Mayer, "Islamic Law as a Cure for Political Law: The Withering of an Islamist Illusion," *Mediterranean Politics* 7 (Autumn 2002): 117–142.

29. See, for example, Amnesty International, *Iran: Human Rights Violations Against Shi'i Religious Leaders and Their Followers,* AI Index, MDE/13/18/97; and Ziba Mir-Hosseini and Richard Tapper, *Islam and Democracy in Iran: Eshkevari and the Quest for Reform* (London: I. B. Tauris, 2006).

30. "Iranian Leader Orders Prosecution of Dissident Cleric," and "Iranian Dissident Cleric Could Be Tried for Plotting Against Regime," *Agence France Presse,* November 26, 1997, available in LEXIS, Nexis Library, ALLWLD File.

31. "Protest Demonstration Against Khamenei Opponents in Iran," *Deutsche Presse Agentur,* November 19, 1997, available in LEXIS, Nexis Library, ALLWLD File.

32. "Political Infighting in Iran Spreads to Holy City," *Agence France Presse,* November 20, 1997, available in LEXIS, Nexis Library, ALLWLD File.

33. An example of how calculations of political interests could override any concern for fidelity to *shari'a* law can be seen in Khomeini's support of the storming of the US embassy in Tehran and the taking of diplomats as hostages, measures in flagrant contravention of Shi'i law. See Roy Mottahedeh, "Iran's Foreign Devils," *Foreign Affairs* 38 (1980): 19–34. It was also clear that *raison d'état* ranked above Islamic law in Ayatollah Khomeini's assertion on January 7, 1988, that his government was free to undertake any actions that it deemed in the interests of Islam. He claimed that Iran's Islamic government was among the most important divine institutions and had priority over such secondary institutions as prayers, fasting, and the pilgrimage—even though the latter are conventionally seen as fundamental pillars of the Islamic faith. See Asghar Schirazi, *The Constitution of Iran: Politics and the State in the Islamic Republic,* trans. John O'Kane (London: I. B. Tauris, 1997), 229–231. Khomeini's command on February 14, 1989, that Salman Rushdie be killed showed a similar disregard for *shari'a* standards of legality. The death edict has never won the endorsement of any distinguished independent Islamic jurists, and after adopting a more sophisticated line on human rights, the Iranian regime has gone to some pains to try to distance itself from the ruling, which even Iran's clerical leaders seem to have realized is indefensible. See Ann Elizabeth Mayer, "Islamic Rights or Human Rights: An Iranian Dilemma," *Iranian Studies* 29 (Summer-Fall 1996): 290–292.

34. Space does not allow discussion of the council here, but it is examined in Schirazi, *The Constitution of Iran.*

35. Examples of the problems of translating the UIDHR can be seen in two attempts to provide literal translations of the Arabic version into English and French,

which have resulted in inconsistent interpretations of important passages. See *Islamo Christiana* 9 (1983): 103–120 (English) and 121–140 (French).

36. In the English-language pamphlet version of the UIDHR published by the Islamic Council, these notes are placed on page 16 after the rights provisions.

37. It will be recalled that the Islamic qualifications included in Iranian constitutional rights provisions were similarly vague and open-ended.

38. In the Arabic counterpart of this article, one discovers that it actually offers a "right" to propagate Islam.

39. *Al-intiqal* in the Arabic, but translated into English as "transfer."

40. See, for example, Abu'l A'la Mawdudi, *Purdah and the Status of Women in Islam* (Lahore: Islamic Publications, 1979), 145–147, 200–209.

41. Sultanhussein Tabandeh, *A Muslim Commentary on the Universal Declaration of Human Rights,* trans. F. J. Goulding (Guildford, England: F. J. Goulding, 1970), 20.

42. This position correlates with standards set in anti-Ahmadi legislation enacted in 1984 by the Zia government in Pakistan. The treatment of Pakistan's Ahmadi minority is discussed in Chapter 8.

43. Tabandeh, *A Muslim Commentary,* 73.

44. Abu'l A'la Mawdudi, *Human Rights in Islam* (Leicester, England: Islamic Foundation, 1980), 28–29.

45. See "Transitional National Assembly Approves Document on Human Rights," *BBC Summary of World Broadcasts,* July 20, 1993, available in LEXIS, Nexis Library, ALLWLD File.

46. *Zaheeruddin v. State,* 26 S.C.M.R. (S.Ct.) 1718 (1993) (Pak.), 1773–1774.

47. Ibid., 1775.

48. Killian Bälz, "Submitting Faith to Judicial Scrutiny Through the Family Trial: The Abu Zayd Case," *Die Welt des Islams* 37 (1997): 149.

49. Constitution of the Islamic Republic of Afghanistan, available at http://www.oefre.unibe.ch/law/icl/af00000_.html.

50. For background, see Nathan J. Brown, "Iraq's Constitutional Process Plunges Ahead," in *Carnegie Endowment for International Peace Policy Outlook,* July 2005.

51. Law of Administration for the State of Iraq for the Transitional Period, available at http://www.cpa-iraq.org/government/TAL.html.

52. "U.S. Commission on International Religious Freedom Tells U.S. Ambassador Draft Constitution Fails to Protect Fundamental Rights," July 26, 2005, available at http://www.uscirf.gov/mediaroom/press/2005/july/07262005_iraq.html.

53. James Glanz, "U.S. Builds Pressure for Iraq Constitution as Deadline Nears," *New York Times,* August 14, 2005, 6.

54. See the translation of the Iraqi constitution, available at http://www.washingtonpost.com/wp-dyn/content/article/2005/10/12/AR2005101201450.html.

55. Khalilzad Speeches, "Iraqi Draft Constitution Balances Islam, Democracy, Envoy Says," August 23, 2005, available at http://iraq.usembassy.gov/iraq/20050823_khalilzad_press_conference.html.

Chapter 5. Discrimination Against
Women and Non-Muslims

1. A valuable introduction to these two aspects of the Islamic heritage is Louise Marlow, *Hierarchy and Egalitarianism in Islamic Thought* (Cambridge: Cambridge University Press, 1997).

2. A summary of the rules on personal status can be found in Joseph Schacht, *Introduction to Islamic Law* (Oxford: Clarendon Press, 1964), 24–33. A survey of sources dealing with inequality can be found in Ann Elizabeth Mayer, "Stratification, Authority and Justice in the Law of the Islamic Middle East," *BRISMES Bulletin* 4 (1977): 82–91; and 5 (1978): 3–19.

3. An example is the condemnation of the principle of equality in the supplement to the first Iranian constitution, signed by a number of prominent Shiʻi clerics. See Abdul-Hadi Hairi, *Shiʻism and Constitutionalism in Iran* (Leiden: Brill, 1977), 221–222, 232–233.

4. I have shown how awkwardly representatives of Arab countries struggle to rationalize their discrimination against women when faced with UN experts, in Ann Elizabeth Mayer, "Internationalization of the Conversation on Women's Rights: Arab Governments Face the CEDAW Committee," in *Islamic Law and the Challenge of Modernity*, ed. Yvonne Haddad and Barbara Freyer Stowasser (Walnut Creek, Calif.: Altamira Press, 2004), 133–160.

5. Abu'l Aʻla Mawdudi, *Human Rights in Islam* (Leicester, England: Islamic Foundation, 1980), 28–29.

6. Ibid., 21.

7. Ibid., 32.

8. The translation is taken from "Constitution of the Islamic Republic of Iran of 24 October 1979 As Amended to 28 July 1989," in *Constitutions of the Countries of the World*, ed. Albert Blaustein and Gisbert Flanz (Dobbs Ferry, N.Y.: Oceana, 1992).

9. The texts cited are 3:64, "None of us shall take others for lords besides Allah," and 49:13, "We have created you male and female." These are not texts that were historically interpreted to mandate full legal equality—nor does Tabandeh, in his critique of the UDHR, interpret them to establish an Islamic principle of nondiscriminatory treatment of women and non-Muslims.

10. Sultanhussein Tabandeh, *A Muslim Commentary on the Universal Declaration of Human Rights*, trans. F. J. Goulding (Guildford, England: F. J. Goulding, 1970), 15.

11. Ibid., 19.

12. Ibid., 20.

13. Jacobus Ten Broek, *The Antislavery Origins of the Fourteenth Amendment* (Berkeley: University of California Press, 1951).

14. For a discussion of this, see Oscar Garibaldi, "General Limitations on Human Rights: The Principle of Legality," *Harvard International Law Journal* 17 (1976): 525–526.

15. Illuminating descriptions of some aspects of early Muslim reactions to and interpretations of the principle of equality and equality before the law are in Hairi, *Shi'ism and Constitutionalism,* 224–234.

16. This was the interpretation of Mirza Muhammad Hussain Na'ini, a leading Shi'i cleric, who supported the Iranian constitutionalist movement and endeavored to show that constitutional rights accorded with Islam. Ibid., 224.

17. Relevant analysis is provided in Courtney W. Howland, "The Challenge of Religious Fundamentalism to the Liberty and Equality Rights of Women: An Analysis Under the United Nations Charter," *Columbia Journal of Transnational Law* 35 (1997): 329–330.

18. For example, the Prophet is quoted as saying that there can be no superiority of the Arab over the non-Arab, of the red (meaning "white" in contemporary American usage) over the black, or of the black over the red save in piety; the Prophet is further quoted as saying that if his own daughter stole, her hand would be cut off like that of any other thief.

19. Because the Arabic and English categories of grounds on the basis of which it is impermissible to discriminate do not correspond and because the English translation is obviously only a very rough approximation of the Arabic, the English cannot be used to clarify the meaning of the ambiguous terms *jins* and *'irq,* which potentially have overlapping meanings. At best, one could presume that in order to avoid redundancy, if *'irq* is taken to mean "race," *jins* should be taken to have some other meaning. The antidiscrimination language in the Preamble of the UIDHR is also not helpful in deciphering the precise meanings of the terms because of a lack of parallelism between the language it uses and that of Article 3.b. For example, the Preamble states that there can be no discrimination based on *asl* (origin or descent), *'unsur* (origin, race, or ethnic status), *jins* (the ambiguity of which has just been noted), color, language, or religion. Because other provisions of the UIDHR mandate sex-based discrimination, reading *jins* in Article 3.b to mean "sex," which would ordinarily be perfectly natural, entails internal inconsistencies in the document. To avoid such internal inconsistencies, one would tend to assume that *jins* should be assigned a meaning other than "sex." However, when one takes into account the frequent inconsistencies in the Islamic human rights literature, one cannot be sure that the authors of the UIDHR would have been troubled by including some provisions barring sex-based discrimination and others mandating such discrimination.

20. *Ansar Burney v. Federation of Pakistan,* PLD FSC, 1983, 73.

21. Ibid., 93.

22. It is interesting to contrast the result of this Pakistani case with the law enforced in Iran after the Islamic Revolution excluding women from the judiciary. This issue is discussed in Chapter 6 on the overall status of women, but it is mentioned here as yet another illustration of the differences among contemporary Muslims about how Islamic law affects women's rights.

23. This same Qur'anic command is included in Article 6 of the Azhar draft constitution and Article 8 of the Iranian constitution, but without any connection being made between it and a right of association.

24. It does not seem accidental that the Western reader, who in most cases is not able to translate the Arabic, is being given a very dissimilar version of the article, one that makes it look much more like a familiar international human rights concept. One sees in this provision yet another example of a pervasive pattern of discrepancies between the Arabic and English versions of the UIDHR where issues of equality are involved.

25. Nuri was active in organizing the revolutionary committees and the Revolutionary Guards, in the debates over the postrevolutionary constitution, and in the Majles after the revolution. This information was kindly provided by Professor Hamid Algar.

26. Yahya Noori [Nuri], "The Islamic Concept of State," *Hamdard Islamicus* 3 (1980): 78.

27. Ibid., 83.

28. Ibid., 70–80.

29. One should not assume that cultural differences make Orwell's ideas inaccessible to Iranians or Muslims generally, or that Iranians do not grasp the inconsistencies and contradictions in Islamic rights formulations. A particularly interesting indication of the fact that Iranians perceive the relevance of Orwell's work to their current circumstances is the enormous popularity that Orwell has enjoyed in Iran since the revolution. By 1984 a Persian translation of *Animal Farm* had become one of Iran's best-selling books, and George Orwell Iran's best-selling author. See "Book Boom in Tehran," *Index on Censorship* (October 1984), 9.

Chapter 6. Restrictions on the Rights and Freedoms of Women

1. The reforms made by the Qur'an are presented schematically in a volume produced at a conference held in Islamabad under the auspices of the Giant Forum and Global Issues Awareness for National Trust in collaboration with the Women's Development Fund, Canadian International Development Agency (CIDA), Islamabad, Pakistan. See *International Conference on Islamic Laws and Women in the Modern World: Islamabad, December 22–23, 1996* (Islamabad: Giant Forum, 1996), 20–21. Hereafter, cited as *International Conference on Islamic Laws.*

2. Fazlur Rahman, "The Status of Women in the Qur'an," in *Women and Revolution in Iran,* ed. Guity Nashat (Boulder: Westview Press, 1983), 38.

3. Naila Minai, *Women in Islam: Tradition and Transition in the Middle East* (New York: Seaview, 1981), 1–24; and Jane Smith, "Women, Religion, and Social Change in Early Islam," in *Women, Religion, and Social Change,* ed. Yvonne Haddad and Ellison Findley (Albany: State University of New York Press, 1985), 19–35.

4. Rahman, "The Status of Women," 37.

5. See the examination of disparities between the original sources and later interpretations in Barbara Stowasser, "The Status of Women in Early Islam," in *Muslim Women,* ed. Freda Hussain (New York: St. Martin's Press, 1984), 11–43; Bouthaina

Shaaban, "The Muted Voices of Women Interpreters," in *Faith and Freedom: Women's Human Rights in the Muslim World*, ed. Mahnaz Afkhami (London: I. B. Tauris, 1995), 61–77; Asma Barlas, "Believing Women," in *Islam: Unreading Patriarchal Interpretations of the Qur'an* (Austin: University of Texas Press, 2002); Fatima Mernissi, *The Veil and the Male Elite: A Feminist Interpretation of Women's Rights in Islam* (Reading, Mass.: Addison-Wesley, 1991); and Leila Ahmad, *Women and Gender in Islam: Historical Roots of a Modern Debate* (New Haven: Yale University Press, 1992). Mernissi argues that Islam elevated the status of women and that women under the leadership of the Prophet and his early successors played active roles, only later to be relegated to the status that they had prior to Islam under the rule of the Umayyad caliphs. Ahmad offers a similar interpretation, although arguing that it was changes under the Abbasid caliphs that precipitated the decline in women's status. The approaches of these two authors are critically appraised in Reza Afshari, "Egalitarian Islam and Misogynist Islamic Tradition: A Critique of the Feminist Reinterpretation of Islamic History and Heritage," *Critique: Journal of Critical Studies of Iran and the Middle East* 4 (Spring 1994): 13–34.

6. Introductions to aspects of women's status in the *shari'a* can be found in Joseph Schacht, *Introduction to Islamic Law* (Oxford: Clarendon Press, 1964), 126–127; Yves Linant de Bellefonds, *Traité de droit musulman comparé*, vol. 2, *Le Mariage: La Dissolution du mariage* (Paris: Mouton, 1965); Noel Coulson, *Succession in the Muslim Family* (Cambridge: Cambridge University Press, 1971); Ghassan Ascha, *Du statut inférieur de la femme en Islam* (Paris: L'Harmattan, 1987); and *International Conference on Islamic Laws*.

7. A summary of these changes can be found in J. N. D. Anderson, *Law Reform in the Muslim World* (London: Athlone, 1976). See also Tahir Mahmood, *Personal Law in Islamic Countries* (New Delhi: Academy of Law and Religions, 1987); and *International Conference on Islamic Laws*, 185–453.

8. A perfect embodiment of this response can be found in Abu'l A'la Mawdudi, *Purdah and the Status of Women in Islam* (Lahore: Islamic Publications, 1979). Many aspects of this literature are reviewed by Ascha, *Du statut inférieur*.

9. For a learned discussion of contraception and abortion in Islamic jurisprudence, see Basim Musallam, *Sex and Society in Islam: Birth Control Before the Nineteenth Century* (Cambridge: Cambridge University Press, 1983).

10. See Abdullahi El-Naiem [An-Na'im], "A Modern Approach to Human Rights in Islam: Foundations and Implications for Africa," in *Human Rights and Development in Africa*, ed. Claude Welch Jr. and Ronald Meltzer (Albany: State University of New York Press, 1984), 82; and Mernissi, *The Veil and the Male Elite*.

11. Examples of feminist literature include Fatima Mernissi, *Islam and Democracy: Fear of the Modern World*, trans. Mary Jo Lakeland (Reading, Mass.: Addison-Wesley, 1991), and *The Veil and the Male Elite;* Ahmad, *Women and Gender in Islam;* Khawar Mumtaz and Farida Shaheed, *Women of Pakistan: Two Steps Forward, One Step Back?* (London: Zed Books, 1987); Riffat Hassan, "Feminist Theology: The

Challenges for Muslim Women," *Critique: Journal for Critical Studies of the Middle East* (Fall 1996): 53–66; Mahnaz Afkhami, ed., *Faith and Freedom: Women's Human Rights in the Muslim World;* Ayesha M. Imam, "The Muslim Religious Right ("Fundamentalists") and Sexuality," *Women Living Under Muslim Laws: Dossier* 17 (June 1997): 7–25; Mahnaz Afkhami and Erika Friedl, eds., *Muslim Women and the Politics of Participation: Implementing the Beijing Platform* (Syracuse, N.Y.: Syracuse University Press, 1997); Ziba Mir-Hosseini, *Islam and Gender: The Religious Debate in Contemporary Iran* (Princeton: Princeton University Press, 1999), and *Feminism and the Islamic Republic: Dialogues with the Ulema* (Princeton: Princeton University Press, 1999); Shaheen Sardar Ali, *Gender and Human Rights in Islam and International Law* (The Hague: Kluwer Law International, 2000); Val Moghadam, "Islamic Feminism and Its Discontents: Toward a Resolution of the Debates," *SIGNS: Journal of Women in Culture and Society* 27 (2002): 1136–1171; Khaled Abou El Fadl, *Speaking in God's Name: Islamic Law, Authority and Women* (Oxford: Oneworld Publications, 2003); Fereshteh Nouraie-Simone, ed., *On Shifting Ground: Muslim Women in the Global Era* (New York: Feminist Press, 2005).

12. This is a consistent theme of Mawdudi's writings. For an example of his arguments, see Mawdudi, *Purdah and the Status of Women,* 21–24.

13. Ibid., 73–74.

14. Ibid., 24.

15. One sign of this might be seen in the patterns of personal status law reform and constitutional guarantees of women's rights in Muslim countries. In most Muslim countries, the choice has been to compromise, keeping some elements of the *shari'a* system of personal status but including many reforms improving the rights of women. See *International Conference on Islamic Laws,* 185–453; and Abdullahi A. An-Na'im, *Islamic Family Law in a Changing World: A Global Resource Book* (London: Zed Books, 2002).

16. See Belinda Clark, "The Vienna Convention Reservations Regime and the Convention on Discrimination Against Women," *American Journal of International Law* 85 (1991): 281–321; and Jane Connors, "The Women's Convention in the Muslim World," in *Human Rights as General Norms and a State's Right to Opt Out: Reservations and Objections to Human Rights Conventions,* ed. J. P. Gardner (London: British Institute of International and Comparative Law, 1997), 85–103.

17. Ann Elizabeth Mayer, "Rhetorical Strategies and Official Policies on Women's Rights: The Merits and Drawbacks of the New World Hypocrisy," in *Faith and Freedom: Women's Human Rights in the Muslim World,* ed. Mahnaz Afkhami, 105–119, and "Religious Reservations to CEDAW: What Do They Really Mean?" in *Religious Fundamentalism and the Human Rights of Women,* ed. Courtney Howland (New York: St. Martin's Press, 1999), 105–116.

18. Sultanhussein Tabandeh, *A Muslim Commentary on the Universal Declaration of Human Rights,* trans. F. J. Goulding (Guildford, England: F. J. Goulding, 1970), 1.

19. See, for example, his comments on Article 16 of the UDHR. Ibid., 41–45.

20. Ibid., 35.

21. Ibid., 41–45.

22. Ibid., 37–38.

23. Ibid., 38–39.

24. Ibid., 40.

25. Ibid., 58.

26. Ibid., 51.

27. Ibid., 57. The alliteration here, it should be noted, is that of Tabandeh's translator.

28. Ibid., 52.

29. Abu'l A'la Mawdudi, *The Islamic Law and Constitution* (Lahore: Islamic Publications, 1980), 262–263; and *Purdah and the Status of Women,* passim, and on divorce, 151.

30. Mawdudi, *Purdah and the Status of Women,* 12.

31. Ibid., 12–15, 26–71.

32. Ibid., 15.

33. Ibid., 73.

34. Abu'l A'la Mawdudi, *Human Rights in Islam* (Leicester, England: Islamic Foundation, 1980), 18.

35. The systematic rapes of women during the strife in Bosnia have heightened the awareness of the need for international law to address such campaigns as violations of human rights and as war crimes. See Donna Sullivan, "Women's Human Rights and the 1993 World Conference on Human Rights," *American Journal of International Law* 88 (1994): 155–156; and Theodor Meron, "Rape as a Crime Under International Humanitarian Law," *American Journal of International Law* 87 (1993): 424–428.

36. Mawdudi, *Human Rights,* 18.

37. Indeed, restrictions on women's testimony in the *shari'a* rules of evidence can make it especially difficult for a woman to prove such an offense and obtain the conviction of an offender because in the case of *hadd* crimes (those for which the penalty is set or implied in the text of the Qur'an), the testimony of women witnesses may be barred altogether.

38. Naturally, the sordid details of these incidents were publicized in India, Pakistan's enemy. See, for example, Amita Malik, *The Year of the Vulture* (New Delhi: Orient Longman, 1972). Mawdudi and his followers backed the efforts of the Pakistani government to crush the movement to establish an independent Bangladesh. The mass rapes of Bengali women, carried out by an army dominated by Punjabis and following a policy aimed at humiliating, degrading, and terrifying the Bengali ethnic group, constituted the kinds of rapes that particularly concern international law. However, far from being moved to condemn these rapes, Mawdudi was trying to deny that they had ever occurred.

39. According to the preface, Mawdudi's human rights pamphlet is translated from a speech delivered on November 16, 1975, at the Civil Rights and Liberties Fo-

rum in the Flatties Hotel in Lahore. Mawdudi, *Human Rights, 7.* Mawdudi and his audience in Lahore, capital of the Punjab, which has traditionally supplied most of Pakistan's military manpower, must have been aware of the Bengali rapes and how they had tarnished Pakistan's image when he made his 1975 speech.

40. See Shahla Haeri, "The Politics of Dishonor: Rape and Power in Pakistan," in *Faith and Freedom: Women's Human Rights in the Muslim World,* 161–174; and Rubya Mehdi, "The Offence of Rape in the Islamic Law of Pakistan," *Women Living Under Muslim Laws: Dossier* 18 (July 1997): 98–108. The sexism of the Pakistani laws on rape in the wake of Islamization is dissected in Asifa Quraishi, "Her Honor: An Islamic Critique of the Rape Laws of Pakistan from a Woman-Sensitive Perspective," *Michigan Journal of International Law* 18 (1997): 287–320. From the standpoint of a Muslim feminist, the laws that Mawdudi vaunts are profoundly problematic.

41. According to the choice-of-law rules in Islam and in the law of Muslim countries, Islamic criteria are used to judge the validity of a mixed marriage. The fact that the religious law of the husband allows such a marriage is treated as irrelevant. Relevant Islamic choice-of-law rules are discussed in Klaus Wähler, *Interreligiöses Kollisionsrecht im Bereich privatrechtlicher Rechtsbeziehungen* (Cologne: Carl Heymanns Verlag, 1978), 157–158. Muslim conservatives today share the view that the validity of a mixed marriage is to be judged under *shari'a* rules. See Mawdudi, *The Islamic Law and Constitution,* 287. This principle is applied as public policy in Muslim countries where the law does not specifically ban such marriages.

42. Examples of such rules are discussed in Mahmood, *Personal Law,* 275–276.

43. These references appear on p. 19 of the English version.

44. For example, see Mawdudi's invocation of this verse; Mawdudi, *Purdah and the Status of Women,* 149.

45. Yves Linant de Bellefonds, *Traité de droit musulman comparé,* vol. 3, *Filiation: Incapacités, Liberalités entre vifs* (Paris: Mouton, 1965), 81–142.

46. In theory, the guardian could also marry off a male ward without his consent, but because of the ease with which a Muslim man could terminate an unwanted marriage, this had little practical effect or significance.

47. Anderson, *Law Reform in the Muslim World,* 102–105.

48. See, for example, Mawdudi, *Purdah and the Status of Women,* 144–155.

49. Noel Coulson, *Succession in the Muslim Family* (Cambridge: Cambridge University Press, 1971), 214.

50. Linant de Bellefonds, *Traité de droit musulman comparé,* vol. 2, 451–470.

51. The translation is from "Constitution of the Islamic Republic of Iran of 24 October 1979 As Amended to 28 July 1989," in Albert Blaustein and Gisbert Flanz, eds., *Constitutions of the Countries of the World* (Dobbs Ferry, N.Y.: Oceana, 1992).

52. Doreen Hinchcliffe, "The Iranian Family Protection Act," *International and Comparative Law Quarterly* 17 (1968): 516–521; and Eliz Sanasarian, *The Women's Rights Movement in Iran: Mutiny, Appeasement, and Repression from 1990 to Khomeini* (New York: Praeger, 1982), 94–97. The situation of women in the aftermath of the

abrogation of the Family Protection Act is examined in Ziba Mir-Hosseini, *Marriage on Trial: A Study of Islamic Family Law. Iran and Morocco Compared* (New York: I. B. Tauris, 1993).

53. *International Conference on Islamic Laws,* 316.

54. Shahla Haeri, "The Institution of Mut'a Marriage in Iran: A Formal and Historical Perspective," in *Women and Revolution in Iran,* ed. Guity Nashat (Boulder: Westview Press, 1983), 231–252, and *Law of Desire: Temporary Marriage in Iran* (London: I. B. Tauris, 1989).

55. Parvin Paidar, *Women and the Political Process in Twentieth-Century Iran* (Cambridge: Cambridge University Press, 1995), 303–335.

56. Ibid., 286–289.

57. See UN High Commissioner for Human Rights, "Situation of Human Rights in the Islamic Republic of Iran: Iran (Islamic Republic of) 15/10/97," A/52/472, available at http://www.iran.org/humanrights/UN971015.htm.

58. "Iranian Team Set for Atlanta Despite Visa Bother," *Deutsche Presse-Agentur,* July 9, 1996, available in LEXIS, Nexis Library, ALLWLD File.

59. The incident described here was reported in the world press, including *The Herald* (Harare) and the *New York Times* on January 22, 1986.

60. Nikki Keddie, "Women in Iran Since 1979," Special Issue, Iran Since the Revolution, *Social Research* 67 (Summer 2000): 417–419.

61. Many studies have been published on the subject of the Islamic Republic's policies affecting women, including Val Moghadam, "Women, Work, and Ideology in the Islamic Republic," *International Journal of Middle East Studies* 20 (1988): 221–243; Nayereh Tohidi, "Modernity, Islamization, and Women in Iran," in *Gender and National Identity: Women and Politics in Muslim Societies,* ed. Val Moghadam (London: Zed Books, 1994), 114–147; Mahnaz Afkhami and Erika Friedl, eds., *In the Eye of the Storm: Women in Post-Revolutionary Iran* (Syracuse, N.Y.: Syracuse University Press, 1994); Paidar, *Women and the Political Process in Twentieth-Century Iran;* Haleh Esfandiari, *Reconstructed Lives: Women and Iran's Islamic Revolution* (Baltimore: Johns Hopkins University Press, 1997); Mir-Hosseini, *Islam and Gender;* and Hammed Shahidian, *Women in Iran,* 2 vols. (Westport, Conn.: Greenwood, 2002). A selective chronology of relevant developments is offered in Elham Gheytanchi, "Appendix: Chronology of Events Regarding Women in Iran Since the Revolution of 1979," Special Issue, Iran Since the Revolution, *Social Research* 67 (Summer 2000): 439–452.

62. See Ann Elizabeth Mayer, "Islamic Rights or Human Rights: An Iranian Dilemma," *Iranian Studies* 29 (Summer-Fall 1996): 284–288.

63. "Iranian Cleric Blasts Taleban for Defaming Islam," *Reuters North American Wire,* October 4, 1996, available in LEXIS, Nexis Library, ALLWLD File.

64. "Iranian Leader Warns Women Against Copying Western Feminist Trends," *Agence France Presse,* October 22, 1997, available in LEXIS, Nexis Library, ALLWLD File.

65. See Mehrangiz Kar, Ludovic Trarieux Prize Winner 2002, available at http://www.ludovictrarieux.org/uk-pages3.1.plt.htm.

66. Mahsa Sherkarloo, "Iranian Women Take on the Constitution," *MERIP Online*, July 21, 2005, available at http://merip.org/mero/mero072105.html.

67. Human Rights Watch, "Access Denied: Iran's Exclusionary Elections. A Human Rights Watch Briefing Paper," June 12, 2005, available at http://www.hrw.org/backgrounder/mena/iran0605/3.htm#_Toc106176111.

68. See "Women Ejected by Force from Iran Stadium," *Iran Focus,* March 6, 2006, available at http://www.iranfocus.com/modules/news/article.php?storyid=6091; "Iran: Women Forbidden to Watch Football Match," *adnkronosinternational,* March 9, 2006, available at http://www.adnki.com/index_2Level_English.php?cat=Culture AndMedia&loid=8.0.271290277&par=.

69. Human Rights Watch, "Iran: Police Attack Women's Day Celebration," March 9, 2006, available at http://www.alertnet.org/thenews/newsdesk/HRW/0ead934ab 6f2e9e124df8d9cb1bdddca.htm.

70. "Sudan: Threat to Women's Status from Fundamentalist Regime," *News from Africa Watch,* April 9, 1990.

71. Ibid.; "Sudan's Capital Bans Mixing of Sexes in Public," *New York Times,* October 27, 1996, 6; Sondra Hale, "Gender Politics and Islamization in the Sudan," *Women Living Under Muslim Laws: Dossier* 18 (July 1997): 51–80; and Sondra Hale, "Legal Aid, New Laws and Violence Against Women in the Sudan," *Women Living Under Muslim Laws: Dossier* 18 (July 1997): 81–92.

72. *The Meaning of the Glorious Koran,* trans. Marmaduke Pickthall (Albany: State University of New York Press, 1976).

73. See, for example, Tabandeh, *A Muslim Commentary,* 51–52; and Mawdudi, *Purdah and the Status of Women,* 185–201.

74. Aspects of the traditional Arab concept of female honor, or '*ird,* and its manipulation to secure male dominance have been studied in the anthropological literature on the Middle East. See, for example, Peter Dodd, "Family Honor and the Forces of Change in Arab Society," *International Journal of Middle East Studies* 4 (1973): 40–54. A critique of mechanisms of oppression in Arab society that analyzes how the concept of '*ird* has been used to deny women their humanity and basic rights can be found in Nawal El-Saadawi, *The Hidden Face of Eve: Women in the Arab World* (Boston: Beacon Press, 1981), 7–90.

75. The other two countries that recognized the Taliban government were Pakistan and the United Arab Emirates.

76. Declarations and Reservations to the Convention on the Elimination of All Forms of Discrimination Against Women, available at http://www.unhchr.ch/html/menu3/b/treaty9_asp.htm.

77. "Religious Police Reportedly Thwart Girls' Rescue in Fire," *Chicago Tribune,* March 18, 2002, 6; and "Saudi Crown Prince Promises Action to Prevent Another School Tragedy," *BBC Monitoring Middle East,* March 15, 2002, available in Lexis, News Library.

78. See an account of the process in Ali, *Gender and Human Rights in Islam and International Law,* 265–272.

79. "Pak SC Strikes Down Clauses of Hisba Bill as Unconstitutional," August 4, 2005, available at http://www.outlookindia.com/pti_print.asp?id=314949.

80. Amnesty International, *Women in Afghanistan: A Human Rights Catastrophe,* AI Index: ASA 11/03/95.

81. See, generally, Nancy Hatch Dupree, "Afghan Women Under the Taliban," in *Fundamentalism Reborn: Afghanistan and the Taliban,* ed. William Maley (New York: New York University Press, 1998), 145–166; and Marjon E. Ghasemi, "Islam, International Human Rights, and Women's Equality: Afghan Women Under Taliban Rule," *Southern California Review of Law and Women's Studies* 8 (Spring 1999): 445–467.

82. See, for example, John Burns, "Sex and the Afghani Woman: Islam's Straightjacket," *New York Times,* August 29, 1997, A4; "Islamic Rule Weighs Heavily for Afghans," *New York Times,* September 24, 1997, A6.

83. See Anne E. Brodsky, *With All Our Strength: The Revolutionary Association of the Women of Afghanistan* (New York: Routledge, 2003); Melody E. Chavis, *Meena, Heroine of Afghanistan: The Martyr Who Founded RAWA, the Revolutionary Association of the Women of Afghanistan* (New York: St. Martin's Press, 2003).

84. Benazeer Roshan, "The More Things Change, the More They Stay the Same: The Plight of Afghan Women Two Years After the Overthrow of the Taliban," *Berkeley Women's Law Journal* 19 (2004): 270–286.

85. Lila Abu–Lughod, "Do Muslim Women Really Need Saving? Anthropological Reflections on Cultural Relativism and Its Others," *American Anthropologist* 104 (2002): 787; Mary Ann Franks, "Obscene Undersides: Women and Evil Between the Taliban and the United States," *HYPATIA* 18 (2003): 135–155.

86. See, for example, Condoleezza Rice's televised comments on the US involvement in the constitution drafting and her claim that "the United States stands for equality for women worldwide," adding, "We've communicated that very clearly to the Iraqi government." Available at http://www.pbs.org/newshour/bb/white_house/july-dec05/rice_7–28.html.

87. See the discussions in Mayer, "Rhetorical Strategies," 104–114, and "Internationalization of the Conversation on Women's Rights: Arab Governments Face the CEDAW Committee," in *Islamic Law and the Challenge of Modernity,* eds. Yvonne Haddad and Barbara Freyer Stowasser (Walnut Creek, Calif.: Altamira Press, 2004), 147–154.

88. Tabandeh, *A Muslim Commentary,* 39.

89. Ibid., 41.

90. Ibid., 51.

91. Ibid., 52.

92. Mawdudi, *Purdah and the Status of Women in Islam,* 113–122.

93. Ibid., 120.

94. Ibid., 121–122.

95. Javad Bahonar, "Islam and Women's Rights," *al-Tawhid* 1 (1984): 160.

96. Ibid., 161.

97. Ibid., 165.

98. Ibid., 161.

99. Ibid., 164. Of course, since he was trying to show the Islamic treatment of women in a positive light, Bahonar neglected to mention that women in the Islamic inheritance scheme receive only one-half the share of a male inheriting in the same capacity.

100. See Ann Elizabeth Mayer, "Islam and Human Rights: Different Issues, Different Contexts. Lessons from Comparisons," in *Islamic Law Reform and Human Rights: Challenges and Rejoinders,* ed. Tore Lindholm and Kari Vogt (Oslo: Nordic Human Rights Publications, 1993), 121–125.

101. Mary Daly, *The Church and the Second Sex* (Boston: Beacon Press, 1985), 85.

102. Ibid., 88.

103. Ibid., 154.

104. Ibid., 115.

105. Ibid.

106. Ibid., 164.

107. Ibid., 87.

Chapter 7. Islamic Human Rights Schemes and Religious Minorities

1. Bernard Lewis, *The Emergence of Modern Turkey* (London: Oxford University Press, 1961), 104–106, 113–115, 131.

2. For background, see Peter Holt, *Egypt and the Fertile Crescent* (Ithaca: Cornell University Press, 1966); Bernard Lewis, *The Middle East and the West* (New York: Harper, 1964), and the sources cited therein; and Elizabeth Monroe, *Britain's Moment in the Middle East, 1914–56* (Baltimore: Johns Hopkins University Press, 1981).

3. The theme that European rule was needed to ensure impartial, fair government and administration of justice and to protect minorities from oppression permeates the thinking in Lord Cromer [Evelyn Baring], *Modern Egypt,* 2 vols. (New York: Macmillan, 1908), especially vol. 2, 123–259.

4. The Casablanca Declaration, available at http://www.al-bab.com/arab/docs/international/hr1999.htm.

5. These attitudes are exemplified in Ayatollah Khomeini's writings and speeches. See generally Imam [Ruhollah] Khomeini, *Islam and Revolution: Writings and Declarations of Imam Khomeini,* trans. Hamid Algar (Berkeley: Mizan Press, 1981).

6. US International Religious Freedom Act of 1998, available at http://www.us-cirf.gov/about/authorizinglegislation.html.

Information on the Office of International Religious Freedom is on the State Department Web site, available at http://www.state.gov/g/drl/irf/.

7. Lee Romney, "Battle Urged Against Religious Persecution," *Los Angeles Times,* October 20, 1997, 1; "Christian Right Urges Sanctions on Persecutors," *Financial Times,* August 27, 1997, available in LEXIS, Nexis Library, ALLWLD File.

8. The circumstances of the early Islamic community are described in W. Montgomery Watt, *Muhammad, Prophet and Statesman* (Oxford: Oxford University Press, 1971).

9. The law of *jihad* is discussed in Rudolph Peters, *Jihad in Classical and Modern Islam* (Princeton: Markus Wiener, 1996), 1–54.

10. For the evolution of *jihad* doctrine, see ibid., 55–159; and Ann Elizabeth Mayer, "War and Peace in the Islamic Tradition and in International Law," in *Just War and Jihad: War, Peace, and Statecraft in the Western and Islamic Traditions,* ed. James Johnson and John Kelsay (Westport, Conn.: Greenwood Press, 1991), 195–226.

11. For background, see A. S. Tritton, *The Caliphs and Their Non-Muslim Subjects: A Critical Study of the Covenant of Umar* (London: Cass, 1970); and Antoine Fattal, *Le Statut légal des non-musulmans en pays d'Islam* (Beirut: Imprimerie Catholique, 1958).

12. Zoroastrians and Sabeans are sometimes also included in this category.

13. A useful review of the rules pertaining to the status of *dhimmis* is in Fattal, *Le Statut légal des non-musulmans.*

14. Joseph Schacht, *Introduction to Islamic Law* (Oxford: Clarendon Press, 1964), 130–131.

15. For a survey of how the Muslim community interacted with non-Muslims on the subcontinent, see Ishtiaq Husain Qureshi, *The Muslim Community of the Indo-Pakistan Subcontinent, 610–1947: A Brief Historical Analysis* (Delhi: Renaissance, 1985).

16. See, for example, the studies in Benjamin Braude and Bernard Lewis, eds., *Christians and Jews in the Ottoman Empire,* 2 vols. (New York: Holmes and Meier, 1982).

17. On the treatment of Jews, see Bernard Lewis, *The Jews of Islam* (Princeton: Princeton University Press, 1984).

18. Introductions to some of the changes in attitudes brought about by nationalism can be found in Albert Hourani, *Arabic Thought in the Liberal Age, 1798–1939* (London: Oxford University Press, 1962); and Lewis, *The Emergence of Modern Turkey.*

19. "Egypt Cracks Down on Muslim Brotherhood," *Asia Times,* April 17, 1997, available in LEXIS, Nexis Library, ALLWLD File.

20. Subhi Mahmassani, *Arkan huquq al-insan* (Beirut: Dar al-'ilm li'l-malayin, 1979), 260–264, 281.

21. Ibid., 260–264.

22. S. M. Haider, "Equality Before Law and Equal Protection of Laws as Legal Doctrines for the Prevention of Discrimination and Protection of Minorities," in *Islamic Concept of Human Rights,* ed. S. M. Haider (Lahore: Book House, 1978), 213–237; Recep Senturk, "Minority Rights in Islam: From *Dhimmi* to Citizen," in

Islam and Human Rights: Advancing a U.S. Muslim Dialogue, ed. Shireen T. Hunter (Washington, D.C.: CSIS Press, 2005), 67–99.

23. Al-Bishri's ideas are discussed in detail in Leonard Binder, *Islamic Liberalism* (Chicago: University of Chicago Press, 1988), 246–292.

24. Ibid., 287–288.

25. Abdullahi El-Naiem [An-Na'im], "A Modern Approach to Human Rights in Islam: Foundations and Implications for Africa," in *Human Rights and Development in Africa,* ed. Claude Welch Jr. and Ronald Meltzer (Albany: State University of New York Press, 1984), 85.

26. Abdullahi An-Na'im applied his Islamic human rights norms to critique the treatment of non-Muslims in Egypt in "Religious Freedom in Egypt: Under the Shadow of the Islamic *Dhimma* System," in *Religious Liberty and Human Rights in Nations and Religions,* ed. Leonard Swidler (Philadelphia: Ecumenical Press, 1986), 43–59.

27. Courtney W. Howland, "The Challenge of Religious Fundamentalism to the Liberty and Equality Rights of Women: An Analysis Under the United Nations Charter," *Columbia Journal of Transnational Law* 35 (1997): 329–330.

28. Sultanhussein Tabandeh, *A Muslim Commentary on the Universal Declaration of Human Rights,* trans. F. J. Goulding (Guildford, England: F. J. Goulding, 1970), 18.

29. Ibid., 15.

30. Ibid., 17.

31. Ibid., 36.

32. Ibid.

33. Ibid., 37.

34. Ibid.

35. Ibid., 70.

36. Ibid., 71.

37. Abu'l A'la Mawdudi, *Human Rights in Islam* (Leicester, England: Islamic Foundation, 1980), 30. He was not inhibited from attacking the "heretical" Ahmadis, even though their "heretical" views should have qualified them as non-Muslims, whose feelings, Mawdudi said, must be respected.

38. Without more specific standards, it would be difficult to determine, for example, whether the Iranian government's harsh denunciations of Baha'is would be deemed in violation of Article 12.e.

39. The translation is taken from "Constitution of the Islamic Republic of Iran of 24 October 1979 As Amended to 28 July 1989," in *Constitutions of the Countries of the World,* ed. Albert Blaustein and Gisbert Flanz (Dobbs Ferry, N.Y.: Oceana, 1992).

40. See, for example, Shaul Bakhash, *The Reign of the Ayatollahs* (New York: Basic Books, 1984), 226.

41. Abu'l A'la Mawdudi, *The Islamic Law and Constitution* (Lahore: Islamic Publications, 1980), 188–189, 274–276.

42. Human Rights Watch/Middle East, *Iran: Religious and Ethnic Minorities. Discrimination in Law and Practice* 9, no. 7 (September 1997), available at http://www.hrw.org/reports/1997/iran/Iran–06.html.

43. Human Rights Commission of Pakistan, *State of Human Rights in Pakistan 1993* (Lahore: Human Rights Commission of Pakistan, n.d.), 45–48.

44. This conclusion is further strengthened by a reading of the section of the Preamble that deals with the army. It provides that the goal of the army is "accomplishing an ideological mission, that is, the 'Jihad' for the sake of God, as well as for struggling to open the way for the sovereignty of the Word of God throughout the world." This is an army with the mission to engage in combat on behalf of the Islamic cause.

45. See "Senior Iran Cleric Calls Non-Muslims 'Animals,'" *Iran Focus*, November 20, 2005, available at http://www.iranfocus.com/modules/news/article.php?storyid =4505.

46. Roger Cooper, *The Baha'is of Iran*, Minority Rights Group Report 51 (London: Minority Rights Group, 1982), 7–8, 10.

47. Ibid., 11.

48. Cooper, *The Baha'is of Iran*; Douglas Martin, "The Persecution of the Baha'is of Iran, 1844–1984," *Baha'i Studies* 12–13 (1984); and Economic and Social Council Commission on Human Rights, *Report on the Human Rights Situation in the Islamic Republic of Iran by the Special Representative of the Commission, Mr. Reynaldo Galindo Pohl, Appointed Pursuant to Resolution 1986/41*, E/CN.4/1987/23. See also the Iran chapters in Amnesty International Annual Reports.

49. "Iran Rejects US Allegation on Violation of Religious Freedom," *BBC Monitoring Middle East*, October 8, 1999, available in Lexis, News library.

50. "Iran: Human Rights Developments," *Human Rights Watch World Report 2001*, available at http://www.hrw.org/wr2k1/mideast/iran.html.

51. Mawdudi, *Human Rights*, 21–22.

52. Mawdudi, *The Islamic Law and Constitution*, 288–291.

53. Ibid., 191–193.

54. Ibid., 297–298.

55. Ibid., 276.

56. Ibid., 287.

57. A fascinating record of materials on the 1953 disturbances and the theological, ideological, and political views of both the Ahmadis and their opponents, including Mawdudi and his Jama'at, can be seen in *Report of the Court of Inquiry Constituted Under Punjab Act II of 1954 to Enquire into the Punjab Disturbances of 1953* (Lahore: Superintendent, Government Printing, Punjab, 1954).

58. The ordinance and the human rights violations that ensued pursuant to the demotion of Ahmadis to the status of impostors wrongfully claiming to be Muslims are discussed in Nadeem Ahmad Siddiq, "Enforced Apostasy: *Zaheeruddin v. State* and the Official Persecution of the Ahmadiyya Community in Pakistan," *Law and Inequality* 14 (1995): 275–338.

59. This case is critically evaluated in Siddiq, "Enforced Apostasy," 275–338; and Tayyab Mahmud, "Freedom of Religion and Religious Minorities in Pakistan: A Study of Judicial Practice," *Fordham International Law Journal* 19 (1995): 40–100.

60. For the text of the 1991 bill, see Rubya Mehdi, *The Islamization of the Law in Pakistan* (Richmond, England: Curzon Press, 1994), 324–329.

61. *Zaheeruddin v. State,* 26 S.C.M.R. (S.Ct.) 1718 (1993) (Pak.), 1773–1774.

62. Amnesty International, *Saudi Arabia: Religious Intolerance. The Arrest, Detention and Torture of Christian Worshippers and Shi'a Muslims* (New York: Amnesty International, 1993).

63. Details of the positions taken on Saudi Arabia and its CPC designation are set forth in the *Annual Report of the United States Commission on International Religious Freedom,* May 2005, 27–37, 113–120, available at http://www.uscirf.gov/countries/publications/currentreport/2005annualRpt.pdf#page=37.

Chapter 8. Freedom of Religion in Islamic Human Rights Schemes

1. See, for example, Mohamed Talbi, "Religious Liberty: A Muslim Perspective," in *Religious Liberty and Human Rights in Nations and Religions,* ed. Leonard Swidler (Philadelphia: Ecumenical Press, 1986), 175–188.

2. Abdulaziz Sachedina, "Freedom of Conscience and Religion in the Qur'an," in *Human Rights and the Conflict of Cultures: Western and Islamic Perspectives on Religious Liberty,* ed. David Little, John Kelsay, and Abdulaziz Sachedina (Columbia: University of South Carolina Press, 1988), 53–90.

3. Subhi Mahmassani, *Arkan huquq al-insan* (Beirut: Dar al-'ilm li'l-malayin, 1979), 123–124.

4. Talbi, "Religious Liberty," 205.

5. Aldeeb Abu Sahlieh, "Les Droits de l'homme et l'Islam," 637.

6. Details on the ratifications and reservations can be found at the Web site of the Office of the United Nations High Commissioner for Human Rights, Convention on the Rights of the Child, available at http://www.ohchr.org/english/countries/ratification/11.htm.

7. The declaration made no mention of the Ahmadis, Alawis, or Isma'ilis. See Statement Issued by the International Islamic Conference on "True Islam and Its Role in Modern Society," Amman, Jordan, July 6, 2005, available at http://www.kingabdullah.jo/news/details.php?kn_serial=3409&menu_id=26&lang_hmka1=1.

8. These patterns are surveyed in Ann Elizabeth Mayer, "Law and Religion in the Muslim Middle East," *American Journal of Comparative Law* 35 (1987): 143–147.

9. Sultanhussein Tabandeh, *A Muslim Commentary on the Universal Declaration of Human Rights,* trans. F. J. Goulding (Guildford, England: F. J. Goulding, 1970), 71.

10. Ibid., 59.

11. The author's translation of a French translation from the Arabic offered in Sami Aldeeb Abu Sahlieh, "Liberté religieuse et apostasie dans l'Islam," *Praxis juridique et religion* 23 (1986): 53.

12. Human Rights Watch/Middle East, *Iran: Religious and Ethnic Minorities. Discrimination in Law and Practice* 9, no. 7 (September 1997): 10.

13. Aldeeb Abu Sahlieh, "Liberté religieuse," 61–66.

14. Sources on this infamous affair include "Shari'a or Civil Code? Egypt's Parallel Legal Systems: An Interview with Ahmad Sayf al-Islam," *Middle East Report* (November-December 1995): 25–27; Nasr Abu Zaid, "The Case of Abu Zaid: Academic Freedom in Egypt," *Index on Censorship* 4 (1996): 30–39; Navid Kermani, "Die Affäre Abu Zayd: Eine Kritik am religiösen Diskurs und ihre Folgen," *Orient* 35 (1994): 25–49; "L'affaire Abu Zayd, universitaire poursuivi pour apostasie," *Monde arabe: Maghreb Machrek* 151 (January-March 1996): 18; Baudouin Dupret, "Le procès: L'argumentation des tribunaux," *Monde arabe: Maghreb Machrek* 151 (January-March 1996): 19–22; and Kilian Bälz, "Submitting Faith to Judicial Scrutiny Through the Family Trial: The Abu Zayd Case," *Die Welt des Islams* 37 (1997): 135–155.

15. Bälz, "Submitting Faith to Judicial Scrutiny," 149.

16. Bjazet [pseud.], "La tradition? . . . Quelle tradition?" *Monde arabe: Maghreb Machrek* (January-March 1996): 23–31; and Kermani, "Die Affäre Abu Zayd," 29.

17. Kermani, "Die Affäre Abu Zayd," 29.

18. Ibid., 35.

19. Ibid., 33–34.

20. Ibid., 33–34.

21. Bälz, "Submitting Faith to Judicial Scrutiny," 149.

22. Kermani, "Die Affäre Abu Zayd," 48.

23. Tabandeh, *A Muslim Commentary,* 70.

24. Ibid., 71.

25. Ibid., 70–71.

26. Ibid., 71.

27. Ibid.

28. Ibid., 71–72. One can find similar defenses being offered by an Egyptian author for the application of the death penalty for apostasy. These are discussed in Aldeeb Abu Sahlieh, "Les Droits de l'homme et l'Islam," 643–644.

29. Tabandeh, *A Muslim Commentary,* 72.

30. Ibid., 72–73.

31. Ibid., 59.

32. Ibid.

33. It should be recalled that Tabandeh's intended audience consisted of persons attending an international human rights conference in Iran.

34. J. Roland Pennock, "Rights, Natural Rights, and Human Rights: A General View," in *Human Rights: NOMOS XXIII,* ed. J. Roland Pennock and John W. Chapman (New York: New York University Press, 1981), 14.

35. The meaning of the phrase *takhdhil li'l-umma* is obscure. A related verb with the same root occurs in the Qur'an (3:160) in the sense of "forsake." However, the verbal noun *takhdhil* seems to mean something like incitement to neglect to aid companions or to be cowardly and weak-hearted. Although one can predict that the prohibited speech targeted here involves ideas and beliefs that are deemed harmful to the Islamic community, just what constitutes this *takhdhil* is open to speculation.

36. How confusing this provision can be is illustrated by the protest made by the International Commission of Jurists (ICJ) over the execution of Mahmud Muhammad Taha, discussed later in this chapter. The ICJ invoked the UIDHR provision granting freedom of religion in its protest. *Human Rights Internet Reporter* 10 (January-April 1985). Apparently, the ICJ imagined that the UIDHR prohibited executions for apostasy. In fact, it has been drafted to allow Muslims to be executed for apostasy.

37. *The Meaning of the Glorious Koran,* trans. Marmaduke Pickthall (Albany: State University of New York Press, 1976).

38. Firuz Kazemzadeh, "The Baha'is in Iran: Twenty Years of Repression," Special Issue, Iran Since the Revolution, *Social Research* 67 (Summer 2000): 535–558.

39. Roger Cooper, *The Baha'is of Iran,* Minority Rights Group Report 51 (London: Minority Rights Group, 1982), 13–15; Douglas Martin, "The Persecution of the Baha'is of Iran, 1844–1984," *Baha'i Studies* 12–13 (1984): 49, 54–56, 58, 65; and Human Rights Watch/Middle East, *Iran: Religious and Ethnic Minorities. Discrimination in Law and Practice* 9, no. 7 (September 1997): 10–15.

40. Martin, "The Persecution of the Baha'is," 54.

41. Cooper, *The Baha'is of Iran,* 13–14; Economic and Social Council, *Report on the Human Rights Situation in the Islamic Republic of Iran,* E/CN.4/1987/20 (January 28, 1987), 20.

42. Economic and Social Council, *Report on the Human Rights Situation,* 21.

43. This translation is taken from "Constitution of the Islamic Republic of Iran of 24 October 1979 As Amended to 28 July 1989," in *Constitutions of the Countries of the World,* ed. Albert Blaustein and Gisbert Flanz (Dobbs Ferry, N.Y.: Oceana, 1992).

44. A useful source on the Rushdie death edict and subsequent controversy is Anthony Chase, "Legal Guardians: Islamic Law, International Law, Human Rights and the Salman Rushdie Affair," *American University Journal of International Law and Policy* 11 (1996): 375–435.

45. Various representative reactions and comments, largely from Muslims, can be found in *Index on Censorship* (May 1989): 7–18. Responses to the order to kill Rushdie are also discussed in Lisa Appignanesi and Sara Maitland, eds., *The Rushdie File* (Syracuse, N.Y.: Syracuse University Press, 1990).

46. See, for example, the book *For Rushdie: Essays by Arab and Muslim Writers in Defense of Free Speech* (New York: Braziller, 1994). The volume includes contributions from many of the cultural luminaries of the Muslim world and a copy of a petition on Rushdie's behalf that had been signed by 127 Iranian writers, despite the danger involved.

47. "Iranian Political Factions in Row over Rushdie Affair," *Agence France Presse,* April 21, 1997, available in LEXIS, Nexis Library, ALLWLD File.

48. "Palestinian Affairs: Iranian Envoy Calls UN Draft Resolution on Human Rights Baseless, Irrelevant," *BBC Summary of World Broadcasts,* December 15, 1995, available in LEXIS, Nexis Library, ALLWLD File.

49. "UN Condemns Iran on Human Rights," *Agence France Presse,* March 8, 1995, available in LEXIS, Nexis Library, ALLWLD File.

50. See Ann Elizabeth Mayer, "Islamic Rights or Human Rights: An Iranian Dilemma," *Iranian Studies* 29 (Summer-Fall 1996): 290–292.

51. A collection of his writings with valuable background material is afforded in Ziba Mir-Hosseini and Richard Tapper, *Islam and Democracy in Iran: Eshkevari and the Quest for Reform* (London: I. B. Tauris, 2006).

52. See ibid., pp. 173–174; "Iran: Prosecution of Independent Cleric Condemned," *Human Rights Watch,* October 11, 2000, available at http://hrw.org/english/docs/2000/10/11/iran683_txt.htm.

53. "UPI Hears," *UPI,* June 1, 2005, available in Lexis, News Library.

54. His views are set forth in a book translated by Abdullahi Ahmed An-Naʿim, *The Second Message of Islam by Ustadh Mahmoud Mohamed Taha* (Syracuse, N.Y.: Syracuse University Press, 1987).

55. Aldeeb Abu Sahlieh, "Liberté religieuse," 51.

56. Abdullahi An-Naʿim, "The Islamic Law of Apostasy and Its Modern Applicability: A Case from the Sudan," *Religion* 16 (1986): 207.

57. Ibid., 209. It is significant to note that the Muslim World League is the parent organization of the Islamic Council, which sponsored and published the UIDHR. According to one account, the Muslim World League later congratulated Nimeiri for executing Taha. Aldeeb Abu Sahlieh, "Les Droits de l'homme et l'Islam," 707.

58. Ibid.

59. *Report of the Court of Inquiry Constituted Under Punjab Act II of 1954 to Enquire into the Punjab Disturbances of 1953* (Lahore: Superintendent, Government Printing, Punjab, 1954), 218.

60. Human Rights Watch, "Persecuted Minorities and Writers in Pakistan," September 19, 1993, available at http://www.hrw.org/reports/1993/pakistan/.

61. Ibid.

62. See Akbar S. Ahmed, "Pakistan's Blasphemy Law: Words Fail Me," *Washington Post,* May 19, 2002, B1. Physicians for Human Rights was one of many organizations denouncing his conviction for blasphemy and calling for his release; their campaign is described in materials available at http://www.phrusa.org/campaigns/colleagues/pakistan_1202.html, and http://www.phrusa.org/campaigns/colleagues/pakistan_112603.html.

63. "Lawyers Observe Strike Against Pakistani Judge's Murder," *Agence France Presse,* October 13, 1997, available in LEXIS, Nexis Library, ALLWLD File.

64. Paula R. Newberg, "Economic, Political Pressures Strain Pakistan's Civil Society," *Los Angeles Times,* November 16, 1997, available in LEXIS, Nexis Library, ALLWLD File.

65. See Amnesty International, *Saudi Arabia: An Upsurge in Public Executions* (May 15, 1993), 6; and Amnesty International, *Religious Intolerance: The Arrest, Detention and Torture of Christian Worshippers and Shiʿa Muslims* (1993), 12, 15–17. In February 1998, even as Saudi-Iranian relations were warming, a Saudi sheikh roundly denounced Shiʿism in the presence of former president Hashemi Rafsanjani during his

goodwill visit to the kingdom, provoking Iranian outrage. "Iranian Official Leads Pilgrims to Saudi Arabia with Warm Words on Ties," *Agence France Presse,* March 17, 1998, available in LEXIS, Nexis Library, ALLWLD File. See also "Saudi Arabia," in *Human Rights Watch World Report 1998,* available at http://www.hrw.org/world report/Mideast–08.htm.

66. Human Rights Watch/Middle East, *Saudi Arabia: Flawed Justice. The Execution of 'Abd al-Karim Mara'i al Naqshabandi,* vol. 9, no. 9 (E) (October 1997).

67. Ibid.

68. Ibid.

69. See Abdul Waheed Wafa and Carlotta Gall, "Afghan Court Gives Editor 2-Year Term for Blasphemy," *New York Times,* October 24, 2005, A3; Griff Witte, "Post-Taliban Free Speech Blocked by Courts," *Washington Post,* December 11, 2005, A24.

70. Carlotta Gall, "Afghans Pick Rival of Karzai as a Chairman in Parliament," *New York Times,* December 22, 2005, A19.

71. Information about the Commission on International Religious Freedom is available at http://www.uscirf.gov/countries/countriesconcerns/index.html.

72. The annual reports of the Commission on International Religious Freedom are available at http://www.uscirf.gov/countries/publications/currentreport/index.html.

73. See US Commission on International Religious Freedom, "The Religion-State Relationship and the Right to Freedom of Religion or Belief: A Comparative Textual Analysis of the Constitutions of Predominantly Muslim Countries," available at http://www.uscirf.gov/countries/global/comparative_constitutions/03082005/03082005_study.html

74. The Annual Report of the United States Commission on International Religious Freedom, May 2005, is available at http://www.uscirf.gov/countries/publications/currentreport/2005annualRpt.pdf#page=37.

75. For a critique of this initiative, see Peter G. Danchin, "US Unilateralism and the International Protection of Religious Freedom: The Multilateral Alternative," *Columbia Journal of Transnational Law* 41 (2002): 33–135.

Chapter 9. An Assessment of Islamic Human Rights Schemes

1. See the Casablanca Declaration, available at http://www.al-bab.com/arab/docs/international/hr1999.htm.

2. Sultanhussein Tabandeh, *A Muslim Commentary on the Universal Declaration of Human Rights,* trans. F. J. Goulding (Guildford, England: F. J. Goulding, 1970), 57. This position was echoed in comments by Ayatollah Khomeini. After denouncing Muslims who wanted to Westernize everything and after condemning Western human rights advocates for their hypocrisy, Khomeini railed against the idea that Muslims should measure Islam "in accordance with Western criteria." Instead, he argued,

Muslims should be loyal to Islam. Imam [Ruhollah] Khomeini, *Islam and Revolution: Writings and Declarations of Imam Khomeini,* trans. Hamid Algar (Berkeley: Mizan Press, 1981), 270–272.

3. "Islam Guarantees Rights, Says Saud," *Riyadh Daily,* June 17,1993, available in LEXIS, Nexis Library, ALLWLD File.

4. Press release of Iran's permanent mission to the United Nations, "Statement by H. E. Dr. Mohammad-Javad Zarif, Deputy Foreign Minister and Head of Delegation of the Islamic Republic of Iran Before the World Conference on Human Rights," Vienna, 18 June 1993.

5. Lawyers Committee for Human Rights, *Islam and Justice: Debating the Future of Human Rights in the Middle East and North Africa* (New York: Lawyers Committee for Human Rights, 1997).

6. The declaration from the meeting is presented in German translation in Bassam Tibi, "Bericht über das Kolloquium Arabischer Wissenschaftler und Schriftsteller: *Multaqa Tunis al-thaqafi 'an al-hurriyat al-dimuqratiya fi al-'alam al-'arabi/* Das kulturelle Tunis-Kolloquium über die Demokratischen Freiheiten in der Arabischen Welt im Centre Culturel de Hammamet, April 1–3, 1983," *Orient* 24 (1983): 398–399.

7. "Doha Declaration for Democracy and Reform," *Daily Star,* June 29, 2004, available at http://www.journalofdemocracy.org/Articles/Documents-Doha-Declaration–15–4.pdf.

8. The serious consequences of the freedom deficit in Arab countries have been analyzed in the studies by the United Nations Development Program and the Arab Fund for Economic and Social Development, see, e.g., *Arab Human Development Report 2002* (New York: United Nations Publications, 2002), also available at http://www.undp.org/rbas/ahdr/english2002.html.

9. See, for example, the statement of Saad Eddin Ibrahim, the prominent Egyptian campaigner for democracy, made in July 2002 before he was yet again dragged off to prison for daring to challenge Egypt's repressive system. "What after the law? Statement from Saad Ibrahim, July 29, 2002," available at http://www.nearinternational .org/alerts/egypt120020731en.html.

10. Mawdudi made a very similar assertion, claiming, "When we speak of human rights in Islam we mean those rights granted by God. Rights granted by kings or legislative assemblies can be withdrawn as easily as they are conferred; but no individual and no institution has the authority to withdraw the rights conferred by God." Mawdudi, *Human Rights,* 15.

11. "Islam Guarantees Rights, Says Saud," *Riyadh Daily,* June 17, 1993, available in LEXIS, Nexis Library, Saudi File.

12. See, generally, Mashood A. Baderin, *International Human Rights and Islamic Law* (Oxford: Oxford University Press, 2003).

Index